ALL AREA ACCESS
Personal Management for Unsigned Musicians

by
Marc Davison

Illustrations by Dan Weinstein

ISBN 0-7935-8134-6

HAL•LEONARD®
CORPORATION

7777 W. BLUEMOUND RD. P.O. BOX 13819 MILWAUKEE, WI 53213

Visit All Area Access Online at
www.allareaaccess.com

Visit Hal Leonard Online at
www.halleonard.com

To Lori and our children, Ryan and Jamie & Cameron

———————————— ‹› ————————————

ACKNOWLEDGMENTS

The following, are names of the very special people whose knowledge in their respective areas of the business are second only to their gracious humanity.

Judith Berger (**My Attorney**). I can't thank you enough for your insights and personal/legal guidance. Your vast knowledge of the music business is surpassed only by your caring and down to earth style.

All at Hal Leonard Corp. including: Brad Smith, Jon Eiche, Nanette Lorenz, Lori Hagopian, Karen Waldkirch, and Richard Slater.

David Schwartz (**Producer/Owner Bermuda Schwartz Productions**), for all your help through the years as well as your input concerning studio time, recording techniques and equipment.

Dan Weinstein (**Funk Factory Art**). After all the years we have worked together I'm not sure where my ideas end and yours begin. You instinctively know what I am looking for. Thank you for all the neat characterizations inside the book.

Jonathan Levine, (**Booking Agent/ Monterey Peninsula Artists**). I thank you sincerely for your keen insights in the chapters concerning band touring, college booking and artist development. Throughout all these years, I have learned more about this business from you than from any other source. You have not only been my close friend but a mentor as well.

Peter Freedman (**Manager/Peter Freedman Ent.**) Thank you for all your consultation regarding chapters 18 & 19. As this book attempts to fill the management void for it's readers, I tip my hat to you as one of the more refined and eloquent managers in today's business. You have rekindled the spirit of true artist development as is evident in the careers of all your acts including "Live and Local H."

Robert Habor, (**Editor, CMJ Magazine**) for all your help on the sections on college radio.

George Tihin (**Screenwriter & Director**) Thank you for making the final edits on the book before being shopped to publishing companies as well as your friendship.

Victor Wlodinguer (**CPA, Wlodinguer Erk & Chanzis**). The honorable rock and roll accountant. Thank you for helping to edit the accounting section of this book. You made yourself available in the height of tax season and I can't distinguish if it was for me or because you wanted to make sure that my readers got the very best advice.

Chris Bubacz, (**Producer/Manager, Bear Tracks Recording Studio**) for your help on the sections concerning studio recording and demo tapes.

William Dirella, (**Manager**) You have been a vast resource of information and the knowledge I gained from many of our conversations, has been dispersed throughout the book..

Gary Bongiovanni, (**Editor POLLSTAR Magazine**) for your help on chapter 14.

Dave Herman (**NY DJ WNEW FM**) for our long interview that helped formulate the history of FM radio in America. Thanks for that and for so many years of great radio.

Rick Dobbelaer (**Recording Artist/ Musician**) for your music which is always an inspiration to me and for all the first hand tales of the trials and tribulations of being a member of a signed and unsigned touring band.

Pete Jameson (**Bass Player/Sound Engineer**) Thanks for your help concerning sound systems equipment and instrument sales.

Dave Ramie (**Drummer**) for the section on drums.

Steve Regina (**Engineer, Bear Tracks Recording Studio**) for your help on chapter 9.

Shawn Meyers, (**Computer Programmer/ ex road manager**) for your help on the Internet.

Tony Johnson, (**Editor, Mind Garbage Denver Co.**) for your help on chapter 7. If there were more editors like you on the east coast there would be more interesting publications on the news stands!

Tony Van Veen (**Marketing Director, Disc Makers**), for years of providing me with great merchandise and service as well as all your information regarding master tape preparation.

To both my mom Bev and my dad Jay for their repeated edits on the book.

Last but not least, to my dear wife Lori Ellen. You are my best friend and I lovingly thank you for enduring a full year without me while I glued myself to the computer and poured my heart out. I will never forget your late night back rubs and loving diversions but most of all for the countless hours you spent reading page after page, making sure it was written in my best and most honest fashion. You devoted a full year of your life to my work; I owe you one!

In addition, I thank the following people who generously gave me their time and expertise: Jeff Walker, (Shorefire Media) Frank Saur, Yasser Dabbagh, Dennis Ostrum, Sales Manager Trutone Labs: Dean Goldman, Keyboard & Synth Tech, Alto Music: Karen Carney, Chameleon Club San Francisco and lastly, a special thanks to **Tamara Singer** who after reading some of my early journals first realized their potential and told me I would be insane not to turn them into a book. Where ever you are Tamara, thanks.

****

This book would not be possible had I not had the privilege to work with four musicians during the late 1980's to the early 1990's. Their music was an inspiration to me as well as all who they came in contact with. They were a classic example of a band that was ahead of their time and unfortunately they could not hold it together long enough to see their visions realized.

Though it has been two years since their disbandment, I still receive mail from new fans who find their CD in record store bargain bins or at friends' homes and hear it for the first time. I still write to at least one new fan a month sending them what's left from the diminishing T-shirt pile and band paraphernalia.

I spent five years on the road traveling with these guys in a van full of energy, eagerness and anticipation. I will never forget the feeling we collectively had come twilight, pulling into the next new town. As the sun would set washing away the dreariness of the long road trip, the quiet lull that hung in the air of the van would dissipate into a combustion of pure energy. The music in the tape deck would switch from the soft vibrations of Enya to the raw crunch of the Smashing Pumpkins as the band members would wake from their afternoon naps. The liquid sky, soaked in shades of pink, red and purple, hid behind it the mystery and magic that we all knew would take place on stage that night. Something big was going to happen and when it felt like this it was the most euphoric feeling one can ever imagine.

I have these memories as well as their recordings which will be with me forever.

Thank You, John, Pete, Rick & Dave

CONTENTS

◄►

———————— ◁▷ ———————— **D**esire is non discriminatory. It is equally shared by all individuals from every walk of life. It comes in many forms and attaches itself to a wide array of possibilities. Achievement of one's desires is a result of a more selective process. In our lifelong pursuit, some of our dreams are realized and some are not.

Musicians are some of society's most profound dreamers. Their offerings spark our imagination and create a porthole through which we, the listener, can escape. Music is a much needed remedy as is evident by the reverence many musicians receive and the amount of time and resources spent listening to and purchasing it.

But tragically, a large percentage of musicians never fulfill their desires of financial independence and public recognition. Their work remains forever hidden in some note pad or on a dusty cassette tape kept in the back of a bookcase.

Why is it so difficult to make it in the music business?

For one thing our society leans more toward immediate, financial gratification rather than inner peace and spiritual fulfillment. Business reflects that sentiment and nowhere is that more evident than in the entertainment industry. Artistic work must be more than just an uplifting piece. It must possess a mass appeal and spew obvious financial possibilities if it is going to attract the backing of the "Industry."

I have come to write this book because the path to success in the music business is not a result of a whimsical journey fueled by a mere few good tunes, but rather it is a destination reached after a long and well-planned trip over a road filled with potholes, detours and speed bumps. Certainly a difficult highway for any young, budding artist to be hitching a ride on.

For you to get your work out to the public you need to be more than just a creative talent. You must be a seasoned businessman, experienced travel agent, articulate negotiator, creative art director, sharp retailer and a convincing salesman. All this you must be, cultivated into a state of perfection in the first twenty five years of your life. At times, it can seem like this is what it's going to take in order for you to get the attention of the presenters of your work to the mass general public.

As I considered this, I wondered if these criteria were essential thirty or forty years ago as a prelude to making it in the music business. Did young musicians have to self-promote their every step or were things easier way back then? Would there have been an Elvis Presley or a Buddy Holly if radio wasn't so eager to play the newest rock and roll song? Would the Beatles have ever made it past the Cavern Club in Liverpool if they had to release their own independent CD, self-fund a tour of Europe, fight to get a mention in the Liverpool press, generate monthly mailing lists and shop the record companies themselves for a record deal? Would they ever have gotten the opportunity to meet a guy like Brian Epstein or a prominent producer like

George Martin who steadfastly believed in them when the rest of the "Industry" didn't?

The answers are as hypothetical as the questions but I can't help but wonder if the steps to the top are indeed so difficult to climb that somewhere, the next Elvis, Dylan or Lennon, despite their brilliant talent, might never get their music out to the world.

Has the music business become so competitive and the bottom line so crucial that labels cannot afford to seek out or even recognize and cultivate great raw talent? In my effort to answer these questions, I traced music back through the last fifty years to see if I could possibly spot a decline in the talent pool to prove a point. My research revealed a marvelous discovery.

I recalled the likes of the early pioneers of popular music who through their means gave young artists a shot at the big time. Their seemingly charitable deeds which brought wonderful music to the airwaves, were but a camouflage for their unscrupulous business practices of paying their artists off with cars, women and empty promises. These men virtually robbed their clients of their integrity with a smile on their face and a sharp pencil between their fingers, by assigning the publishing rights and royalties away from the artists to themselves enhancing their bank accounts while leaving many of these clients penniless.

So, in conclusion, I simply say this: it has always been hard to make it. The term "starving artist" was coined many years prior to 1996. If anything, you, the artists of today, are empowered with an inherent sense of caution and intelligence, bestowed upon you from the perils of those that have walked before. Yes, it may be harder than ever to make it and yes, you need to be much more than just a musician to get to the top of this business. But with all the information available to guide you, in the end you will own your life. You will not be dependent on making deals with the devil because they cannot exist if you don't let them.

It is with this impression that I wish you luck and success in this business. I hope this book may educate a great musical talent like yourself in all the other areas of the business so that you have a shot at bringing your songs into the world.

Good Luck!

1

WHERE I'M COMING FROM

My love affair with music began back in 1962 when I was six years old. It happened one warm Sunday morning in July, when my family and I were on our way to Rockaway Beach for the day. I was riding shotgun, sandwiched between mom and dad in the front seat of their "57" Ford Belair. And, like always, dad had the radio on. He loved listening to singers like Jack Jones, Steve Lawrence, Perry Como and of course the "Chairman of the Board," Frank Sinatra. I, on the other hand, hated that music and would sit with my hands over my ears and hum to myself in an effort to drown out that horrible croon.

On this particular morning my parents were feeling rather sympathetic (considering that my humming was drowning out the radio) and told me that if I stop, I could lean over and change the station to something I liked. Now bear in mind, this was the early sixties and things like seat belts and car safety were not the issue they are today. So I leaned over and aimlessly spun the dial back and forth searching for anything more tolerable than "Mack The Knife."

We were just about to cross the Marine Park Bridge when I stumbled across a sound way different from what I had been tortured with for the first six years of my life. I do not remember what the song was, but I knew immediately that it was not my parents' kind of music. I remained frozen in position with my hand glued to the dial for what seemed like forever. Were they really going to let me keep this station, I wondered to myself. Sure it seemed like a fun thing to do, let little Marc play with the dial for a while, at least it will stop his humming. But to me this was no game. I had just found rock and roll and was hell bent on keeping it.

Slowly, I leaned back into the seat, trying not to cause any attention to the situation. Keeping my head forward, I rolled my eyes first to my left to check out my dad, and then right to check out my mom. They said nothing. The song ended, another came on and another and soon I could see the Atlantic ocean just up ahead. I honestly do not remember the names of the songs that I heard that day, but what I do remember is hearing this odd humming sound coming from my parents.

When we got home, I asked mom to find that station for me on the radio so that I could listen whenever I wanted. It didn't take long before I became familiar with many of the popular songs they played each day. But there was one song that I had heard only the end of once and was dying to hear again. I remember the DJ saying that it was called "The Unicorn" by the Irish Rovers. I told mom how much I liked that song and that we must listen to the radio all day so that I could hear it when it comes on.

Now for me, all day meant just that. **ALL DAY!** But for mom that meant her peaceful three room apartment was converted into a torture chamber, as I took hold of the station dial and raced it across the AM band like I was Mario Andretti at the Indy 500. With the volume level thrust into full gear, that little Emerson did all it could to keep its tiny speaker from exploding. Mom quickly surrendered and took me to the local music store to buy "The Unicorn". When I got home, I immediately took out the little blue portable victrola and placed the record on it.

In colorful limerick, "The Unicorn" told the tale of Noah and how he gathered every animal in the kingdom to the ark that would safely shelter them from the impending flood. Two by two they filed in, "green alligators and long necked geese, humpty back camels and some chimpanzees," all except that is, the Unicorns, who were so busy playing silly games, they didn't hear the final call to board. As the sky turned ominous and the rains began to fall, Noah could wait no longer. He sealed up the ark and drifted into the storm leaving the "loveliest" of Gods creations, to drown into extinction.

As the final chorus ended, a tear welled up in my eyes. After all, I loved that Unicorn and was crushed, thinking how they "all just floated away." Mom, amused by my naiveté, put her arm around me and explained that it was just a story. "Unicorns aren't real and never were" she said while wiping dry my eye, "so there's no need to feel sad." I wanted to believe her, after all, why would mom lie?

She thought it would be a good idea to play the record again and I asked her to write down the words so that I could follow along. I thought perhaps I might find a new ending to the story. Though I never did, the more I played the song, the more I loved it. I spun the record over and over, day in and day out, learning every word by heart. I played it so many times that within weeks, my thick Brooklyn accent was replaced by a heavy Irish brogue. But I never forgot about the poor unicorn, and I wished that maybe one managed to survive.

Weeks later, while riding in the car I was looking out the window when all at once every movement of my body ceased. I was transfixed as I stared at this passing statue so white and noble, poised high atop a Mobil gas station. I stared at the statue, then turned and stared at my mother. I didn't say anything because I couldn't, I was too excited. One Unicorn made it through the flood, and now she owned a gas station!

Since the song never presented me with a definitive description of a unicorn, Mobil's white horse seemed to clearly match the image I imagined, despite its wings and lack of horn. As the car continued away from the station, mom asked why I was twisting my head around so violently. I shared with her my discovery, only to have it shattered by her dissertation into the vast differences between the mythical unicorn and Pegasus, Athena's winged horse.

Did I really need to have my vision shattered for the sake of an education in Greek mythology and literary fable? No! Couldn't mom have let the fantasy ride for a little while until I grew older and figured it out? Of course not! It was like being told Santa didn't exist or that the tooth fairy was really a big hairy man in underwear.

The after effects of this trauma were truly remarkable. For years after this incident, whenever my father would pull into a Mobil station to "fill er up", a blank look would suddenly appear on my face as my eyes would glaze over and my hair would turn a bright orange. I would then exit the car and break into a jig while reciting in Gaelic the lyrics from the Unicorn song. This performance always entertained the man at the pumps and he would occasionally top off the tank for no extra charge. Soon after, my parents sold me off to a circus where I worked as a sideshow act billed as "Conan O'Brien." Years later, after doing voice overs for Lucky Charms commercials, I decided to briefly leave show business for some deep therapy.

Okay, so maybe I exaggerated a bit but truthfully, to this day, I never have "filled 'er up" at a Mobil station.

During that same year, I had a brief flirtation with other pop/children songs like "Puff the Magic Dragon" by Peter Paul and Mary and "Christmas Don't Be Late" by Alvin, Theodore and Simon of the Chipmunks. But these were just mere flings compared to my next encounter, in October of 1963. On my seventh birthday I received as a gift, a blue, hand held, AM transistor radio. WMCA was the hip station and I listened to it all day long. I'm sure I could have named every song on the top 20, but there was one specific song that stood out, affecting my life forever. It was by a group from Liverpool England called the Beatles, titled "I Want To Hold Your Hand".

The song had attitude like nothing I heard before. When it came on the radio I would freak out like I just cooked up and mainlined a whole box of Apple Jacks. I became so over stimulated that I would jump all over my room, bouncing from wall to wall singing and pretending that I was a Beatle. One time I got so loud, mom rushed up the stairs and burst into my room thinking that I was having an epileptic fit. Her look of concern quickly turned to dread when she saw her crazed son standing atop his dresser, wearing one of her wigs and holding a stickball bat for a guitar. No she was not pleased at all but on some level she understood my gravity towards music (she was a dancer before she got married), and in a moment of weakness, took me to the new record store that opened on Ralph Ave where I bought my very first self funded, record.

When we got home, I kept with tradition and immediately got out my pen and paper. I literally had to beg mom to write down the lyrics, which was painstaking for her, since she hated the music and thought The Beatles couldn't sing worth a damn. She obviously did not have A&R ears, since the Beatles went on to become the greatest pop band in the history of Rock and Roll, but I love her dearly for helping make music a part of my life.

Throughout my childhood, there was not a moment when I was without my transistor radio. By the time I was 9, I was making up my own weekly Top 20 and checking against the countdown on the Dan Ingram Show. One Monday in 1968, I was sitting in bible class with my trusty radio, neatly tucked inside my pants pocket. I had cleverly wired the thin, white earphone under my belt, up into my shirt, through the sleeve and into my palm, which then rested up against my ear.

It was 9:55am and there was just me and the infamous DJ "Harry Har Harrison in the morning". "Miro" the named we dubbed our spiritual advisor, was lecturing in front of the class while I sat with my eyes shut, jamming with "Light My Fire." I never noticed that he had abruptly stopped his lesson and was surveying the classroom, wondering what in the world was the annoying sound competing with his voice. My best friend Gary, who was sitting on the other side of the room, knew what I was up to and desperately tried to get my attention. But I was lost in radio land and never saw Miro, in some kind of evangelistic fit, swoop down at me like I was possessed by Satan himself, and whip my arm out causing my head to slam down on the desk. My eyes opened to the sight of this crazed man, with the power of the almighty surging inside him, reach into my pants and exorcise ole' blue from my pocket. And, in a motion that would have made William Blatty proud, he threw it at the blackboard, shattering it and Morrison's voice into bits, spraying blue, plastic shrapnel across the room. On this day in 1968 teen angst was born.

My trauma lasted only until school let out, when I went home and got some of my allowance money together to buy a new radio. After all, tomorrow was Tuesday and it was time for the top 20 Countdown. As it turned out, my mishap was a blessing in disguise since my new radio had FM. Good-bye Steve & Eydie and hello Jimi Hendrix. I never again listened to the Top 20.

At age twelve, I got my first guitar. It was an acoustic and no matter what I did, I could not play anything on it. It turned out that I was left-handed and it was strung for a righty. This revelation came to me at my first lesson with Mr. Lebarker. He decided not to re-string it and made me turn it around and play right-handed. To this day, I wonder how much better I could have been if he just switched the strings.

I had studied for about 3 months when my mom stopped my lessons. It seems that my grades had plummeted worse than the stock market crash of 1929. This was totally devastating to me because Lebarker wasn't boring me with theory or how to read music; instead he was pulling riffs off my favorite Beatle songs and showing me how to play them. This made me the coolist kid in school. Mom wasn't just taking away my lessons, she was robbing me of my status. But I persisted. Even though the lessons were finished, the damage had been done, and I was never without my guitar. Thank you Mr. Lebarker, wherever you are.

Throughout high school and college, I played in bands, practicing my guitar 8-12 hours a day; and by my early 20's, I was giging out live in NYC with a band that was offered a development deal from Polygram records. I cut singles, toured colleges, made 2 videos and finally, in my latter years, managed and consulted acts. I have been involved in music virtually my entire life. I know what drives a young person to music and I hope that with this book I can help all you "Unicorns" not miss the boat. I am very current in what I listen to and at 39, I am drawn more than ever to new music and constantly searching the underground for the latest sounds.

My proudest moment came recently, while driving in my car with my son and daughter. I had a cassette of Disney songs playing for their listening pleasure. In between one of the tracks, I heard a sort of annoying sound that was competing with the car stereo. I looked back at my 7 year old son who was strapped in place with the seat belt, and noticed that he was listening to my Sony Walkman with the headphones on, eyes closed and humming. At the red light I reached behind me, pulled the headphones up and asked him what he was listening to. With both pride and horror I heard him succinctly say "Nirvana dad, 'Smells Like Teen Spirit'." I think I shall write this book for him.

Hey Lord, that's everyone but The Unicorns. Should we cancel the Storm or what? Over"

2

STATE OF MIND

Stripped down to its purest form, the song is man's truest expression of his innermost thoughts and emotions. It is the sacred document of words and music, composed in an effort to communicate these feelings in ways that simple discussion can't.

For thousands of years men and women have taken to this most primal instinct. From the earliest of composers purifying themselves in prayer, to rock's aggressive angst of today, songwriters throughout the ages have tapped the wells of their experiences, personal tortures and intense loves as a form of self-sacrifice, exposing the writer's soul in its barest and most naked form, fragile and innocent, passionate and private.

It was once described to me by a recording artist I managed that his songs were like his children and the manipulation, exploitation and criticism they receive by the industry was heart wrenching. I couldn't have agreed with him more had it not been for just one small point. The second he asked someone, "Hey, I just wrote this tune, what do you think," he crossed the line from personal, private expression to public domain. In fact, when you write these songs and record them for sale you exit the existential world of art and enter into the cutthroat world of the music business. This is not a bad place as long as you come to terms with what happens next and prepare yourself.

In the music business, success brings fame and fortune. We all have dreamed of that at one time or another. But what does it take to turn your ability to write and play music into a successful lifetime endeavor? When you think about it, creating the music is the easy part. With a little inspiration and a bit of talent you can write a song. But once you have the song you might need to put together a band to perform it, find a place to perform it in, advertise to get people to come and see you and then get paid for it. You will need to protect and copyright the songs. You need to come up with marketing plans to keep your band in the public consciousness. You need to secure bookings and make travel arrangements. You will need a bookkeeping system to keep your financial records in order to avoid trouble with your band mates and the IRS. Also, there is merchandising of T-shirts tapes, hats, bumper stickers and mailing lists to consider.

At some point you will need to record your music, as this will be necessary in getting everything from gigs to press coverage, independent radio air play and finally, a record contract.

Before any record company invests in your project, you need to be somewhat of a going concern. What attracts them to you is the same exact thing that attracts a big business to buy up a small business. That is, do you have a product that people want?

Having written a great song is only the first and very last thing you need. Everything in between depends on how well you manage it. You will need to be strong in your convictions, yet open to possibilities and to surround yourself with trusted collaborators to achieve the best possible product. To sell this product so that you can support your very existence you will need producers, a manager, agent, accountant, record company, as well as the support from radio stations, music video, press and most important, the fans to embrace and invest in it. For this, you most certainly will need to be armed with the essential tools and knowledge to get through so you stand a chance of being the next great one without selling your soul to the devil.

Ultimately, if you or your group begin to get some notoriety, your first objective will be to secure a good manager. It is foolish to believe that you can handle the job by yourself. All the important contacts in the music business, prefer to deal with the band's representative and a good professional manager's own skills of negotiation, organization and coordination of people is an essential part of a successful group.

Since most bands start out without one, you have no choice but to do it yourself. Every band would love to have a Brian Epstein or Paul McGuiness as their manager. They are out there, but first you need to have the goods to attract them to you. But even more important is that you should know as much about the business and your career as you can before you ever get a manager so that you'll know if the person representing you is doing the job you are paying them for.

THE RECIPE FOR SUCCESS

Considering the amount of money one can potentially make and how so few bands ever make it, how does one get to the top? Have you ever listened to the radio and said to yourself "I've got more talent and better songs than many of these bands," your head shaking in wonder as to how they got to where they are?

Well, they are where they are because they have, in some fashion, combined the following four ingredients of success.

·TALENT ·POPULARITY · *PERSEVERANCE* · *LUCK*

TALENT

This is a rare, creative, artistic aptitude one has that sets them apart from everyone else. Is it a gift you are born with or is it developed from years of hard, intense work and practice, striving to be the best you can be?

In some cases it's one or the other but in most cases it is the marriage of the two. All of us are born with great talent for something, the secret in life is to find what that is. Aside from our gift there are many other things in life we can master. The worst crime we can commit to ourselves is either never realizing what our talent is or even worse knowing what it is and never cultivating it.

Earlier I asked you if you ever listened to the radio and felt you have more talent than a band you just heard. Remember the band THE KINGSMEN? This was a group from the early 60's that had a hit song called "Louie, Louie." It has to be one of the simplest songs in the history of Rock and Roll. Three chords and some verse lyrics that till this day I can't figure out what they are and a chorus that just repeats the words "Louie Louie." And yet this song is one of the top 100 singles of all time selling into the millions making someone a lot of money. Think you can do it? Try it. Go ahead sit down right now and compose a simple three chord hit song that by next year will make you financially independent. It's so easy, hey I'll give you a few more minutes.

...........................Time's up. What did you come up with? Maybe you actually got something. Well if you did, that's talent. Can you now sell it to a record company, have it released and have everybody in America singing it? That's a slightly more difficult task. The point is, anyone who can slap three chords together with a bunch of silly lyrics, has only one fourth of what it takes to make it.

But what if you had trouble writing even the simplest of songs? Before you even get started down this long road of warm beer and smoke filled bar rooms, be realistic with yourself. Many lives are wasted by people who can't sing, play, write or perform. If you love music there are many things that you can do in the music business that you may have a talent for and excel in. Interning for a record company or talent agency is a good start that may lead to a paying job. If you're in college join the student activities board and work on the concert committee. You can build up a good deal of contacts that may lead to a job in the business when you graduate. Study communications or work at the college radio station. There are trade schools where you can learn sound engineering and recording. If school isn't your thing try to hook up with a band that you believe in and work your ass off to help them. Learn how to do lights or mix sound. You can study guitar or drum repair and be a technician on the road. You can join the union and be a stage hand or if you read this entire book, you might even try to manage a young, up and coming band.

If you love music do not limit yourself to one sole endeavor. Get involved with other projects and become more rounded. It is through experience that one gains a sense of themselves and where their potential talents lie.

POPULAR SOUND

Many people have a talent to write and compose music. What sets one artist apart from another in relationship to making it in the music business is their ability to write music that has a popular appeal. Though you might write a great 50's Do-Wop, it will probably not be widely accepted since it is not a very popular sound today. But that can all change tomorrow. Popularity is such a transient entity because no one knows what determines what is going to be popular. Do-Wop might just come back next year and you will have yourself a hit song. Having a sound out just when it's ready to be popular is called timing. And for the most part, this is everything.

Let's look at what happened musically in the early 90's. There we were, coming out of the 80's and the big thing was commercial, hard rock, hair bands like Van Halen, Motley Crue, Poison and so on. But in the west coast city of Seattle, a sound that has been building for years was beginning to eke its way into the scene. There were bands like Mother Love Bone, Alice in Chains and Mudhoney that were combining elements of Punk Rock, Hard Rock, Metal and Alternative. Some of these bands were signed to small independent record labels and their music was receiving significant air play on college radio. Still for the most part, it was an underground sound until one band, Nirvana, hit with "Smells Like Teen Spirit" and the flood gates opened up. They just had that right combination of great song and perfect timing. The public was ready and primed for this "new" sound. If you were a grunge band that year and had some good songs you stood a very good chance of getting seen and possibly signed to a record deal; certainly more so than if you were writing hook filled, folk rock. But that did not stop the Counting Crows, a hook filled, folk rock band from coming out of nowhere in 1993 and put grunge to the back seat with their monster hit "Mr. Jones." And almost as if grunge never happened, the airwaves were filled with softer bands like Spin Doctors, Toad The Wet Sprocket and The Gin Blossoms, who interestingly enough released "Hey Jealousy" the year before and received no air play whatsoever. But their label held on and re-released the single a year later and the band went multi-platinum.

The true strength of a song's ability to change the public's focus rests entirely on two factors: (**a**) that it's a great song and (**b**) that it appeals to the general public. The reason why Mr. Jones went to number one was simply that. It was an undeniably great song and everybody loved it.

You can't try and figure out what the public likes. The public is only guided by what it's presented with. The record companies only offer the public a small sampling of the tons of material sent to them. The A&R guys are using their best judgment in trying to figure out what offerings to make to the public by combining what musical format is hot along with what is new. This is all they have to go by. No one has a crystal ball that will guarantee a hit song. So the moral of the story is you must write what comes from inside you and hope you have the personal vision to capture mass public appeal.

If you are purposely trying to write popular music, it is a danger to copy the existing format because what is on the radio at this moment was recorded a year ago and written a few years ago. So if you have something comparable you have to figure that at best it will take at least two years before it gets out to the public and certainly by then there's a good chance it won't be popular anymore. By the same token if you are trying to be irreverent and counter popular, there probably exists certain boundaries that might be considered too far to cross especially if you intend on landing a hit song. Chances are if you submit a controversial song to a major record label, though it might be a great song and all your friends love it, there's a very good chance just by a racy title or lyrics the song might never make it to radio.

And don't start blaming the people in the industry by say "they wouldn't don't know a good song if it interrupted their cellular conference call." For starters, they definitely do, the radio is full of great songs and furthermore, it's not a question of whether it's a good song or not. There's just a vast difference between a good song and a commercial hit.

Look at any given Billboard Top Twenty and you will see several styles of popular music from rap to country and metal to alternative. Be honest and write your own music. It will either make it or it won't based on factors outside your control. If you try to compete with the times, by the time the song gets to the public, it will be behind the times.

Besides, radio is only one aspect of this business. For all the money certain artists make from all the radio play, did you know that one of the wealthiest bands in the world, recently written up in Forbes Business Magazine, is the Grateful Dead. Here's a group that hasn't released an album since 1989 and has had only one top ten song in their entire thirty year history. Yet they packed the largest stadiums in America, selling out on multiple night appearances and are worth hundreds of millions of dollars. How's that for popular! All their money and popularity is based on their live show which is the bread and butter of any band. It is the one area of the artists' career of which the record company does not take a percentage.

So whether you're Garth Brooks or Marilyn Manson the one thing they both have in common is that their success was determined by their appeal to the masses.

" Hey Spike get this, Mustang Records rejected our song "The Damn Fridge is Empty Cause We're Freakin' Broke, Cause The Lousy Record Label Won't Give Us a Deal." What are they deaf or something."

FOCUS, PERSEVERANCE AND PASSION

If talent is the match then focus and perseverance must surely be the flame. I especially want to impress those of you who are young and have the goods, to take this seriously. Without a strong will to succeed coupled with a clear and ardent focus toward what you want, your fate may lie swallowed up into the belly of this business and spit out years later, into some lame day job for the rest of your life. I'm not your father and I don't want to lose you by sounding like one, but if music is what you love to do then sanctify it as you would anything else that you love. Maybe more so. There are thousands and thousands of bands across this country, young people from all walks of life trying to get out from under, competing for the precious few record deals that are made. Countless numbers of bands are calling clubs day in and day out trying to get a gig. Sometimes it takes months of not letting up and constantly calling just to get one lousy show in a new town.

The competition gets even more fierce for radio play. Major radio stations might only add two new songs a month into their light rotation. That's got to be tough for the 300 or so albums released each month. You have to work hard at this day after day, sacrificing many of life's frivolities to make it. Can't do it? Too hard? Do you think it's painful to always be practicing, playing at dive clubs, trying to stay straight and not party with all your friends so that you can make smart decisions? You think that's painful? Ask the band *"Live"* who in 1993, just barely out of their teens, sold 350,000 copies of their first album and well over four million copies of their second album, just how painful being serious ultimately was! You show me a lazy musician, irresponsible and not motivated, getting wasted up all the time, not taking care of his money and his spirit and I'll show you a loser or someone staring down the barrel of a gun.

What is pain? Pain is not making it. Pain is not being true to yourself and cutting your chances. Pain is missed opportunities that could have changed your life forever.

If you don't like pain, **FOCUS AND PERSEVERE!**

LUCK

"If only I could get that lucky break," he says while lying in bed in a drunken stupor at 3:00 on a Tuesday afternoon wondering why the record companies haven't been calling non stop in response to that one song demo he recorded at the flea market instant recording studio 6 months ago.

What is luck? Is it some intrinsic gift bestowed upon one individual at birth or is it a result of a series of logical events pooled together into one massive moment in time? Can luck be a god given gratuity that some beings receive while others receive none or even worse bad luck? These are thoughts that I have pondered for many years having seen people I know get lucky who don't seem deserving. Yet upon further investigation what I perceived as lucky, turned out to be either tremendous burdens for them or was a result of a chain of simple events or actions that systematically over time led to one final outcome. To an outsider that would be perceived as a random display of luck. This gave me a new perspective on the concept and how the manipulation of energy can help manifest things both lucky and unfortunately unlucky for oneself.

I do not believe there is any one person that is inherently more lucky than the next. That would imply that there is some force out there doling out good luck to one person, which in effect would then cause bad or no luck to another. Luck surrounds us all. It is the manifestation of thoughts, actions and energy. The extent of our luck or the frequency with which it appears, is directly related to the matter we are concentrating our energies on. It is up to us to individually learn how to connect with the universe and make use of the power within it. It is around you right now. Feel it and connect with it.

In life we all have things that we are meant to be doing. When you get on the right path toward your destination all the things necessary to get you there will fall into place. This is what we interpret as luck. If you are constantly banging into walls, never catching breaks and not going anywhere then I think it's a sign that you are not on the right road; and that in itself is luck. Your instinct to recognize that sign increases your potential for luck. It's all in how you use and interpret the power of the universe.

I don't know you personally but know this: your mind supplies you with all the answers to all the questions you ask it. Train your mind to think positive and ask of yourself positive questions like, "What can I do today that will get me further along in the music business"? I guarantee you that a person who concentrates on these thoughts taps into the positive energy that is around, will see results and be perceived as someone that is lucky. On the other hand if you constantly say to yourself, "I'm such a loser; how come I never catch a break?" Guess what? You never will because you are focusing in or tapping into a negative energy. Your answer is going to be, because you're a loser and you will never get anywhere.

You make your own luck. You will never be in the right place at the right time if you are never anyplace but your bedroom, dreaming.

MIXING THE INGREDIENTS

Whether you are a solo artist, a group, a manager, lawyer or anyone trying to make it in the business, you need to get out there and make contacts and use them to make more contacts. Be confident, personable; and above all be professional. Only professionals make it all the way in this business and if you want to be taken seriously and treated like a professional, present yourself as one.

Here are some tips on getting yourself out there.

 SEND ARTICLES, DEMO TAPES, NEWSLETTERS AND MONTHLY GIG CALENDARS TO MUSIC BUSINESS CONTACTS.

Keep them abreast of your progress and create a buzz.

 STUDY OTHERS THAT HAVE MADE IT TO THE LEVEL YOU WANT TO GET TO.

Read their biographies and become inspired. If they could do it so can you. Try to repeat the things that they did to make it.

 GO TO CLUBS AS OFTEN AS YOU CAN AND WATCH THE COMPETITION.

 SIGN ON TO INTERNET AND LOOK INTO ALL THE VARIOUS WEB SITES AVAILABLE FOR MAKING INDUSTRY CONTACTS.

There is a whole network of services from Record Labels to Marketing groups to Indie bulletin boards. What are you waiting for, get some Sex Wax, polish up your mouse and get surfing. (See end of Chapter 12 for a listing of dozens of cool sites including mine)

 GO TO THE VARIOUS SEMINARS THAT TAKE PLACE THROUGHOUT THE YEAR.

These are great opportunities for you to make contacts and learn about the business. There are usually many guest speakers from the industry that give seminars on every single topic concerning the music business. If you are in a band, apply for a performance slot at the seminars that feature the kind of music you play. It is imperative that you know about them, attend them and if you can, showcase at them.

Below is a list of national and regional seminars that take place throughout the year:

NATIONAL

CMJ (College Music Journal) **(516) 466-6000**

Convention held in NY in September.

FOUNDATIONS FORUM (212) 645-1360

Heavy Metal, Hard Rock & Alternative held in Los Angeles alternating months.

SOUTH BY SOUTHWEST (512) 467-7979

Rock and acoustic showcases, panels and trade shows held in March in Austin TX.

NACA CONVENTION (803) 732-6222

National Association of Campus Activities: Meet all the talent buyers who book college concerts. Panels, showcases and more. Held in Feb. but always in a different city.

(MASS) MID-ATLANTIC SOUND SURF AND SKATE
SYMPOSIUM (910) 256-4653 ask for Terry
Sponsored by Juice Magazine. Held in June.

Some of the most important people in sports, music, fashion and film gather in Wilmington North Carolina for five days of band showcases, panels, seminars, skateboarding, surfing, wakeboarding car show fashion and film.

E-mail Juicesss@AOL.com

Web site: www.juicemag.com

MUSIC BUSINESS SEMINARS (800) 448-3621

Two day seminar focusing on promoting your band.

REGIONAL

WINTER MUSIC CONFERENCE

March, Miami Beach Florida • (954) 563-4444

GAVIN SEMINAR

California in Feb location changes evey year • (415) 495-3200

CUTTING EDGE MUSIC BUSINESS CONF. Sept. New Orleans • (504) 827-5700

PHILADELPHIA MUSIC CONFERENCE Philadelphia PA • (215) 587-9550

SOUTHEASTERN MUSIC CONFERENCE April/May Tampa Fl • (813) 989-1472

UNDERCURRENTS May, Cleveland Ohio • (216) 463-3595

Keep in mind that this is current information this writing in 1997. As with all good things these seminars may indeed change over time. For up to date information check with my web site at
http://www.allareaaccess.com

In the following chapters you will get years of experience that can hopefully save you from the many pitfalls that await you. There is a school for this stuff it's called hard knocks. Your tuition is your blood, sweat and tears, and hopefully this will be your textbook and I, your personal coach to help you graduate.

3

STARTING THE BAND

I choose to start here because this is the very beginning, where it all happens. It's the point in your life where you have either consciously or unconsciously decided that you want to spend a better part of your time playing music. I feel that any decision is a good one as long as you make it sober and with a plan. If you want to play recreationally, many of the points in here will absolutely still apply but you can skip chapters. If you are going to take this seriously, then read it all.

It seems as though the best bands have been made up of long time friends or family members. People who have known each other for a long time develop a subconscious level of communication that is crucial in making and performing music.

Due to the tremendous amount of time you spend with your band mates, it makes for a more successful situation if you know each other. Not to say that this still wouldn't happen, but the most common break up of a band besides not making any money is that they don't get along.

Usually the nucleus of a band will form rather unceremoniously when a few friends get together to jam. Sort of an adolescent form of playing poker with the guys. Unless you are fortunate that among all of you each instrument is covered, you are going to have to seek out one or more players to complete the group.

In order to do that, the core group you have must now decide what type of band you are and what kind of music you are going to play. If you are focusing on being a Metallica tribute band and you need a vocalist, your friend Mary Joe, who is into country and western should not be your first choice.

On the other hand, if you are going to be writing and performing your own music, you are going to need players that have original ideas. Though similar influences may be a good starting point for an original band, be careful not to end up writing music or sounding just like the band you are all so influenced by. Sometimes bringing in a player who you get along with personally but has slightly different musical roots, might very well give your music a whole new feel. There have been some great bands throughout the years made up of radically diverse members that pooled all their influences together to make one common great sound: Faith No More, Traffic, Smashing Pumpkins to name a few.

If you don't know anyone around that could fill the open spot, here is a list of how you can begin your search

"Dudes meet Hiram. He's gonna be our new lead singer.
The only thing is we're gonna have to play acoustic"

HANG POSTERS UP AT YOUR LOCAL HIGH SCHOOL OR COLLEGE

Before you hang up anything you must check in with the office and get approval to post a flyer and in some places you will need to get your flyer stamped before they can be posted. Failure to do this will probably result in the posters being torn down before enough people get a chance to see them.

PUT POSTERS UP AT THE LOCAL MUSIC STORES

ASK FRIENDS

HANG POSTERS AT THE LOCAL CLUBS AND BARS

PLACE AN AD IN A LOCAL MUSIC PUBLICATION OR CLASSIFIED SECTION OF A NEWSPAPER

GO OUT TO CLUBS TO SEE OTHER BANDS IN HOPES OF SPOTTING MUSICIANS IN ANOTHER GROUP. IF YOU SEE A PLAYER THAT FITS YOUR STYLE, CASUALLY INTRODUCE YOURSELF AND INVITE THEM OVER TO YOUR NEXT REHEARSAL

CLASSIFIEDS

When you make up a poster the goal is to try to say a lot in very few words. Chances are wherever you're going to put them, there will be a shortage of space. So don't tell your band's life story and design it to stand out.

VOCALIST NEEDED

FOR FIVE PIECE ORIGINAL ROCK BAND.

18-21 years old.

Attitude & Presence a must

Call Joe Cabot at: 777-9911

I'm sure that with a bit more flair and originality you can style this to fit your band's image but this will work for both posters and newspaper ads.

AUDITIONS

As potential band members begin to call you, an interview over the phone will be necessary. Have a conversation about influences, equipment, the opposite sex, whatever. A good conversation will be one good indicator for things to come musically. By the end of the interview set up a time when you are going to get together. It is important that when you begin jamming with a potential new member, that aside from the standard blues progressions, you will have found within your conversation common musical elements and can begin to throw in some cover material to see how well they learn and execute parts. If you are an original act, it might be a good idea to make simple tapes of your rehearsals so that you can supply potential new members with your music prior to them coming over to jam. This way when you do get together you can tell how well they learned the song and if the parts they write add or detract from the song.

Other things to be looking for are:

 HOW WELL THE PLAYER CONTROLS THEIR VOLUME.

 HAVE THEY LIVED UP TO THEIR DESCRIPTION OF THEMSELVES OVER THE PHONE?

 HOW GOOD IS THEIR EQUIPMENT?

 DO THEY SEEM TO DISPLAY THE SAME DRIVE AND CONVICTION AS THE REST OF YOU?

 DO THEY WRITE AND HOW COMPATIBLE IS THEIR MATERIAL TO YOURS?

 DO THEY HAVE BAD HABITS, LIKE CHAIN SMOKING IF THE REST OF YOU ARE NON - SMOKERS?

Remember nobody's perfect and yet don't settle for second best. You are depending on each one of the band members for your life. Make sure these are people you trust.

With the members in place, choosing the correct musical direction and style of the band will now determine what your next moves are going to be.

DETERMINING YOUR MUSICAL IDENTITY

I will spend a lot of time in this book focusing on original bands but there are other types of rock groups out there making all kinds of money and enjoying different levels of success. They are as follows:

 COVER BAND

This band plays a varied selection of popular recorded songs. Usually there will be some theme to them such as an alternative cover band playing sets comprised of songs from The Cure to Pearl Jam or a top 40 cover band playing the hotel circuit doing a more dance and ballad style set. These bands need to perform the songs as close to the original recordings as possible. The ones that do it the best become the most popular.

Cover bands in general make more money per night than an unsigned original group and will probably have an easier time getting a booking. Club owners know exactly what they are getting when booking a cover band and crowds tend to respond better to a cover band playing material off the radio than to a new original band whose music they never heard before. A good cover band can make anywhere from $500-$3000 a night. Chances are as a cover band this is as far as you will ever go in the business and your longevity is based solely on how current you stay musically.

 TRIBUTE BAND

Essentially the same as a cover band but with one distinction. The basis of your act is the recreation of the music and many times the appearance of only one band. (For example, Beatlemania playing tribute to the Beatles or The Machine as Pink Floyd). Bands of this nature will go to great lengths to sound exactly like the group they are playing tribute to by using the same equipment and putting on a similar style of performance. Many of these acts are quite good and eventually hook up with booking agencies securing dates throughout the year making very good money.

The main drawback is none of these groups will ever get a record deal so all your income is made on the road from live performances and merchandising, which is where you will live for a good part of the year.

Another drawback is that group you're paying tribute to, for a time might be a hip band to cover but what happens if over time their popularity decreases? It's very difficult for tribute bands to change direction without the risk of losing a good portion of their audience.

❸ ORIGINAL BAND

This is the hardest but ultimately most rewarding way to go. It is very difficult to get gigs especially when you are unknown, simply because audiences have never heard your material before and club owners who have large overheads (business costs) need to keep their audience happy and drinking in order to stay in business.

For the most part when you are starting out, the pay is 50-75% less than cover bands. As you begin to get more popular the pay will always be relative to the amount of people you draw to the club. In some cases original bands have been known to buy tickets from the club and sell them to their fans in order to get on stage (Pay to Play).

Times are always difficult for original bands even after they sign a record deal. When you record your first album and go on the road to tour, in the markets where you have not developed any business you will only get anywhere from $50-$200 depending on how good your booking agent is. Of course this scenario does change, as you get more popular and as your single begins to climb up the charts. Someday if all goes well you may be worth anywhere from $10,000-$250,000 a night!

❹ TRACK ACTS

These type of acts perform live to pre recorded music which is on tape and supplied to the house DJ to spin while they perform. Track acts usually specialize in dance oriented music be it alternative rave, hip hop, Latin or disco. Their show is centered around a stage production of dance and lighting. A fairly popular track act can earn as much as Tribute bands do in a club circuit and can quite possibly earn more if they score a hit song on a dance oriented radio station.

Each style brings with it risks that you must deal with. But there is no rule that says you can't change direction if something isn't working or that if you are a cover band you can't play an original song or vice versa. Bottom line is look out into the crowd and focus on what is working and what isn't. These people paid to see you play. The more entertaining you are the more successful you will be.

When you are getting started it is as important now as it will always be that you maintain and strive for perfection. The following four things are the most common problems young bands face.

BAND NAME

There are some really great band names that I can think of that stand alone as great names. Then, there are names that have become great due to the greatness of the band. Whatever you choose as a name, keep in mind that it does and will play an important role in the first impression everyone from fans to labels has of the group.

In the end, it is always about the music but the name does carry with it a great deal of responsibility. From first impressions to the marketing and promotions of a band, the name manny times is the cover in which your musical book is judged by. Choosing the right name for your band should invlove a great deal of thought and foresight.

When choosing a name you should consider the following:

 EVERYBODY IN THE BAND LIKE IT.

It's very difficult to come up with that great name and sometimes it's the band that makes the name great. Unless you unanimously agree within your group to become the name, it will never really become part of you.

 IT IS EASILY SPELLED AND PRONOUNCED.

You'll never know how important this is until you start playing out at clubs and finding your name misspelled on the marquee or in the newspapers. One group that I represented had a name that sounded like five other possible names. At times, especially when calling out of state where accents are different, the first 3 minutes of a phone call was spent on just trying to get the name right. Even after all that, we would arrive in town only to find that the marquee had the name still spelled incorrectly. Finally I had to insert in our contract rider as the very first provision, the adherence to the correct spelling.

 IT COINCIDES WITH THE STYLE OF YOUR MUSIC.

To get noticed over and above your competition your band name is one of the first things people hear or see. A great name advertised in posters or in the papers will also help to attract people to see you and also define you to a certain clientele. Graphic styles and band logos are also very important in helping your band be defined by its name. After all it's not a coincidence that bands with strong names like Tool or Corrosion of Conformity play a hard style of music or groups with softer names like The Cranberries or The Cardigans play a softer style of music. These names serve as a calling card to the musical community they are trying to attract. So if you are a Polish Polka band, the name "Brutal Rage" might be a poor choice .

 IT EITHER DOESN'T BELONG TO ANOTHER BAND OR VAGUELY SOUND LIKE ANOTHER BAND'S NAME.

This is more of a legal infringement than just bad judgment. As you would copyright a song so will you eventually trademark your band's name. By naming your group "You Two" or "Share" you are inviting a legal recourse that can carry severe penalties. You will at some point be contacted by the legal arm of U2 and Cher with a cease and desist letter to immediately stop using the name.

To make sure you have not infringed on another group's name you will need to do a trademark search. This is costly and will require an attorney. Trademark search organizations such as the following will issue reports to attorneys on trademarks registered with the United States Patent and Trademark Office in Washington, DC.

"Brutal Rage, these guys are more like a Lawrence Welk cover band!"

```
TRADEMARK      →THOMPSON & THOMPSON
SEARCH              500 VICTORY ROAD
ORGANIZATIONS      NORTH QUINCY, MASS 02171     (617) 479-1600
                   or

        →       THE TRADEMARK RESEARCH GROUP
                300 PARK AVE SOUTH
                NEW YORK, NY 10010               (212) 228-4084
```

Due to the overabundance of names and trademarks it is difficult to decide whether names are similar in regards to the law. Check with an experienced trademark attorney either to conduct a search or to defend you in the event of a lawsuit.

EQUIPMENT

The trend right now with bands is to down scale the size and flash of their equipment. This is reminiscent of the late seventies and early eighties when punk first reared it's angry head with bands like the Sex Pistols, Ramones, Generation X and the Clash who cast aside the rock star image for a low budget anti endorsement look and sound. Remember the B52's? Their guitarist Ricky Wilson played a two string Mosrite guitar through a Fender Twin. As if the late 90's music isn't already taking a cue from the punk era, I recently saw The Presidents Of The United States live and experienced deja vu seeing their guitarists create a great sound with beat up guitars and a total of five strings.

Equipment is only as good as the person using it. Top of the line, custom made Diaz amps sound great but so does the $350, 80 watt, Ampeg Rocket with one 12" speaker that I just bought last week. If expense is an issue you should look to buy used. In fact searching through the classified ads will probably help you uncover the equipment of your dreams for a lot less money than buying new at the store.

The advantage a music store offers is that you will receive a warranty as well as a selection. Guitarists, if you are looking to buy new but money is an obstacle, there is a wide range of moderately priced electric guitars that believe it or not will function just as good in a live situation as a top of the line Fender with Lace Sensor pickups. Fender for instance manufactures a mid-priced American standard, a slightly cheaper Japanese model as well as guitars manufactured in Mexico that retail for under $300. Other good playing inexpensive models are manufactured by Gibson (the Epiphone line), Ibanez, Aria, Yamaha, Peavey and Washburn. I am not endorsing any of these companies but I have played selected models from all of them and there are characteristics about all of them that I like and dislike. My personal guitar is a

Fender American Standard in Sunburst finish that I paid $400 for and wouldn't trade for anything in the world.

Amplifiers are important pieces of equipment due to the fact that they are responsible for projecting the sound coming from the guitar. Though there are brands that I would strongly recommend avoiding, I would suggest that before you purchase any amp, you play *your* guitar through it. Each piece of equipment has its own personality and you can't buy it based on its looks or brand name. Though I love the look and sound of Marshall amps, I never owned one because I couldn't get *my* sound out of it. Aside from Marshall, some moderately priced amps are put out by Crate, Peavey, Fender and Ampeg that have at least 40 watts or more of power and come equipped with good speakers.

Drums are acoustic instruments and rely more on materials and craftsmanship for sound and durability. The type of wood, the brand of heads, the hardware and the overall construction all determine the quality of your sound. Of course you can put down big bucks and order a hand made GMS kit in a custom color made from hollowed out tree trunks, or you can get a Pearl or Tama 5 piece drum set that will get the job done and still be able to eat for the year as most of you drummers out there know.

Shopping for keyboards requires a more technical approach than buying guitars or drums. You first need to determine what the full range of uses are and what piece of equipment will do the job.

Some keyboards are "closed systems" where they come pre loaded with 100-300 various different samples of sounds already programmed into it. Price ranges change radically from year to year. In 1994 the new wonder machine selling for $1,500 is old news in 1995 on sale for $750.

If you are looking for a machine that you can use both as a performance instrument as well as a writing/recording instrument then you might be more interested in a Keyboard Sampler. This type of machine allows you to record multi tracks of whatever you are composing on it. This is great for studio work and home recording.

There are many hybrids of both these machines that perform some functions from both styles. All in all you should really try to buy new equipment from a reputable and knowledgeable dealer especially if you are a first time buyer. If you are educated in this area then you don't need me to tell you that you can buy last years models very cheaply from the want adds.

So do not go into hock to get top of the line equipment. Like the guy who spends thousands of dollars fixing up his car so that he can do 0-60 in 3 seconds on residential streets where the speed limit is 35, you will not need tons of great equipment until you are signed and touring around.

IMAGE

The image of an individual band member and to a larger extent, the image of the band, is a major ingredient in determining the group's overall potential. Bands must realize that aside from the music, image is the most important element that fans identify with. The stronger the image, the wider the appeal. The wider the appeal, the better the chances are of success.

Image refers to both stage presence and personal statement. Think about some of the most popular groups and their members throughout rock history. Elvis, Beatles, David Bowie, U2, Guns N' Roses, Nirvana etc. Aside from the music, what was it that set these groups apart from their contemporaries? The answer is a strong, identifiable image. Just the mere mention of these bands' names and you can immediately conjure up strong images in your mind that describes them. Another point to consider is that the description of these bands can be done in one sentence. In other words their image is so concise that you need only a few words to describe them; like blues rock for The Stones or Grunge for Nirvana. If you need a full paragraph to describe your band, then your image is too scattered and ineffective.

Where does image come from?

It comes from the individual members' ability to highlight marketable traits within their personality. Traits that set them apart from others; that attract others to them.

But be careful. Your image cannot be a false or dishonest one. You cannot be what you are not because people will eventually see through the pretentiousness and laugh at you. Remember Milli Vanilli?

You cannot try to be what you are not simply by applying makeup or wearing cool clothes. If you need cool clothes to be cool than *you're* not cool. Your clothes are. These applications will only work if they are truly an extension of your personality.

Image is so important that at times image may supercede the music and can launch a band's career faster than a band with better music but no image. The nineties rock music scene witnessed a direct correlation of this early on by the rise of the Seattle and Jam bands into the mainstream. One never would have guessed that the hard grunge or "Hippie" bands would within a few years come to be considered popular let alone mainstream. But it did and I believe that it was due in part to the bands having such strong, identifiable images, one that reflected those they were performing to. Bands like Alice in Chains and Blue Traveler have sold millions of records and attracted millions of fans with music that was considered by radio programmers, not prime candidates for "hit radio" programming. Nevertheless they gained commercial success by successfully tapping into a growing movement. The most successful of these groups were the ones who combined great image with great songs.

Just remember, do not just pick an image out of a hat. It has to be what is a part of you.

COMMITMENT

You don't have to sign your life away in blood, but other people do depend on you for rehearsal, new material, financial responsibilities, etc. Everyone involved in the project needs to share in the responsibility. Just because you write all the lyrics and don't play an instrument does not exclude you from lugging equipment at a gig. All band duties should be divvied out ahead of time so that everyone knows what is expected of them. I can't count how many times bands have finished a show, packed up and left only to arrive at their next destination minus a snare drum because they had no system to check if they had left something behind. If there is a weak link, address it. It will only get worse.

4

REHEARSAL

Now that you have your group assembled and the jamming is going great, it's time to begin making the most out of your rehearsal. There is definitely a right and wrong way to do this and if done improperly you are just wasting valuable time, money (if you're paying for rehearsal space) and energy.

I have assumed up until now that you have a place to rehearse and let me further assume that it is in the basement or garage of your parent's house. If so, consider yourself lucky. For many who live in the inner cities where there are only apartment buildings or private homes built one right next to the other, you are going to have to find a studio to rehearse in. I'd like to briefly go over the advantages and disadvantages of both and how you can make the most out of them.

HOME REHEARSAL

WORK OUT YOUR REHEARSAL TIMES IN ADVANCE.

At the end of the last rehearsal of the week, make a new schedule for the upcoming week. It is important to get on a steady schedule so that band members as well as household members know when rehearsal is so that it won't interfere with private, personal functions.

BE CONSIDERATE OF THE COSTS INCURRED BY YOUR REHEARSING.

Amps use electricity and though they probably won't accept it, it would be respectful to offer a small contribution to the homeowner to help offset the cost. Offer to mow the lawn or do a spring clean up. A little thought goes a long way.

WATCH YOUR VOLUME.

In time, the high frequencies will radically damage your eardrums possibly causing Tinnitus the inner ear disease that has affected players like Pete Townshend. Use a good set of ear-plugs that filter out the middle and high frequencies. At first it will be uncomfortable but in time you will get used to it.

If you are too loud you will miss certain nuances of the music not to mention disturbing neighbors or residents of the house.

PROTECT YOUR EQUIPMENT.

Basements that are below ground will at times get humid especially in the summer. This will wreak havoc on the wood and possibly the electronics of your instruments. If it's really bad you can either keep a dehumidifier on (which uses a lot of energy) or at least take your guitars and keyboards home after practice. Leave the drums and amps covered to protect them from the humidity as well as the dust that can accumulate.

 ## MAKE SURE THERE ARE NO WATER LEAKS.

This is a common problem in basements of private homes especially after a strong rainfall or snow melt. I recommend spreading old carpets on the floor to protect you from shocks caused by contact with the moisture. If the area you're playing in does have a water problem, do not turn any electrical equipment on until you have checked (especially under the carpet) for a buildup of water.

 ## MAKE SURE THAT THERE IS ENOUGH ELECTRICAL SUPPLY AND OUTLETS.

A shortage of each could cause a fire. Use surge protectors to plug all your amplification in. Unplug the amps after each rehearsal to further prevent damage. Make sure everything including your equipment is properly grounded.

 ## CREATE A MOOD CONDUCIVE TO A GOOD REHEARSAL.

Most basements are not acoustically balanced or properly lit and you will need some creative decorating (if allowed) to improve the acoustics and ambiance. To deaden the bouncing sound of amplified equipment try hanging old blankets on the wall. To improve the lighting, get some strands of white x-mas lights and run them above you on the ceiling. You now have created a subdued, club like, environment to rehearse in.

Use the rehearsal space as if it were a stage and use your imagination to dress it up. It could end up being a springboard for stage set ideas later on.

 ## REHEARSAL PA SYSTEM.

If the band has a vocalist they will need some form of amplification for the vocals. Mic's, cables, mic stands and an amp are the least amount of equipment you can get away with. As you begin to pool your money together you will want to invest in a simple vocal PA system. This will not only come in handy at rehearsals but in the event you should play at a party or a club that has no sound system, you will avoid having to rent one.

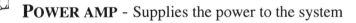 **POWER AMP** - Supplies the power to the system

MIXING BOARD - The console that mixes and controls the volume, tone, balance and effects of all incoming sounds. In some models the Power amp and mixing board come as one unit. You should use one that puts out at least 250 watts of power.

SPEAKERS - These should be full range cabinets with at least one 15" woofer and one horn. Some of the better speakers to use are: JBL, Altec Lansing, Crate & TOA.

CABLES- The connecting wire from the microphone to the mixing board. They should be about 15' long to reach from where you are singing to the board.

MICROPHONES - There are a full range of microphones priced anywhere from $19 to thousands. For rehearsal purposes all you really need is the durable Shure SM 58 .

MIKE STANDS

This is all the equipment you will ever need for basement rehearsals. You can find many if not all components of a PA in the classifieds so check there first before you buy it new. I do advise that you educate yourself about sound equipment. There are so many systems for each level of need. **One word of caution**: a sound system is only as good as its weakest point. This means that all the components should match in terms of wattage so that it will deliver its maximum potential. For example if you have powerful speaker cabinets capable of 500 watts of power equipped with two 15" sub woofers, 10" midrange speaker and a treble horn and you have a 25 watt power amp to drive it, you will end up with horrible sound and the speakers will end up sounding like they are broken.

The proper set up for the PA should be up against the far wall with the speakers facing you. This way you will be able to hear the vocals over the instruments as well as reducing the feedback caused by microphones. The correct position for mic's should be facing away from the speakers at a 180° angle.

As things progress and if your live performance requires you to bring your own system, you will need to look into purchasing effect racks, equalizers, pre amps, and snakes as well as monitor speakers.

RENTING A STUDIO

➳ CHECK THE YELLOW PAGES OR YOUR LOCAL MUSIC SHOP FOR A LOCATION.

➳ CHECK OUT THEIR RENTAL RATES.

> The prices range drastically from place to place so shop around. Some places rent by the hour and some have package deals if you rent by the month. I recommend renting by the hour in the beginning so that you get used to the place, and are sure the band lives up to their rehearsal commitments.

➳ MOST RENTAL HALLS COME EQUIPPED WITH A VOCAL PA, SOME EVEN SUPPLY DRUM KITS (MINUS THE SEAT AND PEDALS) AND AMPS.

➳ BOOK IN ADVANCE TO SECURE THE ROOM.

ZEN AND THE ART OF REHEARSAL

Time flies by in rehearsal and you want to keep it that way. If it starts to get boring you will become less motivated. You want to keep things moving, creative and interesting for the best results.

Here are some rehearsal techniques but first I want to preface it with this thought.

Rehearsals are important on two levels. (a) Learning new songs and perfecting them, (b) perfecting the live performance. When you are rehearsing new material or working on perfecting a song you should keep everybody who is not in the band out of your rehearsal. These are private moments for you to work on material. When people are around, you will have a tendency to perform rather than work and the song will suffer. Once the songs are learned and you are trying to perfect the live show it is recommended that you run through a mock performance in front some good friends of the band.

THE FOLLOWING ARE SOME REHEARSAL TECHNIQUES THAT IF FOLLOWED WILL ADVANCE AND MATURE YOUR GROUP AT A FASTER PACE.

➤◉➤ PRACTICE A MINIMUM OF 3 TIMES A WEEK FOR 2 HOURS

➤◉➤ PRACTICE AS MUCH AS POSSIBLE BY YOURSELF.

> At least 2 hours a day for the other four days you're not in rehearsal; learning your parts, writing new parts, improving your skill and writing material.

➤ BEGIN EACH REHEARSAL WITH AN IMPROMPTU JAM

This is a good way to just warm up (about fifteen minutes per one hour of rehearsal time) and explore your musical communication.

➤ TAPE RECORD EVERYTHING AT ALL TIMES

Those jam sessions might contain some brilliant moments that could materialize into a song. Record all the songs you play and listen to the tape objectively for parts that don't work and parts that do, for adjusting volume levels and improving or adding harmony vocals. Besides, making these tapes is the cheapest way to capture your music for passing out to friends, clubs, potential new band members and for copyrighting your material (see chapter 10).

If you are learning a new tune, practice enough times in a row so that you can complete the song without stopping. Then stop and listen to the tape. This will nip any wrong parts in the bud and help get the song tight without wasting time.

➤ GUITARISTS AND DRUMMERS SHOULD REPLACE THEIR STRINGS AND DRUM HEADS OFTEN.

Dead strings and heads produce dead sounds which ultimately affect your volume and tone.

➤ MAKE SURE YOU REHEARSE USING THE SAME EQUIPMENT YOU WILL BE PERFORMING/RECORDING WITH.

Part of rehearsing is getting your live/recorded sound perfected. You are definitely going to run into sound problems if your using different all sorts of different amps. For those of you who have big Marshall stacks, I know what you are up against so at least you can be prepared.

➤ WATCH YOUR VOLUMES

Part of the learning process of a new band requires that the individual members learn how to control their personal volume which will affect the overall band volume. Many times young bands will produce this wall of sound where every instrument is drowning each other out. Music should be like a conversation. When there are solos or lead vocal parts the other instruments should play in such a way that these parts are highlighted. There is no law that says that every single part of a song has to have every instrument playing. Silence allows the song to breathe and it will create a more dynamic effect. Less is sometimes more. Once your levels are established, you will have a volume reference point to start your sound check in when you play live. Of course every room is different and you will have to compensate but it won't be drastic. If there is a sound system in the club you need not worry about the audience. The system will take care of that. You need to just concentrate on the stage volume.

➤ KEEP A WRITTEN LIST OF ALL YOUR SONGS.

From these lists you will compose a set list which is a written list detailing the songs you will play and the order in which you will play them. Set lists take the risk out of the live show and rehearsing these lists and refining the order of the songs help complete the architecture of the event and make the performance flow smoothly.

An effective set list will result in a smooth show, one where the audience's attention is always kept focused on the band. To accomplish this, trial and error is your best bet. Watch the crowd for a lull in their attention. If there is a dud in the set list, you will feel it on stage. Sometimes you think a song is good but for whatever reason it doesn't work on the audience and you need to assess that and alter the list.

HOW TO CREATE AND REHEARSE A SET LIST:

 UNDERSTAND THE AUDIENCE YOU WILL BE PLAYING TO.

If you're playing to a new audience, open the set with three songs that invite the audience in. The last thing you want to do is open up with the weirdest song in the set. You want to get their interest away from the bar or the video game and out on the floor facing you. Once you have their undivided attention, you can take it softer or moodier for one or two songs but then come right back to the up tempo songs building and building to a crashing finish.

 MAKE RECORDINGS OF THE SHOWS AND LISTEN TO THEM TO HELP YOU CONSTRUCT LISTS FOR THE NEXT SHOW.

 DO NOT REHEARSE THE SET LIST TO DEATH.

You will leave yourself no inspiration for the live show. At each rehearsal perform the set twice, working out where in the set you will takes breaks or talk to the audience. Work it out among you who does the talking to the audience so that there aren't two or three of you talking over each other. I don't suggest that you have canned speeches (although many of the big acts rehearse what they say to the audience) but there are some things you need to rehearse like informing the crowd where your upcoming shows are, or what the name of the next song is. It might seem cheesy to do this but up on that stage with lights glaring in your eyes and fans screaming, it's good to have a reference point rather than saying something stupid or give wrong information.

After two practice runs go on to other material. Do this for 7 rehearsals prior to the show. The day before the gig do not do the set list. If you don't have it down by now you should not be playing out. Giving yourself a day off will give the set a new life when playing it at show time.

REHEARSING NEW SONGS

I'll be the first to tell you that writing a song is a most personal endeavor and I will not offer any hints on how to write one. What I will list for you are some pointers on how to turn your written work in to the group and make it a finished product. Whether you're writing lyrics or music it would be a good idea to document it down on paper. If you write music you should own some kind of small tape recording device so that you can get your ideas out of your head and on to tape. This really applies to guitarists and keyboard players. I would imagine it difficult for a drummer to do this.

Once you have this song on a tape, to make best use of your rehearsal (especially if you're paying by the hour), make copies and give them to your band members so they can begin the learning process at home on their own time. This method allows them to work on their parts without pressure and without using up precious rehearsal time. Once everybody works on their parts you can then start the rehearsal, putting it all together.

JUST A BRIEF PASSAGE ON BAND POLITICS. DEMOCRACY IS A WONDERFUL IDEOLOGY BUT AT TIMES IT CAN CAUSE PROBLEMS FOR BANDS THAT WEIGH THEMSELVES DOWN BY NOT ELECTING A LEADER. CERTAIN DECISIONS REQUIRE A SINGLE INDIVIDUAL'S INSIGHT AND NOT A UNANIMOUS DECISION BY THE ENTIRE BAND. ONE AREA THAT WOULD BENEFIT BY THIS TYRANNICAL APPROACH WOULD BE THE INTRODUCTION OF NEW MATERIAL.

NEW SONGS PRESENT A UNIQUE PROBLEM TO BANDS. WHAT IF IT'S NOT A GOOD SONG OR WHAT IF THE SONG IS TAKING THE BAND IN A DIFFERENT MUSICAL DIRECTION THAN IT'S PRESENTLY ON?

WHAT IF THE SONG HAS POTENTIAL BUT SOME OF THE PLAYERS ARE WRITING PARTS THAT ARE NOT WORKING? WITH EGOS AS FRAGILE AS THEY ARE MANY TIMES BANDS END UP PLAYING SONGS THAT EITHER DO NOT BELONG IN THEIR REPERTOIRE OR DO BUT SOME OF THE PARTS ARE WEAK BECAUSE EVERYONE IS AFRAID TO SUGGEST OTHERWISE TO EACH OTHER.

WHO IN THE BAND WILL ASSUME THE ROLE OF PRODUCER? WELL IF THE BAND HAS A LEADER THEN THAT PERSON PROBABLY ASSUMES THAT ROLE. BUT WHAT IF YOU ARE A BAND OF EQUAL PARTNERS? WELL THE ANSWER IS SIMPLE. DIVIDE UP YOUR PARTNERSHIP AND TAKE CHARGE OF DIFFERENT AREAS OF THE BAND. WHO EVER IS HANDLING THE BOOKINGS OR THE FINANCES IS DOING SO BECAUSE THEY HAVE GRAVITATED TOWARD THAT POSITION BASED UPON NEED AND THE ABILITY TO DO IT. WELL SURELY THERE IS ONE OF YOU THAT HAS THE GIFTED EAR. PERHAPS IT'S THE MEMBER THAT WRITES ALL THE MUSIC AND HAS THEIR OWN LITTLE 4 TRACK MACHINE AT HOME. IN MY OPINION THIS PERSON NEEDS TO LEAD THE REHEARSALS AND PREVENT TUNES FROM STRAYING TOO FAR OFF THE BAND'S BEATEN PATH.

THIS MAY SEEM RADICAL BUT I HAVE WITNESSED MANY REHEARSAL SESSIONS WHERE SO MUCH TIME IS WASTED BECAUSE THE BAND DOES NOT HAVE A MUSICAL LEADER. FURTHERMORE, THIS IS A VERY GOOD PREPARATION FOR THE FUTURE WHEN YOU ENTER INTO A PROFESSIONAL RECORDING SESSION WITH A PRODUCER. IN THAT SCENARIO THE PRODUCER WILL MAKE MANY SUGGESTIONS ON YOUR SONGS TO EITHER IMPROVE THE ARRANGEMENT OR DECIDE THAT IT IS NOT PROPER FOR THE ALBUM. YOUR ABILITY TO WORK UNDER THESE CIRCUMSTANCES WILL BE GREATLY ADVANTAGED IF YOU HAVE MASTERED THIS CONCEPT.

Regardless of how you approach rehearsals here are some tips for making them the most productive they can be.

✓ Throughout the rehearsal of the new material, keep listening to your tape to key in on the parts that do not work.

✓ Look for areas where adding a part or a vocal harmony in the chorus might improve the song. Be realistic. Some songs don't work and just do not represent the musical direction of the band. If this is the case scratch it and move on.

✓ Listen to each other's criticism without being defensive. It ultimately doesn't matter if the drummer has a good idea for the bass player, or if the guitarist writes the singer's melody.

All that matters is you all work together and make the song happen. The crowd could care less who wrote what part.

COVER SONGS

If you are in a cover band, try to stay as musically current as you can. Interpret the songs by playing the parts as close to the original as possible. Choose material that is most popular and then you will be more in demand.

If you are an original band and you want to play a cover song, try picking songs that don't detract from the image or aura of the band. I can't tell you what to play but I would advise against performing material that is currently out on the radio.

If you are trying to make it as an original band, playing current material is risky because it sets up competition with your own songs and in my opinion shows a lack of musical depth. After all, there are 40 years of recorded rock and roll music out there. Surely you can find something from the past that you can resurrect. That would be a lot cooler and show that you have a knowledge of rock history.

If you are compelled to cover a current radio hit, I recommend interpreting it in your own way. It will definitely show off some originality and musicianship.

Now that you're rehearsed let's get some gigs.

5

BOOKING THE GIG

So you have been rehearsing for months, writing your own songs and learning some cover tunes. You've got a set list together and it has about 45 minutes of material on it. You've had some friends over and they're telling you how great the band is. Word is spreading around town and as you look outside your rehearsal room window, you see crowds of curious onlookers waiting to get a glimpse of the next musical superstars.

You now know it's time to get out there and book yourself into a club. Hopefully many of you know at least one place in your town, where you can just walk in and ask the owner if he can give you a gig. So let's start at a club where you really want to play and have no contacts. Before you attempt to book gigs you should gather up some information about how clubs work and how the owners or bookers of the club think.

THE CLUB & CLUB OWNER

A nightclub, a bar or any small size venue that you are going to call upon is first and foremost a business. The owner is someone who has invested a good deal of money and is working long hours so that after the overhead (bills) is paid, there's some profit left over for themselves. They are probably in the business because they enjoy music, but if music were their only motivation, they would be in some other job listening to the radio while they work. They are in business to make money.

The way clubs make money is by charging admission and/or selling drinks to their clientele. The amount of patrons a club can attract is a result of the type of entertainment and atmosphere the club provides. When a club owner looks to hire a band to perform, the decision on hiring revolves around the entertainment value the band can provide. A band's value is based on (a) *How many people will they draw? (b) Will they entertain the regular clientele?, (c) Does the band have a following and are they big drinkers?*

Ask any club owner and they will tell you that a great band is one that brings in a big crowd. A band that plays great but doesn't draw anyone is an out of work, great band.

The days of clubs working hard to develop an act are for the most part long gone. Locally, you might find a place that will give you a start on an off night like Sunday or Monday, but it's up to you to bring the crowd. Due to the high cost of rent, insurance, liquor and security just for opening the doors, club owners will not offer you much in the way of pay to just come in and perform for no one.

Many clubs today will put anywhere from 3-6 bands together on a bill to maximize the audience. If each band can draw 25 people, then 6 bands can draw 150 people on the night. Of course it doesn't always work out this way and some bands will draw more than others. But unless you can pack the house on your own, sharing the bill is a fact of life.

There are many different types of clubs, bars etc., and for the sake of this conversation, we need to concentrate on the type of place you will first be looking to play in. Whether you live in a big city or a small town, chances are that you can find a small drinking bar that has at least a 75 person capacity, a small stage, some lights and a small dance floor. This should be a room that aside from a regular clientele of bar flies, younger people go there occasionally to see a band.

The owner of this establishment like every other club no matter what size, is probably inundated with requests from more bands to play than there are available dates. The decisions on who to book are usually based on the following:

❧ THE REPUTATION OF THE GROUP

If you are an already established band, the word on the street and through the club circuit on how well you play, or what size crowd you bring, will determine whether you have a good reputation or not. Usually club owners know of each other and due to their competitive nature are always checking who's playing at the other guy's club. If the band has a good reputation they will be preferred by the clubs over a new untested act, especially if they're vying for a booking on the same date.

❧ THE TAPE AND PRESS KIT

These are the two most important marketing tools your band has. They serve as proof of your accomplishments documented in a professional manner for everyone from club owners to the press, all the way up to the record labels. The press kit contains a bio on your group, band photo, press clippings, along with any other vital booking information. This will be accompanied by a demo tape of your music. The club owner looks at this material, listens to the tape and determines whether they want to offer you a gig. If your band is new or has never played in the area before, the club owner takes a very big risk in booking you. The reputation of the club is based on many things including the kind of music it features. Having never seen you before will supersede any guarantee you make as they take a financial gamble by hiring you.

❧ YOUR SALES PITCH

The fact is, some of the most successful people in the world are salesman. Whether you're selling computers, cars, ideas or yourself, to truly be successful at it, you will need to possess certain communication skills and concepts. Club bookers are very busy people and do not have a great deal of time to look for quality in a band if it is not easily found.

Furthermore, due to the vast amount of phone calls club bookers receive it helps if you can offer something that makes you and your group stand out.

To develop an edge so that you can get through the maze of tapes and press kits on their desk you will need to possess the following traits:

➤ PROFESSIONAL ATTITUDE AND PERSONALITY

First you need to come off like a winner but without being cocky and arrogant. You are not the first group in the world that writes their own music and you need not try to sell yourself with the line "we're the best band you've ever seen." Trust me you are not the best band they've ever seen and you never will be if at this stage of the game you already think you are. The club booker has seen and heard it all. Allow them the chance to come to that conclusion on their own. Let your music do the talking.

Allow yourself to take criticism. Club owners are just one of the many people who you will be approaching for help and in turn they will offer their opinion on what you need to do to improve. You should not change yourself with every opinion thrown your way, however, if enough people comment on a particular characteristic of the group, consider its conquest to be the next rung you need to climb on the ladder to success.

Upon calling me, many musicians open with the line "we are so much better than everybody else out there, we just need a break." When I hear that, I get turned off. My feeling is if you are better than everybody else, the breaks should be and will come. I prefer that you let your music do the talking and not words of bravado. If you feel you are better than everyone else that's great but keep it inside as an inspiration for yourself. A healthy positive attitude is magnetic and it draws people to you.

➤ TIMING

They say this is everything but they are only partially right. If you look at most successful people and listen to their story, you'll find out that when they hit it big, yes timing was everything , but you should also realize all the times that they tried and failed. Like a baseball player, the more times you get up to bat the more chances you give yourself to hit the ball. But not every time up at bat will yield a base hit. Eventually if you keep at it you just might get that pitch that you will meet with the perfect swing and boom, it's outta there. So really it's not just timing, it's putting in the time that is everything. When making your calls, don't call one club. Call 5 clubs. Make it your goal to book at least 3 shows a week and don't stop until you do. If you call 15 clubs and book 5 of them, you are batting 300, and that, my friend, will get you in the Hall of Fame.

➤ KNOWLEDGE/UNDERSTANDING

Know your opponent. It's war out there. If you're going into battle without knowing your enemy, then to whom do we send your belongings?

Before you attempt to book a club, try to find out as much about the place as you can even if it means going there at night and hanging out. The worst thing you can do is book yourself into a club that is not right for your music. It will happen sometimes but each time it does, you will learn something from it.

Learn about the booking habits of the owner. Find out what the minimum draw is. If the owner expects bands to draw 100 people at the worst, do not even attempt to contact this place until you are at 75 people.

I keep stressing to you that the people who book and own clubs are inundated with phone calls. Your window of opportunity is 60 seconds on the phone at best. You better know what you're going to say and minimize what you have to ask so you can get right to the point and make your pitch. Unless you can talk your talk and walk your walk, do not dial that dial.

PATIENCE

Last but not least, something all bands need to have is a little bit of patience. You are not going to get booking agents or club owners on the phone the first time you call. Or the second or third. Just keep leaving your name and number and continue to ask when is it a good time to call back.

Do not get frustrated. If after 10 calls you don't get a response move on. It's not meant to be. Use your time and energy on your next conquest. Just do not take it personally. These people do not know *you!* In time when your reputation is stronger you will come back to this club and find yourself pleasantly surprised as to their willingness to work with you.

With all this in mind, let's start at the beginning.

THE CHICKEN OR THE EGG

In trying to answer the question of which came first the chicken or the egg, many groups have asked me "How can we get a gig without a tape and press kit and how do we make a press kit without a gig?" Obviously you will need to have played some shows and received press, have photographs taken and made some kind of demo tape. While all this is true, I feel that in the beginning the only thing you really need to get a gig is a demo tape. This does not have to be a great master recording from a 48 track studio. Use the best of your rehearsal tapes to at least pass around for now until you raise enough money to make a good studio recording.

(HOW TO MAKE PRESS KITS AND DEMOS WILL BE DISCUSSED IN CHAPTERS 7-9).

YOUR FIRST BOOKINGS

 APPOINT ONE PERSON IN YOUR BAND TO ASSUME THE ROLE OF MAKING CONTACTS AND BOOKINGS.

It is important to split up jobs within the group. But it is equally important that the jobs do not cross each other otherwise it will cause conflict. The best choice of individual to assume the role of band booking agent should be the one member that is comfortable on the phone and able to do what it takes to *sell* the band. It helps to have a likable personality as well as some knowledge of the music business. With that I am not just referring to the way business is conducted but to also know what is going on in the industry as a whole. It would certainly help your conversation skills if you read issues of Billboard magazine, R&R, CMJ, etc.

HOOK UP WITH A LOCAL ESTABLISHED BAND.

Inquire if they have a local show coming up and if you can be the opening act. This will help break the ice with the club allowing them to see what you've got without a press kit. It also gives you that chance to play in front of audience, and hopefully pick up new fans.

You should have a prepared set that has at least 40 minutes of music. If you consider audience applause and time in between songs, you can possibly push the set to 45 minutes which is the usual time allotment for an opening act.

If the group is willing to let you open up for them do not discuss money at this point. Most bands need every penny they make and they are already doing you the favor by getting you in the door. This is something you can't buy. If you bring up the money there is a good chance you won't get the gig.

If you do not know a band that can help you, this is the way to proceed:

LOOK FOR A CLUB, PREFERABLY IN YOUR HOME AREA CONVENIENTLY LOCATED, SO THAT ALL OF YOUR FRIENDS CAN COME.

Make sure the admission age is low enough so that it doesn't exclude many of your fans. Don't forget, that for this first show you are going to want to bring in as many people as you can, so that you can begin developing that good reputation.

Make sure that the club features bands so that they are used to loud volume levels. The last thing you need is to be constantly reminded to lower your volume   or in a worse case scenario, be told to stop playing altogether.

CALL THE CLUB AND INQUIRE AS TO WHO DOES THE BOOKINGS.

Get their name, the club address and the hours in which the booker works. Ask how long after they receive your tape should you call back for booking information.

It is not necessary to speak to the club booker at this time. All you will get out of the call is instructions to send your tape and press kit and call back in two weeks. So why waste your time and theirs. First mail in the tape and then ask for the booker.

If you live close by you can consider dropping off the tape. For one thing it gives you a chance to step into the venue and see it, especially if this is your first time. If you're lucky, the booker will be there and might even listen to the tape right away. If not, then perhaps the person behind the bar who you will leave the tape with will become a good contact and if you enter into a good conversation that could be an asset to you.

CALL BACK AT THE TIME YOU'VE BEEN INSTRUCTED.

It would help if you remember or even jotted down the names of the people you met when you were at the club or spoken to on the phone. If they should answer the phone and you remember their voice and refer to them by name, you will have made a very big impression. Ask to speak to the owner or the person that books the shows. Do not lie or exaggerate the size of your following. Be honest and let them know you are just starting out and would like the chance to open for a more popular group so that you can start adding on to your following. If this is indeed your first show you still should be out telling all your friends, family members and whoever else you can about this event so that you can count on some kind of initial following.

THE EVENT

If the club has received your tape and you are now in conversation to book the show, there are three main points you need to address.

 PAYMENT   **DATE**   **TIME**

Thursday, Friday and Saturdays are by far the best nights of the week. Depending on where you are, Sunday might not be so bad (but is usually affected by people having school or work the next day), and Monday and Tuesday are terrible.

If this is your first show, you are somewhat at the mercy of what the club booker offers you. Chances are it's not going to be on a Friday night at 11:00 for $500. It could be a Monday at 7:00 PM or worse at 2:00 AM.

Though you may be able to come up with many reasons why this time slot won't work for you, you need to understand that there is no reason why the booker should offer you anything different. You have no reputation and he has no way of knowing for sure what kind of crowd you will bring so why should he take any chances. Remember the club has to pay its bills. Unless you can supply him with documented proof like a press kit legitimizing your group and describing your drawing power, I'd say take what you are offered. Consider it an audition for the club to get in and impress whoever is there with your ability to turn it on in the face of adversity.

As far as pay is concerned, unless you have a reputation and have established a going rate for your band (based on what you've been paid for the past five shows), the deal they offer is the deal you take. Payment is based entirely on how many people you draw and not just for the first show. You will need to prove that you can bring in good business every time you play. Once you prove yourself, you should be getting your area's going rate for bands. The most useful tool you have negotiating your pay is the amount of people you bring through the door. Based upon admission price, times the amount of people, you can estimate how much money the club is making on your crowd.

$5.00	admission	
x 75	people who came to the show	**Sample 1**
= $375	amount made at the door	

What are you entitled to?

That will depend entirely on the club policy, your area's going rate and your reputation. If you are asked how much you are looking for, you should take the equation from sample 1 and receive anywhere from **25% -100%** of that money. To figure out the percentage use the equation in sample 2.

SAMPLE 2   Gross x percentage = amount or $375 \times 25\% = \$93.75$

Your job will be to negotiate this, based on many factors including: your reputation, club policy and going rate. You will have to because the club will certainly never offer you your value.

WHAT TO EXPECT FROM THE CLUB

Basically the club functions as a room that you are borrowing to put on a show. Don't depend on the owner for anything other than maybe some advertising. It is your job to bring in the crowd.

It is important that you understand this fundamental rule. Although ethically you should be paid every time you play because it is work, you are really working for yourself so who in reality should be paying you? As with any new business starting out you have to develop a clientele. This is usually done through advertising which for any new business can be a costly undertaking. In this case your advertisement is your performance, a pretty cheap way to build clientele if you ask me! Besides, get used to it, throughout your career there are going to be other types of dates where you might play for free like seminars, agent/record company showcases etc. just to gain exposure.

The following are some of the many types of pay structures offered in clubs:

 PAY TO PLAY

In this scenario you will be asked at the time of your booking to purchase in advance x amount of tickets from the promoter of the show. This amount ranges from city to city and in NYC where I'm from, it's around **$250- $500**. Once you get the tickets it then becomes *your* responsibility to sell them to fans not the club's. In the case where you purchase **100** tickets for **$500** that makes each ticket cost **$5**. This insures the promoter and the club profit for that night. For you to make profit on the show you will have to raise that cost to let's say **$7.00** a ticket.

This is a sleazy way for promoters to do business and I advise you to steer clear of these deals, however as these promoters put it, they are offering you a place to play and an opportunity to make money taking some of the pressure and financial liability off themselves. It definitely gives you some insight into the workings of the business and it puts the pressure on you to succeed. So it's not altogether horrible, but if you can find a reputable promoter who isn't lazy and works to promote the show, you are better off.

NO PAY

Sometimes a band needs to play out live to showcase themselves for a club owner or booking agent. Due to the high cost of running a business, a club won't take a risk on paying a band that they have never seen or heard of. Many clubs offer open mic or audition nights on a certain night. You'll get around a half an hour or so to play and the club will see what kind of crowd you bring in and if you're good enough for a pay gig.

I don't often recommend that bands give their show away for nothing but at times under the right circumstances, if you really want to get into a place on a regular basis, this is a very good way to do it.

If you are not going to get paid there are some trade offs you can ask for. The willingness of a booker to concede to some will give you some indication as to the type of club and individual they are:

> → **Ask the owner if the club regularly take ads out in the paper**
>
> If so they can give you some mention in an upcoming ad. This alone is valuable in your press kit.
>
> → **Try to get some perks out of the club like a guest list.**
>
> → **Try to book a tentative future date at the time of the show.**
>
> This way should there be a good crowd happening and they are giving you a good response, you can advertise your return date right there, maximizing the potential draw for the next show.

PERCENTAGE OF THE ADMISSION PRICE BASED UPON REDEEMED PASSES

Passes are those 4"x 5" postcards used by bands and clubs the world over to advertise the show. They are passed out at clubs, on the street and through the mail giving friends and fans alike information about an event. On the night of the show the club will have someone at the door collecting passes and admission money. At the end of the night the club will then count up all the collected passes and pay you a percentage of the passes with your name on it. Fair deal right? ....wrong!!!

First, unless your father owns the club or the door man is Mother Theresa, you can't really trust the club to account for every pass redeemed. Imagine over the course of a busy night how easy it is for a doorman to misplace 15 passes and not realize it. Are you going to be the one to accuse this 8ft gorilla who eats steroids for breakfast and punks like you for lunch, that he purposely threw some away in the garbage? I think not. And if you try to convince the club owner that you drew more people than cards collected and therefore expect them to fork over more money, you will be attempting a kind of surgical procedure that even Dr. Beverly Crusher has not heard of.

You will therefore need to take the following precautions.

→ **Find the biggest, badest, but level headed friend you can and post them near the doorman.**

Have them collect the passes as they are handed off to the doorman. If that isn't permissible they should carry their own counter and check off the amount of people redeeming your passes. Sometimes having this person looming in the background who is not easily intimidated is enough to keep an otherwise dishonest club owner or doorman straight.

→ **Try to be original in the style, color and even size of your postcard.**

If you have a disagreement with the owner after the show, you might want to look around the front door area, dance floor or even in the trash for your very recognizable postcards.

Percentage deals are the standard in the club circuit but here are some tips on negotiating them to work in your favor.

To start with, your cut of the passes will usually be around **20%** of the admission price. So if the admission is **$5** you'll get **$1** per card. But what if you draw **200** people? Shouldn't you get a higher percentage than the **$1** per ticket? Yes you should. What you need to do here is negotiate an accelerated percentage per amount of people you bring in. So that after let's say you draw 50 people you get **25%** and after you bring in **100** people your entitled to **30%** and so on. A club should be open to this negotiation at the onset, when you book the gig.

IN SOME AREAS OF THE COUNTRY, ADMISSION PRICES TO THESE SHOWS ARE SOMEWHAT EXPENSIVE.

And if you're appearing on a bill with other acts chances are you are not going to get a lot of time on the stage. In order to entice some of your fans to come down you might want to work out a deal with the club owner that offers your friends a cheaper admission price. In return you will accept either a slightly lower percentage or what I recommend is a larger draw amount before your percentage goes up. So instead of a **$7** cover charge you can offer on your postcard a **$5** charge. In return the club will only pay you **$1** on your pass or bump you up to **25%** after you go over **80** people instead of **50**.

What you are hoping to accomplish is showing some business smarts as well as an appreciation for his club. After all, you are trying to draw the most amount of people. The booker might be more interested in getting a true count of what you brought in. You also cost less money and in showing you their appreciation they might be more prone to doing right by you. Keep in mind, many of the clubs have themselves been burned by plenty of bands ripping stuff off from the clubs and defacing their property. You've got to show them some respect before you can expect them to show you some back in return.

PERCENTAGE OF THE ADMISSION PRICE.

A slightly better deal usually reserved for more reputable bands. The club will pay you at the end of the night a percentage of all the door receipts.

Depending on how many bands appear that night and at what spot your band played in (opening act, middle acts or headliner) will determine what your percentage will be.

So let's take a **$5** ticket price and 6 bands. It's three o'clock in the morning and you finally sit down with the booker. Your told that **95** people paid all night to see all the bands. **95** people on a **$5** ticket comes out to **$475**. If you were promised **50%** of the gross receipts then you would get **50%** of **$475** or **$237.50**.

SET PAY

Some clubs that have a good reputation will usually offer to start a new band at a set price. Usually around **$50**. If you are just starting out trust me it's decent money and take it. Until you develop a following and begin to make the club money, you have nothing to bargain with. In most cases a club that offers you a starting pay is a club that cares about its acts and will do more to help develop you a following. These types of venues will advertise you in the local papers and if you ask them nicely might give you the names of music reviewers so that you might invite them down to review your band.

SET PAY PLUS A PERCENTAGE OVER

Now you are starting to get in with the club or have a good reputation as a band that draws a big crowd. Let's say the deal is the club will pay you a set salary of **$500** plus **50%** of the collected door money over **400** people. So, in effect you will get **$500** no matter what happens. If the club draws **575** people on an **$8** ticket you will get **50%** of **175 x 8,** (175 being the difference between **575** and **400**) or **1/2** of **$1400** which equals **$700**. So now your total pay for the night will be **$1200** (your contracted price of **$500**. plus **$700** over). Of course you have to rely on the club's honesty as always but keep in mind that if you are doing the club this much business, they themselves are making good money and will not try to do anything to upset you. The tides do turn as you get more popular and you'll notice the clubs will become like home to you and your fans.

THE DOOR

This very simple arrangement is where your group will supply someone at the front door and he'll collect the admission as it comes in. At the end of the night you keep everything that you collected. You usually get this kind of deal only if you are a fairly popular band with enough of a reputation to demand it and the only band on the bill. It is more common in suburban areas and college towns than in bigger cities where there is more of a tendency for the clubs to do the door themselves and give you a percentage.

There are many other deals that will incorporate a little of each one of these with perhaps a new twist of its own. I know a promoter in Colorado who books a number of popular clubs in the Denver area. For many of the new acts that are booked, their pay (regardless of their draw capacity) is $100. But included with that they get a big ad in the main music newspaper as well as a 1/2 page write up!........ Brilliant!! To me, this is promotional material that in most places, money can't buy. In fact the $100 seems almost a bonus when you consider how valuable the write up and ad is to their press kit.

Of course all good deals are not without some drawbacks and in this example, the promoter only books bands that have their own CD out. They need not be a signed band, just a band that has reached the level of marketing their own merchandise. That as we will see later on in the book is a positive signal in the industry that the band has made it through some of the first stages of development.

NEGOTIATION

What is your recourse in the event that you feel you have been unfairly handled be it pay or otherwise? When it comes to pay you are at a disadvantage especially in the beginning when you have very little performance options and are at the mercy of the club. Each negotiation is unique unto itself. To be successful you must not attempt to outsmart your opponent but rather match wits with a good argument based upon facts and a good sense of business etiquette.

Supposing you go to settle a show that you were promised 50% of the gross door receipts. From the stage you can see the 350 capacity room is so packed that the line by the door needs to be manned by two bouncers instead of the usual one. As you now sit in the office watching the clock turn 3:00 AM, waiting to get paid, the booker enters and after offering you a drink says you did okay drawing 95 people. Your pay is $235. You stare ahead wondering which one of their two heads you should address.

Instead of hitting the roof, inquire how that is possible when the club was obviously filled to capacity. The booker will no doubt combat that with all kinds of excuses ranging from half those people were regular customers and do not pay, to you must be blind and don't tell me how many people were in my club. What you must keep in mind is that if you honestly drew a huge crowd, the booker would be a fool to piss you off to the point where you vowed to never perform there again. So with an armful of confidence you can offer this possibility.

There are other clubs in town that would appreciate your 300 fans and if there is no way to settle with you then you will happily play for the competition. A fool would end the conversation here so they will respond one of two ways. If your bluff is called you know what you have to do. If on the other hand you're asked what you think is fair, let me offer you one solution.

"Paid, no no, I never said paid, I said sprayed"

You were offered payment on 95 people and you feel that club maxed out at 350. Offer to split this down the middle and have him pay you the percentage on 222 people which is roughly the difference. You arrive at the difference by adding 95 + 350 then dividing the total in half.

The booker's reaction may be positive or they may come back to you with an offer which might end up being another split down the middle. The argument might be that x amount of dollars was spent on advertising and there is no way that you drew that many people. Explain that you also spent x amount on advertising. Proceed to show the mailing list pages from the night with the multitudes of signatures to drive your point home.

What you are hoping to achieve here is much more than financial. Let's face it, neither of you can really prove how many people came in through the door unless there were tickets sold and the show sold out in advance.

In a courteous tone you want to establish that you are not to be jerked around and that you are not a fool but rather someone who is taking care of their business. In the end you will get more respect from the club, keeping them honest in the future. The final result of this negotiation should put a bit more money in your pocket, raise some respect for you and hopefully culminate in a better arranged deal for the next show you perform there.

I want to point out that although this may happen from time to time there are many very reputable clubs where it is a pleasure to play at and where the bands are treated very fairly.

As far as the many other circumstances that bands find themselves disadvantaged by, the same level headed techniques need to be assimilated. Always direct your problem to the person directly responsible for correcting it. Yelling at the bartender because you are being denied drink passes is not proper procedure. As you will see later in this chapter and chapter 6, there are methods to booking a show, documenting and confirming all the things you discussed with the booker on the phone so that you are in less risk when you arrive at the club.

PROMOTION AND ADVERTISEMENT

The concept of publicity is one that may truly escape the budding musician, and yet it is the vehicle upon which you ride toward success in the music business. You may have the greatest songs in the history of music but if you do not have a grip on how to alert the public, no one will ever know. Band promotion is truly an art in itself and a musician should not feel compromised in any way by taking steps to advertise. Everything you do from a live performance to mailing out gig flyers falls under the category of promotion and marketing. Be as creative as you can. The heap is high and you need to be seen to get to the top.

The following is a list of ways to go about promoting your band.

WORD OF MOUTH:

Most bands at the onset rely on their friends and word of mouth. It starts with telling all your friends about an upcoming show and they in turn tell their friends. This is a very cheap but effective way to promote yourself. If you have some recordings from your rehearsals pass them around.

FLYERS:

If you or a friend have some artistic talent, try making a really creative flyer that you can hang up on telephone poles, or at the shopping center, music stores, record stores, pizza stores and most certainly at the club. You must stick to certain rules of advertising in designing the flyers so that your message is clear and understood. Be sure to list:

→ THE DATE, DAY & TIME OF THE GIG MUST BE CLEARLY PRINTED.

→ THE NAME OF YOUR GROUP AND LOGO PROMINENTLY DISPLAYED.

→ THE CLUB NAME AND ADDRESS & PHONE # WHERE YOU ARE PLAYING.

→ THE SPECIFIC CLUB ADMISSION POLICY LIKE 21 & OVER ONLY.

→ YOUR PHONE NUMBER FOR MORE INFORMATION.

→ THE ADMISSION PRICE

Here is a sample flyer generated by computer:

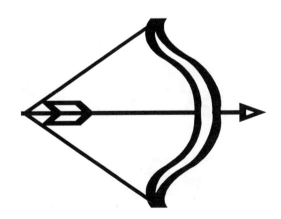

FRIDAY JUNE 15

SLIM JIM

and the

BEEF JERKY BLUES BAND

appearing at the

THE SLAUGHTERHOUSE SALOON

1234 Hickory Avenue Dallas TX

555-5555

Doors open: **10:00 PM sharp**

18 to get in and 21 to drink

Web site: www.cowchip.com

$5.00 admission with this pass

Bring this flyer to a printing shop and for about ten cents a copy you can make as many as your budget will allow. You can also ask that they reduce this to a smaller 4x5 size and print it on a postcard so that you can mail it out to all the people on your mailing list.

If you are playing a show out of town or far enough away that you cannot physically get there until the night of the show, ask the club owner if you can mail a bunch of posters to hang in the club. You should make a note of how many you send the club so that when you arrive you will be able to check and see if the club hung them up or not.

 ## NEWSPAPER ADS:

With a little coaxing you can get the club to run an ad in one of the local music trade newspapers. This is a costly form of advertising as any local retail business owner will tell you. For new bands I really don't feel you should take out the ad unless it is a heavily read newspaper and they are offering a pre-designated space for a reduced rate, as they sometimes do in the papers in the NYC area. In this case if you have the few extra bucks (no more than $35.) go for it. In fact sometimes a band will take out that space and just run their name week after week. Exposure is the name of the game and the more name recognition you get, the better.

 ## MAILING LIST:

This is a list that you begin making from your very first show and continue on until you can sell out The Garden. Start with a spiral notebook or a clip board with paper or even with small postcards spread out around the club. Its purpose is to get patrons of the club to fill out their name and address so that you can communicate with them in the future about upcoming shows.

Here are some effective ways to distribute the mailing list.

 ### DO NOT JUST ARBITRARILY PASS THE LIST AROUND THE CLUB.

You will only end up with names like Beavis and O.J. with false addresses that will end up wasting your money in postage and printing bills. Have a friend solicit the crowd during the show targeting those who by their behavior (dancing or staring wide eyed) appear into your band.

 ### DO NOT LET IT OUT OF YOUR SIGHT.

If it just gets passed around without being attached to somebody you might never see it again. Also there is the possibility that a member of a rival band might be in the club and might just need to borrow that book for a while.

 ### REMOVE COMPLETED PAGES AND INPUT THEM INTO A COMPUTER.

This will be invaluable when you need to do a mailing. The computer will be able to print all the labels for you, saving you hours of work.

LEAVE THE MAILING LIST EITHER BY THE MERCHANDISING BOOTH OR STAGE.

During the show announce the mailing list and where it is. Encourage people to sign it.

MAKE SURE PEOPLE PRINT THEIR NAME CLEARLY.

You don't want to find a ton of names scribbled all over a beer stained sheet of paper.

The following is a sample mailing list Postcard:

PLEASE JOIN OUR MAILING LIST

Place stamp here

Your Name_____

Your Address_____

_____

_____

Send to:

◁ **SUCTION** ▷

PO BOX #8

NYC, NY 10021

Just leave these around the club and you will be surprised how many people will take them home fill them out and mail back to you. Besides they come in handy if you have something urgent you need to get out to your fans, you can always use these postcards.

Just slap a stamp on it, write your message on the flip side and you're done.

When you are printing, make sure you print at least 500 at a time. They run out faster than you think and it's a whole lot cheaper when you print in bulk.

Also make sure that you use postcard stock paper or 67lb stock. Anything lighter than that and you might have a problem getting them through the mail.

Another mailing list option is as follows:

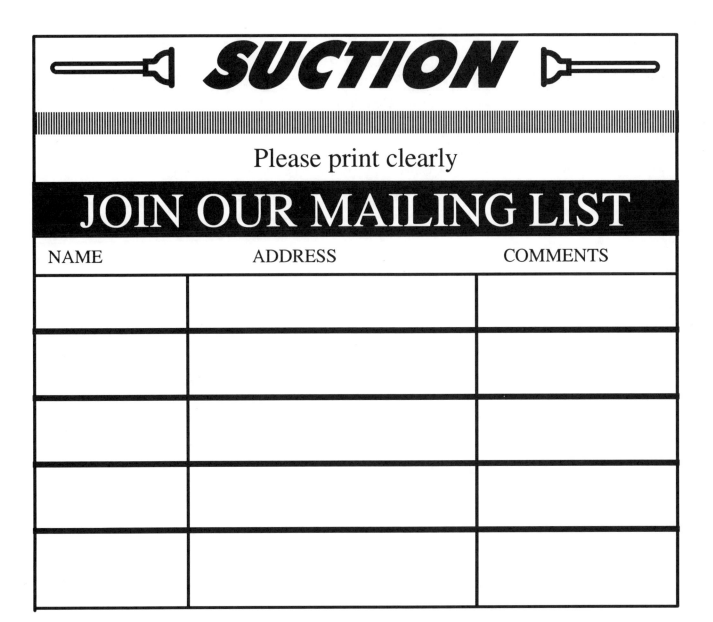

MONTHLY CALENDAR

The main purpose of the mailing list is for you to keep in contact with your fans about upcoming events. The most common events of course are the gigs as well as merchandise purchase information, the upcoming release of your new CD and whatever other news you may want to share with your fans.

The way you keep this contact is by printing up a monthly calendar or list of the gigs you have booked for the following month. The styles in which you decide to design the card are entirely up to your artistic approach. Whether you choose to type it out on the computer or infuse art into the design, make sure that the following information is included: • NAME OF BAND • DATE OF SHOW •NAME OF VENUE •ADDRESS OF VENUE • PHONE NUMBER OF VENUE •ADMISSION AGE FOR EACH VENUE •TIME OF SHOW •TICKET PRICE.

HERE IS A SAMPLE:

FEBRUARY 1999

Wed 2 Chestnut Cabaret 10:00pm 38th & Chestnut. Phili, PA 215 688 4600 21 & over **$5.00**

Thu 3 Penn State 11:00pm State College PA Student union 717 555-9876 all ages

Fri 4 The Bitter End 10:15pm 157 Bleeker St. N.Y.C. 212 673-7030 **$3.00**

Sat 5 The Barre Chord 11:15pm rte 37 & Garfield Ave Toms River, NJ 908 929 0221

Thu 10 930 Club 11:00pm Sharp 930 F St. Wash DC 202-363 5277 (w/ Flush) 21 & over

Fri 11 Hammerjacks 11:30pm 1101 S. Howard St. Balt MD 410-752 3302 **$10.00**

Sat 12 Chameleon Club 10:00pm 223 N Water St Lancaster PA 717 299 9684 18 & over

Sun 13 J.C. Dobbs 10:00pm 304 South St Phili PA 215 925 6679 (2 Sets) 18 & over

Mon 14 El-N-Gee Club 9:30pm 86 Golden St New London CT 203 437 3800 21 & over

Wed 15 7 Willow St 11:00pm 7 willow St Portchester NY 914 939 1473 21 & over

Thur 16 Pearl St 10:15pm 10 Pearl St North Hampton MA 617 492 7679 (w/ Drool)

Fri 17 T.T. Bears 11:00pm 10 Brookline St Cambridge MA 617 547 0620

Sat 18 CBGB's 1:15 am 315 Bowery NYC NY 212 982- 4052 21 Over

Tue 22 Loop Lounge 10:00pm 373 B'way Passaic Park NJ 201 365 1394 (1 hour set)

Thu 24 Zodiac 10:30pm 410 Allentown PA 215 435 1591 18 over **$3.00** Adm.

Fri 25 Khyber Pass Pub 11:15pm 56 S Second St Phili PA 215 440 0932

Sat 26 The Bayou 11:30pm 3135 "K" St Wash DC 703 663 1900 (Headline)

Mon 28 TBA call hotline for information

Once all your dates are confirmed start putting this calendar together. Whether you do it on computer or write it out by hand it really doesn't matter. Your mission is to print the cards in *enough volume*, in *enough time*, *mailed* and *delivered* to the fans at least five days before the first date listed.

The cheapest way to create a post card is as follows:

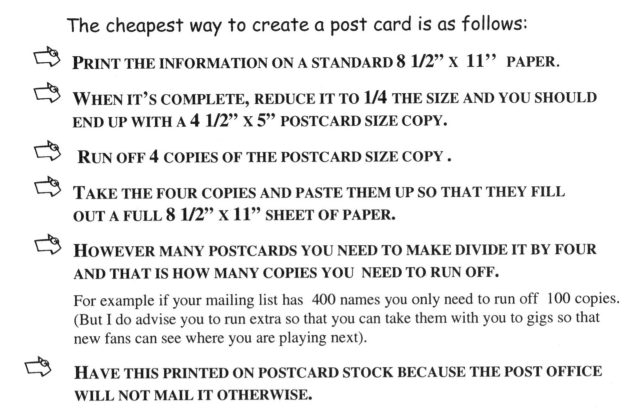

➥ PRINT THE INFORMATION ON A STANDARD 8 1/2" X 11" PAPER.

➥ WHEN IT'S COMPLETE, REDUCE IT TO 1/4 THE SIZE AND YOU SHOULD END UP WITH A 4 1/2" X 5" POSTCARD SIZE COPY.

➥ RUN OFF 4 COPIES OF THE POSTCARD SIZE COPY .

➥ TAKE THE FOUR COPIES AND PASTE THEM UP SO THAT THEY FILL OUT A FULL 8 1/2" X 11" SHEET OF PAPER.

➥ HOWEVER MANY POSTCARDS YOU NEED TO MAKE DIVIDE IT BY FOUR AND THAT IS HOW MANY COPIES YOU NEED TO RUN OFF.

For example if your mailing list has 400 names you only need to run off 100 copies. (But I do advise you to run extra so that you can take them with you to gigs so that new fans can see where you are playing next).

➥ HAVE THIS PRINTED ON POSTCARD STOCK BECAUSE THE POST OFFICE WILL NOT MAIL IT OTHERWISE.

Most printing places will need at least two days to complete the job so figure this into your schedule.

Once the job is done, instruct the Printer to cut the cards for you. Most decent size Printers have a cutting machine that will cut many pages at once. If you have to do it, it will take forever and look like crap.

Print out your mailing list names on labels, adhere them to the cards and use postcard postage stamps to mail. Figure into your schedule about 2-3 days for them to arrive by mail. So if it takes 3 days for mail delivery and 2 days for printing, that's already one full work week. If your first gig is on Feb 2 and you want it to arrive one week prior to that, you should start the whole process by Jan 15 which means all your gigs should be confirmed by the 14th. Which really means that you should have begun booking February in late November early December.

SETTING UP A MAILING LIST FILE SYSTEM

If you are storing your mailing list on a computer data base (which I very strongly recommend) you should create separate files for each state and for some larger states with multiple cities, sub files by each city. This way names and addresses can be easily found and if you're playing in one area, you can just print out labels to that one area only rather than having to always print out all the labels.

You may choose to code by location using either by the first few letters of the area or it's recognizable initials. For instance:

SYRACUSE , NY IS CODED TO READ	**SYRA**
ALBANY NY IS CODED TO READ	**ALB**

Print out a list of these codes and leave it by your computer as a directory otherwise you will forget some of the codes you do not often use. For states that you regularly play where there are a lot of major cities and college towns, it pays to create lists for each city or area. This way if you are playing Buffalo NY, you might decide to only send postcards to the Buffalo area rather than the whole NY state. Let's face it, no one is going to travel from Long Island NY to Buffalo unless you're the Grateful Dead. On the other hand if it's a small state like Delaware or a state where you are only playing in one city, than you can create the file just for the state and wait till you either expand the area or begin getting names from another part of the state.

The latter is a very crucial piece of the booking puzzle. Let's say you play in Philadelphia in one particular club. It's your third time there and the past two times you have collected about 45 names on your mailing list. After the show you went home and keyed the names into the computer and noticed that all of the addresses were from Philadelphia and its immediate surrounding area. (You noticed that by looking at the zip codes). But on this third visit, as you where typing in the names and addresses you came across a zip code whose numbers are a bit off from what you had in the past. So you either get out your map or call the post office only to find out that the three people who signed up are from Monroeville Pa, which is a suburb of Pittsburgh. Well what do you do? Do you file this in the **PA** file or do you begin to split up **PA** into sub files?

What I have done is simply this. Split the **PA** file into two files. Create **PHILI** for all the existing files that are in the Philadelphia area changing their codes to **PHILI** and start a second file calling it **PITTS** because it's the nearest big city. I would then put the three names in this new file. The very next thing I would do is try to find out if there are any rock clubs in Monroeville or in the nearest vicinity including Pittsburgh to book the band into. I have to figure I have at least three people that might come to see the group and possibly more if they bring friends. When you are booked in a new town that could be at least 300% more people attending than in a place where you have no names on the mailing list. By becoming a mailing list detective you will be able to get a feel for where your band should be expanding itself into.

SETTING UP A DATA FILING SYSTEM

As you begin to book shows, you must start a filing system and keep records of all your contacts.

For starters you should have a daily planning book that dedicates a full page to each day of the year. In it you will log your phone calls, things you need to do, appointments etc. When a phone conversation results in your having to call back in two weeks, advance the books to that day and log in that reminder to call so & so.

As you begin to establish key contacts and confirmed dates, your next step is to transfer this information to a data form. This can either be a printout from your computer or a plain white piece of paper you write on. This data form will contain everything from the club name, address and telephone number to the club contact, details concerning your last conversation and your thoughts and feedback. This is vital information for a number of reasons.

YOUR CAREER IN MUSIC IS BASED ON CONTACTS AND FRIENDS.

In the course of a day you might call 20 clubs trying to get a show and talk to forty people. It is impossible to remember each conversation and the name of the person you spoke with. If you have this form in front of you, marking down information as your phone call progresses, your memory will instantly be refreshed when you make your follow up call. Your amazing recall will undoubtedly impress the person on the other end of the phone separating you from the many bumbleheads that call and elevating you to a level of receiving more respect. This can only translate into one thing; getting a gig.

HAVING ALL YOUR FACTS IN FRONT OF YOU WILL PREVENT YOU HAVING TO ASK FOR THE SAME INFORMATION AGAIN.

If you have a computer, setting up a data form is fairly simple. You start a file and title it by the name of the club. You then use the format below as a basis for logging in information. Due to the turnover of employees at many clubs, over a few years' time, you will probably deal with a number of different booking people (unless the owner does all the booking) and having a computer with a printer will eliminate a lot of crossing out. If you are doing this by hand, set the forms up as I have (see next page) and make a stack of copies. You will need a separate page for each club you talk with and eventually more pages per club that you deal with most often.

I can't stress the importance of noting key elements of a conversation especially personal comments made that might help you break the ice during the second phone call. For instance, you make your call and the person tells you that Randal (the booking agent) is out sick with the flu. Determine that there is no one else you can talk to, display your concern over his illness and then reply that you'll call back showing a sign of intelligence by not asking when you should call. The person on the other end probably has no idea when Randal will be well and back to work, so assume that. Now in your notes mark down that Randal has the flu. In your daily planner, advance to the following week and mark down to call Randal, that this is your second phone call and that he had the flu the last time you called. When you call back in a week you can open up the conversation by asking how he is. This sounds like basic common sense, but this is the type of thing that gets lost if its not written down especially if you have made dozens of other calls between the last time you and now. This will set you apart from the others and begin to establish a link between yourself and the club.

You can set up your Data Form in the following manner.

```
CLUB NAME: _____

ADDRESS: _____

PHONE: _____ FAX: _____ CONTACT: _____

BEST TIME TO CALL: _____ DO THEY HAVE LIGHTS: _____

DO THEY HAVE SOUND: _____ HOUSE SOUNDMAN: _____ NAME: _____

ADMISSION AGE: ____

OTHER INFORMATION:

WHEN I SHOULD CALL BACK: _____
```

So you've called a club and got some information. Let's record it.

```
CLUB:            101 club

ADDRESS: 101 5th Ave NYC NY 10010

PHONE:  212 555-5555    FAX:    212 555-5556 CLUB CONTACT: Randal

BEST TIME TO CALL: Mon, Tue, Thur after 5:00pm DO THEY HAVE LIGHTS:   Yes

DO THEY HAVE SOUND: Yes  HOUSE SOUNDMAN: Yes   NAME:   Dante

ADMISSION AGE: 18 but 21 over to drink

OTHER INFORMATION:  Good conversation!! Spoke with Mike the guy behind the bar.
Randel  wasn't  in he's sick with the flu. They received my tape but he's not sure if it was
listened to yet. They are booked up for the next two months.

WHEN I SHOULD CALL BACK            Next Thursday
```

CONFIRMING THE SHOW

At some point during one of your phone calls, you will get a booking for a show. Congratulations! Having agreed on the night, the time slot and the pay, you should then ask if you can send some flyers to post up in at the club. This is one way to confirm the agreed time and date as well as give the club the impression that a professional band has just been hired.

Now you have your work cut out and you should spend the next two months concentrating on nothing else but the show. But what about the promoter you booked the show with. They speak to hundreds of bands a week. There is no guarantee that they will remember you much less remember all the promises made to you on the phone. There is a good chance that the person you spoke with might very well forget your entire conversation. To make matters worse the person you spoke with might not even be employed at the club in two months when you arrive there to play. So what can you do to protect yourself?

Well first you will want to get down all of the promises made to you by the booker in writing. Things that you discussed in your phone call about the event such as pay, stage times, billing and all of the other things you talked about.

These arrangements are for the most part verbal agreements made on the phone by two people who most often have never met each other. Unless your band is an important one with a reputation of bringing in big business, **don't trust a verbal commitment**!!

To avoid getting ripped off or finding out your gig is canceled the day before you are supposed to play, ask for a signed confirmation. You can provide them the form by using the one below and faxing it to them. This just represents a record of the conversation. It is not meant to be a legal binding contract but rather a show of professionalism from you and a deterrent from them screwing you. Just ask them to please sign it and fax it back to you for your records. You should have this computer generated and printed on your band letterhead.

SUCTION

CONTACT NAME: _____

ADDRESS:_____

ARTIST NAME : _____

PERFORMANCE DATE:_____ VENUE:_____

ADDRESS (of venue): _____

TERMS: _____

CLUB CAPACITY: _____

SHOW TIMES: _____ _____ minute sets w/____ _____ minute/s break/s

DOORS: _____

TICKET SCALING: _____

BILLING: _____

BUYER: _____

PHONE:_____

SIGNATURE OF BUYER: _____

Confirmation

OCTOBER 11, 1998

SAL MINELA

C/O THE BACTERIA LOUNGE

1101 PERDUE PLACE

PTOMAINE GARDENS, NY 11901

NAME:	Sal Minela
ADDRESS:	1101 Perdue Place Ptomaine Gardens NY 11901
ARTIST:	Suction
DATE :	November 18, 1998
VENUE:	The Bacteria Lounge
ADDRESS:	1101 Perdue Pl., Ptomaine Gardens NY, 11901
TERMS:	$300.00 flat guarantee. Sound & Lights provided.
CAPACITY:	600
SHOW TIMES:	**2 60** minute sets w/ **1 15** minute break
DOORS:	8:00PM
TICKET SCALING:	$8.00 in advance $10:00 day of the show
BILLING:	25% special guest
BUYER:	Sal Minela
PHONE:	(516) 687- 4934

_____   _____

SIGNATURE OF BUYER   **SIGNATURE OF ARTIST**

MD MANAGEMENT PO Box 210 NY NY 10010

NEW YORK
BEVERLY HILLS
NASHVILLE
LONDON
ROME
SYDNEY
MUNICH

WILLIAM MORRIS AGENCY, INC.

1350 AVENUE OF THE AMERICAS · NEW YORK, N.Y. 10019 · (212) 586-5100

ESTABLISHED 1898
XXXX

Cable Address:
"WILLMORRIS"
TELEX 620165
FAX (212) 246-3583

July 17, 1990

Selling Agent: Jonathan Levine

Shah Management
Marc Davison
120 McNamara
No. Hempstead, NY 10927

Per our conversation and your confirmation, we are issuing contracts for the following:

ARTIST: The Last Tribe
DATE: July 28, 1990
VENUE: WORLD STAGE/PHONE: 914-425-7321
ADDRESS: 302 North Main Street
CITY/STATE: Hillcrest, NY

TERMS: $500.00 (FIVE HUNDRED DOLLARS) FLAT GUARANTEE PLUS
               LOCAL SOUND & LIGHTS TO ARTIST SPECIFICATIONS.

BINDER: None
DEPOSIT: None   Turn House: No

CAP: 900   Ticket Scale: 782 @$15/118 @$22.50   App. GP: $
14,385.00
SHOW TIMES: 1- at 9:00PM DOORS PERF. TIMES: Perf:10:00PM

BILLING: 75% SPECIAL GUEST   SHOW ORDER: Open
ON BILL WITH: MEAT LOAF

BUYER: Gary Katz/WORLD STAGE
               302 North Main Street/Hillcrest, NY 10977
               C/O Stan Levinstone/Stan Levinstone Presents
               Stan/Woodridge, NY 07075

PHONE: 201-939-5454
LOCAL CONTACT: Gary Katz

ADDITIONAL INFO: PRODUCTION CONTACT: Stan Levinstone (201)
939-5454.

With best regards,   cc:

CONTRACTS AND RIDERS

There are two important rules to abide by.

1- DON'T TRY TO OUTSMART YOURSELF 2- GET THE OFFER IN WRITING.

As a young act you may attempt to inform the booker that a contract from you will arrive in few days to be signed and mailed back. (This is how it's done for national acts). However, you're probably going to hear a laugh from the other end of the receiver followed by an offer to headline next Sunday's comedy night.

Why? As I already pointed out when you are starting out, the clubs don't need you. And there is really no way the booker is going to bother with a contract for a band with no reputation and furthermore the booker is not going to lock themselves into a legal agreement with a band they have never done business with before, especially since a better offer may come in from a more popular band for the night in question.

The best you can hope for is the club throwing you a few free beers and a chance to play in front of some people. But I can promise you this, if you bring in 50 or more fans the first time out, chances are you can secure a second show before you leave with some kind of set pay. And if your next show brings in more people and the next brings in even more, you'll soon own this place and you'll be able to negotiate with strength. When that time comes, all of the provisions you need as a band will be presented in the form of a contract and rider to the contract. The contract spells out the major points discussed about the show and the rider is the document that spells out the specific terms of the contract and the event. When you become a big star, your contract will be very similar to the one you will use now but your rider can be as long as 30 pages detailing every nuance from ticket price to catering.

At this level, your rider is merely a request form that rides along with your contract that the band would like to have under the best of conditions. This is more or less a game many times, because in most cases you'll get the rider sent back with everything crossed out, but is was worth the shot.

Another important reason for a contract is if you are planning on spending money on promotion of the show. You need to make the booker aware as to how seriously you are taking the show and that you are planning some promotion for it. You want their assurance that you will be taking the stage at the agreed upon time and be receiving the agreed payment some of which will be used to compensate yourself back for what you spent on promotion.

The following will include a blank contract, one filled out and a simple rider.

THIS CONTRACT for the personal services of musicians on the engagement below

is made on the _____ day of _____, 199__ between the undersigned:_____ herein called "Purchaser" and the band

_____ herein called "Artist".

1. The ARTIST agrees to render to the purchaser personal services and the **PURCHASER** agrees to hire the **ARTIST** on the following terms and conditions:

Place of engagement _____ **Telephone**_____

Address _____

Date of Engagement_____**Showtime**_____**Load in**_____

Set Length_____ _____ minute set(s) with ____ _____minute breaks

Compensation_____

_____**Type of Engagement**_____

2.Production_____

3. Age of admission_____ **4. Venue capacity**_____ **5. Tix price**_____

6. Purchaser will make payment as follows:

A) _____ shall be paid by purchaser via cash, certified check or University check made out to _____

as deposit for the event.

B) The remaining _____ balance, plus all percentages, shall be paid in cash or University check on or before conclusion of engagement directly to **ARTIST** or **ARTIST MANAGEMENT**.

6. No performance shall be recorded, reproduced or transmitted in any matter without specific written permission from **ARTIST** or **MANAGEMENT**.

7. It is hereby agreed that the undersigned **ARTIST** is an independent contractor and not an employee of the undersigned **PURCHASER**.

8. The agreement of the artists to perform is subject to proven detention by sickness, accidents, riots, strikes, epidemics, acts of god, or any other legitimate condition beyond control. If this occurs deposits shall be returned in full to purchaser.

9. PURCHASER understands that s/he is obligated to pay for services of ARTIST unless it becomes impossible for the purchaser to provide a place of performance due to an act of god.

<u>10. This contract shall be governed by the State of</u> _____

IN WITNESS WHEREOF, *the parties hereto have set their names and seals on the and year first written above*

_____

Purchaser's Full Name

_____

Signature of Purchaser

_____

Street Address

_____

Phone Number

_____

Name of Artist or Representative

_____

Signature of Artist or Representative

_____

Street Address

_____

Phone Number

THIS CONTRACT for the personal services **of musicians on the engagement below**

is made on the   11th day of **October,**   199**8** between the undersigned **Sal Minela** herein called "Purchaser" and the band **SUCTION** herein called "Artist".

1. The **ARTIST** agrees to render to the purchaser personal services and the **PURCHASER** agrees to hire the **ARTIST** on the following terms and conditions:

Place of engagement   **Bacteria Lounge**   Telephone **(516) 687-4934**

Address **1101 Perdue Place Ptomaine Gardens NY 11901**

Date of engagement **Nov 18th** Showtime **11:00pm** Load in **6:00pm**

Set Length **2   60** minute set(s) with **1   20** minute break(s)

Compensation $**300.00 flat guarantee.**   Type of engagement **Indoor club**

2. Production **Purchaser to provide sound and lights**

3. Age of admission **21** 4. Venue capacity **450** 5. Tix price **$8.00**

6. Purchaser will make payment as follows:

A) **$300.00** shall be paid by purchaser via cash, certified check or University check made out to **SUCTION**   as deposit for the event.

B) The remaining **$0.00** balance, **plus all percentages**, shall be paid in cash or University check on or before conclusion of engagement directly to ARTIST or ARTIST MANAGEMENT.

6. No performance shall be recorded, reproduced or transmitted in any matter without specific written permission from ARTIST or MANAGEMENT.

7. It is hereby agreed that the undersigned ARTIST is an independent contractor and not an employee of the undersigned PURCHASER.

8. The agreement of the artists to perform is subject to proven detention by sickness, accidents, riots, strikes, epidemics, acts of god, or any other legitimate condition beyond control. If this occurs deposits shall be returned in full to purchaser.

9. PURCHASER understands that s/he is obligated to pay for services of ARTIST unless it becomes impossible for the purchaser to provide a place of performance due to an act of god.

10. This contract shall be governed by the State of _____

IN WITNESS WHEREOF, *the parties hereto have set their names and seals on the and year first written above*

SAL MINELA   **MARC DAVISON (MNGR)**

Purchasers Full Name   *Name of Artist Representative*

_____   _____
Signature of Purchaser   *Signature of Artist or Representative*

1101 Perdue Place, Ptomaine garden NY

Street Address   _____
                                                    Street Address

516 687-4934

Phone Number   _____
                                                    Phone Number

78

RIDER TO CONTRACT

ADVERTISING:

a) Artist shall be billed as ***SUCTION*** in all print ads

b) Artist shall receive 75% headline billing and no less than 25% opening act billing in all advertising, publicity and promotions for this event.

c) Purchaser will not commit any member of Suction to personal appearances or interviews without prior consent from **MLD management**.

ACCESS:

a) Artist must have access to venue five hours prior and two hours after the show.

STAGING:

a) Promoter shall provide a free and clear stage, minimum of **24**' wide by **20**' deep and a minimum of **2**' high.

b) A drum riser shall be provided for stages no lower than **2** ft.

c) A carpet of rug **8' x 8'** shall be provided for drums.

MERCHANDISING:

a) Artist must be provided with a free and clear well lit area to display and sell all merchandise. Promoter shall take no more than 10% of all merchandising sales.

b) Artist reserves the right not to trade merchandise to any employee of the venue in exchange for venue privileges.

INSURANCE:

Purchaser shall indemnify and hold artist, and their crew safe and harmless from any loss, damage, personal injury or expense incurred or suffered by or threatened against as a result of any claim for personal injury or property damage by or on behalf of any third party, person, firm or corporation as a result of or in connection with the engagement, which claim does not directly result from artists' active negligence. This provision may never be waived.

GENERAL INFORMATION:

a) Purchaser shall notify artists of any laws, or rules governing specific regulations that could affect performances, including: pyrotechnics, decibel levels, curfews, lighting, crowd control and other performance restrictions.

b) Artist shall have exclusive control over the production, presentation and performance of this engagement and sole control over the concert room prior to and following the engagement.

c) The person executing the contract and rider has authority to do so.

d) In event of a breach of any part of this contract by purchaser, management may cancel this engagement and purchaser will be obligated to pay the full contract price to artist.

e) In case of an outdoor show, the stage and PA wings should have a roof covering adequate to withstand heavy rains and not dampen equipment.

HOUSE SOUND:

a) PA system shall be sufficient to supply a house sound pressure of 100db at the rear of the hall.

b) There shall be a graphic equalization on the house system, separate from the monitor system.

c) The minimum number of inputs for **SUCTION** shall be **16**

d) There shall be Reverb and delay on the house sound system if artist cannot provide one.

e) Artist will need to patch into the house sound system all effects and necessary sound gear.

f) Artist sound man shall have full use and control of all house sound equipment.

g) House shall provide a sound engineer to operate system if artist cannot provide one.

MONITOR SYSTEM:

a) Monitor shall have a minimum of **12** inputs on the mixing console.

b) A minimum of **6** separate monitor mixes are needed

c) A minimum of **5** monitor wedges are needed. Each must be capable of supplying a sound pressure of 110db at 10 feet.

LIGHTING:

a) Promoter shall provide a back lighting with a minimum of **9** instruments and full stage washes.

b) Promoter shall provide gel frames and a variety of colors

c) **SUCTIONS road manager** shall have control over all house lights.

d) **SUCTION** may also request the use of a lighting operator.

ARTIST RESERVES THE RIGHT TO:

a) Assign a minimum of **ten** names on the guest list

b) Choose the recorded music to be played before, during and after the performance

c) Have final approval of all opening acts.

DRESSING ROOM AND CATERING:

Artist requires at least one, large, private dressing room. This room is for the exclusive use of artist and crew and cannot be used by any other artist, employees of the club, etc. This dressing room should contain adequate heating, air conditioning, comfortable seating, mirrors and a lock on the door.

DRINK: **Two gallons of Orange Juice**

Two gallons of spring water (Evian)

One case of Rolling Rock or Bud

Plenty of clean ice and plastic cups

FOOD (for 9 people) Choose one

    Chinese (separate veg and meat dishes)

    Pasta with salad and bread

    Hot turkey or chicken dish w/ potato and bread

    Three large pizzas (plain, veg, meat)

If meals are not possible a ten dollar per person buy out is acceptable

WE HOPE THIS RIDER EXPLAINS OUR NEEDS IN FULL.
THANK YOU.

_____   _____

Purchaser   **Marc Davison**

                                 P.O. Box 218

                                 NY NY, 10010

The contract in its completed form, should be filled out by you after receiving all the specific details concerning the show.

You should sign and send it ASAP to the person that booked your show (the name that appears at the bottom of the contract).

You should have these contracts in triplicate so that after it's signed by the purchaser, they will keep one copy sending two back to you. You then keep one filed away and the third copy gets filed in your **Confirmed Gig File (see next page)** which is the copy you then bring with you on the night of the show. This is your insurance in case the person that booked you and signed your contract isn't present at the club or is and conveniently forgot the deal you both agreed upon. In case of a dispute over set length or payment or anything detailed in your contract, you simply refer to your contract and expect it to end all arguments.

The above contract and rider deals with some intricate technicalities that do not apply to young bands starting out. As I have previously mentioned, unless you are worth something to the club as in the case of a national act (band with an album out on a national release from a major or independent record company) or you are an extremely popular unsigned act that is touring around, the provisions included in the rider such as sound and lighting requirements, private dressing room privileges and catering, are not yours to ask for in the beginning of your career. Your rights, however, do include that the club owner pay you according to your arrangements and that you are treated fairly and without danger to you or your equipment.

Once you are at a level where you are making the club money by the substantial crowds attending your shows, you are certainly well within line to expect the club to provide many of the things spelled out in the rider. Keep in mind that your rider needs to be flexible and that many venues simply cannot comply to every request. The purchaser will usually red line (draw a red line through) any provision he will not or can not offer.

When you receive the contract and rider back in the mail, put it in your gig file and go book another show.

CONFIRMED GIG FILE

You should also set up a separate filing area where the entire club file folder will be transferred to, once a show has been confirmed. This will be known as the Confirmed Gig File. When you confirm a show, the file should be transferred to this area with all its contents, in sequential order by date of the live event. This way it is outside your file cabinet and easily reached should the club call or should you need to file more things in it. What I always used was a plastic milk crate that had slots built in on the inside that the folder would fit right into (purchased at Staples). I kept it right on the end of my desk so that whenever the band came over they could see what had been confirmed and what the correspondence looked like.

BAND CONFIRMATION FORM

Once the show is confirmed I'm sure you are going to call all your band mates and tell them the good news. But I recommend one further action. Since you are doing all the bookings you are on top of the information on a constant basis, but your band members are not. A simple form detailing only the most important information should be supplied to them so they can prepare themselves for the show in their own way. The form should be as follows.

BAND CONFIRMATION FORM

DATE OF SHOW:_____   DAY:_____   TIME:_____

CLUB NAME_____

ADDRESS:_____

PHONE #:_____

HOW MANY SETS:_____   OPENER OR HEADLINER (CIRCLE ONE)

NAME OF OPENER OR HEADLINER:_____

PAY:_____

This simple form given to each member of the band at the very next rehearsal, advises them of all key points of information concerning an upcoming event. Should there be other information needed that is not contained on this form, then create a line and insert it. Each band member should have their own personal gig file where they will store this information.

ADVANCING THE SHOW

When you land a gig and verbally confirm it on the phone, you will need to prepare the advance sheet for the show. The advance sheet is the list of everything you need to know in advance before you walk into the club, so that you will be fully prepared for the event.

These items are somewhat different from the information on your contract. They are specific details concerning the night including directions to the club, load in time, phone numbers, etc.

You can begin filling out some of the general information on the advance sheet like club name, address and phone number but the bulk of the advance sheet need not be filled out until three days before the event. This way you can make some necessary contact with the club to remind them you're alive, and get any last minute info or if there have been any changes on the night that you were not informed of. If you wait until the night of the show it will be too late to resolve.

This form should be stapled to the outside of the club file folder and placed back into the confirmed gig file until you are ready to leave for the show.

So about two or three days before the show you call the club and ask to speak to the manager (your contact). Tell them that you are from the band that will be playing on Friday night and you want to "advance the show". Don't waste time with idle chit-chat. Get right down to business.

Have the following form ready and just go down the list asking the questions and writing in the answers.

The following is your advance form.

DAY / DATE:

VENUE:

ADDRESS:

DIRECTIONS:

PHONE: **FAX:**

PROMOTER: **PHONE #:**

CLUB CONTACT: **PHONE #:**

SOUNDMAN: **PHONE #:**

LIGHTMAN: **PHONE #:**

CAPACITY:

PRODUCTION CO.:   **PHONE #:**

DEPARTURE TIME:

ARRIVAL TIME:

LOAD IN: **LOCATION:**

SOUND CHECK:

STAGE SIZE: **RISER:**   **WILL YOU GET IT:**

DOORS OPEN:

SHOWTIME:

SET LENGTH:

CURFEW:

DRESSING ROOM: **HOSPITALITY:**   **BAR:**

OTHER ACTS: **HOW MANY:**

NAMES:

GUEST LIST:

LODGING:

ADDRESS:

INTERVIEWS

NAME: **COMPANY:**   **PHONE:**

AFTER SHOW

ATTENDANCE: **FLYERS POSTED:**

          CLUB RESPONSE:

Day/ Date: **Wed Oct 22**

Venue: **The Ballroom**

Address: **970 W. Belmont   Chicago, Ill 60657**

Directions: **65 north to 94 west. Exit east at Belmont. Go straight to Shefield Ave. On right**

Phone: **312 555-5555**   Fax: **312 555-5556**

Promoter: **Mr. Blonde**   Phone: **312 666-6666**

Club Contact: **Mr. Pink**   Phone: **" "**

Soundman: **Mr. Brown**   Phone: **" "**

Lightman: **Mr. Orange**   Phone: **" "**

Capacity: **250**

Production Co.: **In house**   Phone:

Departure time:

Arrival time: **5:00**

Load in: **6:00**   Where: **Side door**

Sound check: **7-7:30**

Stage size: **20 x 18**   Riser: **yes**   Will you get it: **yes**

Doors open: **9:00pm**

Showtime: **11:00pm**

Set length: **1/45 minute set**

Curfew:

Dressing room: **Yes**   Hospitality: **2 pizzas**   Bar: **Free beer**

Other acts: **Yes**   How many: **2**

Names: **RUKUS** (headliner)   **Spasm (Co-Headliner)**

Guest list: **10 names   See attached list**

Lodging: **Ask Mr. Blonde when you get to the club for best hotel and directions**

Address:

<u>Interviews</u>

Name: Company: Phone: Location:

Nice Guy Eddie   Chicago Music Mag   **8:00 at the club**

AFTER SHOW

Attendance: **175**   Crowd response: **Great**

Flyers Posted: **We sent 2 dozen. There were about 6 around the club**

Club response: **Loved us and wants us back in Nov. will give us a Friday night.**

"Hey Spike I told you everything would fit. You owe me five bucks"

6

Whether you're a big name act or a young unsigned band, the day of a show is always special and full of excitement. A lot of hard work on your part has gone into making this day go well. Combined with the excitement, there is also some stress associated in hoping that everything from the weather to your broken down van making it to the gig, goes well and works in your favor.

Hopefully, you have gone through your checklist of all the things you must do prior to the show and in the proper time sequence. There are things that, if left to the day of the show, might come too late and can screw up the whole event. There are also things that can only be left for the day of the show and we will cover both of these categories in this chapter.

It is important that from the onset you treat this day as if it were special. Performing in front of people is one of the most challenging things you can do in life. Throughout the course of a performance you will be reaching inside yourself to bring forth a tremendous amount of energy. It is therefore imperative that you spend a good portion of the day doing things that build up your energy level and uplift your spirit. After all, you not only have a responsibility to yourself, but you owe it to your band mates and the audience to be on top of everything.

It would be ideal if you could sleep late into the morning, and wake to a fruit and nectar breakfast in bed, followed by a dip in the pool and Jacuzzi. Your personal masseuse could then show up for a two hour full body massage. You then eat a soft lunch and devote yourself to a quiet yoga and meditation session. You wind up just in time to get dressed and hop in to your limo which will whisk you off to the venue for sound check.

While for some this might be a reality, for most of us the day is usually spent working at some day job where your boss is probably bent that you have to either leave early or will be in late the next morning, tired and a little hung over. You get out of work, hungry and beat, and rush out to the club, hopefully in time for sound check.

This is the reality for most of you so take solace in the fact that you are not alone. The secret is to remember that in a sense you are two people. There is the day job persona where you are whatever your boss and job require you to be. But then there is the other you, perhaps the real you. The artist/performer, struggling to make it not just for the money but for a realization of a life long dream.

It is therefore really important that if you are working during the day of the show, that when you leave for the gig, you consciously let go of the day job persona and transform yourself into your artist/performer mode. Many of you already do this in one form or another. I just want you to be more aware of the transition and find some kind of ritual that helps complete the transformation. This is an empowering act, and I believe that any form of spiritual rite is good for the soul and charges you up in a positive way. This is just a good way to get yourself focused on the night and make it possible for you to deliver the best show you can.

Though meditation and positive, creative visualizations are keys to creating success, there are some important tribal rituals that you must consider as a method of transforming yourself, as well as a bonding process with your band. Like a native tribe would prepare for a hunt, you and the group must make preparations so that your hunt for success is fruitful.

The following pages are a laundry list of preparations combined with some tribal philosophy to help you get ready for your personal hunt out there in gig land.

TRANSPORTATION

Unless you own a van, you will need to give the transportation of all your equipment and your band members some consideration.

A group should depart from their home base to the show together at all times. There is a lot of nervous energy on the day of the show and when the band members are together riding to a gig, a synergy of that energy occurs, uniting the band. The results will be apparent in their performance. If you all arrive separately, this may not occur and may create a tension that will feed into your energy and rob it of positive vibes. One example might be the effects on a band by the late arrival of a band member. Sound check has been delayed causing the remaining members to get hassled.

There are also equipment considerations. Unless you are each responsible for loading in your own equipment (which is uncool since drummers have many more pieces than the singer), a late-arriving member will not have been there to help with the load in. And in closing, since I have traveled with bands for years I know first hand how bands get in sync through the nonsensical banter that takes place during the trip to and from the show. So regardless of how you arrive at the show, do it in unison.

If you do not own your transportation, you'll have to rent or hitch a trailer to your car.

TRAILER

These boxes on wheels (U-Haul) come in a variety of sizes, though the most popular are 4x6, 5x8 and a 6x12. You will need a ball hitch on the back of your vehicle to hook the trailer up to, and you will need electrical connectors to hook up the brake lights from the rear lights of your car to the trailer.

These are very inexpensive to rent and you do not need to be a certain age as you would when renting a van. The main difficulty is that many people rent trailers and use them on one way trips, like renting one in New York to move belongings to Seattle and dropping it off there. So often, rental companies will not have a variety of trailers available; therefore, you will need to start calling agencies that rent trailers days in advance to line one up. *If the rental company has one and it's two days before the show, go down and put a deposit on it so that they will hold it for you. Do not depend on the rental agency to hold it for you based on a friendly phone conversation unless you want to learn the hard way!* You will be awfully disappointed when you get down there one hour before you need to leave for the show and find out nobody remembers ever talking to you and they don't have a trailer your size.

When you go down to put a deposit, find out the following information.

HOW MUCH IS IT FOR A ONE DAY RENTAL?

They range from about $10 to $25 a day depending on size, destination and if you're dropping it off at a new destination or bringing it back to where you rented it from.

WHAT TIME THE FOLLOWING DAY DO THEY EXPECT IT RETURNED?

IS THERE A DEPOSIT REQUIRED?

HOW LONG WILL IT TAKE ON THE DAY YOU PICK IT UP TO PROCESS THE PAPER WORK AND HOOK UP THE TRAILER TO YOUR CAR?

Give yourself plenty of time because I have known instances where it took two hours to get processed due to a waiting line and only one employee behind the counter.

FIND OUT EXACTLY WHAT KIND OF BALL HITCH IS REQUIRED ON YOUR CAR AND IF THEY SUPPLY THE WIRING TO HOOK UP THE BRAKES.

Once this is all in place, on the day of the show you just need to drive down, get hooked up, go back to load in your equipment and proceed to the show. Hopefully, one of you has had some experience in driving with a trailer. There is no problem driving forward however when backing up things can get confusing. Remember one simple rule. To angle the trailer in one direction you must position your car in the opposite direction. So in other words, if you want to park and you need to reverse to the left you must turn the car steering wheel to the right and back up. This will position the trailer to angle to the left and vice versa. My advice is do not put yourself in a situation where you have to reverse. Either park on the corner of the street, or if you are in a parking lot, park in a space where you can easily go forward to pull out.

VANS

If you look in the Yellow Pages under van rental or automotive rental, you will find most of the rental agencies in your area that rent vans. There are two types of vans available that will suit your needs:

 CARGO VAN - A van that has a driver and passenger seat with the back empty for all your equipment.

 PASSENGER VAN - A van that has two to four rows of seats for accommodating many passengers.

There is very little difference in rental price between the two and their advantages and disadvantages are quite obvious. In the beginning when money is very tight your main concern is to get everyone plus your equipment down to the show as cheaply as possible. Yes, you can all drive separately and each bring your own equipment and that will certainly solve the immediate financial concern. But at some point when you start playing gigs fifty miles or more from your home this method will be **(a)** more expensive and **(b)** not philosophically correct. Therefore you are going to have to rent a van if you do not own one. In that case, to keep the cost down if there are more than two members in the band, accommodating yourselves and the equipment will require some creative packing techniques.

In the case of one of my clients, they found a small couch and put it behind the front seats of the cargo van and then loaded up the equipment behind the couch. As time went on they eventually rented a U-haul, hitching it to the back of the van and adding more seats to the van so that everyone could ride in comfort.

Vans, like trailers, are rented by the day, but with vans you will also pay for the mileage. The cost ranges from area to area and certainly from agency to agency but it would be safe to say that it is 15 to 25 cents per mile. Some agencies will offer free miles (like the first 50 miles free). This is an attractive plus in choosing which agency to rent from because the miles will add up.

You will also be asked if you want to take out an insurance policy. They run about $10 to $15 extra on top of the rental charge but it is extremely important that you take it. The policy will usually limit your liability to about $500 on a major accident. You need to confirm with the agency exactly what the liability is, but whatever the case, it's better than having to replace the entire value of the van.

To rent a van you will need the following:

A VALID LICENSE

BE OF A CERTAIN AGE

Many agencies will not rent to anyone under twenty five years of age and they require that whoever does the renting also do all the driving.

HAVE A MAJOR CREDIT CARD FOR THE DEPOSIT.

Deposits are in the neighborhood of $300, refundable when the van is returned.

VAN ETIQUETTE

I hope this following paragraph does not fall on deaf ears. I preface this by saying that a vehicle is a weapon in the wrong hands. Going to a show is exciting and certainly being in a band and heading off to play a show is an exhilarating experience. Don't ruin it by acting like a fool, which can, at best, delay your arrival if you're caught speeding or at worst, kill you or somebody you don't know by driving recklessly.

I had a rule that was heavily enforced with an act that I managed which was "No beer or alcohol allowed in the vehicle." If it wasn't followed, I would immediately cease booking any live shows and drop them as clients. My concerns were justified in so far that I cared for their safety and for the responsibility I had to the van company. Remember, this is not your van and if you ever want to rent one again from the agency you are dealing with, you need to make sure that upon return there are no signs of illegal activity. While I might not necessarily agree with the law as it pertains to controlled substances in a private matter, I do believe that when we are responsible for the safety of others, we must think a bit more globally and act accordingly.

One particular agency where I rented from has a $100 fine if any beer bottles are found in the van. The sign in the office reads, " $100 fine for every beer bottle or can found. If you have a problem with that, call a cop."

DEPARTURE

Now that you have your travel arrangements secured, we need to load up the equipment and head out. Prior to load out, you should take an inventory of everything you are going to bring with you to the show. Make a list of each and every individual carry-on piece including: luggage, briefcase, merchandise case, etc., and assign a number to it. You must then affix that number on to the corresponding carry-on piece. Begin with number one and go as high as your equipment goes. Use either a spray paint or a good adhesive tape like duct tape, to apply the numbers. If you have a case that you do not want numbered, replace it with a case that you can number. The individual pieces with their identifying numbers should then be listed and checked off as they get loaded into the van.

If you are bringing along something like a camera or a tape recording device, and it is only for this particular show, then you do not need to paint a number on it but you should add it to the list at the bottom. This way you are reminded of it as you load into the van both before the show and of course after the show is over.

Your list should look something like this:

	Date	in	out	Date	in	out	Date	in	out
#1 Fender Twin									
#2 Mesa Dual Rectifier									
#3 Mesa 4x12 cabinet									
#4 Mesa 8x10 cabinet									
#5 GK 800									
#6 Les Paul									
#7 Fender Precision									
#8 Fender Strat									
#9 Drum Hardware									
#10 Rack tom									
#11 Bass drum									
#12 Snare									
#14 Floor tom									
#15 Effects rack									
#16 Tool box									

✓   The list is designed to be used for more than one show. Include the date so you can trace any lost piece of equipment.

✓   Attach list to a clipboard along with a good flashlight (Maglight) and secure it somewhere by the back door of the van after all the equipment is loaded in. It will be much easier for you when you're loading out in the dark at 3:00 AM.

✓   Assign one person to check off each piece as it gets loaded in.

If you have put the confirmed gig file in a routing file system, pull the file and take out the information that you need to bring with you to the club.

ADVANCE SHEET

The form you filled out days ago for all the last minute show information.

CONTRACT

If you have a signed one, bring it. Do not depend on the club owner or booking agent to have saved their copy.

MAILING LIST

The mailing list forms should be either in a spiral notebook or a loose leaf notebook. It should be stored in one of the merchandising cases or your brief case.

ALSO INCLUDE THESE FOLLOWING ITEMS AS WELL

TOOL BOX.

Every band should invest in a tool box that contains pliers, screwdrivers (especially small jeweler size), wire cutters, soldering iron, solder, extra cables, hammer, glue and wire. This is essential and should be with you at every show.

DUCT TAPE

This extra strength tape is the most common used adhesive on stage. It is used for everything from taping down all your guitar and microphone cables to the floor but also for mending or repairing equipment, hanging up flyers, set lists, hanging backdrops, etc.

EXTRA BATTERIES

Keep plenty of extra batteries on hand at all times for your effects and tuners.

BLANK CASSETTE TAPES AND TAPE RECORDER

At some point after sound check you are going to ask the sound man if he can record your set either through the board or hook up your recorder to the board. You should try and get a live recording of every show you play mainly for constructive criticism and posterity.

EXTRA FLYERS

Bring along more flyers in case you do not find any of the ones you sent or put up yourself. Put some posters around the club and in areas outside the club where postering is permitted. It's a good idea to have some band posters that only include the band's name and some blank space at the bottom where you can write in by hand new information. (See next page)

GUEST LIST

When you advanced the show one of the questions you asked was "do you have a guest list and how many guests are you allowed?" For a new or unproved act you should get a minimum of four guests or one guest per band member.

APPEARING LIVE AT

You should inquire about an **"Industry Guest List."** This is a separate list for invited members of the music industry such as someone working for a record company, booking agency, press, producer, etc. All clubs should honor this list and keep it separate from the band's regular guest list.

Your guests will be admitted to the show with the admission price waived. The list should be compiled before you leave for the show and all guests should be informed that they are going to be guests. You should write their names down on a sheet of paper which will be handed to the doorman prior to the doors opening at the club.

All guests must be of admission age and most definitely will need to bring their ID. Being on the guest list does not mean you can get in if you are underage.

 ### Extra Guitar Strings

Stock up on plenty of full packs as well as individual strings. Keep the strings in order in a small box. Use the individual strings to replace broken strings during the set. This way you won't be breaking up a whole pack. Use the full packs when you are replacing all the strings at once.

 ### Change of Clothes

For after the show to change out of your sweaty clothes.

OTHER ITEMS INCLUDE:

 ### Merchandise

T-shirts and tapes packed in a box or case and marked with a umber on your equipment list.

 ### Money for Tolls, Gas, Food

 ### Business Cards

 ### A Staple Gun

Or an aerosol can of spray glue (3M) found at most large hardware stores for posting flyers.

ARRIVAL (Load In)

As we have discussed earlier in the book, one member of the band should be elected as the liaison to the club. If you have a manager or a road manager, that person is the liaison and the band members just do as they are instructed. If you have neither, than your elected liaison should be holding on to the gig files. When you have reached your destination these are the following actions you need to take:

CHECK THE ADVANCE SHEET AND FIND THE CORRECT DOOR WHICH YOU WERE INSTRUCTED TO LOAD IN FROM.

 PULL YOUR VAN OVER TO THAT DOOR AND PARK.

Do not unload until you check inside making sure this is the correct load in door.

 ENTER AND LOCATE THE CLUB CONTACT.

Announce your arrival and ask if you can begin to load in. Only one band member need enter at this point establishing that they are the representative of the group. Club employees may appear a bit grouchy and when an entire band converges on them with questions, it's generally a sure sign of their unprofessionalism and the manager can reciprocate with an attitude.

 CONFIRM YOUR SOUND CHECK TIME AND ASK WHEN YOU CAN BEGIN TO SET UP THE STAGE.

If you are the opening act you will be the last to sound check. Club managers will schedule the bands to arrive at different times so that they do not get in each other's way.

 IF YOU WERE TOLD WHEN YOU ADVANCED THE SHOW THAT YOU WILL GET A DRESSING ROOM, THIS WOULD BE A GOOD TIME TO CONFIRM THAT AND FIND OUT THE LOCATION.

This way if there is a lag time between load in and sound check, you have a place to go and collect yourself.

 **CONFIRM WITH THE CONTACT IF THEY ARE THE PERSON THAT PAYS YOU AT THE END OF THE NIGHT.**

If so, then establish at what point after your performance do you meet and where.

Once you have all the information you need proceed to load in.

STAGE PLOT

You may be asked to submit your band's stage plot. This is a diagram outlining your stage set-up and detailing your equipment requirements. It is required in certain situations where you are performing with multiple bands or opening up for a national act. In most cases the production manager is renting a backline that will be used by all the acts performing to reduce the amount of set changes and time between sets. By viewing the stage plot the production manager can determine what type of equipment to rent that will suit all the bands on the bill.

A tech list should be included with your stage plot. It should outline your requirements for the house PA system. You also want to list the desired rack effects for the vocals as well as which instruments should be included in the monitor mix. It is also helpful for you to list your backline.

```
┌─────────────────────────────────────────────────────────────────────────┐
│┌────────────────────────────────────────────────────────────────────────┐│
││                              □    [] monitor 4                            ││
││                            Drums                                         ││
││                                                                          ││
││         □                    □                    □                      ││
││      Lead Gtr             R. Gtr                Bass                     ││
││ Stage Right   [ ] monitor 1      [] mon  2        [] mon 3    Stage Left ││
│└────────────────────────────────────────────────────────────────────────┘│
└─────────────────────────────────────────────────────────────────────────┘
```

┌───┐
│   │
│ **SUCTION**   **TECHNICAL RIDER** │
│   │
│ **Front of House:**   │
│   │
│ Console, At least 24 inputs, with at least 3 bands of E.Q. with Sweepable midrange control per channel. │
│ At least 2 pre fader aux. sends per channel for stage monitors (if stage mix is from house position) │
│ At least 3 post-fader aux. sends per channel for fx sends.   │
│   │
│ Outboard Processing,   │
│   │
│   1- Digital Delay (SPX-90 or Equivalent).   │
│   │
│   1- Digital Delay (with at least 1 sec. delay time)   These are all effects for the vocals │
│   │
│   2-Compressors (dual channel unit ok)   │
│   │
│   2- Channel noise gates (optional)   │
│   │
│ **Stage:**   Monitors, Four mixes plus side fills in house with separate monitor mixes │
│   │
│   MIXES   MICROPHONES   │
│   │
│   Mix 1 - Lead Vocals (stage left)   -   SM58 (type of microphone) │
│   │
│   Mix 2 - Background - Vocals (stage right) - SM57   "   "   │
│   │
│   Mix 3 - Bass (stage left) - Bass direct taken from back of amp. │
│   │
│   Mix 4 - Drum (drum riser) SM 57's snare, Sen 421 or EV n/d on toms, AKG d-112, Sen 421, │
│   ATM-25 or EV RE20 on kick drum Guitar Mics should be SM57's │
│   │
│   **Backline:** 2 Roland Jazz Chorus 120 (ev's), 1 GK Bass Head, 1 Hartke 4x10, Tama 5 pc, Hi hat, │
│   ride, 2 splash, 2 crash, 1 china.   │
│   │
└───┘

This is a sample list I used for one particular client. Everything listed is suggested equipment for *their* optimum sound. Most clubs don't carry such a wide array of gear and unless you are a national act with a significant amount of record sales most clubs or promoters will not make your choices available to you. It has been my experience that when it comes to renting a backline, production managers usually go with the standard popular models like Marshall, Fender or Roland amps and Pearl or Tama drums. Drummers are allowed to use their hardware and guitarists will be allowed to use their effects.

SETTING UP THE STAGE

When you begin to set up your stage there is some simple etiquette you should follow. If you are the opening act, there is a good chance that the headline act's equipment will be on the stage and most probably will remain there throughout your performance. This can be disappointing because whatever size the stage is, the room left for you to set up can, at times, be cut in half. You wonder how in the world you're going to fit all your equipment in this little space and pull off a performance. Well, if you consider yourself creative, here is the chance to prove it.

Sharing a stage is a fact of life for bands at all levels of their career. Even as a signed act touring with a bigger named act, if you're the opener you may not get the full stage. It belongs to the headline act, the band all the people are there to see.

If you absolutely need more space, say for instance there are eight members in the band, you may get some consideration from the soundman or the headline act if you approach them with a cool head. However, the reality is that most headline acts will not move their stage set up very much. I have seen large bands where the front line members are standing on the floor, in front, off the stage.

An important need on stage aside from room is the riser for the drummer. Because drums are acoustic and not really amplified except for what is going through the P.A. system, the overall sound of the band thrown to the audience is enhanced when the drums are raised up. For cosmetic reasons, being that the drummer is in the back, not only behind the band but behind his kit as well, putting the drummer on a riser gives them a chance to be seen by the audience as well.

Once the drums are sound checked and all the levels are set in place on the sound board, the drums can be moved off the riser for the next band. This will be determined by the soundman, the headline act and the specifics of their performance contract.

I've seen many arguments over who gets the riser and as far as I'm concerned the whole thing is nonsense. If it was promised to you when you advanced the show (hopefully, you have it in writing on your confirmation), then take it up with the house sound man and not the other band. The stage belongs to the house and the soundman is the proper channel. If you state your case in a calm manner you are more apt to get results.

Sometimes there are compromises made to appease everyone. It may be suggested that the drummers share one kit to avoid problems. If it is agreed upon by all drummers, this can actually be a positive thing. It will reduce the time in between sets and you will probably get a better sound out of the kit if it stays permanent on the stage.

If you do not get the riser then so what! It's more impressive when a band plays their guts out in the worst of conditions, but not having the riser is certainly not one of them. If you're a young act, don't get cocky. Just get up on the stage, set up close to each other, and bang out the best set of your life. Before you know it you'll be the headline act and the riser will be yours to do what you like.

In most cases the headline act's amplifiers will also stay on the stage. All you need to do is place your amps in front of theirs. They should remove any floor effects they have leaving the area by the mikes clear for you. This is standard practice as you will notice if you go into any club on a double or triple bill show.

Once you have all of your equipment on stage, **DO NOT** all start playing. There is a time and place for that and this is not it. Drummers can tap their kit lightly to make sure everything is in place and guitarists may strum lightly to make sure everything is in working order. You need to wait for instructions from the house sound man to begin the sound check.

SOUND CHECK

The sound check is to establish the proper sound level for the band and make sure that all the line feeds from the board to the microphones are working. This is not an opportunity for the band to rehearse or for individual members to flash their prowess on their instrument. This is a crucial exercise that if done improperly will result in an off balance final sound mix that will make your band sound horrible at showtime.

The best person to mix your sound is the house soundman. Every room has its own acoustic personalities as does every sound board so the house sound man who has probably been mixing in it for a while, will know how to compensate at the board.

The two basic checks you're going to do are:

 LINE CHECK

This check is for all the lines connecting the mic's for vocals and your amps to the main board. The soundman asks you to play on your respective instrument, to check the signals and make sure that each line is working. As the check proceeds the sound of each instrument will be adjusted establishing effects and balance.

It is imperative that during the line check all instruments remain silent except for the one instrument the sound man is checking. If the drummer's floor tom is being checked for example, the lead guitarist cannot be whacking out a solo. This is rude and pointless since the bleed over of your sound will affect the drummer's mix. If your fingers cannot stay idle, then just take all the volume off your guitar and play silently. Disturbances in the sound check will only delay your check and quite possibly leave you little time for the overall sound check.

OVERALL SOUND CHECK

This occurs after the line check. All the instruments have been individually checked and if there's time, the sound man will ask you to play through a song to mix the sounds together.

✓ Prearrange which songs you will play in sound check. The songs should be in your set list and should include harmonies and lead guitar parts. These are crucial parts of a song and it is important that to check them in sound check.

✓ It would help if there's a secondary ear, perhaps a friend of yours that comes along with the band, that can give you information on how the mix is from the floor. Even though the sound man knows the room, they may not know your band and what it should sound like.

✓ Keep in mind that when you sound check, you are probably doing so in an empty room. This will create a sound mix that may at first sound a bit cold, but that will be corrected when the room fills up with people. Just make sure that the vocals are not too low and if there is more than one vocalist make sure that their levels are all balanced.

✓ Usually a typical five piece drum set with three cymbals will not get sufficient amount of mic's for the whole kit. So it's important that key elements of the kit come through like the snare, bass drum and cymbals. Also a common problem in quick sound checks are that the drums will sound tiny or too loud.

✓ You should make sure that the lead guitar comes across during the solos. The sound man should know who is the lead guitarist in the group if there is more than one guitar player. A good sound man will be able to pick up on the solos and boost the lead level at the appropriate times.

✓ It is important to note that you must adjust your stage levels during sound check and leave them that way throughout the course of the show. By changing the settings you are either increasing or decreasing the sound level coming from the main board and offsetting the balance.

✓ It is also important to regulate the stage sound. If you are too loud on stage you will override the PA thus rendering it useless. You obviously need to hear yourself on stage and if the room itself requires a lower stage volume you can point your amps in towards you as opposed to pointing them straight out into the audience. After all, what the audience hears is not your stage volume but the sound from your amp through the board and out of the PA speakers.

MONITOR MIX

The monitors are the speakers on the stage that are facing in toward the band. They are primarily used to amplify the vocals back toward the band. The vocals do not come off of any amp on stage. They are amplified through the club's sound board and out the speakers that are in front of the band in a mix for the audience. The only way the band can hear the vocals is through the monitor speakers. In a perfect world each player would have at least one monitor in front of them. But in the club world you'll probably get two up front and one in back for the drummer.

The sound mix for the monitors is different than the mix from the PA to the audience. In bigger venues the monitors are mixed off of a separate sound board usually located on the side of the stage instead of in the middle of the room where the house sound board is. A separate soundman will operate the monitor, mixing the instruments and vocals for the band to hear on stage. But in the smaller venue, the monitor mix is included on the one main board mixed by the one soundman. In this case there will be a limited number of mixes for the stage that will usually incorporate vocals and some guitar. This will help the player from stage left receive the signal from the player on stage right if they are having a hard time hearing each other during the performance.

Most small house boards do not have enough inputs to fully mix the whole band on stage for the monitors, so you'll have to deal with what's available. Down the road as your reputation gets bigger, you might want to invest in a full PA system that you bring on the road with you and set up every night so you can get the perfect mix.

Sound checks are not lengthy events and sometimes you may get only five minutes for one. So be quick to set up, don't step on each others' toes and respect the soundman. Remember your sound is ultimately in their hands.

DOWN TIME

When sound check is over, follow instructions on where to put your equipment in case there is another band sound checking after you.

 PUT AWAY ALL YOUR ROAD CASES, GUITAR CASES, BAGS AND ANYTHING ELSE LYING AROUND.

The smaller stuff can go into your dressing room or get locked up in the van. The bigger cases will probably get rolled over by the side of the stage.

DEPENDING ON WHAT TIME YOU GO ON, YOU MAY HAVE ANYWHERE FROM 20 MINUTES TO 8 HOURS UNTIL SHOWTIME.

If you are hungry and have catering from the club, this is the time to inform the club manager that you are ready to eat. If not, plans should be made for some kind of meal to either be brought in or go out for. Since you have thousands of dollars worth of gear on the stage, there should always be a band member standing by keeping an eye out. So whatever you do until you start playing, you should do it in shifts so that nothing disappears.

 SUBMIT YOUR GUEST LIST TO THE CLUB MANAGER FOR APPROVAL.

Guest lists should be written up by listing the names of the guests (first & last). If they are bringing a guest you would then list it as follows: Butch Coolidge +1.

Most bands spend their time after sound check sleeping, reading, eating, playing video games or drinking beer. Sound like your band? Well, how can this possibly help your career?

By the time you hit the stage you are most likely played out. Here are some management suggestions to make this downtime more productive and inspiring.

 POST UP THE EXTRA FLYERS YOU BROUGHT AROUND THE CLUB.

Make the club look like your place tonight.

 IF YOU HAVE A BAND BANNER HANG IT BEHIND THE DRUMMER.

 LOOK FOR THE HOUSE LIGHT MAN AND DISCUSS YOUR SET.

Give him some cues on lighting effects for your show. If you have your own light man with you, confirm their permission to use the board.

 MAKE COPIES OF THE SET LIST AND POST IT ON-STAGE.

 SET UP YOUR MERCHANDISING BOOTH.

 TALK TO THE CLUB BOOKER ABOUT UPCOMING EVENTS.

Inquire about any upcoming nationals acts coming through town or if there is a hot local band that you could share the bill with. Let them know that you are eager to play and assure them that you will promote the event. Use tonight's event as an indication of the bands drive.

 GO TO THE NEARBY COLLEGES AND PUT FLYERS UP.

You're bound to run into people who will be curious. Take this opportunity to talk about your band and invite them to the show.

 PICK UP THE LOCAL NEWSPAPERS (IF YOU'RE OUT OF TOWN) AND SEE IF YOU CAN GET SOME INFORMATION ABOUT OTHER CLUBS, BANDS, AND MUSIC REVIEWERS IN THE AREA.

FIND OUT WHERE THE LOCAL RECORD STORE IS AND GO DOWN AND TALK TO THE MANAGER OR THE OWNER.

Introduce yourself and perhaps even invite him/her to the show. Put them on the guest list if need be. Listen, there's no guarantee they'll come, but this is a good contact for you down the road if you ever come back to the area to play. One day you might even release your own CD and by establishing a relationship now, you may be cultivating a location to sell the CD's from.

One of my key successes was building relationships with record stores. I visited or contacted every record store in every town that my clients played in. Some store managers were really receptive to me and others pretended like they were too important to honor me with a moment of their time. In that case I just moved on. Eventually I had built a network of record stores that looked forward to the band coming to town and they were always invited into their stores to do live in-store acoustic performances during the day of the show. When one of my clients got signed, they hit pay dirt because they had dozens of record stores that immediately ordered and stocked the record.

Establish a correspondence with the record store that takes place in the future when you book the club again. Ask if they would display some postcards announcing the show. If you come up with some good promotions like "Bring one friend for free with one paid admission and this card," you will get an idea if the cards are working for you. Any promotion that involves the club should be cleared by the club first, but in most cases they will be more than happy to honor it. If they see you busting your ass to make the show successful, it may motivate them to give your band priority gigs in the future.

Realizing that the most important part of making it, lies in the quality of the performance, I suggest that you split the band up to take care of all these tedious chores, so that when showtime comes you are not all worn out from running around. You certainly need to take some precious time out to relax and compose yourself.

So wrap up at least one hour before showtime to get back to the club and prepare for the show. You and your band should regroup with each other about a half hour before show time. Have a beer, relax and be positive because you are doing everything you can to make it.

When showtime approaches, if your crowd has not arrived yet and you are going on first you may want to push the starting time back a few minutes. You need to see the club manager about that. Do not just decide on your own and disappear so that no one can find you to tell you to go on. You will endanger your set length because the sound man will cut you off before your set is over to make up for lost time.

Sometimes you may get a few minutes but not always. There are other bands after you so be considerate. When it's time to hit the stage make your entrance and "kill."

SHOWTIME

There's not much written anywhere on how to perform on stage. When I thought about what to write I almost decided to skip this part and move on. But then I remembered all of the bands I've seen in my life and what the really good ones all had in common and what the really bad ones had in common. Some of this stuff takes time and just naturally develops, for instance just feeling comfortable on stage and learning how to move about. Some of it is just bad habits or not realizing what you are doing.

So without further ado I present to you the following:

 HAVE ALL YOUR STAGE EQUIPMENT IN PLACE PRIOR TO TAKING THE STAGE

Either *you* do it or if you're fortunate enough to have a roadie, have them do it. Be subtle when you go on stage especially if there are people in the audience. You want to make your entrance when you are announced and not before.

 WHEN ARRANGING YOUR EQUIPMENT DO NOT PLUG IN YOUR INSTRUMENTS AND START PLAYING. THIS VIOLATES RULE #1

 MAKE SURE THAT YOUR GUITARS ARE TUNED BEFORE YOU TAKE THE STAGE

Hopefully you own a tuning device that silently tunes your instrument. The worst transgression you can make on-stage is to come out and face an eagerly awaiting audience only to stand there and tune your instruments.

 WHEN YOU ARE ANNOUNCED, MAKE AN ENTRANCE

This doesn't mean coming on stage in a tank and blowing your lead singer out from the turret. I merely suggest that you don't stumble on out in dribs and drabs, clumsily searching for your place on stage.

If you are not announced, chances are you'll walk out on stage while the juke box or DJ is playing music. Have someone cue the club to slowly turn down the house music. Time it so that when the house sound is down you either introduce yourself or just start playing. You just want to avoid a lull if you can.

'HEY SPIKE, THIS CROWD JUST DOESN'T GET IT." "WHAT'S HIPPER THAN A SET OF ACOUSTIC LOVERBOY COVERS!"

As you begin to get more sophisticated you can bring in your own recorded music and use it to start off your set. This way you are pre-rehearsed so that when it ends you will know the cue and can begin your set.

PLAY YOUR SET FROM THE SET LIST AND TRY NOT TO DEVIATE

However, if you sense that the audience is not going where your set list is taking them, be prepared to deviate. In other words if it's five songs into your set list and the audience is finally up on their feet and moving and the next two songs are ballads, I think the band should make some quick adjustments. It might not be a bad idea even while you are initially making the set list that you figure in some alternative songs in place of the slower ones just in case this happens. The reality is most people come to a live show to *see* a band, as opposed to *hearing* a band. While it might very well be that your best songs are the slow ones, I've learned that bar crowds judge songs a bit differently when they're out as opposed to when they're listening to the radio. I am not telling you not to play slow music, I'm just instructing you on learning to read a crowd.

DO NOT TAKE FOREVER IN BETWEEN EACH SONG.

Practice the transitions in rehearsal. All the extra time you spend in between each song is coming off your set time, which can be costly if you've only got a 35 or 40 minute set.

USE THE CLUB'S LIGHTING TO ENHANCE THE STAGE EFFECT.

If there are lights in the venue, instruct whoever is doing the lights to kill them (shut them down) after each song, and start them again when the next one begins. This really adds atmosphere to the performance and makes you appear more professional.

TALK TO THE AUDIENCE.

Make sure that twice in the set you announce what your band's name is for all those in the audience that just happened to stumble in, and that you have a mailing list. Point out where the mailing list is and influence them to sign up. If a song gets a really great response, acknowledge it to the crowd and announce the title. This way they can yell for it at your next show.

SHOW ENTHUSIASM.

If you appear as though you aren't into it, the crowd will pick up on that. Look intense, smile, make eye contact with fans and band members.

LET THE CROWD KNOW WHEN YOU GET TO THE LAST SONG OF THE SET.

If they liked you which I'm sure will be the case, it will motivate them to give you all they have as a crowd. This way when the song ends they will be ready to call you back for an encore. I say this half in jest because many times the crowd just doesn't have their act together and fails to call for an encore even though they loved you. So don't be disappointed if they aren't tearing down the walls to call you back. If it's the first time the crowd has ever seen you, be glad they stayed for your show and showed any interest.

 ALERT THE CROWD TO ANY UP COMING SHOWS IN THE AREA.

Do it either right before the last song or directly after the last song ends. The latter might also buy you some precious time after your set ends, to delay the house DJ from turning on the house music and it might coerce the audience to ask you to play one more song.

POST SHOW WRAP UP

Great show; but alas, your work is far from over. If there is a band going on next, you must get all your gear off the stage quickly. This will require every band member to pitch in even if one of you does not play an instrument. And keep your eyes open! As you are taking your equipment off, the next band is bringing their stuff on. This makes for a very crowded stage and you need to pay attention so that none of your equipment walks.

As you are taking apart your stage, there is a good chance that some audience members will approach you. This is a very important part of your job since after all you are trying to attract people to buy tickets to your shows and hopefully buy your album one day. I just want to remind you that while you are talking to a fan, do not lose sight of your equipment both on stage and down off the stage. There are plenty of untrustworthy people out there who wouldn't think twice about ripping you off.

When you are taking your equipment down from the stage, it is a good idea to have the mailing list book nearby, so that as you are approached by fans you can ask them to please sign it.

LOAD OUT

Once all your gear is off the stage, you should immediately bring it backstage to a secure place (if you plan to remain in the club), or load it out to your van. As each piece of equipment is loaded into the van, its corresponding number should be checked on your equipment list. Make sure you have everything including your mailing list book, which might still be in the club. If you had a guest list you should go to the door man and ask for it back. You want to check and see if all your guests showed up and were crossed off the list, especially "Industry" guests.

Do not leave the van unattended even after all the equipment is loaded and the door is locked. In 1979, I had a 63 Strat, a 67 Gibson SG, a Fender Twin, all my effects and a suitcase full of clothes stolen out of our van parked outside CBGB's in less than 10

"You guys are so hot! I love that thing you do, you know when you trip on your guitar chord and fall into each other. And then when you knock each other down on the stage, that's really cool, and blah blah blah blah blah"

minutes of the van being unattended. This was a hell of a way to learn a lesson. When the van is loaded it is time for the band liaison and another band member to go and settle the show (get paid). Good luck.

SETTLING THE SHOW

This will be your final moments at the club. Though it may last for hours because your contact will probably make themselves very scarce and keep you waiting till the very end of the night to pay you. It's generally the nature of many club owners to think that the longer they hold on to your pay the more you might forget to ask for it. This is why it's a good policy to determine when you arrive at the club, where and when during the night you should expect to get paid.

Generally you and one other member of your band (for safety and support reasons) should meet in the office or some room away from the public when you transfer money. I'm sure you will get into a conversation regarding your set and an attentive owner will have seen some of it so that they can constructively criticize you as well as get a better idea on how to book you and with what type of group you can double bill.

When it comes time for payment you should only accept cash. If you are presented with a check, unless you can cash it at the club (which is usually the policy), do not accept it. When you get paid by check you will be asked for your social security number or a business tax ID number. It is better to have the latter so that this income is not added to your own personal income and subject to taxes at the end of the year. If you do not have a business ID number, give your social security number and don't worry about it. Chances are it won't be for a lot of money and this is certainly not going to happen all that often as to push your yearly income into a higher tax bracket.

If you are denied payment or check cashing privileges, you're screwed. Most reputable clubs that deal with live bands and that have been in business for a number of years, will probably not resort to this (unless they are going under). But there are plenty of bars and small venues run by sleazy operators that do not adhere to certain unspoken and accepted business practices.

Your best bet is to state your case and be as firm as you can, but beware. A situation occurred once with an act of mine that was playing dates with Gene Loves Jezebel, both of whom were booked by the William Morris Agency. The last show of the tour took place in an eleven hundred capacity room in our own home town. The poor excuses for club owners went out of their way to make my clients uncomfortable because, as they put it, "You are a local band; you should have purchased tickets (pay to play) to sell to your fans like all other local acts that play here." It never occurred to them that the band had a record out and was a national act. That they lived locally was of no importance except for the fact that they were probably going to be responsible for filling up the room.

Their blatant disregard for our contract and personal safety raised real concerns. I began to fear that the night might indeed have a violent conclusion. They denied the band their sound check, dressing room privileges and slashed the guest list down to one person per band member which meant only four guests were honored. The final straw came when I was told that in order for us to set up merchandising I would have to give all 10 of the stage hands and club personnel, free t-shirts.

Having been involved in the music business for most of my adult life, I took this as a personal insult. Needless to say each one of these events led to constant confrontation which began the moment we walked in at 5pm straight on to midnight that night.

When the set ended we found to our surprise all of our belongings missing from the coat room, we covertly acquired to use as a dressing room. Under normal situations things never would have gotten this bad, since I would simply have the band pack up prior to performing and split. But there were hundreds of fans of the band present and there would have been a riot had the group not played.

The crescendo came in the coat room when I went face to face with the owner demanding with my now horribly hoarse voice that the police must be called to investigate the theft. She threw insult after insult, waving and slapping her hands in the air. Finally I raised mine to ward off her more fervent attacks when these steroid infested Neanderthals who flanked her on both sides, misinterpreted my defensive gesture and without warning attacked me like sharks on bloody chum. Their vicious blows to my head and face left me sprawled out on the floor within seconds, unconscious in front of my pregnant wife, band members, and about thirty fans and friends.

Later, as I lay in the ambulance on the way to the hospital, I was comforted by my wife who assured me that there where many witnesses who offered their names and numbers in case it went to court. A few years later I received a sizable settlement, but the big award came just one month after the incident occurred when I read in the paper with my one unbandaged eye, that this club had to shut its doors when no reputable agent would book any acts there after hearing about what had happened.

Almost one year later to the date, while attempting to settle a New Years Eve show, the managers of this relatively new club in NYC, made me wait for payment until 3AM, when they finally told me that there was no money for my two clients that performed that night. My disbelief quickly reverted to anger as I aggressively demanded payment. The argument digressed to bodily threats issued by both parties. When it seemed clear to my adversaries that I was not about to leave without money, the silent figure to my left stepped out of the shadows and issued a rather poignant threat assuring me the loss of a most cherished part of my anatomy if I did not vacate the premise immediately. The warped smile that emanated from his crooked face emphasized his conviction. I became instantly clear-minded and decided that speaking with a high pitched voice and winning lawsuits was not the way I wanted to spend the rest of my management

"I don't care what your flyer says, you aint booked here tonight or any night"

career. Intact, I left the office and greeted the crisp NYC dawn having learned a valuable lesson for the new year.

You must be selective in choosing the proper clubs to book your groups. Big money offers can sometimes mean further investigation is needed and signed contracts may not be worth the paper they are printed on if a club has Ray Luca as its owner. As it turned out this was the last night the club would be open for business. They used my act's drawing power to line their pockets before they closed up for good, disappearing into the night.

So the moral of the story is: try to stay out of brand new clubs or clubs with a notorious reputation. If you get into confrontational situations, don't take it too far. The end result is never good. Pack your ego into your road case and never play there again.

GOING HOME.

As the night comes to an end, you should establish the ritual of your whole band traveling home together. I dissuade you from splitting up and going home fragmented. The ride home is an important time for the group. You will need to talk about the night while it is fresh in your mind. If it was a great show you should all rejoice in it together. And if it was not a great show, this is the time to talk about it and iron out the problems.

If you taped the show, you should listen to it on the ride home. Especially if you have a show coming up in the next day or two, you need to refine the sour points and accentuate the positive ones.

Whatever transportation you came down in, if the equipment is going to one main place like a rehearsal studio, then you all should be there to help unload it.

If you are in a rented vehicle, you should return it after you unload and not wait until 8:00 in the morning, when most rentals need to be back before they start to charge you for another day. So it would be a good idea to clean out the van completely and fill it up with gas and return it. Most places have key drop off slots and you can show up later in the afternoon to pick up your deposit.

THE DAY AFTER

Today your tasks are very simple.

 TAKE OUT THE ADVANCE SHEET AND FILL OUT THE BOTTOM PART THAT CONTAINS INFORMATION REGARDING THE SHOW.

After Show

Attendance:　**175**

Crowd Response:　**Great**

Flyers Posted:　**We sent 2 dozen. There were six posted when we arrived.**

Club Response: **Loved us and wants us back next month on a weekend. Should call in two weeks.**

 FILE ALL YOUR PAPERS FROM THE SHOW BACK IN THE MAIN CLUB FILE.

 MARK DOWN ANY APPOINTMENTS OR PHONE CALLS YOU NEED TO MAKE AND THE DATE YOU NEED TO MAKE THEM.

 IF YOU RECEIVED BUSINESS CARDS FROM ANYONE THE NIGHT BEFORE, ADD THEM TO THE CLUB FILE AND TO A SEPARATE PHONE NUMBER DIRECTORY.

It is important to add them to the club file because after some time you may accumulate many, many names and the where and when of how you met these people may become jumbled. If they are listed in your club file, you will always have that information and be able to contact these people every time you pull that file out and schedule another show.

 IF YOU PROMISED TO SEND OUT ANY BAND LITERATURE LIKE A PRESS KIT OR A TAPE DO IT TODAY! DON'T DELAY

 IF YOU RECEIVED COMPENSATION PREPARE AN ACCOUNTING OF THIS MONEY.

(See Chapter 16 for more information)

 IF YOU RENTED A VAN AND RETURNED IT, GO GET YOUR DEPOSIT.

 START SCHEDULING YOUR NEXT REHEARSAL. KEEP THE MOMENTUM GOING.

 PICK UP THE PHONE AND BOOK SOME MORE SHOWS.

 BRING BACK ALL MUSIC RELATED PUBLICATIONS

When you were at the club and if you spotted a newspaper, magazine or any literature that had your band name associated with the performance, either as a club listing or advertisement, cut it out and add it to your press kit.

"No press again! What are we supposed to do play a gig or something"

7

PRESS AND THE MEDIA

Promoting yourself is a major necessity in the music business. Especially at this early stage in your career, understanding how the press works and how to utilize it for your gain is imperative.

The need for press is two dimensional. On one hand it is a medium to be used for publicizing your band (paid advertisements) and secondly, receiving press coverage of your group validates what you're doing by someone you do not know, who is in the position of judging quality. Let's face it, though all your friends will tell you how great your band is, having it confirmed by a complete stranger in the paper, takes it to another level.

To begin with, "The Media" refers to printed publications such as newspapers, magazines, fanzines, newsletters, as well as electronic publications such as television or radio. Any time your band is featured in any one of these mediums, it is referred to as "getting press."

The importance of press is immeasurable. Whereas you might reach a limited amount of fans with your mailing list or word of mouth, once you appear in some form of public press, you are reaching far more people than you ever could on your own.

Look at how the entertainment business works on a national scale. Months prior to an album's release, a marketing plan is coordinated. This will include interviews, press releases and news stories followed by major print advertising, electronic advertising and public appearances. Take a cue from how it works in the big time and scale it down to where it can be effective for you.

There are numerous mediums in which to get press and countless ways to get press on your group, even at a very early stage in your development. You are going to need to be creative in your thinking and do a bit of detective work to locate every possible publication in every area you want coverage. Every town and city has a newspaper and every big city has at least one major music publication. By tracking down and viewing these publications, you will get a fairly good idea as to the music and club scene in that area. This will be the basis for your finding out about which are the right places for you to perform in and who the features writers are that are covering the music scene. Contacting these individuals and inviting them to either review your live show or your tape, is the easiest and simplest way to start getting press.

By checking your local library you may come across some of the following sources to help you locate the correct publications in the towns you're looking to play in:

THE RECORDING INDUSTRY SOURCE BOOK

6400 HOLLIS ST.,   SUITE #12   EMERYVILLE, CA 94608

(800) 472 7472

MUSICIANS GUIDE TO TOURING & PROMOTION

1515 B'WAY NY NY 10036

* ## GALE'S DIRECTORY OF PUBLICATIONS AND BROADCAST MEDIA

Published by International Thomson Publishing Co.

(Directory that lists the circulation and descriptions of most American publications and broadcasting stations)

* ## 1996 WORKING PRESS OF THE NATION

Lists over 7,690 daily and specialized newspapers in America

* These two sources found at most libraries list most of the major news reporting publications. You will find some papers that deal with arts and music like the Village Voice located in NYC but many of the underground hip papers like Fear and Loathing in Atlanta will not be listed.

TYPES OF PRESS

So what am I referring to when I talk about getting press. There are many different ways that you can utilize the press for coverage and many different elements of what you are doing for the press to cover. For instance:

SELF PROMOTION

For one thing, you want to let the world know that you exist. Putting flyers around, sending out mailers and word of mouth are just some of the grassroots approaches you

can take to give yourself publicity. So when it comes to the press, why not use the same street psychology and apply it to the media.

Instead of printing a big flyer why not take out a small ad in the classifieds, or a small display ad in any one your local music papers. The cost for a 2" x 3" can run anywhere from $5-$70., depending on what type of publication it is. This type investment buys you many things that can be summed up all under one heading; perception. The ad can say anything you want. It can just be the name of your band and nothing else. Imagine the curiosity it will raise if week after week this little ad appeared in the paper:

Week after week until finally you change the ad to this:

What you are doing here is using the press to gain public awareness to your product. The fruits of this type of campaign may not be realized the first or second time you play, but, I can assure you that your group's name is unconsciously being implanted on the readers mind and that is what your immediate goal is.

So basically this type of advertising is self promoting in that you are the instrument of your own marketing which carries with it a certain value in the reader's mind. Readers will respond slower than let's say to an ad taken out by the biggest promoter in your area advertising a major concert event with you as the headliner. But do not underestimate its value either. (See: How Do You Get Press)

Advertising is a very professional thing to do and by you taking this step you are in a sense saying that you are a business person and that you are taking the proper steps to motivate your career.

 REVIEWS

As far as value goes, this is the next level up. Here your product (band, music) is being brought to the public's attention via someone else's word. This carries weight not just in the public's eyes but in the music industry as well. After all, the more reviews you get, the more publicity you receive. If the publicity is good then that will lead to you gaining a good reputation which helps get you gigs, and possibly a record deal. If the publicity is bad, evaluate it to see if the criticism has merit. If it does, try and correct the problem. Never think that you are flawless. You can always improve, even if the critic is off base and does not understand what you are going for there may still be something there that you did not notice and can improve. But remember this: Bad publicity is still publicity and publicity is good.

Two aspects of your career will be reviewed:

 Your Recorded music.

 Your live performance of it.

Both of these are intertwined and yet can act distinctly independent from each other as well. While your music can be reviewed during a live performance, it can also be reviewed on its own if it is sent in on a tape. Ironically, each scenario may result in a different review. Some bands sound great on tape but their performance of their songs is horrible while other bands do not have good recordings but live, they kick ass. Make sure that you evaluate which one represents you the best so that you can position that part of you for a review.

 Feature Story

Finally, this is a piece is very much like a review only told either in interview form or written as a story. In either case it carries the most value because it says to the reader that of all the things the paper could be writing stories about, they chose your band to cover.

The Big question I'm sure you're asking is, HOW DO WE GET PRESS?

Sure taking an ad out is easy but how do you get the paper to write about your band? An even tougher question to answer is, HOW DO YOU GET PRESS WHEN YOU DO NOT HAVE A DEMO OR PRESS KIT?

HOW DO YOU GET PRESS

Aside from performing in the nude and getting arrested thereby resulting in bad press getting press on your group takes a certain finesse. The act of getting press is refereed to as "working the press."

To start with, choose someone in the band who is good with people, conversation and someone who is sincere. You do not want to approach this with a game show host mentality.

Now if you refer back to the previous page where we discussed taking out you own ads, I wrote about not underestimating it's value. Here is what I mean.

Suppose you called up the paper and said "**Hi my name is Christine and I am in the band WINDOW PANE can you do a story on us?**", the chances are, they will instruct you to send in a press kit and tape and curtly hang up the phone. However, suppose you call and say, "**Hi may I have the advertising department please?**" you will hear, "*Hang on one moment please*"

    While you are put on hold let me explain what you are about to do.

This is what I call getting in through the back door. As you discovered, the editorial department had no time to talk with you. They could care less about your little band, demo or gig. However, the ad department is very different. They want to hear all about you and your band because you are about to spend money with them.

"Hi can I help you"

"Yes my name is Christine and I would like to place an ad in next week's paper can you give me some rates please"

"What kind of ad are you taking out"

"Just an ad for my band WINDOW PANE"

"Wow that's a great name where are you guys from"

"We're from right here and we just finished recording our new demo and will be putting on a big show at the Factory"

"That sounds cool" ....

Do you see where this is going? In the spirit of taking out an ad, you are telling someone at a newspaper all about your band. I will bet that by the end of this conversation, providing that you placed even a small ad, you will be saying the following,

"That's great, I really appreciate your time, if you would like to come down to the show I'll have your name +1 listed on the guest list."

Of course this invitation is only applicable if the person on the other end of the phone is a someone interested in your kind of music which should be the case if you are calling up a music publication.

If you guide the conversation correctly, I am sure that you will find a person who would anticipate receiving your music. Both these end results are what makes taking out the ads so important. It is a one hand washing the other concept.

Once this first contact is made, either send the tape or invite them to the show and then follow up with a call of professional courtesy to see if they either received the tape or came to the show. If they did and like what they heard or saw, kindly ask if they can help instrument a review in the paper. Sometimes for local independent papers, the ad person also write reviews and I am telling you that this is the case for many, many music publications.

By taking out that stupid small ad for $30, $40 or even $70., you just increased your value by the contacts you just made.

While this is a good way for you to begin getting some press as well as a method for getting press in new markets, I certainly do not expect you to go around buying press everywhere you go. You need to be resourceful and utilize other methods as well.

CLUBS ADVERTISEMENT

When you book yourself into a local club, request that the club owner call the local paper (music paper, regular paper but in the entertainment section) and have your band listed in the entertainment section. This is usually a free or at worst a very inexpensive way for the club to advertise. Your next step will be to call the paper and ask for the entertainment editor. Once they are on the phone briefly explain who you are, what band you're from and that you are playing at a certain club on a particular date.

Extend the reviewer an invitation to come down and see the band for a possible review. You will probably be asked to send in a demo tape, which, as we have already established, you do not have yet. You can reply with "We're in the process of making our demo, but it won't be completed by this date but we would still appreciate if you could come down to see us anyway." Assure them that their names will be on the guest list plus one in case they come. (If you do have the demo and press kit then just forward the package over.)

If you live in a small town and there are more of these than big cities in America, there stands a good chance that they may actually come down. There's not always a lot of things going on in small towns so anything can become news. I know this to be true because I live in a small town and I received tons of press out of my local papers. You can follow up prior to the show with a brief phone call inquiring if they received your package or that you are reminding them about the show.

When the gig is over, check your guest list to see if their names were crossed off. If it was, then there was a good chance the reviewer was there.

If they did come down to see you perform, if they liked what they saw, they will write a review. Keep an eye out for it by purchasing the paper and checking. There really is no need to call and pester them. If you do not see any reviews after a month or so, it may either mean that they were not present at the show, not that impressed or had many more pressing things to write about.

Wait then until you have the demo tape you promised to send and you have booked another show at the club. About two weeks prior to the next show call back and begin the conversation by reminding them of who you are and extending another invitation. Forward over the demo tape you promised in the original conversation and hope for the best.

Chances are you will catch an attitude and probably still be ignored. Keep in mind that you are now dealing directly with editorial and that you have not put anything in their hand like you did when you took out the ad. That was an exchange that put both of you on a level playing field. Here it is not level, they have the upper hand. And they will play that out until you prove to be a great group one that would make a great story and them, just the person to write it.

Do not expect editorial to just drop everything they are doing for you or your group. As frustrating as it is sometimes, it's something you have to deal with. People in the music business have a "follow the leader" mentality. Very few venture out on their own searching for new talent. It's due in part to the reality that there are way too many groups, with a large percentage of them unfortunately lacking in talent. Then it becomes like finding a needle in the haystack.

By telling people how great your band is, you really do absolutely nothing in generating interest. However, if someone else tells someone else who tells someone else, now we're talking. You see, the way things work many times in the music business, is that a band will not get any attention until people start talking about them. This is referred to in the business as a "Buzz." It's hard to pinpoint where the buzz starts or how to start one. But I can tell you that if your band is really good and you are attracting crowds of people to your show, the buzz already has begun.

I remember a few years back a particular unsigned group was playing the local club scene here in New York. It seemed that every time I opened the paper, I would see their name advertised in the club listings. Articles began appearing in all the different local music papers. When I started to ask around about them, it seemed everybody knew of them, heard of them or saw them. Finally after seeing their name so many times I had to go see the group live to find out what the hell was going on. This is the result of a buzz. Their buzz was so strong that it attracted record companies and landed them a major recording contract which later resulted in three top ten singles and a multi platinum debut record album. But this happened only after years of working hard.

So keep this in mind as you try to attract press. They are busy and will probably not be that motivated until they start to hear things about you. But once they do, they will jump on the bandwagon to cover the story. And once they do, if they write a favorable article, the professional thing to do is reciprocate with a sincere letter of thanks without loading it down with too much kiss ass either.

If an article does appear in an out of town paper and you have a correspondence going with the writer, you can ask them to mail or fax you a tearsheet of the article. If you feel uneasy about asking the author, just call the paper and ask for the circulation department and tell them that you were featured in the paper and would like a copy of either the whole paper or a tearsheet of the article.

MUSIC PUBLICATIONS

Aside from the standard news publications, there are many papers that deal solely with the music business. Papers like New York City's **"Village Voice"** are published weekly and sold at newsstands and through subscription. These are full service papers offering feature articles as well as music news and information about the local club scene.

There is also a plethora of underground and free papers that are available anywhere free counter space is provided for them. These publications are small and have limited circulation but since they report mainly on the local scene, their readership is a dedicated one. Because these publications are for the most part free, the sale of advertising space is the only thing that keeps them in business. For the majority of these papers, the advertising clients they rely upon are interestingly enough, their own readers; local bands and local clubs. While it may be very difficult to get anything other than an ad mention in the major music publications, you stand a better chance of getting a review and possibly even a feature story in these smaller papers.

But it's still not easy. In most cities there are more acts looking for press than there are pages printed. Editors are besieged with requests from throngs of local bands trying to get front page coverage of their Tuesday night Bowling Alley Bar gig. Hence the editors remain selective of the stories they publish and will only feature bands that are popular. After all, even though these papers are free, who is going to read them if there is nothing inside but trash. To be successful with these publications, your group needs to have something going on and your approach to them needs to be cultivated.

Let's start with first finding these publications. Aside from checking the newsstands and local deli and pizzeria counters, what you need to do is go to any of the more popular venues featuring your style of music. Especially if the club is a frequent advertiser. The standard practice is that the clubs who advertise, usually get copies of the paper shipped to them so that they can display their ad in the club. This helps the club advertise themselves further and also helps the paper gain popularity. Common sense says, the more popular the paper becomes the more advertising it can sell.

Many of these small free papers spent years as underground publications but through their efforts to bring their readership good stories, they have grown to become the area leading music publication like Denver's free **"MIND GARBAGE"** or New Jersey's **"EAST COAST ROCKER"**.

Now if the papers are servicing the local clubs to gain popularity, you should do the same. Go and hang out at the local clubs. Bring a back pack so that you can grab up a copy every free paper, newsletter and fanzine that you find. And do this in every town and city you play in. Familiarize yourself with the name of the writers and the style of music these papers prefer to cover.

Once you get home, study these papers and document the following:

ALL THE REVIEWERS' NAMES THAT REVIEW YOUR STYLE OF MUSIC.

ALL THE CLUBS IN YOUR AREA THAT FEATURE YOUR STYLE OF MUSIC.

With this information you can intelligently choose what the best clubs are to play. When you book yourself there, your band's name will begin to appear in the ads that the clubs are running. By performing in these clubs your band stands a better chance of getting reviewed because the paper is going to give the clubs that advertise in them, more review space than a club that doesn't. The more often you perform at these clubs, the more familiar your band will become to the writers of the paper and the easier time you will have getting them to do a feature or review of you.

Another way to invite the press is via the fax machine. To obtain the fax number simply call the main office number of the paper and ask for the fax line of the person you want to contact. If they ask who you are, simply state your name and that you represent the band so & so. Fax invitations are a common practice in the business. If you are going to do a fax invitation it should read something like this:

```
┌────────────────────────────────────────────────────────────────┐
│                              FAX                                 │
│                         (212) 555-1234                           │
│                                                                  │
│ FROM:      Marc Davison                                          │
│                                                                  │
│ TO:        Chili Palmer                                          │
│                                                                  │
│ RE:        Shorty                                                │
│                                                                  │
│                                                                  │
│ MESSAGE:  For Immediate Release: The band SHORTY will be         │
│ appearing Sat June 10 at  The Mobster Club.                      │
│ Showtime is 10:00pm. Your name will be at the door on our guest  │
│ list plus one.                                                   │
│ Thank you:                                                       │
│ M D Management  PO box 210  NY NY,  10010                        │
└────────────────────────────────────────────────────────────────┘
```

This is a form of press release and a much more professional way to get some attention.

It is also important to pick the right shows to invite press to. The bowling alley event has amateur written all over it. Even though I urge you to book yourself wherever you can play, you should minimize the exposure of certain events while maximizing the exposure of others. The immediate face value of how good a band is, is measured by their bookings as well as their business manners. By highlighting the choice clubs in your area, and inviting the press and industry to these quality events, you will be giving out a positive impression of your group. It is through this impression that you increase your chances of getting the press and other members of the industry to see you.

OTHER IDEAS FOR PRESS

Another way to get some press without a tape or press kit is to look around for any kind of local event like a summertime outdoor festival or street fair. Perhaps even a high school charity event as I did one year for the American Cancer Society. I called them up and offered to do a concert at the local high school where my clients all graduated from. All the proceeds would go to the charity after the band's expenses like the PA system, flyers & lights. After 3 months of planning, the show sold 600 tickets at five and seven dollars. The group of course benefited since they not only got full coverage from the school paper, (which when cut out and pasted up in their press kit, appeared as a very impressive review), but they also got front page coverage with a full color photo in the area's major Gannett Newspaper.

The show was so successful for all involved that the following year I approached the very same high school and offered to put on a concert for the senior class to help raise money for their yearbook. Of course you can imagine the somewhat negative response from the band for having to play at their old high school again. But after considering how many new fans they would be cultivating as potential buyers of a future CD, not to mention how much press they would once again receive, they became very receptive. By the end of the show I think they also learned the importance of giving back something to the community. Tickets sales where overwhelming, and the band netted about two thousand dollars for the graduating class after sound and lights, advertising, ticket printing and security was paid.

As a footnote, this group went on to sign a record deal about 6 months later. Within the second week of the release of their CD, they made the top ten seller list at the local Tower Records. At one local mom and pop shop, their CD was selling at about 50 units per day for the first three weeks of release, outselling every other major title.

These creative booking concepts, created so many press interviews and stories that it began to have some significant impact on the "Industry" (the buzz). The bottom line is that no matter where you come from, be it a small town or big city, if you have something or do something that is drawing press attention and making the headlines, record companies begin to take notice and wonder if perhaps you have what it takes to make it on a national level. So when you look at newspapers as a big brick wall that is hard to crack, it only takes the power of your imagination to knock it down.

COLLEGE PAPERS

As with every high school in America, so does every college have a paper. You can get the listings of these papers simply by calling the college. For a listing of all the colleges in America, check the library or ask any high school guidance counselor. You can also get a subscription to **POLLSTAR** magazine. This publication comes to you by first class mail supplying you with phone numbers of key company, booking university, clubs in every and concert tour listings also supply you with weeks a year on things business). For a yearly

> **POLLSTAR**
> **4333 North West Avenue**
> **Fresno CA 93706.**
> **(800) 344-7383**
> **Calif.: 209 224 2631**

throughout the year, names, addresses and people in every record agency, college and city in America, club and much more. They weekly newsletters (50 happening in the subscription send $295.

They also offer a 3 month trial subscription for $95 and a directory at a non-subscription rate of $37.50. I guarantee you will be using these directories every day and for every aspect of your band's career.

FANZINES

These smaller independent publications are written by fans and enthusiasts. They are printed on cheaper paper and for the most part are very localized and circulated by mail from a small mailing list.

In the past, some have grown up from newsletters and have become national and international publications like Relix which caters to the Grateful Dead fan. Fanzines are very one-dimensional in that they tend to cover either one band or one style of music. It is difficult to locate all the Fanzines that are out there but if you look in the back of Rolling Stone or other popular rock and roll magazines, there will be ads from Fanzines offering information about their publications.

As you play clubs from town to town and city to city, you will at times be approached by nerdy guys telling you they publish a Fanzine and wonder if you would be interested in having an article written about you.

Some words of caution and advice. As you get more popular, you will want to gain some control over **what** is written about the group and **where** it appears. But in the beginning when press is hard to come by and you can use all the exposure you can get, these Fanzines are a really good outlet.

Some however are not what they appear to be and some of these so-called publishers write like they never finished 6th grade. You should definitely request a few back issues to look over, as well as a copy of the mailing list to verify how many copies he mails out. If this turns out to be something he prints up for his parents, siblings and a few close cousins that live in Kentucky, I think it's pretty cheesy and could do your band more harm that good.

You should also beware of the Fanzines that charge bands a fee to have an article written about them. I'm not saying not to do it since many of these Fanzines need to raise some kind of money to print and mail out. Just look at all the qualifications I mentioned above and make sure this is something you want to be a part of.

NEWSLETTERS

Whereas a Fanzine is usually multi-pages, a newsletter is usually one page. It can either be printed by one member or all the members of your group and sent out to the mailing list covering updates on upcoming shows, events and band news. Though I really wouldn't constitute this as press, it is a great marketing tool and if you have a really good newsletter, aside from mailing it to your fans you should bring them with you to your shows and keep them out in the open for people to pick up and read. I have seen some really interesting newsletters that featured great artwork, poetry and well written articles left over at clubs. Though I had never heard of most of the groups, some newsletters were so captivating (like GWAR) that I did some research to find out more about the group, either for possible management or to just check out their music and see if it was as good as their newsletter.

Press comes in all fashions, from one-liner mentions to full page articles and interviews. The most important thing I can stress is to leave calling cards around the club (be it the mailing list postcards, business cards, posters, flyers or newsletters). Any of these things that have your name, address or phone number or all three, are leads you purposely create, that trace back to you.

I once received a postcard back from a club, six months after the band had played there. (I knew that because I would mark every card I left in the club with the date and club name, so that I would know where it was coming from). The message on the card was from someone who was putting the final touches on the first issue of a monthly newspaper/magazine. They had seen the band six months ago and now wanted to do a feature story/interview for the first issue. I invited him down to the band's next big show in New York City, where they did the interview and a photo shoot. The article was so impressive that it became a feature in the band's press kit and many of the quotes that were used in the band's press releases, came from this article.

Two months later I was called up by this same editor who asked if the group would be able to perform at the paper's press release party that was being planned for the following month. The party was held at a very popular club and was by invitation only. The paper featured a large full page ad which highlighted the group. So, all those elements and tedious details that went into the show, paid off here in a very big way.

INTERVIEWS

I want to discuss this very delicate matter and I suppose this would be the best place to do it in. Interviews are great to do and are very important to a band's career. They are very much like a performance but in some ways much harder. In a performance, you are playing rehearsed material, however in an interview, chances are you don't know what is going to be asked of you. Therefore your answers are not rehearsed and sometimes the interviewer will ask for information you do not have, resulting in your coming across, dull, burnt, uninformative or the opposite: pretentious, full of yourself and put on.

So here are some suggestions for successful interviews.

CHOOSE AMONG YOU THE BEST SPOKESPERSON FOR THE BAND.

This should be someone with wit and charm, a good memory for recalling dates and places and someone who is interesting. I know that in many cases everyone in the band wants to do interviews but sometimes it's not possible and you need to be realistic. Everyone can't be the lead guitarist either. These interviews put you under a microscope and only certain personalities can handle them with flair. So be smart and put your best foot forward at all times.

 WHEN THE WHOLE GROUP IS REQUESTED, DECIDE IN ADVANCE WHO WILL ANSWER WHAT QUESTIONS.

This way everyone get a chance to speak. It is very important that when a question is asked of the band, all of you do not all start chiming in on top of each other. This will make you all look unprofessional and cause unnecessary tension. For instance, decide who in the band will be the band historian, so that when you are asked "how did you guys meet? ", the designated historian answers that question.

 THE PERSON DOING THE INTERVIEWS SHOULD BE ABLE TO ANSWER QUESTIONS ABOUT THE MUSIC, THE LYRICS AND THEIR MEANINGS.

If your band spokesman is not the songwriter then the head songwriter should accompany the spokesman to answer the questions concerning the songs and their meanings.

 YOU SHOULD SUPPLY THE INTERVIEWER WITH A PRE-WRITTEN LIST OF QUESTIONS.

These questions, composed by the band, are tailor made to cover the topics you want discussed. They should cover topics that will make your band interesting and sell your show. If the interviewer fails to ask the right questions you won't make the impact you need.

FOR INSTANCE:

? HOW DID YOU ALL MEET?

　　This is a good way to break the ice. In case this is a full band interview, this is a good opportunity for one of the less eloquent members to answer.

? HOW LONG HAVE YOU BEEN TOGETHER?

　　Use this question only if the band has been together for at least six months. I believe fans will take a band more seriously if they have a history rather than a band that has been together for 6 weeks.

? WHO ARE SOME OF YOUR INFLUENCES, BE IT MUSICAL OR OTHERWISE?

Point of reference question as well as a chance to really win over some fans who might have never heard of you. If your list of influences are similar to the readers/listeners, it might spark a curiosity that will entice them to come see you.

? WHAT WAS THE MOST MEMORABLE SHOW YOU PLAYED TO DATE?

This question that gives you a chance to convey some real significant historical band facts as well as allow you to boast about some of your accomplishments. It's a chance to talk about the Halloween show you played in the Wellesley College gym in Massachusetts where over 1000 people bought tickets and went insane. Elaborate on the story and describe in detail what your concert experience is like, baiting the listener or reader to come and check it out for themselves.

? HAVE YOU DONE ANY SUPPORT FOR ANY MAJOR ACTS?

This is a good next question but only if you have done support. List some of the most current events and only the most popular bands you played for. This will give you some real credibility.

? WHERE ARE SOME OF THE PLACES YOU'VE PLAYED SO FAR, OR; HAVE YOU BEEN OUT ON ANY EXTENDED TOUR AND WHERE DID IT TAKE YOU?

If you have never been out of your home town then do not use this question. If you have played some interesting cities I want you to name them. It's lends more credibility especially to the fan who has never been out of town.

? WHAT DO YOU LIKE ABOUT TOURING?

Give this answer some real though. Perhaps talk about the different people you got to meet and some of the places that really make you appreciate your own hometown (if this is a hometown interview) or how it makes you appreciate the fact that you're in a band and can visit places like this (if your being interviewed away from home).

Talk about how certain places have influenced your music or how being in new cities has given you a chance to see great local bands that have influenced you and your music as well.

? WHAT SONG BEST DESCRIBES THE OVERALL VIBE OF THE BAND?

These next few questions are designed to give the fan a reference point in your live show. The songs you talk about are the songs they will look for at the live show. If people came to the show as a result of the interview, you may notice a better response at these songs especially if you announce the title prior to playing it.

WHAT SONG GETS THE BEST REACTION FROM THE CROWD?

This just gives another opportunity to talk about your songs attempting to capture the imagination of the listener by its description.

WHICH DO YOU LIKE PLAYING BETTER CLUBS OR COLLEGE?

Since both places are great to play, rather than pick one over the other, point out the cool things about each so as to not alienate any place. If you're doing an interview for a college radio station prior to a college show, put the emphasis on the college gigs. If you're about to do a club gig, then put the emphasis on the club. Your goal is to try and make the event that you're promoting, special.

WHAT ARE SOME UPCOMING DATES?

Promotion, promotion, promotion! "nuff said"

HAS THERE BEEN ANY LABEL INTEREST IN THE BAND?

This question is listed because it might be asked by the interviewer and I want to guide you though the answer.

First, what is label interest? Is it really anything concrete? No not really. Either you have a deal or you don't. Everything else is in between and that's fine. If you truly are in some kind of negotiation, my advice is to stay pretty closed mouthed about it. It seems to me like so many bands I spoken with always seem to have some interest. They say "this guy from one label and that guy from another label is interested in us." Funny things as time goes by none of these groups ever get signed and end up breaking up without ever having any interest from anyone except the buildings elevator operator or the mailroom employee who represents himself at a show as an A&R scout. If you have something going on, good for you. But be discreet. Wait until you sign the papers. When you do, then announce it. You will come off looking like sweet and gain respect and awe as people wonder "how did they do that?"

HAVE YOU BEEN IN THE STUDIO YET AND CUT ANY DEMOS?

If you have, say yes and talk about your CD or cassette. If this is a radio interview have the DJ cue up a tune from the tape you brought and play it.

IS YOUR CD GETTING ANY AIR PLAY ON ANY RADIO STATIONS?

 If it is, list some of the stations so that people can call up and request it.

These are just some ideas. I do not know you or your group so I'm sure you can think of answers that are more personalized than the ones I've listed as well as some more interesting questions that can further exploit your band.

Your first set of interviews will be a bit shaky but like anything else, with a little practice and the desire to make it work, you will have the press right in the palm of your hands.

PRESS RELEASES

A press release is simply the format in which you will alert the press to an upcoming event or news story. It should be prepared on your band's letterhead, typed out and double spaced for easy reading and faxed to whom ever you want to read it. The information within should cover who you are, where you are playing, when you are playing, any news blurb associated with the event. To further guarantee action, you should send in a glossy photo and press kit if you have one. The purpose of this is to get some form of mention in a publication at worst, and some coverage of the event at best. To do this successfully you should have all this sent in allowing plenty of time to avoid missing the publications deadline (about 2 weeks before it goes to the printer).

Here is a sample press release:

SUCTION

◁— ⊏   ⊐ —▷

12/3/98

To: Barry Check

Editor of: DNA (Discoverer of New Artists) Music Press

RE: CD RELEASE PARTY • TUES. DEC 9 • 8:00PM • CBGB'S 315 BOWERY NYC

Suction, the 4 piece band from Brooklyn NY., has been playing to packed houses throughout the east coast for the past two years. They will release their debut CD **"PLUNGE OF ALLEGIANCE"** on Defense Records DEC 7, 1995.

You are invited to join them for an open bar celebration between 8pm & 9:00pm on Dec. 9th at CBGB'S followed by a one hour set featuring songs off the CD.

FOR MORE INFORMATION CONTACT: MARC DAVISON AT (212) 555-1234

◁— ⊏   P.O. Box 210 NY NY 10010 (212) 555-1234   ⊐ —▷

8

PRESS KIT

A press kit is a multi-functional, media package, documenting your band's accomplishments. The press kit will contain news clippings, band biography, photographs, tour history and other unique information that will distinguish your band from the others. As you continue to supply it with new data (updated articles and touring information), it will act as the first impression many receive on your group. The better the information is, the stronger it will be in defining and promoting your band.

The press kit gets its name from its obvious function. As you begin to receive favorable press on the band, you should cut out the articles and put it in a folder. When you send these articles to a potential club owner for a booking or a writer for press coverage, they will look over the articles to get ideas as to what kind of band you are and what would be the best way to promote you.

However, with the competition you have out there today, a press kit has to do and be much more than a compilation of good articles. It must be a comprehensive documentation covering the most essential areas of your band's history, presented in a concise, chronological format. Your press kit acts in many ways as the representative of the band, and its overall appearance and contents will be the basis on which your band will be judged. But understand that the press kit is only an extension of the band; it cannot be all the band is.

I have come across many groups that have been all press kit and no substance. You cannot rely on just the flash of your press kit to open doors for you. It must be more than great looking. It must have content. This will get your group the respect and attention you're looking for.

To put together a functional press kit, keep in mind that not everyone in this business will take the time to read everything or even anything in your press kit, therefore you must learn how to sequence the information and highlight things in a way that will catch the reader's attention, whoever it might be. Let's face it, after a while all press kits start to look alike. The bands are different but the reviews all say the same "how great the band is" thing. Remember you're not the only band submitting for a show or a record deal.

The sequencing of the press kit and the type of material you include inside will help pave your way through many important situations. Suppose you are on tour. You will likely be sending the press kit out to newspaper publications and club managers for promotional use. A well stocked press kit will give anyone interested in promoting the band enough material to do a complete job.

Take your photograph for instance. After a date is confirmed at a club, you might instruct the owner to take your photo out of the kit and post it in the front window with a sign that says: Appearing next month. Or if you are trying to get some press on your band, when you supply the writer with your press kit, he will have a photo of you that could be included next to the article. Other information in your kit, like the tour history or college radio play list, give the reader plenty to promote your group with.

If you are trying to get some press on an out of town show, your bio will come in very handy to feature writers who have never heard of your group before. They might even borrow a line or two from one of the articles already written about the band. This will happen quite often when you tour colleges for example and submit your press kit to a college newspaper or college radio station newsletter. The writers of these publications will find suitable phrases from previously written articles within your press kit, so as not to have to spend time coming up with a piece on a band they need to write about but don't know about. This also gives you better control as to what is being written and said about the group.

This is only a sampling of how the press kit serves you. The documentation of your tour history, merchandising sales and radio play, will also help entice potential booking agents, managers and record companies.

The one major point I want to stress concerning the press kit is that each page be clear, concise and truthful. Most recipients of your kit will not have the time nor the patience to read every single article and document within. It will more than likely be skimmed over in search of anything that quickly stands out. This is why we are going to set up the kit in a way that even with a quick glance, the fine points will shine through, establishing your kit and band as the cream of the crop.

THE FOLDER

The saying "you can't judge a book by its cover," applies to many things, but not when it comes to press kits. The cover or folder that your information will be stored in, is indeed important, for it will be the first visual image one will have with your band. The first important qualification for the folder is that when you open it, both the right and left hand sides have insert compartments for your data. Since I recommend displaying the enclosed data in two separate piles, this is an important criterion.

The press kit folder should also be of a certain color and texture. I suggest staying away from the bright neon colors, folders with graphic designs or theme covers like outer space pictures, since they are too flashy and trendy. The common colors widely used in the industry are black and white since they are clean and professional. As for texture, I have always used a linen finish which has character without the flash. The average stationery store has a decent selection, but with the advent of office superstores (like Staples &Office Depo) cropping up everywhere, you will find a bigger selection for less money.

Folders can run as high as $3 each, so if you're thinking of getting overly creative producing your own custom designed folder with a holographic logo on the front cover set over a 3-D image, you are looking at a considerable amount of money. If you have these great artistic concepts use them in a poster that you include within the press kit, your CD cover art or even make a big band backdrop for the live show. Too much emphasis on the front cover will divert attention from what's inside.

LOGO

Your logo refers to the band name and the style in which it is written for instance, Led Zeppelin's Zeppelin, or The Dead's skull & roses.

You should display your band name and logo on the front cover of the folder. Unless you know a talented artist that will draw your logo on each folder, you should look into purchasing some simple band bumper stickers and apply them to the front cover (See merchandising for more info). If bumper stickers are not in your budget and you cannot draw, I would then advise you to take your business card and glue it onto the front of the folder about 2 inches from the top.

You should not leave the front blank, under any circumstances. As you will eventually realize, press kits are a considerable expense to a band and many times you will find yourself supplying a club with the same kit more than once. Often the booker will use your unmarked folder for their own purposes, misplacing the documents within. By not giving a club any reason to break up your press kit, you stand a better chance of it staying intact.

PHOTOGRAPHS

As soon as you can, you should be taking photographs of your group. This is a significant promotional tool that you will be supplying to clubs, newspapers, agents, managers, etc. To create the most appealing photographs you must consider pose, clothing, location and the photographer as key ingredients. The picture should capture you looking like a band not a bunch of losers hanging out at the local 7-11.

 POSE

Your goal is to take a photo of the band in as natural of a scene as possible. Use familiar surroundings and take a varied amount of photographs in as many different poses as you can afford. Any photographer will tell you that out of one roll of film they are lucky if they get one great shot. It may seem uncomfortable at first but in time you will learn how to position yourselves to get the best looking shot. Look through your CD collection, rock and roll magazines and posters to get ideas that you can adapt to your situation.

It's is important to position the band members with the strongest visual personality up front as the focal point of the pose.

CLOTHING

When taking a band photo, all the members should dress as they do when they perform. Keep in mind that this photo will be used for press copy as well as posting at clubs so you must pay close attention to the image you want to project. You should pay close attention the color of the shirt that you wear. If you are shooting with black and white film (which I strongly suggest) with a light colored background, you should wear darker clothing. If the background is dark like a brick wall for instance, wear lighter clothing. This will create a striking contrast and bring out your faces. If you are shooting in color, pay close attention to the surrounding colors and attempt to wear opposite colors. For instance, if you are outside during the day and the sky is a deep blue, certainly don't wear a deep blue shirt. Try red or yellow as an example.

LOCATION

Scout around and look for places that complement the vibe of your music and image of your band. A gangster rap band might look out of place taking publicity shots in the Amish country.

If you are shooting outside you should also consider shooting during a time of the day when the sun is not at its full strength (in the morning before 11am or in the afternoon after 3pm). This will eliminate squinting eyes and overexposure.

If you shoot indoors with color film and are using a flash, don't aim the flash directly at the subject or they will end up with red eyes in the developed picture. You need to diffuse the light by having it facing away from the subject and bouncing off a white background.

PHOTOGRAPHER

Choosing the right person to take the pictures is essential. They not only should have good photographic ability but they also should be able to make you feel comfortable in front of the camera. The less conscious you are about posing the better your pictures will come out.

Here are some tips on choosing and locating a photographer.

POST FLYERS AT A NEARBY COLLEGE, ART SCHOOL, CAMERA SHOP/ LAB.

When you get a response, set up a meeting at one of your rehearsals. It is important that the photographer see the group perform. This will help define your image to them and inspire the mood needed to create a visually effective photograph.

Ask that they bring a portfolio of their work. The quality of their past work will be a factor that determines whether you hire them or not. The more you respect their work, the more you will be able to trust their direction during the photo shoot. If they have never done a band photo before, use some common sense in making the decision to hire them. It is a lot harder than you think to set up a really good press photo. If you are paying this person, you are going to want to get good results. If you are left with only one option to hire someone who has never shot bands before, judge their photos for clarity, framing, subject matter and image interpretation.

 OCCASIONALLY CHECK YOUR LOCAL MUSIC PUBLICATION OR TOWN NEWSPAPER FOR COOL PHOTOS TAKEN BY THEIR STAFF PHOTOGRAPHER.

If you see a photograph that grabs your eye, look below the photograph. If it was shot by a staff photographer, their name will likely be listed. You can call the paper to find out how you can get in touch with them. Since most staff photographers prefer to be discreet about their side jobs, I would advise against leaving a detailed message when you call the paper. In many cases you will find a more than eager individual that would gladly take on a side project.

SEEK OUT OTHER BANDS AND ASK THEM WHO SHOT THEIR PRESS PHOTOS.

As with everything else try to get recommendations and contacts.

PAYMENT

Once you have found the person you want to use, you need to arrive at some kind of payment. Many young photographers will be glad to shoot just for the experience providing you pay for the film and all the development costs. After all, if they are serious about photography, and the pictures come out great, it would make for a very nice addition to their portfolio.

If they insist on getting a fee, depending on their level of expertise and the cost of development and film, I would agree on somewhere around $35 -$50 per roll of film which includes the developing, contact sheets and three 8x10's. You should make this fee contingent on your approval of the negatives.

Most photographers insist on keeping their negatives so do not be alarmed if they tell you that. When the negatives are developed they should then prepare a contact sheet. This is a sheet of photographic paper, containing developed strips of negative sized prints. It is from these contact sheets that you will view all the pictures taken and choose your favorite. Standard practice would be to include in the price, the development of three 8x10 glossies of the three best shots. Generally after you view the three blown up 8x10's, if you request additional shots developed, there will be an extra charge.

8X10 GLOSSIES

Once you have picked the photograph you intend to use, you will need to have copies made. The average price for an 8x10 black and white with a glossy finish is about 5-$8 each, or if you run off 100 copies it would be in the $3 per piece range. This is based on averages taken from one-hour photo labs and national franchises like Moto Photo. DO NOT USE THESE ESTABLISHMENTS FOR THE REPRODUCTION OF YOUR FILM!!!! You will pay through the nose. You need to look in your local yellow pages under photo labs. These are primarily used by professional photographers to develop film in large quantities for a much cheaper rate. You will also find ads in the Village Voice (published in NYC) as well as Rolling Stone magazine from time to time from photo labs.

HOPKINS STUDIOS.	(212) 929-0800

Located in NYC, the above lab is one I recommend. They have been in business for over 35 years and are very reputable. A hundred 8x10's will run you approximately $.50 per photo provided you supply them with good negatives and the band info is already typeset.

Print the photo with a white border around it. At the bottom there should be room for your logo and contact information. The typesetting for that can be done at your local printer. Just supply them with a sample of your band's logo and any other information, and they will typeset it to the correct size to fit under the photo.

If this is not in your budget, you can resort to using a photocopy machine. Use a good machine, the kind found at Staples or at your local printer, rather than the ones found at Woolworth's for five cents a copy. You can copy right off the 8x10 and in many cases with a little creativity you'll get some cool results. I would not consider using these shots for all occasions like submission to a record company or using it for a press article, but it will work fine for bookings. Even if you have the 8x10 glossies, it might not be a bad idea to have some photocopies anyway to use in situations where it would be a waste if you send the 8x10.

BIO

This one page document is the most important piece of literature in your press kit. As the name implies it should describe in detail the band's biography. The problem here is exactly how much biography is really necessary and how you can make it interesting enough to read. The unfortunate truth is that most people really do not care about the band's biography and many bands seem to really get into publishing their whole life story, producing a very ineffective situation.

A good bio should read more like a press release on the group, utilizing some of the following techniques to enhance it and make it interesting and, above all, serve a further purpose down the road. Since most people do not read your press kit in depth, I feel that if you design your bio to be a capsulated version of everything in the kit, you stand a better chance of the recipient reading the most important facts about the group.

So how do we do that?

 GLANCE THROUGH ALL OF THE PRESS WRITTEN ON YOUR BAND.

Highlight the best quotes in each article. Gather two or three of the best ones and begin the bio with these quotes. (See example bio on next page). End the quote with the name of the author followed by the publication the article appeared in. Skip a line and write in the next one.

The purpose of this is to extract the most potent part of the story and highlight it. This increases the chances of it being read. If you bombard a club owner with a press kit full of information, there is too much they must to wade through before they get to the part that says how great you are.

 FEATURE THE NAMES OF THE BAND MEMBERS, THEIR AGES, RESPECTIVE INSTRUMENTS AND A BRIEF HISTORY OF THE BAND.

DO NOT list the make and model number of your guitar, how many years of lessons you had, or that you volunteer at the hospital on weekends. I have seen this stuff and it serves no purpose.

Include some of your past <u>band</u> credits and worthy accomplishments, like if you toured with a national act, if you won any Battle of the Bands or if you sell out at a good-sized, well established club. This is the pertinent information that a club owner needs to read in order to evaluate whether or not to give you a gig. If you don't have impressive credits, don't list anything and certainly do not make things up. In time your credits will get more impressive, then you will update the bio.

LIST ACCOMPLISHMENTS SUCH AS COLLEGE RADIO AIR PLAY OR CD SALES.

Don't be modest here. If you have some really good sales numbers or are tracking on a lot of radio stations, you want people to know this.

 FINALLY, CLOSE WITH A POWERFUL STATEMENT.

If you have something coming up in the near future like the release of your own 8 song CD, this would be the place to mention it. You might choose another quote that you may be using as a slogan in some of your posters.

Another effective closer would be to describe the live show detailing what you do that is special like a special effects light show, that would make having you play at the club a memorable event.

 AFTER THE FINAL PARAGRAPH, LIST THE DATE. THIS WAY THE READER KNOWS HOW CURRENT THE INFORMATION IS.

As you gather more credits and accomplishments you should add them into your bio. As you do bigger and better things, take out the old and replace it with the new.

The bio, as with every other data sheet in the press kit, should be copied on band letterhead. This way if a sheet gets separated from the rest of the pack, it will be identifiable as your band's material.

The following examples are mock bios using the technique I've suggested.

These are by no means the only blueprints for a making a quality bio. They just stand as guidelines in helping you to craft one for yourself. Regardless how you approach making your bio remember that it is a one of the most important marketing tools you have and that it has to be very effective in hooking the reader into giving you a listen.

Always remember what the bio's function is. Don't be too consumed with writing a novel. The end result will not serve your needs and actually turns some people off.

SUCTION

***For Immediate Release*:**

"Suction is a young band out of Brooklyn New York, impressing those in the know with their hard hitting, infectious, Rock and Roll sound."

--- Jo Simpson, The Cutting Edge

"Suction manages to combine intricate melodies, hard guitars and socially conscious lyrics into one cohesive, thoroughly engrossing, musical mind trip."

---- Paula Barby, In Tact

Troy (20): vocals, Chris (21): lead guitar, Kelly (19): bass and Will (20): drums, grew up within a few miles of each other. Their backgrounds are similar and their commitment to the music is genuine. Performing together throughout high school, **SUCTION** has been playing to a loyal and expanding following. From their current 50 song original set list, **SUCTION** has headlined clubs and colleges from Vermont to South Carolina, with 150 dates booked in 1994 including support for Hole, Our Lady of Peace, Tripping Daisies, Spin Doctors and Blind Melon.

In July of 1993, **SUCTION** released a 7 song CD titled "Plunge of Allegiance" which sold out its first pressing of 1000 copies within the first month. These initial recordings have since been re-pressed and have sold over 5000 copies to date. Both college and mainstream radio stations have welcomed the material. These stations include: ***WFCS*** New Britain, CT, ***WONY*** SUNY Oneonta, ***WFNP*** SUNY New Paltz, ***WMWC*** Frederickburg, VA and ***WHTG*** Asbury Park, NJ. Many of these stations have reported **SUCTION** to *CMJ in their top ten rotation.

SUCTION'S commitment to themselves and their audience is borne out of their desire to perform. From college Frat houses to the Limelight in NYC, **SUCTION** "puts on one of the most exciting and intense live performance of any band today."

"I've born witness to many of the best bands of our time. Among such company as Nine Inch Nails, Pearl Jam, Jane's Addiction, or the Red Hot Chili Peppers, there is one group that stands out with an intoxicating intensity that will captivate you and force a stunned 'damn!' from your lips. I'm talking about **SUCTION**."

---Keyser Soze - Suspect Magazine

March 21, 1998

PO BOX 120 BROOKLYN NEW YORK 11063 718 555 5555

*CMJ which is the College Music Journal is the Billboard magazine for college radio. It compiles all the top twenty play lists from all the 300 plus reporting college radio stations in America. For more about college radio see chapter 15

Another option is to go with a conceptual Bio as follows:

MENTAL GENTLEMAN

Case # 00010

In over 30 years of research never has there been such an extreme case of shoudhaveaious a recordcontractitus. There have been only five other cases of this rare affliction documented in these psychiatric journals.

DIAGNOSIS:

Multiple testing and lengthy theraputical sessions have detected a repressed neurosis present in patients, Moss (24): vocals, Floss (21): guitars, Ross (26): drums and Gloss (22): bass. Subjects display highly acute vocal harmonic capabilities and an unusually advanced stage of musical ingenuity. When symptoms flare up, patients are prone to depression and severe insomnia resulting in their need to perform in smoke filled rooms surrounded by large crowds of adoring people.

TREATMENT:

The only known cure for this disease is extensive touring and releasing their musical recordings. For the last five years 1989-1994 **Mental Gentlemen** have done just that. Having performed over 1500 live shows, **Mental Gentleman** released their CD **"I'm Not Okay & You're Totally Wacked,"** which has sold 8000 copies to date. In May of 1994 their single "White Padded Cell," was released to college radio and by October had charted on over 100 college radio stations from coast to coast including: *KBOO Portland, OR, WWUH West Hartford, CT, WCDB Albany, NY, KCSS Turlock, CA.* Headlining clubs from DC to Austin, TX., **Mental Gentleman** have also opened for **311, Rage Against the Machine and Rust.**

OTHER PHYSICIANS CONSULTED ON THIS CASE HAVE HAD THIS TO SAY:

"By balancing often bleak subject matter with aggressive and animated arrangements, singer Garret Moss is the key to Mental Gentleman's diversity."
---- Mia Wallace, Pulp Fiction Journal

"The group somehow manages to combine intricate melodies, scratching guitars, harsh vocals, and socially disturbing lyrics into one cohesive musical mind trip..."

----Karl Childers, MmmMm Magazine

From the very first verse of <u>White Padded Cell</u>, "The fever drips from my parched lips, the stories I can no longer tell, of life and love inside the hell, the pale cruel silence of your white padded cell..." To the disturbing truth of <u>Killing me with Kindness</u>, ... "Take back your handshake, it just leaves me one arm short to protect myself," Moss guides the listener through a dark sarcastic journey covering the spectrum of emotions with a blanket of despair.

Having risen from the ashes of depression, **Mental Gentleman** have the prescription to cure your musical ills.

PO BOX 10 WASHINGTON DC 98765

202 555-5555

6/24/97

"Hey Spike, I'm almost done with our bio, is "This is a warning not a threat" a good sentence?"

These bios describe fictitious bands, but they give you a good example of how it can be put together. As you can see they are streamlined versions of everything that would be contained within the press kits. The manner in which I have chosen to compile it, should make for easy reading and should assist anyone looking to write press on the band with all the information they need all on one page.

You should also take notice as to the way I have typeset, to highlight the band's name in bold, listing the college stations in italics and using a larger font for the quotes. I feel that it will draw the reader's attention directly to areas in the bio that warrant it. Of course, as with all areas of your promotion use this only as a blueprint. The bio is very personal and should highlight *your* career as much as possible.

ITINERARY

This list should begin to be compiled as soon as you start playing your first show. The list should be titled at the top with the name of your band and centered underneath it, should read the present year and "Itinerary." Skip a line and separate the page into three columns. Then begin to log in the information as follows:

◁ *SUCTION* ▷

1998 Itinerary

DATE	CLUB	LOCATION
Jan 4	CBGB's	NYC, NY
Jan 18	Chameleon Club	Lancaster, PA
Jan 23	Hammerjacks	Baltimore, MD
Feb 1	Wetlands	NYC, NY
Feb 2	7 Willow St.	Portchester, NY
Feb 3	Delta Chi Delta	Syracuse, NY
Feb 4	Buffalo State College	Buffalo, NY
Feb 6	Penny Arcade	Rochester, NY
Feb 7	Granny Killams	Burlington, VT
Feb 10	9:30 Club	Washington, DC
Feb 15	Chameleon Club	Lancaster, PA
Feb 25	Penn State	State College, PA

PO BOX 120 Brooklyn NY 115063   718 555 5555

The purpose of this is to show the reader your band's activity. If you are only playing one or two gigs a month, I want you to still keep compiling this list but do not put it in the press kit until you are performing 6 shows or more. Obviously the more shows you do the more impressive this list becomes and the more impact it will have on whoever reads it.

When you begin to look for a booking agent, this list is the most crucial one you can supply. However, for the agent you should keep an exact duplicate of this list, only create a fourth column. This one will be titled **compensation**. Here you will list the exact amount you were paid for each show. You will show this to no one except your booking agent and manager. Since an agent's job is to book shows which they take a percentage of as their earnings, you will need to present your "tour history," which is the itinerary plus the compensation. Showing good numbers will be a key factor in attracting an agent. It will be very difficult for you to go back and try to remember all the dates and what you got paid so you really need to stay on top of this list.

CLUB, COLLEGE AND COLLEGE RADIO LISTINGS

This page should have two columns. The left hand side should list all the clubs and colleges you've played and their locations. The list should not be in alphabetical order but should be listed in the order of the state the club is in, and then in an order where you list the most prestigious club first. The right-hand side should list all the college radio play you're getting, once again listed by state. If you have been playing out for a number of years and have played in more than 50 clubs, there is no need to list every one. The point is to highlight those clubs that are considered prestigious to play in or at the very least tough places to get a gig in.

This list might seem redundant when you have your tour history but what it provides is a quick overview of your routing and regional coverage. One of the things labels look for is a band that is out there spreading their music around. A band that is playing over and over again in 6 states for example has the potential to sell 6 times the amount of records upon release than a band that is playing one state. Also, a band that is booking themselves successfully over a large region is likely to have more press contacts and booking contacts than a band that has only played in their home town. This bodes well for a band and presents them in a very strong light to labels as well as booking agents and clubs.

The following example is how the list should appear:

SUCTION

CLUBS AND COLLEGES

Irving Plaza	NYC,NY
Webster Hall	N.Y.C.NY
Wetlands	N.Y.C, NY
Tramps	N.Y.C., NY
CBGB'S	N.Y.C. , NY
7 Willow St	Portchester, NY
RCC College	Suffern, NY
Stone Pony	Asbury Park, NJ
Fastlane	Asbury Park, NJ
Court Tavern	New Brunswick, NJ
Club Babyhead	Providence, RI
9:30 Club	Washington, DC
Club Chameleon	Lancaster, PA
Penn State	State College, PA
The Sting	New Britain, CT

RADIO

WNYU	NY, NY
WFNP	New Paltz, NY
WCDB	SUNY Albany, NY
WFCS	New Britian, CT
WHUS	Univ of CT
WLVR	Lehigh Valley, PA
WMWC	Mary Wash Col, VA
WFCS	Baltmore, MD
WHTG	Asbury Park, NJ

PO BOX 120 Brooklyn NY 11063   (718) 555-5555

COLLEGE RADIO

In chapter 15 we will discuss college radio at great length. For our purposes here, we will assume that you have approached college radio and have received some air play. If this is the case you will want to get your hands on the written playlists or charts that show your music in rotation. This can be achieved in a number of ways.

 STAY IN TOUCH WITH THE DJ THAT IS CHARTING YOU AND ASK THEM TO FORWARD YOU A COPY OF THEIR PLAY LIST.

Once in your possession you can make copies and insert it into your press kit.

 READ CMJ (SEE CHAPTER 15 FOR MORE INFORMATION)

This is a publication that among many things publishes the charts of reporting college radio stations. It is a highly respected publication within the industry and you should get your hands on a subscription if you plan on focusing on college radio. If you are charting and your band appears in the playlists, then in my opinion you have a very valuable piece of press kit information. After all if you are an unsigned band and you are charting with the likes of signed bands, that's a good piece of bait for record companies. Once you receive the play list, set up a CMJ page by posting the CMJ logo from the magazine itself at the top of the page. Then below it, paste in the cut out play list which includes the call letters of the radio station (WFCD for example). Cut out the volume number, issue number and date and paste that in above the call letters. Lastly, with a yellow highlighting pen, highlight your band's name as it appears in the play list. See below:

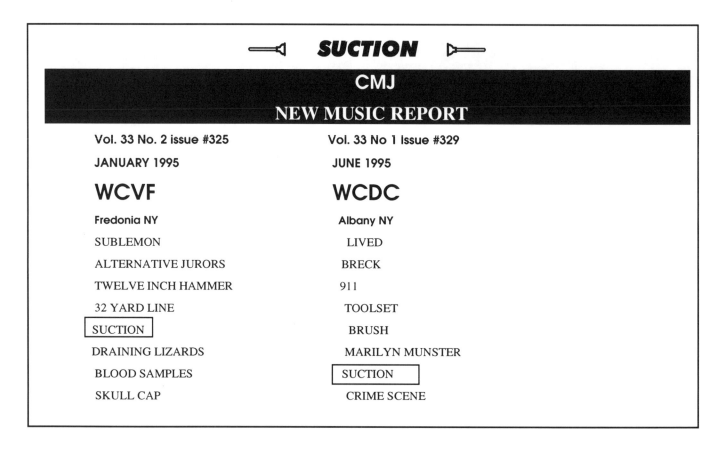

These are a couple of fictitious samples but I think you get the idea. Keep the page neat and hopefully full. If the page fills up, either make reductions at the printer or take some of the old play lists off replacing it with the current ones. As with all these data sheets in the press kit, it is important to keep updating it with new material.

CLUB LISTINGS (optional)

When the clubs you are playing at take out ads in the paper, you should cut these ads out neatly and paste them on a separate sheet of paper. The purpose of this page is to show club owners that you have indeed played the places you say you have. This page is not necessary until such time as you are headlining major venues or opening a major act at a popular venue.

PRESS CLIPPINGS

When you cut articles out of the paper, you must also remember to include the title, any photograph, and the name of the publication it appeared in, as it appears on the front cover. If the article is more than four paragraphs long, you should examine the article to see if you can eliminate some of it. As I have already pointed out, since most people will not read the entire article, you will increase your chances if it is short and to the point. Here are some methods for editing your articles:

 IF YOU USE THE ENTIRE ARTICLE OR PARTS OF IT, BE SURE TO HIGHLIGHT THE KEY QUOTES WITHIN THE ARTICLE THAT YOU WANT SEEN.

EDITING A FULL FEATURE STORY

These extended articles are great for the ego but too cumbersome to be read. Cut out the unnecessary fluff of the article and paste a new edited version of it together. This might mean only keeping the first paragraph or two or only using the third paragraph or using only the last paragraph. In any case, abbreviate the article and once again highlight the best quotes.

Now let's take this even a step further. Suppose you have a pretty decent article. It could be a great article if the writer didn't put in that one line describing something negative. Well if this one line bothers you, edit it out. The easy way to do this is to go to the printer and enlarge the article by 50%. Take this new enlarged copy and with an x-acto knife (found at any art supply store) carefully cut out the sentence or two that you do not like. Now carefully paste the separated pages back together over a blank sheet of paper. Make another copy so that you can white out the black lines that might appear around your little surgery, make another copy reducing it back to normal size and magic, a happening article.

CADAVER
SUCTION

Headlining Friday night at the SUNY ALBANY Spring Fest was LA's Cadaver. Their last stop on a murderous 60 city tour was performed like it was their first as the band ripped through a set of 15 killer songs, many of them off their latest CD, "Autopsy Turvy," to a loyal and revved up crowd.

Opening up the show was Suction, a relatively young band from Brooklyn NY. The energy from this young band whose members are barely in their twenties seemed to ignite the crowd into a frenzy. Except for the first two songs which were drawn out self indulgent noise, the rest of the set steadily improved to grand finale.

Performing a brief thirty five minute set, Suction reached into their bag of influences and pulled out a strong set that kept the crowd on their feet. Though young and at their first college show you can almost see what this band will become. It's a good feeling to be able to say that you knew them when.

This is a relatively decent article with a lot of potential. It mentions you with a national act, and most of what is written is positive except for that line about the opening songs. It's a shame that many good reviews are marred by one negative comment so if you feel it   detracts from the article, you can delete it out.

The following is an edited version as an example.

> **Opening the show was Suction, a relatively young band from Brooklyn NY. The energy from this young band whose members are barely in their twenties seemed to ignite the crowd into a frenzy.**
>
> **Performing a brief thirty five minute set, Suction reached into their bag of influences and pulled out a strong set that kept the crowd on their feet. Though young and at their first college show you can almost see what this band will become. It's a good feeling to be able to say that you knew them when.**

I did not alter any of the words. I just edited out a sentence and took out portions that would bore the reader.

PUT AT LEAST TWO ARTICLES ON A PAGE.

This would reduce the amount of pages, for each press kit, and in case the recipient breezed through the first few pages, they would at least see more than one article. Each article on the page should be separated by the enlarged photocopy of the paper or magazine's logo followed by your article directly underneath it.

Though I recommend pasting up more than one article on a page, you should keep in mind that in order to do that, you might have to reduce the size of the articles. If you have reduced it to the point where it is hard or uncomfortable to read, it will be worthless. You are better off keeping it to one or two articles per page.

POSTER

In the last chapter we spoke about having a standard blank poster that just has your band logo on it which you send in advance as well as bring along with you to clubs. If your budget permits, enlarge the poster to an 11x17 size. When you send your press kit to a club fill in the poster at the bottom with the club's name on it then fold it in half and include it in your folder. If you get the gig, instruct the club owner to take the poster out and post it somewhere in the club adding the date that you will be playing.

If you're sending the press kit to anyone else, include the poster as well if for nothing more than to show that your band is conscious in marketing and promoting itself.

BUSINESS CARDS

Last but not least you should have a band business card that has the band logo, your name, address and phone number.

PUTTING IT ALL TOGETHER

Now that you have all the information for the press kit here's the order in which everything should appear starting with the first item on top.

 INSIDE LEFT

Photo (top page)

Tour History (Itinerary) (second page)

Band poster. (Third page)

 INSIDE RIGHT

Bio (top)

Club, College, Radio list (second)

Press clippings (third)

Business card attached to the right inside jacket by a paper clip.

COST

If it costs **$.10** a copy and if you have 13 pages in your press kit, that comes to **$1.30** for copies. Add in **$.50** for the photo and **$1** for the folder. This comes to **$2.80** per press kit not including tax. Doesn't seem like a lot, does it? Well, if you're calling 15 clubs a week and they all want press kits that comes out to **$42** a week, not counting the **$2** postage and the envelope.

PRESENTATION

Here are just some instructions on how to make good looking copies and how to properly paste up articles along with all the tools you'll need.

 **GLUE STICK**

This glue comes in a container that looks very much like chap stick. You need only apply it to the corners of anything you are gluing and press it down gently onto a clean surface. If you make a photocopy right away you can examine the copy to see whether or not it is on perfectly straight. This type of glue will allow you to lift the item off the paper providing you did not initially press too hard.

 ## X-ACTO KNIFE

This is a cutting devise that has a thin metal handle about as long as a pencil and the tip is a sharp pointed blade which can be replaced when worn out. You hold it like a pencil and run it across the surface of anything you want to cut. It's great for cutting out articles and especially good for the intricate type of cutting like getting into an article and removing sentences.

 ## WHITE OUT (CORRECTION FLUID)

It comes in a small plastic container about the size of nail polish. The cap opens and a little brush is attached to it. You just dab some of the liquid on to the area you're correcting and in a few seconds when it dries you can write on it.

You will find that when you make copies, a black line appears around the edges. This can be easily corrected by applying white out on the black line of the copy. When it dries make a second copy which should come out clean. You must do this with all your paste up for the press kit. It will just give it a much cleaner look and will make for a better presentation.

RULER

For cutting straight lines. A metal one is preferred. Place the ruler along the area you want to cut and run the x-acto knife across the ruler and you should end up with a straight cut.

 ## STAMPER

With you band name and return address so that you do not have to hand write that information on every piece of mail you send.

 ## YELLOW HIGHLIGHTING PEN

Use this to highlight the quotes within the article that you want the reader to focus on. *Be sure to highlight the copy not the original.* If you highlight the original, when you make a copy it will reproduce with a black smudge line across the area that you highlighted, rendering it unreadable.

ENVELOPES FOR MAILING PRESS KITS.

Envelopes are just another expense for you in the long line of expenses. You will need an envelope big enough to fit your press kit inside. If you have one of those office superstores in your area, that's where you will find the best prices on envelopes and all the other things I mentioned above. You will need two types of envelopes.

 **LARGE WHITE UNPADDED**

These are fairly inexpensive and can be used for sending out your press kit. Since most standard press kit folders are 8 1/2" x 11 1/2," you need to buy the very next size which should be either 9 1/2" x 13 1/2" or 10" x 12." Buy the ones that have a glue seal rather than the tin clasp for closure.

 YELLOW PADDED

These are fairly expensive about $1 a piece at the post office or about 65 cents a piece at a superstore for the 10"x 12" size. You should use these envelopes for mailing photographs (you might even tuck inside some card board on both sides for extra protection) and for mailing your press kit if you are including a cassette tape, CD or DAT.

 THERE IS ALSO A 6X9 SIZE YOU SHOULD USE FOR MAILING YOUR TAPES.

Save any padded envelopes that you receive in the mail. Just take off the stamps and rub some magic marker over the previous addresses and it's ready to go.

COSTS

 COPIES - Generally run about **$.05** per copy for a standard 8x10 and **$.25** for an 11x17. Enlargement and reductions cost around 25 - 75 cents depending on where you have it done.

 POSTAGE - For a standard press kit/tape in a padded envelope cost is **$2 - $3.** For a press kit mailed in a plain envelope without tape cost **$1.25 - $2.**

 STAMPERS - Approximately **$2 - $3** each for a wooden handle one and **$15 - $18** each for the self- inked depending on how many lines of type you put on the stamp. The most you need is three. Your band name and two lines for your address. If you want your logo there will be a set up charge somewhere between **$5 - $30** depending upon the complexity of the art work.

 TYPE SETTING - Differs from place to place. If you do not own a computer you are going to need the typesetting services of your local printer for your bio, business cards, stampers etc. They usually charge by the line so a bio is going to run much more than a business card. Business cards are roughly **$20** for **500** cards. Price depends on the style of card and the weight of the paper you choose.

 COMPUTER LABELS (aprox. **$10** for 5000 labels.) **X-ACTO KNIFE** ($2 -$4.)

 YELLOW HIGHLIGHTER (**$.50 - $2.**) **WHITE OUT** (Under $2.)

CORRESPONDENCE

**WITH YOUR PRESS KIT, ENCLOSE A BRIEF LETTER, COMPUTER GENERATED IF AT ALL POSSIBLE**

Keep it short only one paragraph or two at the most. Refer to your recent conversation and that this is the follow up. Be specific as to what your exact purpose is and close the letter with instructions that you will call in the prearranged time you discussed in your last phone call.

MAKE A COPY OF THE LETTER

This is for your own records to be stored in a file marked by the name of the club or whatever the destination is of the letter. ***Make sure you put a date on the letter*** and proofread it for errors and grammar.

MAKE SURE THAT YOU MAKE A NOTATION IN YOUR DAILY PLANNER ON THE FUTURE DATE THAT YOU HAVE ARRANGED TO CALL BACK

There are as many different styles and techniques for setting up a letter as there are different types of matters you will need to address. The one rule is to be as direct as you can using the shortest amount of words possible.

Here is a sample letter sent directly after a phone conversation inquiring about booking a date.

Unless you have been requested to supply them with additional information, the contents of this letter will do. You have reminded them of your phone conversation, stated a valid reason why you want to play the club and have supplied them with your available date to play. Sign it after you print it out.

All other correspondence should begin the same way with the date, the name of the person, their position (if they work for a company) followed by the address.

If your budget permits, I advise you to have letterhead stationary printed for all your correspondence. You can have your logo printed on nice 20lb bond stationary which can been done at your local printer. If you own a computer, you can design your logo from software and insert it on everything you print out. Any office stationery store should stock varieties of nice stationery for around $10 for 500 sheets.

If you do not own a computer, have your band name type set, so that it would fit nicely on top of a standard 81/2 x 11 sheet of paper. Purchase a ream of paper (500 sheets) from the office superstore or stationery store (should be under $7.00) and paste the logo on one sheet so that you can make copies of it.

Once you are ready to mail the press kit, place the letter of correspondence directly on top of the closed press kit and insert it into the envelope and mail it first class. It should normally take about two days for it to reach its destination. So you should start counting from this point the days until you were instructed to call back.

Good Luck!

9

THE RECORDING STUDIO

The first time I ever walked into a recording studio I felt like a kid at Disney World. It was 1978 and the studio was a 4 track set up in the basement of a grade school in Pomona, NY. Little did I know that this recording session would launch my group into becoming one of the more popular club bands in NYC during the new wave revolution that launched bands like Television, Blondie and The Talking Heads.

It took three eighteen hour days to record and mix three songs. The studio was, by today's standards, a very simple one. We recorded live on to 1/4 inch reel to reel tape. There were hardly any effects to speak of, just compression and reverb. But the thought of being in a recording studio gave me purpose and made me feel legitimate, like I was doing this rock and roll thing for real.

By the third day when our time and money ran out, I felt like I'd ridden Thunder Mountain for the 3,000th time. I was totally fried and swore I would never do this again. I couldn't wait to get back to the live stage show where I felt the most comfortable. In retrospect I know why the studio was so harrowing for me. The main reason was that prior to that session I had never recorded anything I played before. When you play live, the experience is much more visual and any mistake or slight deviance in the music will be overlooked or forgotten by the next song if not the next note. In the studio however, every note, sound, inflection and nuance of the music is under a microscope. Errors that might be accepted in a live setting, stick out like a sore thumb, on tape. Looking back, the band was very uneducated about the studio and clueless as to how to achieve a polished, finished product.

To the engineer's credit and the fact that we were a well-rehearsed band (playing eight hours a day, six days a week, since we all lived together), the final product was actually very good. We pressed a single from the tape which went on to become a big club and college radio hit charting on 120 stations.

That was 1978. Today, recording studios are far more technologically advanced, equipped with digital multi-track recording, random access multi-track editing, DAT mix down and more. A band need not have a degree in recording technology to get through the recording experience. But you should have some understanding about what some of the equipment is and what it does, what you should be paying for, how to prepare for the recording, and how to maximize time and get the most for your money.

CHOOSING A STUDIO

If you stop and think about what makes a song great, the first place you have to start at is the song itself. The melody, tune and lyrics are the crucial ingredients that make up a song much in the same way plum tomatoes, fresh basil, garlic and olive oil make a great marinara sauce. Whether or not this combination of great ingredients will ultimately reproduce a great end product will depend on who's doing the cooking and how the individual ingredients are mixed.

For this recipe the ingredients are the musicians, the recording studio is the sauce pot, and the recording engineer is the chef. During a recording session, the engineer will record your instruments and vocals on separate tracks (designated areas on the tape that isolate these individual musical components) using various effects to enhance the sound quality. Upon completion of the recording, all the separate tracks will be mixed together to produce the finished product. If it sounds easy, believe me, it's not. It is usually rare that an artist ends up with a finished product that they are completely happy with. What you hear in your head is a very complex thing to translate to tape. But with the right combination of good song, musical clarity, good engineer and good studio you will get awfully close.

To choose a studio, consider the following:

COST

BY THE HOUR

This is just what it says. The meter begins ticking from the moment you begin setting up until the last note is played for the day. It is the most profitable way for the studio owner and can be most efficient for you if you only have a few hours of recording to do.

BLOCK TIME

If you are working with a tight budget and extreme time restraints, block time should be considered. The studio will then set aside for example 5 hours on Saturday afternoon between 3:00pm and 8:00pm. It's good for the studio in that they can book a session during an off time and bring in income. Chances are the studio will take their per hour fee and reduce it.

DAY RATE

A day rate will be approximately 12 hours. The studio should cut you a better price than the per hour fee.

Studio fees are determined by equipment, quality and engineer experience. This fee can be as low as $10 per hour and as high as hundreds or thousands of dollars. The higher end studios primarily used by major recording artists are combination high tech studio/retreats. Set in remote areas, they provide the artist the best of the recording technology along with a spectacular environment and hotel-like accommodations. The lower end studios are commonly found in the basement of someone's home.

Of course, there is a cornucopia of choices priced in between. The beautiful part of this is that for your purpose as an unsigned band, the lower end studios can supply you with exactly what you need and for the purpose of this book these are the type of studios I want to concentrate on.

AMBIANCE

When choosing a studio it is important that you visit the room and feel the vibes. Studio rooms give off an energy from what has transpired there in the past and this can affect you in either a positive or negative way. Chances are when you go to record, you will spend up to 12 hours a day in the process. That is a lot of time to spend in any one room and it can be very tense if you are not comfortable. At the worst, the studio should have a separate smoking area, a comfortable couch, a refrigerator for food and drinks, and a TV to help pass some of the time while you are not recording. If the studio is in the basement of someone's home, chances are they have all the things I mentioned upstairs in their house. You should inquire if they are available for you to use.

ACOUSTICS

Acoustics is a scientific term that deals with production, emission, control, reception and effects of sound. In English it refers to the way the room is designed using different ceiling and wall heights, angles and materials to conduct the sounds made in the room. A simple example of acoustics is standing in the stairway of a large skyscraper and shouting. The result will be a reverberating echo because of the endless room and concrete that the sounds will bounce around in. In reverse, if you cover yourself inside a sleeping bag, the sounds are totally muffled because the material soaks it up and it has nowhere to go. Well you can imagine the chaos a studio would have if did not control the bounce of the sound or if the room soaked up all the sound. Even basement studios can be built with acoustical considerations using tiles or padding on the walls to help balance out the sound. With all this in mind I should tell you that poor acoustics is usually a minor concern and can be solved by the use of a good digital reverb unit.

You can determine acoustics just by standing in the room and talking, listening to the sound of your voice. Further testing will include asking the engineer to play some music through the system so you can hear its effects in the room.

ENGINEER

This is the person that will sit behind the mixing board and run the machinery that will record your music. This is their primary function. Though they may have other qualifications, if you are paying them to engineer then that is all they will do. Their job is not to suggest ideas or sounds. It is your job to ask what are the different options available. You may ask for their opinion but many times they will offer neutrality. Perhaps after you've worked together for a while the engineer may participate more, but generally the engineer will refrain from suggestions. You are expected to know what you want so that the final result will be your responsibility.

Speaking of responsibility, it will be yours and yours alone to choose an engineer that has the kind of qualifications necessary to produce a quality product. A resume concerning where they have worked and who they have recorded are important but what is most important is that they know the equipment they are working on in the studio you will be recording in. Time goes by quickly in the studio and if problems should arise or if you are not happy with a particular sound, the engineer's expedient delivery of a solution is your most prime objective. The rich kid down the block whose dad just loaned him ten thousand dollars to set up a studio will make for a disastrous situation if they have no idea how to use the equipment.

Ask around for recommendations from others that have recorded in the past. Listen to their tapes and judge for yourself. It might be worth it to travel 30 miles to record with someone who is highly respected for their abilities, equipment, price and results.

When you speak with a potential engineer, you should be looking for someone who looks to understand what you want and works in conjunction with you to achieve it rather than someone who will try to force their ideas on you in hopes of leaving their own musical impression on your recording. One true acid test of their abilities lies in the work that they have previously done. Therefore you will ask to have some music queued up that they have engineered in the past. Hopefully they have engineered something in the past that resembles your style of music so that you can get a feel for their recording technique. You should inquire about the equipment they are using so that you can judge by industry standards if they have the equipment capability to record you properly as well as equipment that is not obsolete.

Though we will discuss studio equipment, I want to preface it by saying that equipment is only as good as the person using it. With the cost of a very decent home recording studio being so affordable (around $10,000), virtually anyone can put one together. Engineering is an art that requires talent and I feel that while good equipment, ambiance and acoustics are important considerations, the most crucial element is the person who is engineering the system. Go on recommendations from other bands that have recorded demos and be picky. It's your music.

EQUIPMENT

There are some basic pieces of equipment that studios should have as well as some select added pieces to help add fidelity, quality and personality to your recording. The following is a laundry list of outboard gear (effects and processors) and basic recording equipment and what their function is in the studio.

 **MICROPHONES**

The entry point of your music in the recording process. A good microphone is a key piece of equipment, especially vocal microphones. There are good mikes that start at $100 and there are great microphones that start at $1000. Though this is just one piece of the puzzle, you might want to look for some quality names in the microphone business. Companies such as Neumann, AKG, Micro Tech and Shure all make good quality products. It would not be a bad question to ask the engineer what type of vocal mic he uses. You can list the information and double check at your local music store. Keep in mind, if the studio has a top of the line $1000 mic, the chances are that the cost will be reflected in the studio rate you are quoted. Yes a $1000 Neumann is a great mic but I have been through sessions where the engineer used a $150 vocal microphone and got a great sound by over-compensating with their technique and use of effects. This is the person you ultimately want to find.

One common vocal problem in a studio is sibilance. This is caused by a singer making an overly pronounced "essss" sound while singing. This can be solved by using a very good mic or the singer working hard on reducing his natural sibilance. If the studio does indeed have cheap microphones it would be important to check if it has a de-esser. This is a limiter that can reduce the "esss" somewhat.

 MASTER TAPE FORMATS

There are various different taping formats available today mainly due to our ever-expanding quest for perfection in sound quality. It seems that with every great breakthrough, there is one disadvantage that keeps a large portion of the consumer community from jumping aboard. In recent times D.A.T. (digital audio tape which looks like a miniature cassette) was expected to compete with the CD format but that has not happened. Yet it has become the format of choice in recording studios.

Your main objective in the studio is to record music. Since rock and roll has been successfully recorded since the 1950's, conceivably you can use recording equipment from the 50's. Well not really. If you have in mind to reproduce these recordings into cassette or CD for distribution one day, you will need to have your recording prepared in a format that will be acceptable by the pressing plant that converts the signals of your master tapes and duplicates them. The success of your final product will then rely on how up to date the studio is and how compatible their tape format is with the pressing plants you are using. With all the modern recording equipment available today, you need not worry that much. You should inquire what master tape format the studio offers. If you are going to be pressing

CD's or cassettes you should be lining up which pressing company you will use and make sure that they can reproduce from that format.

 ## TAPE DECK

This is the piece of equipment that will house the particular format of tape you are recording on. Whether it be reel to reel or SVHS which looks like a VHS cassette, you will want 16-24 track capability. Since each instrument is being recorded on its own track, 16 tracks is recommended and here's why. Suppose you are a 4 piece band. Chances are your drummer alone will require about 7-8 tracks if it's miked correctly, two tracks for each guitarist, possibly more if they record in stereo, bass track, vocal tracks, and more tracks for over dubbing.

In keeping up with the latest technology you should look for a studio that has a D.A.T. mix down. It is a good medium right now for transferring the finished product off the master tapes. A good D.A.T. machine will cost a studio around $800 to purchase as opposed to a 2 track reel to reel which is in the $1500 and up price range. This cost differential will be reflected in the price you are going to pay for a recording. The D.A.T. format will preserve the integrity of your music as there is minimal to no generation loss from the transfer off the master. You can reproduce from the D.A.T. and make CD's and cassettes now without having to make copies off the master reels. The only drawback to D.A.T. is that this format cannot be edited or spliced like the reels. This will only affect you if the order in which you place the songs on the D.A.T. changes when you go to press CD's or cassettes since the pressing plant sets up the D.A.T. and lets the tape run. This means if you decide that the third song on the tape should be the first song and the second song should be the third song.

 ## CASSETTE DECK

When you are done recording for the day bring home and listen to. Glance over to where the cassette deck is and see if it is a Fisher Price or something decent. Check the brand of cassettes the studio uses for copies. You will most probably have to pay for them, but to save you the trouble of going out and buying your own there should be good quality tapes.

 ## HEADPHONES

You will spend a good deal of the time in the studio wearing headphones. Decent headphones are not terribly expensive. They should be comfortable and there should be enough headphones for each member of the band to use. You might want to ask how many headphone mixes there are off the board. You will need at least one, this way each member hears all the recorded tracks. Each additional headphone mix offers the capability to send the different isolated tracks to a particular headphone. For instance, with a four headphone mix, each member of the band can get their own instruments sent to their headphone in a separate mix where as in a one headphone mix you can't isolate the tracks.

SOUND BOARD

The board is the control panel for all the equipment. There are types of boards that range in price from $500 - $1,000,000. The board should have at least as many channels as the number of tracks on the tape deck. Inquire as to the name of the board and then you can inquire at the music store what the price range is. The purpose by the way is to determine he quality of all the equipment and to get an idea on the cost of the system so that you can judge whether you are paying a fair price or not. If you are being charged $100 per hour on a 10,000 studio then you are way overpaying unless you are using a top of the line engineer. Once again the cost of the board and the ultimate capability of the board will be reflected in the hourly rate and will only be as good as the person using it.

SPEAKERS

A studio should be equipped with at least two to three pairs of speakers. They should range in sizes from large (with 12" woofers for bass frequency response), 8" speakers in bookshelf size cabinets to simulate the home stereo and a small pair like the size of a Walkman to simulate the car stereo. The purpose for this assortment is to help stabilize the sound of the tape to fit all the obvious places that the music will be played in. If the studio contained huge pillar like speakers that cost $10,000 a piece, you will get a very false impression of what the tape really sounds like.

OUTBOARD GEAR

These are the effects that the engineer will use to control and enhance the music.

REVERB

There are three kinds of reverb. Plate, Spring and Digital. Most if not all the studios you will be working in have only digital reverb. This effect's primary function is to acknowledge or introduce into the recording a desired acoustic that is not present in the room you are presently recording in. This can be true for almost any room since a room only has the one basic acoustic personality of itself. If for creative purposes you want a big open air sound of a huge ballroom you can create that with a reverb unit..

Digital reverb is a necessary piece of equipment in a lower end studio simply because many of these rooms have no real acoustic quality to speak of and if it were not for a little reverb the music would sound very flat.

DIGITAL DELAY

This effect is primarily used for vocals but can be incorporated to affect other instruments. What a digital delay does is simply regulate the length of time of a particular sound. For instance if you say the word "Ah" with no delay the word sounds like "Ah." If you now adjust the time delay slightly you would end up with something similar to "Ah...Ah," or four "Ah's" in a second.

COMPRESSORS

Removes and smoothes out the volume peaks. For instance the vocalist letting out a scream that might pin the needle on the recording and distort on the tape. The compressor will soften the scream and bring it back into range without destroying the effect of the scream.

This is all a studio really needs effect-wise to give you a desirable tape. It would help if the studio has a few digital delays hooked up but it's okay if it does not.

Effects are no doubt fun toys, but I strongly recommend that you know what you want out of an effect in relationship to the song before you go in to record. You will waste precious time experimenting and I can tell you that these experiments in the hands of a novice will bring poor results.

STUDIO PREPARATION

Now that we have dissected the studio, let me tell you that it will all be for naught if you and the group are not thoroughly prepared both mentally and musically. The following is a list of studio preparations:

♪ **MAKE SURE THAT YOU HAVE BOOKED TIME THAT YOU CAN AFFORD**

It will haunt you if you're under budget and have to stop in the middle and wait for more money. Momentum and timing are very important. It's okay to take a few days off or at most a couple of weeks but if you let more than six months go by in between recording sessions you are going to lose touch with the project.

To create a budget you must become familiar with all the costs associated with a recording session.

To keep your costs in line try to adhere to some sensible techniques.

From start to finish, a song should take no more than a day and a half to record (18 hours). This includes setting up, sound checking and tracking. If you are paying **$25** per hour and spend **18** hours recording a song then you have spent **$450** to record the song.

Once the song is recorded, you also have to mix. That should take at most **5** hours if you are doing **24** tracks. That will adds **$125** to the price. In total, the cost of the song from beginning to end is **$575** (at **$25** per hour) Right?

Wrong! Don't forget about the master reel that costs about **$100.** And what about incidentals like the food, beverages, transportation, cassettes, guitar strings, drum heads, etc. They all add up as well.

You need to add the **$100** tape fee and the incidental amount (approximately **$100**) to the cost of the song. The total then is approximately **$775** per song. Quite a lot of money!

So now you're saying "no way can I afford **$775** to record a song" or "no way am I going to spend **18** hours recording a song." Right! These two things should not occur but they do because musicians tend to loose track of time in the studio. Though much depends on the quality of recording you are ultimately trying to get, you most definitely can record for less money. In fact you can record three songs for **$775.** But to accomplish this you must prepare your budget, determine how much you can ultimately spend, and then stick to it.

Stay conscious of the time you're spending in the studio. When you are recording don't experiment. Your experimentation should be done in rehearsal where time is much cheaper than the studio. Looking for a cool effect is okay but not if you spend three hours working on one note! Remember this is an independent production. While you should try and make the best quality recording you can certain sacrifices must be made.

With regard to mixing, try to negotiate a lower price for the mixing session. It probably won't be offered but if you know to ask you may be able to negotiate a reduced rate.

The general rule is one day of mix (5 hours) per song. Sure you can cram in five song mixes all in one night if you don't mind staying up until sunrise and having the last three songs sound like crap. If you are working within a thin budget which I'll assume most of you are, don't mix more than three songs in a twenty four hour period.

♪ PICK YOUR SONGS WEEKS AHEAD OF GOING INTO THE STUDIO

Deciding on which of your songs to pick will be determined by what purpose you are recording for. If you are making a club demo for getting gigs, then I would choose those songs that best represent you live. If you are making a demo to shop for a record deal you might want to consider what songs get the most audience reaction along with what you think has a good commercial appeal and yet reflects the band's sound and identity.

The most important criterion is that the choice of songs have a musical continuity. This means that if you write Ballads, Rap, Metal, Funk, Punk, Fusion and circus music, don't flatter yourself by recording one of each. An important part of a band's image is the definition of what their image is. If you record all types of music on a demo no-one from clubs to fans, from press to record labels will have any idea what to make of you. Furthermore even if they liked all the music how in the world would a label market you and who would they market you to. It is rare that a band can appeal to punkers, rappers, head bangers, 40 year old housewives and children of all ages.

Group your music and record with a theme. Some bands naturally have a theme and will tend to discard a new tune if it varies from their theme. Imagine how out of character it would be for "Marilyn Manson" to record 10 tracks of acoustic love songs. So if your group has a variety it is a good idea to begin deciding who you want to be.

Making demos and positioning them is a difficult task. In your career as an unsigned act, the chances are good that you will be making more than one demo recording and in time you will find a song formula that works best for you.

♪ REHEARSE THE SONGS

This is the big secret of a successful recording. Once you have picked the songs and evaluated how much money you have, determine the amount of songs you are going to do (which should be at least three), and practice the hell out of them. Record every rehearsal on a boom box and analyze the recordings.

"What's wrong with you freaks, You've been here for 18 hours already and haven't recorded a thing"

I also want you to practice the songs two different ways.

→Play them minus the vocals. You will most probably record parts of the song this way in the studio and besides, playing the song without the vocals will help you learn the song even more and aid you in a quicker recording time, which will translate into saving money.

→If you own acoustic instruments, try playing the songs acoustically. For one thing this would be good practice for when you become a rock star and have to perform on MTV unplugged. Secondly what better way to really learn a song and locate the bad notes and weakest parts than when you are playing acoustic. When your amp is cranked and the floor effects are on, you really mask a lot. You won't realize this until you record in the studio where every note is highlighted. Strip down to acoustic guitars, light vocals and drums played with brushes, and I will make this one guarantee (which is the only time I will guarantee anything in this book), that you will hear the song a whole new way and improve upon it thus saving you at least two hours of studio time.

When you rehearse the songs acoustically and without the vocals, you should be recording on a boom box. This will help you hear how it sounds and determine if you are keeping proper time or not. This will also be a good opportunity for you to work on your vocal harmonies if you have them. The vocalists should get together when the band isn't recording and play the tape and sing their parts. This exercise mimics the way it will be done in the studio.

♪ SUPPLY THE ENGINEER WITH YOUR REHEARSAL TAPES

This should be done when you first meet the engineer. It would give you both a chance to listen to and discuss the music and the direction of the production once you enter the studio.

A few days before going in to record you should give the engineer another tape in which you have recorded the rehearsal versions of the songs you plan on recording. Your hope is that the engineer will listen to these tapes and be prepared when you arrive to record.

♪ MAKE SURE THAT ALL THE GUITAR STRINGS ARE REPLACED AND TUNED THE DAY BEFORE GOING IN

Have all your amps checked and effects checked; (batteries included). Change all the drum heads, clean up your cymbals and supply yourself with sticks. Bring your guitar tuners with you in case the studio does not have one. Vocalists, do not go out drinking the night before. Get a good night's sleep so you are fresh and well rested.

RECORDING

So you are all prepared and today's the day. You should arrive at the studio a half hour before your set time to assure that you are not late. Some places will start charging at the set time whether you are there or not. Load in your equipment and follow the engineer's directions as to where to set up. Hopefully within three to five hours the drums will be miked up and sound checked. They usually take the longest to sound check. There are many variations of the way the instruments can sound and you are going to try to reproduce one that will best add to the song. Keep in mind that you can search for days for that one perfect sound. Chances are you don't have days for that so do the best you can within a sensible time limit.

RECORDING TECHNIQUES (LIVE VS. TRACKING)

These describe the alternate ways of recording. They each have their advantages and disadvantages and I also give you my advice on why you should choose one over the other.

 ## LIVE TO TWO TRACK

When you record live it basically means that the band will play the song as it does when they are performing. When you record "Live To Two Track" this means that the band as a whole is being miked as opposed to each individual instrument being miked into their own separate track. The theory is to capture the live feel of the song. The advantage to this style is that if you are a really tight band, and can nail the song within a few takes, you can conceivably record your entire demo in one day. Depending on how good you are, if you have 12 hours of studio time booked, first deduct about 6 hours for line checks. If you have on the average 4 minute songs and at worst require 5 takes a song to nail them, technically you can record about 2-3 songs an hour or 12-18 songs in the day. The disadvantage to this style is if you go through the song and every part is hot except the singer flubbed one line for example, you cannot get in and fix the flub. You will have to perform the whole song over again, and again and again until you all get it right. When it comes time to mix you are only dealing with 2 tracks instead of 24 so you can probably mix the entire tape in one day as well. So for the price of 1 song you can record a whole albums worth of material.

Be aware that this shortcut will have some compromise on the overall sound of the tape. That is why I suggest you only record this way if you are preparing a tape for getting gigs and for passing it around to your friends. After all, the clubs only really care about how you sound live. And what better way to show them than through a live recording.

 ## LIVE TO TRACK

This is similar to the example above with the one distinction that each instrument will be miked to record on its own separate track. You will retain the live feel and you gain the ability to repair any mistakes without the entire band having to play the song again.

 ## LAYERED TRACKING

This refers to the recording technique where you perform the song together live, but the engineer will only concentrate on one instrument at a time, for instance the drums. You might go through the song a dozen times until the drummer feels that they nailed it. At that point the drummer will step aside and the engineer will then bring in the next player, let's say the bass guitarist. They will put on a pair of headphones and play their parts on a new track along with the drum tracks. Once the bass is done, then each additional instrument will step in and record in the same fashion. Then last but not least, the singer will lay down their tracks over the recording of the instrumental version of the song. Once these main tracks are complete then you can go and record over dubs (secondary parts) and more vocals, harmonies and whatever else.

The advantage to this style of recording is that by isolating the individual instruments, the engineer can better control the recording dynamics, effects and sounds. Any mistake or slight musical deviation can be erased at the exact point of error and a new part can be punched in its place.

You will end up with a superior quality recording and this is the recording style you should use if you are going to shop this tape to an industry executive.

The disadvantage to this style is that it's the most time consuming and expensive method. Once again if you are not well rehearsed or have no idea as to how the final arrangement should be, stay out of the studio. If you are going into the studio in hopes that during this recording session the scrambled ideas you have in your head will miraculously come together onto tape, transforming into a solid gold hit then I say, "What drugs are you on"?

Seriously, for the last time, do not rush into the studio. Keep taping yourself in rehearsal until the song is completely arranged and as perfect as it can be. Then and only then should you make the investment in the recording studio.

MIXING

When all the tracks are completed, you basically have 16 or 24 tracks filled with music. Mixing is the process of incorporating all the individual elements of the song together to create the final product. This is a specialized process that in the larger scope of the music business is usually performed by a separate individual and sometimes even done in a separate studio. You may notice with major recording artists that their record was produced by so an so and mixed by someone else. In a lower budget project of course, the mixing and engineering are done by the same individual at the same studio.

The engineer and band should if time allows, take a full day off after recording before you start the mix. This will give your ears a chance to rest up and be fresh. Your mixing goal is to combine all the tracks and yet have each instrument stand out clearly defining their role in the song. Trouble may arise in mixing when all the band members are just focusing in on their own parts trying to make sure that their parts are way up front. I don't need to tell you how destructive that mentality is. The song will suffer if you attempt to make the drums as loud as the lead guitar and the keyboards as loud as the vocals.

If you have never been in a studio before, let the engineer mix the tracks without all of you hovering around. The engineer is removed enough from the song to be able to hear what it needs in terms of a final mix. Once that is done you will be invited back to listen. Many times an engineer will make more than one mix for you to compare. When you are listening, pay attention to the song first and then the individual instruments second. If the overall sound of the song is hot, then focus on the individual instruments to see if anything got lost. The guitars and vocals might be the first instruments you hear so listen closer for the high hat, bass drum and cymbals that tend to get overlooked.

The engineer will probably play you these mixes over a few different sets of speakers in the studio to give you different formats in which they might be played under. I recommend bringing a Walkman or small boom box to the studio to sample the tape through as well. Most people do not have the type of sound system at home that is there in the studio and that type of set up can give you a false sense of what the song sounds like. Another suggestion is to mix the song down to cassette and bring it out to your car stereo. This is where you probably spend a good deal of your time listening to music and your ears will pick up discrepancies between your tape and others. It would not be fair to expect your recording to sound as good as one recorded in a 64 track studio by a world renowned producer. But it should have fidelity, clarity and no distortion.

If you are uncomfortable with the engineer mixing on their own then I recommend that the band elect the one or two members of the group who wrote the song to be present. Remember, too many cooks spoil the broth.

THE FINAL PRODUCT

When all is done make sure that if you mix down to D.A.T. that you record the songs in the order you will want them to appear on the CD's or cassettes you will eventually make. Do not pass the D.A.T. around and play it for people. It is your master copy and you do not want to wear any of the frequencies out. Ask the engineer to make a few copies onto cassette for you to listen to at home and pass around. Secure your D.A.T. master in a safe place until you make arrangements for the manufacturing and further duplication of the music.

As a final note, as soon as you're done in the studio begin saving your money for the next time you want to record. Your music should be fresh and up to date should you find yourself in a situation where you are asked to submit a tape for a possible career breaking situation and you are stuck with old material written and recorded a few years ago. I know how much it sucks to give someone a tape and then have to preface it by saying "Here's our tape but just keep in mind that it was recorded last year and we have so many new songs that sound so much better blah blah blah". To avoid this embarrassing confrontation shoot for a new recording once every sixteen months. If you learn your way around a studio and find a good one that is not too expensive, you can do it.

10

COPYRIGHTING MADE EASY

WHAT IS A COPYRIGHT?

Copyrighting refers to the registration of your written work for protection against usage by others. The definition of copyright as defined by the Copyright Office in Washington, DC is "the right to copy." In other words, when you create an original work whether it be a song, play, book, movie or even an original pattern for a clothing line, you own the exclusive rights to that work.

To begin with, under the 1976 Copyright act, your songs are considered protected as soon as they are written or recorded. But this is a very weak form of protection. Suppose you write a song, record it on your home boom box for your own enjoyment. You play it for your friends and find that they really seem to enjoy it. But for whatever reason you don't pursue a musical career and eventually forget about the song. Then a few years later you're listening to the radio and you hear a good portion of your song being played as a part of a whole song. Further investigation leads you to find that one of your friends had borrowed the tape and played it for their friend who was in a band. They in turn used ideas from the song to record their own version that has now become a hit. Well under the law you can sue for infringement providing that you can prove you were the original songwriter. Unless you stored the tape along with a date to prove when you wrote it, the 1976 Copyright act will not be enough.

POOR MAN'S REGISTRATION

To gain better protection against infringement, upon completion of the material whether in written form or recorded on tape, you can go to the post office and mail it to yourself by registered mail. When you receive the package, don't ever open it. The sealed contents inside postmarked by the United States Post office will be proof enough of exactly when your work was completed. The disadvantage to this form of copyrighting is that your work is not traceable for anyone who is interested in acquiring information regarding copyright ownership. This will hinder your ability to make the material available to someone who may want to pay you for recording one of your songs. That is why I strongly suggest you fill out copyright forms.

COPYRIGHT FORMS

These forms are obtained from The United States Library of Congress by writing to: ➔

You can also call **202-707-3000 or (202) 707-9100** for information on all the forms available. If you have access to the Internet you can download forms by typing in >**http:\\www.loc.gov.**

> **REGISTER OF COPYRIGHTS**
>
> **COPYRIGHT OFFICE**
>
> **LIBRARY OF CONGRESS**
>
> **WASHINGTON D.C.**
>
> **20559-6000**

HOW TO FILL THE FORMS OUT

To copyright a song you will need to fill out **FORM PA**. This is the application form created by the Copyright Office for the registration of works that fall into the category of Performing Arts. The form must be filled out exactly as the copyright office requires or it will be sent back to you along with a note that checks off what you have omitted or filled out incorrectly.

You should note that your written work will be not considered copyrighted until the office receives your completed form, a check for $20 and a copy of the work. It can take months before you are assigned a copyright number so I advise you to make sure you have the form filled out correctly before you send it in. If it does come back for corrections it can delay the copyright for a few more months.

Your work can be sent in written on sheet music or by a recording of the song on tape. The tape does not have to be a master from the recording studio. A relatively decent recording made in your rehearsal room will be sufficient.

The following example will be a copy of **FORM PA** filled out and then explained so that in case some of your information differs from mine you will know what to write in. I will use the fictitious band SUCTION along with their fictitious names and addresses so that I can fill in the blanks. Note that for the purpose of this example I will establish that all the members of the band will list themselves as the writers of the song. I will do this because if you encounter the same, you will find that Form PA only gives three spaces for authors. If there is a fourth author that needs to be listed then you will need to ask for **FORM ___ /CON** which is the continuation form for **FORM PA.**

FORM PA

For a Work of the Performing Arts
UNITED STATES COPYRIGHT OFFICE

REGISTRATION NUMBER

_____

PA _____ PAU _____

EFFECTIVE DATE OF REGISTRATION

_____

Month _____ Day _____ Year _____

DO NOT WRITE ABOVE THIS LINE. IF YOU NEED MORE SPACE, USE A SEPARATE CONTINUATION SHEET.

1

TITLE OF THIS WORK ▼

Sway

PREVIOUS OR ALTERNATIVE TITLES ▼

NATURE OF THIS WORK ▼ See instructions

2

NAME OF AUTHOR ▼

a) Troy McCoy

DATES OF BIRTH AND DEATH
Year Born ▼ 1971 Year Died ▼

Was this contribution to the work a "work made for hire"?
☐ Yes
☑ No

AUTHOR'S NATIONALITY OR DOMICILE
Name of Country
OR { Citizen of ▶ USA
Domiciled in ▶ USA

WAS THIS AUTHOR'S CONTRIBUTION TO THE WORK
Anonymous? ☐ Yes ☑ No
Pseudonymous? ☐ Yes ☑ No
If the answer to either of these questions is "Yes," see detailed instructions.

NATURE OF AUTHORSHIP Briefly describe nature of material created by this author in which copyright is claimed. ▼
MUSIC

NAME OF AUTHOR ▼

b) Kelly McCoy

DATES OF BIRTH AND DEATH
Year Born ▼ 1971 Year Died ▼

Was this contribution to the work a "work made for hire"?
☐ Yes
☑ No

AUTHOR'S NATIONALITY OR DOMICILE
Name of Country
OR { Citizen of ▶ USA
Domiciled in ▶ USA

WAS THIS AUTHOR'S CONTRIBUTION TO THE WORK
Anonymous? ☐ Yes ☑ No
Pseudonymous? ☐ Yes ☑ No
If the answer to either of these questions is "Yes," see detailed instructions.

NATURE OF AUTHORSHIP Briefly describe nature of material created by this author in which copyright is claimed. ▼
LYRICS

NAME OF AUTHOR ▼

c) Chris Tanner

DATES OF BIRTH AND DEATH
Year Born ▼ 1972 Year Died ▼

Was this contribution to the work a "work made for hire"?
☐ Yes
☑ No

AUTHOR'S NATIONALITY OR DOMICILE
Name of Country
OR { Citizen of ▶ USA
Domiciled in ▶ USA

WAS THIS AUTHOR'S CONTRIBUTION TO THE WORK
Anonymous? ☐ Yes ☑ No
Pseudonymous? ☐ Yes ☑ No
If the answer to either of these questions is "Yes," see detailed instructions.

NATURE OF AUTHORSHIP Briefly describe nature of material created by this author in which copyright is claimed. ▼
MUSIC

NOTE
Under the law, the "author" of a "work made for hire" is generally the employer, not the employee (see instructions). For any part of this work that was "made for hire" check "Yes" in the space provided, give the employer (or other person for whom the work was prepared) as "Author" of that part, and leave the space for dates of birth and death blank.

3

a) **YEAR IN WHICH CREATION OF THIS WORK WAS COMPLETED** This information must be given ◀ Year in all cases.
1997

b) **DATE AND NATION OF FIRST PUBLICATION OF THIS PARTICULAR WORK** Complete this information ONLY if this work has been published.
Month ▶ _____ Day ▶ _____ Year ▶ _____
◀ Nation

4

a) **COPYRIGHT CLAIMANT(S)** Name and address must be given even if the claimant is the same as the author given in space 2. ▼

Troy McCoy 631 E 57ᴿ St Brookly N.Y 11234
Kelly McCoy 631 E 57ᴿ St Brooklyn N.Y 11234

b) **TRANSFER** If the claimant(s) named here in space 4 is (are) different from the author(s) named in space 2, give a brief statement of how the claimant(s) obtained ownership of the copyright. ▼

See instructions before completing this space.

APPLICATION RECEIVED

_____

ONE DEPOSIT RECEIVED

_____

TWO DEPOSITS RECEIVED

_____

FUNDS RECEIVED

DO NOT WRITE HERE
OFFICE USE ONLY

MORE ON BACK ▶
• Complete all applicable spaces (numbers 5-9) on the reverse side of this page.
• See detailed instructions.   • Sign the form at line 8.

DO NOT WRITE HERE

DO NOT WRITE ABOVE THIS LINE. IF YOU NEED MORE SPACE, USE A SEPARATE CONTINUATION SHEET.

PREVIOUS REGISTRATION Has registration for this work, or for an earlier version of this work, already been made in the Copyright Office?

☐ **Yes** ☒ **No** If your answer is "Yes," why is another registration being sought? (Check appropriate box) ▼

a. ☐ This is the first published edition of a work previously registered in unpublished form.

b. ☐ This is the first application submitted by this author as copyright claimant.

c. ☐ This is a changed version of the work, as shown by space 6 on this application.

If your answer is "Yes," give: **Previous Registration Number** ▼   **Year of Registration** ▼

DERIVATIVE WORK OR COMPILATION Complete both space 6a and 6b for a derivative work; complete only 6b for a compilation.

a. Preexisting Material Identify any preexisting work or works that this work is based on or incorporates. ▼

b. Material Added to This Work Give a brief, general statement of the material that has been added to this work and in which copyright is claimed. ▼

See instructions before completing this space.

DEPOSIT ACCOUNT If the registration fee is to be charged to a Deposit Account established in the Copyright Office, give name and number of Account.

Name ▼   **Account Number** ▼

CORRESPONDENCE Give name and address to which correspondence about this application should be sent.   Name/Address/Apt/City/State/ZIP ▼

Kelly McCoy
631 E 57ᴿ ST
Brooklyn N.Y 11234

Area Code and Daytime Telephone Number ▶   Fax Number ▶

CERTIFICATION* I, the undersigned, hereby certify that I am the

Check only one ▼

☒ author

☐ other copyright claimant

☐ owner of exclusive right(s)

☐ authorized agent of _____ *Kelly McCoy*

Name of author or other copyright claimant, or owner of exclusive right(s) ▲

of the work identified in this application and that the statements made by me in this application are correct to the best of my knowledge.

Typed or printed name and date ▼ If this application gives a date of publication in space 3, do not sign and submit it before that date.

Kelly McCoy   Date ▶ 16.11.97

Handwritten signature (X) ▼

Kelly McCoy

Mail certificate to:

Name ▼
Kelly McCoy

Number/Street/Apt ▼
631 E 57ᴿ ST

Certificate will be mailed in window envelope

City/State/ZIP ▼
Brooklyn N.Y 11234

*17 U.S.C. § 506(e): Any person who knowingly makes a false representation of a material fact in the application for copyright registration provided for by section 409, or in any written statement filed in connection with the application, shall be fined not more than $2,500.

CONTINUATION SHEET FOR APPLICATION FORMS

- This Continuation Sheet is used in conjunction with Forms CA, PA, SE, SR, TX, and VA **only.** Indicate which basic form you are continuing in the space in the upper right-hand corner.

- If at all possible, try to fit the information called for into the spaces provided on the basic form.

- If you do not have space enough for all the information you need to give on the basic form, use this Continuation Sheet and submit it with the basic form.

- If you submit this Continuation Sheet, clip (do not tape or staple) it to the basic form and fold the two together before submitting them.

- Part A of this sheet is intended to identify the basic application.
  Part B is a continuation of Space 2 on the basic application.
  Part C (on the reverse side of this sheet) is for the continuation of Spaces 1, 4, or 6 on the basic application.

DO NOT WRITE ABOVE THIS LINE. FOR COPYRIGHT OFFICE USE ONLY

A — Identification of Application

IDENTIFICATION OF CONTINUATION SHEET: This sheet is a continuation of the application for copyright registration on the basic form submitted for the following work:

- TITLE: (Give the title as given under the heading "Title of this Work" in Space 1 of the basic form.)

Sway

- NAME(S) AND ADDRESS(ES) OF COPYRIGHT CLAIMANT(S) : (Give the name and address of at least one copyright claimant as given in Space 4 of the basic form.)

KELLY McCoy

B — Continuation of Space 2

d

NAME OF AUTHOR ▼	DATES OF BIRTH AND DEATH
William Trivelli	Year Born▼ 1970 Year Died▼

Was this contribution to the work a "work made for hire"?
☐ Yes
☑ No

AUTHOR'S NATIONALITY OR DOMICILE Name of Country
OR Citizen of ▶ USA
Domiciled in ▶ USA

WAS THIS AUTHOR'S CONTRIBUTION TO THE WORK
Anonymous? ☐ Yes ☑ No
Pseudonymous? ☐ Yes ☑ No
If the answer to either of these questions is "Yes" see detailed instructions.

NATURE OF AUTHORSHIP Briefly describe nature of the material created by the author in which copyright is claimed. ▼
Co author of Music

e

NAME OF AUTHOR ▼	DATES OF BIRTH AND DEATH
	Year Born▼ Year Died▼

Was this contribution to the work a "work made for hire"?
☐ Yes
☐ No

AUTHOR'S NATIONALITY OR DOMICILE Name of Country
OR Citizen of ▶ _____
Domiciled in ▶ _____

WAS THIS AUTHOR'S CONTRIBUTION TO THE WORK
Anonymous? ☐ Yes ☐ No
Pseudonymous? ☐ Yes ☐ No
If the answer to either of these questions is "Yes" see detailed instructions.

NATURE OF AUTHORSHIP Briefly describe nature of the material created by the author in which copyright is claimed. ▼

f

NAME OF AUTHOR ▼	DATES OF BIRTH AND DEATH
	Year Born▼ Year Died▼

Was this contribution to the work a "work made for hire"?
☐ Yes
☐ No

AUTHOR'S NATIONALITY OR DOMICILE Name of Country
OR Citizen of ▶ _____
Domiciled in ▶ _____

WAS THIS AUTHOR'S CONTRIBUTION TO THE WORK
Anonymous? ☐ Yes ☐ No
Pseudonymous? ☐ Yes ☐ No
If the answer to either of these questions is "Yes" see detailed instructions.

NATURE OF AUTHORSHIP Briefly describe nature of the material created by the author in which copyright is claimed. ▼

Use the reverse side of this sheet if you need more space for continuation of Spaces 1, 4, or 6 of the basic form.

CONTINUATION OF (Check which): ☐ Space 1 ☐ Space 4 ☐ Space 6

C

**Continuation
of other
Spaces**

**MAIL
TO**

**Certificate
will be
mailed in
window
envelope**

Name ▼

Kelly McCoy

Number/Street/Apt ▼

631 E 57ᵗʰ ST

City/State/ZIP ▼

Brooklyn N.Y 11234

D

**Address for
return of
certificate**

August 1995–150,000

☆U.S.COPYRIGHT OFFICE WWW FORM: 1995

TITLE OF THIS WORK:

Write the title of your song

PREVIOUS OR ALTERNATE TITLE:

Leave this line blank unless you have copyrighted the song before under a different title. If you title a song "My Girl is Red Hot" and it becomes a hit there is a chance that a female might want to cover it one day but alter the gender and change the title to "My Guy Is Red Hot" If you assume this might happen you would list this as an alternative title so that if a third party should search for its copyright origination and never heard your first version they will be able to find it listed as your song under the alternative title.

NATURE OF THIS WORK:

If you are submitting a song that contains both lyrics and music write *Words and Music*. If it is an instrumental than just write *Music*. If it's just words you're submitting just write *Song Lyrics*.

NAME OF AUTHOR:

List your name in full (first, middle, last)

DATES OF BIRTH AND DEATH:

List the year you were born and if you're still alive leave "year died" blank. If you are submitting work on behalf of a deceased author, fill in the year of his death.

Was this contribution to the work "made for hire:"

A "work made for hire" is material you write either under contract to someone else or in the case where you might be an employee and this was part of your job. For instance, a theme song for a movie or a TV commercial. You are considered the creator of the work but by contract and under the copyright law the author will be your employer.

There are nine categories of work for hire. They are as follows:

1) Contribution to a collective work; 2) Part of a Motion Picture or other audio visual work; 3) Translation; 4) Supplementary work; 5) Compilation; 6) Instructional text; 7) Test; 8) Answer material for a test; 9) An Atlas

Under the normal conditions of you writing the song for yourself, just check No. If you checked yes, you must give the full legal name of the employer.

AUTHOR'S NATIONALITY OR DOMICILE:

Write in the Country you are a citizen of. In this case it would be USA.

WAS THIS AUTHOR'S CONTRIBUTION TO THE WORK ANONYMOUS OR PSEUDONYMOUS:

If the author's name is not identified with the work it is considered anonymous. If the author is identified with this work under a fictitious name, then it's pseudonymous. If either of these apply check Yes. If you checked yes then in the line above (**Name of Author**) either leave the line blank or write anonymous next to your name. If you checked Pseudonymous then in the line above (**Name of Author**) write your fictitious name with the word "pseudonymous" next to it.

If you want to be known by your real name as the author which I would imagine you would, check No.

NATURE OF AUTHORSHIP.

Whichever part of the song you wrote, whether it's the **Words & Music**, or just **Words** or just **Music**, write that in. As you see in the form on the previous pages, songs that are co-authored need to have these lines specified by each individual contribution. If two or more authors work on the lyrics and music together, they will then fill in **co-author Words & Music.**

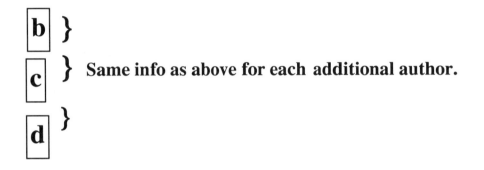

3 a YEAR IN WHICH CREATION OF THIS WORK WAS COMPLETED:

Fill in the year that you completed writing the song. If you wrote the lyrics in 1987 and completed it with music in 1993 then list 1993 as the year.

b DATE AND NATION OF FIRST PUBLICATION OF THIS WORK:

As the instructions say, unless the song has been published don't fill anything in.

4 COPYRIGHT CLAIMANTS:

If you wrote the song and have not transferred it to anyone as you would when you sign a publishing deal, then list *your* name and address. If you had assigned it to a publisher, the publisher would probably be filling this out for you and would list the name of the publishing company followed by "By written contract" above the line that says **Transfer**. In the scenario where there are multiple authors then list at least two names under copyright claimant.

PREVIOUS REGISTRATION   5

If this is the first time you're registering the song, just check No and move on. If you had submitted this song previously and obtained a copyright and are now resubmitting it, for reasons that you have changed the lyrics or you are adding portions to the song, then check yes. Right below, fill in the registration # from the previous copyright.

DERIVATIVE WORK OR COMPILATION: **6**

If you borrowed music or based some of the melodies on older pieces of work you list the song title of the borrowed piece on line 6a.

On line 6b below, **Material Added to This Work,** you would add what you borrowed and what you changed for instance: "Revision of melody, added new words".

DEPOSIT ACCOUNT: **7**

You would leave this blank unless you have an account set up where your copyright fee can be withdrawn. This only applies to people who copyright material on a frequent basis like a Publishing Co.

CORRESPONDENCE:

In case the application needs to be sent back to you, fill in your name and address. The name and address here can be different than the names on the front if in fact you have someone like a manager that takes care of copyright registration. Make sure you list your area code and telephone number below the last line.

CERTIFICATION*:   **8**

The copyright office requires your handwritten signature on the application stating whether are the author of the song check author. Type and clearly hand write your name/s below a long with the date.

Where it says "Handwritten signature" Sign your name.

MAIL CERTIFICATE TO: **9**

Here you will fill in the name and address of where you want the stamped and registered copyright form to go to. If you are the sole author and are handling this yourself fill your name in. If you are part of a group and have co-authored the song have the band liaison or manager that handles all the files receive it.

****

Upon completion make out your check of $20 to Register of Copyright and mail it to the Library of Congress.

If you have filled everything out correctly give it about 2-4 months before you receive your forms back with the registration #.

This exercise needs to done for each and every song you want to copyright. Now I know what you are thinking. If I make a demo with 8 songs will it cost me $20 to copyright each song for a total of $160? Good question. The answer is no not at all. There is a form called **FORM CA** that you can use to register many songs at once. What you need to do is the following. Instead of sending in one song for copyright make a cassette with all the songs on it. When you fill out **FORM PA** in Section 1 where it says **TITLE OF THIS WORK,** instead of writing in the title of one song, write in a phrase that describes the group of songs you're sending in. For instance you can call it "SUCTION SESSIONS" or "PLUNGE OF ALLEGIANCE," or whatever you want.

There are a few drawbacks as follows:

 ALL THE SONGS MUST HAVE THE SAME COPYRIGHT CLAIMANT.

This means that all the songs must either belong to the same publisher or if they are "work for hire" they should be for the same employer.

 ALL THE SONGS MUST HAVE BEEN WRITTEN BY THE SAME AUTHOR AND IF THERE WERE MORE THAN ONE AUTHOR AT LEAST ONE OF THEM HAS TO HAVE WRITTEN AT LEAST A PART OF EVERY SONG IN THE COLLECTION.

So if the demo in question has 8 songs, 7 of them were written by the singer but the eighth was written by the drummer, you can't submit them on a **FORM CA.** What you can do is submit the 7 as a collective work on **FORM CA** and then submit the eighth by itself on **FORM PA.** This will still save you a great deal of money.

Fill the rest of **FORM PA** out the same exact way and mail it in. When it comes back to you in three months, take out your **FORM CA** (which you should order at the same time you order your **FORM PA**), and fill it out as follows:

FORM CA

A **TITLE OF WORK:**   Plunge Of Allegiance (The same as on the FORM PA)

REGISTRATION NUMBER: Copy over the # from the FORM PA you just received back.

NAME(S) OF AUTHOR: Copy the name/s from section 4 of FORM PA "copyright claimant"

B **LOCATION AND NATURE OF INCORRECT INFORMATION:**

Leave this part blank unless you have to correct an error made in the original FORM PA. If you are correcting a mistake, list the line # and Line heading the mistake was on, followed on the next line by the corrected information followed by the explanation of the correction.

C **LOCATION AND NATURE OF INFORMATION IN REGISTRATION TO BE AMPLIFIED:**

Line Number............................. Line Heading or Description...........................

Here you fill in   line #1   and "Title of This Work" in the space above.

Then below where it says **Amplified Information,** fill in each separate title of each of the individual songs in the collection. **FORM CA** also costs $20 which you will include and mail it back in. So for a total cost of $40 you have copyrighted $160 worth of material. Of course if you want to do this with 15 or 30 songs the savings only increase much more dramatically.

Now that you are copyrighted make sure that whenever you send out your material, you signify it's copyright by printing:

Copyright © 1997 (or whatever year) by Troy McCoy

LENGTH OF COPYRIGHT

If all goes well and your song becomes copyrighted you will own that copyright for your entire life plus fifty years after you die. So in effect if you live to be 80 years old and the song becomes a hit in the year 2110, your great, great grandchildren can reap its rewards. This will apply however only to songs that receive their copyright after Dec. 31 1977, when the copyright laws changed to expand this length of time.

YOUR RIGHTS AS A COPYRIGHT HOLDER

There are five exclusive "rights to do and have others do" that the U.S. Copyright Act gives you, the owner of your songs. They are as follows:

© **THE RIGHT TO REPRODUCE THE COPYRIGHTED WORK IN COPIES OR PHONORECORDS.**

This gives you the right to (and to authorize others to) reproduce copies of your song. This can be in the form of Records, Tapes, CD's, D.A.T. or whatever audio technology they come up with in the future. This also gives you the right to reproduce sheet music. If someone else wants to reproduce your song they will have to contact you, get permission and of course arrange the proper payment.

© **THE RIGHT TO PREPARE DERIVATIVE WORKS BASED UPON THE COPYRIGHTED WORK.**

Very simply, if you take a piece of music that is in public domain which means that the copyright has passed its statute of limitation and is no longer held by the original writer as in the case of a song that was written 150 years ago. If you put new lyrics to the old music you may obtain a copyright on that piece of work. This does not imply that you now own the music. That still remains in public domain; however your arrangement will be protected by your copyright.

Another example would be if you have a piece of copyrighted music that was popular. Some author comes along and gets your permission to use the music adding their own lyrics and it becomes popular. This has now become a derivative work which can be copyrighted. This will be good for you because now you have a second source of income from your one song.

© **THE RIGHT TO DISTRIBUTE COPIES OR PHONORECORDS OF THE COPY-RIGHTED WORK TO THE PUBLIC BY SALE OR OTHER TRANSFER OF OWNERSHIP, OR BY RENTAL, LEASE OR LENDING.**

What this means is that not only do you have the right to make copies of your work, but you have the right to give others permission to copy your work such as publishing companies and record companies.

© **THE RIGHT TO PERFORM THE COPYRIGHTED WORK PUBLICLY, IN THE CASE OF LITERARY, MUSICAL, DRAMATIC AND CHOREOGRAPHIC WORKS, PANTOMIMES, MOTION PICTURES AND OTHER AUDIOVISUAL WORKS.**

This is your right to perform your music publicly and no one else. However much of an artist's income is generated from the performance of their music via the radio, jukeboxes, DJ's etc. While it is difficult to track all the cover bands that may be playing your material, there are three performance rights societies that are watchdogs for the rights of copyright holders. You may have heard of them; they are ASCAP, BMI and SESAC. They charge licensing fees to whomever uses music publicly like stadiums, convention halls, roller skating rinks, radio stations, bars and night clubs, concert halls, TV and more. The fees collected are then divided up among all the songwriters that belong to these respective societies. Each society has their own way of monitoring, collecting and dividing up the money.

You will have no need to worry about joining up with a performance rights society until such time as you have a song that is about to be featured in any one if not all of these examples.

For more information on these societies you can write to them at:

- ### ASCAP:
  1 LINCOLN PLAZA • NEW YORK, NY 10023 (212) 621-6000

- ### BMI
  320 W 57TH ST • NEW YORK, NY 10019 (212) 586-2000

- ### SESAC
  421 W 54TH ST, 4TH FLOOR • NEW YORK, NY 10019 (212) 586-3450

When the time come for you to consider joining one of these societies there are a few things you should ask them about so that you can judge for yourself which one would best suit you.. Here are a few slected questions to ask:

Can I become a member if I am not signed to a label?

What is the length of your contract agreements?

Can I become a member if I do not have a song on the radio?

What are all the different formats you survey and what formats do I collect on. How do I know what radio stations, clubs, performances fall into your survey?

Must I have all my songs registered with you or can I have other songs listed with the other societies?

Are there penalities and what are they if I leave for another society during our contract?

If I leave can I take my songs that are registered to you with me?

© **THE RIGHT TO DISPLAY THE COPYRIGHTED WORK PUBLICLY, IN THE CASE OF LITERARY, MUSICAL, DRAMATIC, CHOREOGRAPHIC WORKS, PANTOMIMES, PICTORIAL, GRAPHIC OR SCULPTURAL WORKS, INCLUDING THE INDIVIDUAL IMAGES OF A MOTION PICTURE OR OTHER AUDIOVISUAL WORK.**

This right deals with the use of your music for visual display rather than audio. For instance the printing of your lyrics on a t-shirt to the use of a piece of sheet music in a book. Even karaoke which displays your lyrics across a screen as the music is played in the background has to get a license and pay for its use.

So to sum it all up, be careful when you write a song that you use original ideas instead of copying licks or lyrics from previously recorded material. This will either create an infringement on another artist's rights or you will have to go through a search process to locate the artist and make an arrangement to use their song. This has happened before to famous artists such as Michael Jackson and George Harrison to name a few, that have been sued (at times successfully) by unknown writers that claim their original composition written years prior was the basis for the stars hit song.

It is entirely possible that two people can write a similar piece of music. It is also possible that they both can be written about the same time of each other and even sent in for copyright around the same time. Should one of them become a hit, a successful lawsuit would have to depend on the proximity of both songwriters to each other and if either one of them has any connection with the other. If one writer lived in Alaska and the other in Key West, you can bet that the suit would be dropped. On the other hand, if a relative of the writer in Alaska were to take a vacation in Florida and had a tape of the song with them, which was played on the beach while the other songwriter was at the same beach looking for musical inspiration, the suit will have merit so long as this ridiculous scenario can be proven.

Copyright your songs in bulk if you are prolific and write more than 1 or two a year.

Whenever you submit material to anyone make sure you list the © to acknowledge that it is copyrighted.

"Hey Spike, you should have made the sign bigger"

11

MERCHANDISING

If you look through your dresser drawers I'm sure you'll find at least one if not many, T-shirts displaying a band name or logo. Maybe you own a baseball cap or a bumper sticker or even a key chain or bottle cap opener with your favorite band's name and logo on it. Whether you purchased it at a store on main street or at the concert itself, you have bought into the secondary form of income for bands known as merchandising. It doesn't matter whether the band is a huge national act or a young unknown act, they both rely heavily on the income and advertising that results from their merchandising.

THE KEY TO SUCCESSFUL MERCHANDISING RELIES ON TWO FACTORS.

THE POPULARITY OF THE BAND

THE LOOK, QUALITY AND PRICE OF THE MERCHANDISE

Popular bands that are on tour generate a great deal of merchandising sales mainly due to the fact that their fans want mementos of the show. How much overall merchandise they will sell will be determined by how many people attend the event and how cool the merchandise is. There are some really clever bands out there that have done more than just make merchandise with their name on it. They have created a look that defines the band and the fans want to inherit that look for themselves.

As far as T-shirts are concerned, the fact is people always need clothing. For an average price of **$10** for a T-shirt for a club band and **$18-$30** for a national act T-shirt, you're not talking about a major investment on the fan's part. For an unknown band, selling T-shirts is a challenge that requires designing a look that attracts the consumer.

The investment into T-shirts are large and the return is usually small (after all the giveaways) and the sales are few and far between. Yet ultimately it is very important to merchandise yourself not only for the little profit you might make, but for the advertising of your band which in my opinion is the most important. If you disagree, then what band immediately comes to mind when you see a tie-dye T-shirt?

Unlike the national acts that have merchandising deals with companies like Brockum or Winterland to manufacture and sell products at shows for a cut of the profits, unknown acts must make their own investment, sell the merchandise themselves, account for their own money and keep track of their own profit so that they can reinvest and make more T-shirts. In this chapter I want to discuss the two most common merchandising items, T-shirts and CD's or cassettes and how to present them to the public for sale.

T-SHIRTS

T-shirts are first and fore most one of the most impotent marketing tools you can have. If the designs are hip and people wear them, the advertising punch that this has is immeasurable. But it comes with a price. T-shirts are expensive to make. And because they are expensive they should be handled and designed very carefully. Careful considerations must be given to everything from the color of the shirt, what size they should be, what kind of design you should have where it should go on the shirt, what material the shirt should be made from and finally, who will you hire to do the screen printing.

SHIRT COLOR

Approximately 90% of all the music t-shirts sold are on black or white colored shirts.

I don't know why. There are some great colored shirts out there but they really do not sell that well. If I had to guess I would say the colored artwork look best on black or white. They are also the cheapest shirt to by from the manufacturer so their retail cost is lower than a custom dye or stock colored shirt. Whatever the reason, go with the stats. Your investment will be large and you want to make your money back. Do not experiment with colors that may or may not sell.

SIZE OF THE SHIRT

If statistics are our guide then lets use them here as well. The most popular sizes by far are large and extra large. Small and medium do not sell well they are too small for the average adult fan. As far as the oversized shirts like xxl, they are more expensive to buy than the L and XL and unless your fan base is made up of Sumo wrestlers, they won't sell.

QUANTITY

So you want to place an order. The salesman is showing you all these price breakdowns based on how many dozens you buy. Sure buying one hundred dozen will get you a great price but where are you going to get the money to pay for them. Besides unless you are a national touring act and playing 300 dates a year you are going to have these shirts around for a long time. Some will get damaged, stolen and many will get given away. In the end you will never recoup your investment.

Ordering in quantities of 6-12 dozen are the most sensible way to get started. These amount are small enough to unload over a period of a few months and will give you a chance to test out your designs and see if they are popular. I suppose the best argument for not printing higher quantities would be the problem of a design that is just not going over well with the consumer. You are selling these shirts in hopes of having people wear them.

THE SILK SCREEN

Have you ever bought a shirt and found the artwork to be a thick glob of paint that wears heavy on the skin despite many washing? This is probably a result of too many colors, poor application and bad advice from your screen printer. To avoid this, make sure that you get samples of their work, preferably sample that contain similar colors on the specific shirt you are considering.

THE SHIRT

Have you ever noticed how some garments are soft to the touch while others are stiff? Or that some wear out fast while some retain their color for a long time? Dye, yarn, fabric all play an important role in how a shirt wears. When you look through your collection of band T-shirts you may notice that the shirts manufacturers name tag has been replaced by the T-shirt company that does the groups merchandising. This is too bad because it would aid your decision in choosing which manufacturer to go with.

There is a wide assortment of manufacturing companies that make a wide assortment of shirts. Some that are 100% cotton while some are a blend of polyester and cotton. You will find that one companies 100% cotton feels entirely different than another. Try to look at as many sample of shirts as possible before making a decision. Find out how each shirts wears and compare. Some really soft shirts are that way because they are made from a thin weave and will fall apart after a few washings.

To answer the question of which shirt manufacturer I recommend, I think that it is really up to your taste and budget. For me, I have always used shirts manufactured by Anvil or Oneita. They are very good quality, mid priced shirts commonly used by screen printers. I would advise against using shirts whose names are synonymous with underwear. This is strictly a personal thing but to me it clashes with the desire to put out a hip line of outerwear.

CHOOSING A SILK SCREENER

When you are ready to make shirts, you will have to put a lot of consideration into who will do the printing. It is from a wealth of experience that I convey the importance of choosing someone reputable. You will be relying on them to reproduce your designs to your exact specification, on the quality shirts you have chosen and printed at the time and date that you were promised.

When choosing a printer, use reputation and recommendation as your guide. Don't judge a company by it's size as to whether or not they can do a good job for you. Some big screen printers may not give your small order the attention it requires while a small firm may not have the shirt selection or competitive price.

With regard to production schedules, it is vital that you are assured of prompt delivery of your order. What a disaster it would be if the hundreds of dollars of T-shirts you had made for the upcoming road trip is lost because the shirts aren't printed yet.

CHOOSE YOUR SILK SCREENER CAREFULLY!

Interview them. Ask for a client list so that you can check them out. Ask to see a selection of shirts and compare their prices to other printers. When comparing pricing you should be comparing the same shirt manufacturer otherwise you will not get a fair comparison.

There are thousands of silk screeners around. As in any service business some printers are very reputable and some are not. Your best bet is to use a local printer. Get recommendations from local businesses that have printed shirts like a service station or restaurant. If you need to search outside your local area you can search the Internet or check out the ads in the back of rock and roll publications. But truthfully you have no way of qualifying them. So if you cannot find a decent local screen printer take a recommendation from me. The following source is the printer that I use. Aside from their independent t-shirts printing service, they hold licenses to print shirts for Playboy and other prominent companies. Just call Phil and tell him about this referral.

PRICING

When you are selling merchandise you need to understand some fundamental business concepts in order to be successful. Success can be measured in different ways. One way is by how much money you make. Another is by how much volume you sell. For your purposes, the latter is more applicable. The more T-shirts you can push out, the more people are wearing them and the more advertising you are doing. This can translate into more ticket sales at your shows. While it is true that the overall profit is being deferred until a later date, if you go through a full run of T-shirts and break even or even make a few dollars, then you are successful.

Since you are doing this mainly to advertise yourself, there are going to be situations where you will be giving away product. If you take into account what your cost is (on the first run your cost will be higher to include set up fees) and how much you can sell it for, you will be able to come up with an amount of free merchandise you can allot yourself before you begin to lose money. Remember your goal is to get your shirts out there and also to recoup your initial investment so that you can make a second and third run of shirts.

So if you buy **100** shirts for **$6** each your total cost is **$600**.

$$\$6 \times 100 = \$600$$

If you sell all of them at **$10** each your total possible gross is **$1000**

$$\$10 \times 100 + \$1000$$

The first **60** shirts sold at **$10** will recoup back your initial investment of **$600**.

$$60 \times \$10 = \$600$$

This will leave you with **40** shirts that if sold at **$10** each would represent a total profit of **$400** that can be used for sale or which you can use for giveaways.

$$40 \times \$10 = \$400$$

RETAILING

In a retail business, the standard formula for figuring out your sale cost is to double or triple your purchase cost. This is done to incorporate into the sale price the cost of doing business; mainly rent, utilities and payroll, etc. So for example if you buy an item at **$6** you should sell it for **$12-$18**.

We need to alter this formula slightly here because we are affected by one constant factor. There is a unwritten fixed price rate for T-shirt sales for unsigned bands. This price is around **$10** a shirt. Under normal conditions, the public will not pay much more than this. The average wholesale cost (your cost of manufacturing) for a two sided printed T-shirt is around **$6** (Depending on the amount of shirts you run off, the price will be either a bit higher or lower). So the formula is slightly off since you have to sell them for less than twice the cost.

But this is okay because other than the cost of the product, you do not have any operating costs like rent or utilities that need to be paid so you can make less than double and still end up with the same percentage of profit.

As I alluded to earlier, included in the cost of your first run of shirts is the art work and setup fee to make the screens. This is a one time charge usually around twenty five dollars per screen. You will need a separate screen made for each image you want on the shirt. So if the front logo is different than the back logo you will need 2 screens. If the logo requires more than one color, you will need a screen made for each color. One way around this expensive, multiple color dilemma is to avoid color separation by using one screen and applying multiple colors to the screen with a gradation method. This will work extremely well if for instance you want to create a twilight sky effect. If you apply a coat of dark blue across the top quarter of the screen followed by a lighter blue followed by a red followed by a pink, after a couple of brush strokes the colors will start to flow together forming a really cool visual image. And the best part is that it's 4 color art for the price of one.

Once you figure your profit line, in this case the balance of **40** shirts left over after you sold **60** shirts, make sure that you sell at least an additional 10 for the full price of **$10** each or **$100**. Add to the initial **60** shirts or **$600** you sold and you will be able to increase your next order by **$100** to **$700** worth of shirts, or an extra **16** shirts.

If you do this on a consistent basis, increasing the volume of your order, in time you will be purchasing shirts for a cheaper price and increasing your profit. The key is to keep reinvesting the profit for more product. In the example above, the remaining **30** shirts can be used for either give away or sales at reduced prices for family and friends. The money you earn from the remaining sales should be put into the purchase of more shirts as well.

TAPES

Recording your music and making it available to the public on tape or CD, is the most surefire way of advertising and promoting your band. Record companies have been doing this rather successfully for 75 years.

No matter how cool a T-shirt or poster looks and no matter how great the band name might be, the music is what it is all about. I can safely say that any audience member after seeing a band for the first time will be hard pressed to name songs or sing a passage. But if they had a great time and liked what they heard, they will buy a tape and be able to spend quality time with it and really get into the music.

For bands that do not have record deals but are successfully booking themselves around and are playing to decent size audiences, tape sales have in many cases subsidized their traveling costs. Many bands, create their own sub culture of fans and independently have sold their tapes in huge numbers attracting the big labels to offer them deals.

The major expense is the recording costs for the tapes and if you are pressing CD's then this too is a major expense; as we will discuss in the next chapter.

Whichever medium you're carrying be it CD or cassette, there is a basic price fixed on the retail end at your show. Cassettes usually sell for **$6-$8** and CD's **$10-$12**. These figures are based on a 6-10 song cassette or CD. Most bands can't afford to record more than that and I do not recommend you do.

You must apply the same mathematical formula you used for T-shirts to tapes to figure out how many you need to sell to recoup your investment so that you can determine how much you need to sell to earn profit.

MARKETING YOUR MERCHANDISE AT THE SHOWS

SETTING UP A BOOTH

To sell merchandise at a show you will need to secure an area that has a heavy traffic flow, is within eyesight of the band and near some lighting. This is the ideal situation.

These are some of the things you need to create a good display.

 BAR TABLES TO DISPLAY YOUR WARES

 HANGERS OR A WALL TO HANG THE T-SHIRTS ON

 DUCT TAPE

 OVERHEAD LIGHT FIXTURE WITH HOOK ON CLASP AND EXTENSION CORD

To light up the merchandising table. Use a 40 watt bulb and no higher. You do not want to disturb the ambiance of the room and this will provide enough light for viewing the shirts.

 SIGNS FOR YOUR MERCHANDISE

You should have a large signs that lists all the information. For example:

100% all cotton (large & extra large) **SHIRTS** ▷ *SUCTION* ◁ **Black / White** **$10.00**	**TAPES** *"PLUNGE OF ALLEGIANCE"* 10 new songs **Cassette $8.00** **CD $10.00**

Make smaller signs on cardboard or paper no larger than 5" x 8" that you pin to the T-shirts. They should just read **FRONT** and **BACK** so that when you hang the shirts, the designs will be self explanatory. If you do not have a back logo then an alternative would be   to just write the price of the shirt.

 HAMMER, NAILS, THUMB TACKS, WIRE.

Whether the club has cement walls or wood paneling you are going to have to rig up some way to hang your T-shirts. If the club permits, you can either put thumb tacks in and hang the shirts from them, or hammer in a couple of nails and wrap a wire from one to the other creating a clothes line and hang the shirts from that. If you can't do any of these then use the surface of the display tables and keep the shirts out unfolded.

Most if not all clubs will allow the bands to set up their merchandising. Most will allow you to use one or two of their tables for display and in many cases will have a pre designated place for you to set up. Some places provide a merchandising booth like the VW bus inside Wetlands in NYC, where bands are required to sell their merchandise from.

If you are setting up your own booth you need to plan the display as though you were a merchant setting up a retail store on Main St. Your wares must be displayed clearly, with signs that describe what you are selling and prices listed.

A FEW TIPS ON SETTING UP YOUR MERCHANDISING TABLE

SET UP YOUR MERCHANDISE BOOTH AFTER YOU SOUND CHECK.

Before you pick any spot ask the club manager where they suggest. If at all possible it should be near to the stage or at least within eye sight of the group.

GET SOME BAR TABLES AND SECTION OFF THE AREA

Use the tables for displaying your mailing list, band newsletter, etc. It would be wise to post someone you know and trust to man this area throughout the night. They would be responsible for collecting money on sales as well as answering any band related questions the fans have.

PROCEED TO DISPLAY YOUR SHIRTS

By either adhering them to a wall behind you or across the table in front of you. You might want to put little signs that say **Front** and **Back** so that people know what they are looking at.

DISPLAY YOUR CASSETTES OR CD'S WHICHEVER YOU ARE SELLING.

Remove the music inside leaving the empty case with the cover art. Adhere some duct tape on the back in a way that the sticky part is facing out. Then stick it right on the wall or on the table. Remove the tape or CD so that if someone attempts to rip off the case they won't get the music.

KEEP STORAGE OF EXTRA SHIRTS AND TAPES UNDER THE TABLE.

This is the pile that you will sell from so that your display stays in tact throughout the night.

CLUB PERCENTAGE

Most clubs are cool about letting you set up your merchandising and many will expect a cut of your sales; about **10-25%** to be exact. If they insist on more than that they are way out of line so do not even bother setting up. You may just want to covertly do it from the stage after the set. Even **25%** is high unless the club has their own merchandising booth and will display and sell your wares for you. The clubs that have their own booth will insist that you sell from there and in most cases you are probably better off. You can always raise the price by the percentage cut the club is taking so that you can retain your profit structure.

As far as collection, if you set up your own booth, you may be asked how many shirts you have sold when you get paid. Based on what you say, the percentage will be deducted at that point. If you have used the clubs booth, the club % will be deducted when you pick up the remaining shirts and whatever sales money there may be.

MERCHANDISE ACCOUNTING FORM

When you set up your merchandising, whether you do it at the club's booth or your own, fill out a merchandising account form prior to the start of sales. The form accounts for what merchandise you're selling.

Here is a sample of a merchandise form I used for one of my bands.

T-SHIRT SALES

DATE:_____   VENUE_____

STARTING AMOUNT: _____

AMOUNT SOLD: 1 2 3 4 5 6 7 8 9 10 11 1 2 13 1 4 15 16 17 18 19 20

At what dollar amount: $___ = $___ - venue____% $____ total $____

GIVEAWAYS: __ REMAINING SHIRTS: start __ - sold __ - free __ = __

TAPE SALES

START AMOUNT: CD's ___

AMOUNT SOLD: 1 2 3 4 5 6 7 8 9 10 11 1 2 13 1 4 15 16 17 18 19 20

AT WHAT DOLLAR AMOUNT: $___ = $___ - (venue)____% $____ total $____

GIVE A WAYS: __ REMAINING TAPES: start __ - sold __ - free __ = __

START AMOUNT: CASSETTES_____

AMOUNT SOLD: 1 2 3 4 5 6 7 8 9 10 11 1 2 13 1 4 15 16 17 18 19 20

AT WHAT DOLLAR AMOUNT: $___ = $___ - (venue)____% $____ total $____

GIVEAWAYS: __ REMAINING TAPES: start __ - sold __ - free __ = __

Here's one filled out:

T-SHIRT SALES

DATE: **OCT 11**   VENUE **SIDEBAR**

STARTING AMOUNT: **25**

AMOUNT SOLD: 1 2 3 4 5 6 7 (8) 9 10 11 1 2 13 1 4 15 16 17 18 19

AT WHAT DOLLAR AMOUNT: **$12.** = **$96.** - (venue) **10%** or **$9.60** = total **$86.40**

GIVE A WAYS: **3** REMAINING SHIRTS: Start **25** - **8** sold - **3** free = **14**

TAPE SALES

START AMOUNT: CD's **15**

AMOUNT SOLD: 1 2 3 4 5 6 7 8 9 10 11 (12) 13 1 4 15 16 17 18 19 20

AT WHAT DOLLAR AMOUNT: **$10.** = **$120.** - (venue) **10 %** or **$12.** = total **$108.00**

GIVE A WAYS: **0** REMAINING TAPES: START **15** - SOLD **12** - FREE **0** = **3**

START AMOUNT: CASSETTES **20**

AMOUNT SOLD: 1 2 3 4 5 (6) 7 8 9 10 11 1 2 13 1 4 15 16 17 18 19

AT WHAT DOLLAR AMOUNT: **$8.** = **$48.** - venue **10%** or **4.80** = total **43.20**

194

In the event that you have more than one style or color of t-shirt, just add in an extra column in the T-shirt section. It's a good idea to separate sales of color shirts from white shirts or different logo shirts from each other, to give you an idea as to what is selling and what isn't.

FREE SHIRTS

There is no doubt that you will be accosted at the club from club employees to fans and everyone in-between for free shirts. When that happens what should you do? Well, you have your allotment of free shirts to take from but if you give them away to everyone who asks, you will have nothing left for those you want or need to give to. Always go on the assumption that if someone really wants something they would pay for it and anyone who expects it for free just wants the free and not the thing.

Free shirts should be given to those who do not expect it or ask for it. It should be given to someone who hooks you up and this is your way of thanking them. For instance:

 CLUB MANAGERS THAT GO OUT OF THEIR WAY TO BE COOL.

 HOUSE SOUNDMAN THAT REALLY GIVES YOU A GOOD SOUND CHECK COULD GET ONE AS A TOKEN OF YOUR APPRECIATION.

If you are playing an important show you might consider giving the soundman a shirt prior to sound check only if you think it might make a difference in the attention they give to your set.

 YOU SHOULD RESERVE THE FREE SHIRTS FOR COLLEGE RADIO STATION DJ'S AND PROGRAM MANAGERS AS A WAY TO PROMOTE MORE AIR PLAY.

 INCLUDE T-SHIRTS IN WITH PRESS KITS TO BOOKING AGENTS AND RECORD LABEL PEOPLE.

They are accustomed to this sort of thing and appreciate it. By doing it, shows that you understand the game and can play along.

Fans should pay for merchandise. Sometimes you can lower the price if someone wants to buy a few at one time. Just keep in mind that this stuff cost you money and you need to sell them.

I advise you not to bring more than you need with you to the show. Many times your merchandise can get ruined by drink spillage, spoiled by cigarette smoke, wrinkled or stolen. If you run out during a show and there's still a demand for more, take down names and addresses or give them yours and have them send you a check in the mail. Include $2 for postage and you will send it to them or they can come to the next show where you will have more.

When I got pestered by club personnel for free stuff I would tell them that the shirts were made for the band by an investor who expects an accounting of every shirt, otherwise I have to pay for them myself. Offer them a shirt for cost ($6-$8) instead of the retail price. That is the best you can do.

If you are a good soul and have extra cash just laying around, your last alternative is to print up an extra dozen or two shirts on cheaper 50/50 cotton/poly blend, with a simple one color logo for giveaways only. Do it on a white shirt because they are a bit cheaper than colored and you will make everybody happy.

*We will discuss free tapes and CD's in the next chapter.

12

MANUFACTURING AND RELEASING YOUR MUSIC

Preparing your recorded music as a final product for presentation to the public is a multi-dimensional task. While the recording end of it is probably the most taxing, you need to be aware of all the other ingredients that go into creating the final product.

Keep in mind all of the reasons why you made the tape and all of the people you plan on giving or selling them to. Whether for fans, the press, clubs, representation or record labels, the finished product's appearance and sound quality must achieve a certain level of competitiveness. To achieve this level you will need to focus on much more than the musical content. Choosing the mastering plant to press your product, deciding which is the best format (CD, Cassette or Vinyl) to go with, and the visual image you want to design your product with are all important decisions to consider.

The time when all these considerations should be figured out is around the same time you have decided to go into the studio to record. As you will find out, there is a lot of free time spent in the studio as well as the presence of high artistic energy, so why not use both to tackle the latter half of the process? This way, when the recording process is completed, you can immediately begin manufacturing your product.

In order to send the tapes out for manufacturing, there are certain criteria that you or your studio engineer should adhere to, that will make the transition from master to finished product faster, cheaper and higher in quality.

When you are done mixing, the tape needs to go through some processes before it is ready for mastering and reproduction. The following are some tape preparation guidelines for the different types of formats you may have used.

D.A.T. (DIGITAL FORMAT)

If your masters are recorded on reel to reel (which is the analog format), but have been mixed down to two track and transferred to D.A.T. (which is a digital format), you have done what most bands are doing these days. Digital recording is a process that takes music and transfers it to electronic signals. These signals, when read by the playback machine (which is a type of computer), will analyze the signals and reproduce it back in the exact state it was recorded in. This is why it is such a popular format. There is no generation loss in this process. So, in effect, you can make many duplications of the music and they will always sound as good as the original recording.

Have you ever recorded from one cassette to another and noticed the slight reduction in sound quality from the original to the recorded version. This occurs from analog transfer which is one of the reasons why vinyl records have lost their popularity. They never sounded as good as the master.

If you are planning to mix down to DAT, the following is a preparation list to ensure a high standard of reproduction.

RECORDED ONTO THE DAT, IN THE EXACT ORDER YOU WANT IT TO APPEAR ON THE CD OR CASSETTE.

MAKE SURE THAT THE SPACING BETWEEN EACH SONG IS THE SAME LENGTH OF TIME. THE OPTIMUM TIME SHOULD BE 2 - 4 SECONDS.

AT THE VERY BEGINNING OF THE TAPE, RUN IT ON RECORD FOR ABOUT 15 SECONDS OF PRE LEADER TIME.

At the end, let it run for 15 seconds for post leader time. Set the DAT machine to record and set the levels to peak at 0 (zero) dB for total silence. Make sure that during the mix, the overall volume level is the same for every single song. In other words make sure that when someone listens to your tape, they won't have to keep adjusting the volume because one song is louder than the other.

PREPARE A TIME LOG THAT DOCUMENTS THE BEGINNING AND THE END TIMES OF EACH TRACK ON THE TAPE.

You must include the pre -leader and post leader times as well. For instance:

PROGRAM	TIME	
1. Pre Leader	Start	0:00
	End	0:15
2. 1st Song (title of song)	Start	0:15
	End	3:15
3. 2nd Song " "	Start	3:18
	End	7:25
4. 3rd Song " "	Start	7:28
	End	10:56
5. 4th Song " "	Start	10:59
	End	16:32
6. Last Song " "	Start	16:35
	End	18:51
7. Post Leader	Start	18:54
	End	19:06

The purpose of this log is to help the engineer find and distinguish each song that is on the tape.

CALIBRATION TONES

Depending on where you press your masters, they may or may not need calibration tones on the tape. This tone helps the pressing plant calibrate their duplicating machines to the frequency on your tape. It's like tuning your guitar to an album that you want to play along with at home. If the pressing plant requires a tone it will probably be at -12 dB.

SAMPLING RATE

The DAT format converts the analog signal off the reel to reel and transforms it to digital, by taking a sample of each analog signal. For the resulting DAT copy to sound exactly like the analog master it must take in a certain amount of samples at one time.

If you are going to press CD's, you must be aware that CD's play at a sampling rate of 44.1 kHz, (the sample of the analog signal was taken at 44,100 time per second). Since many DAT decks sample at 48 kHz which is fine for cassette reproduction, it is unacceptable for CD's. A conversion can take place but it can become another extra charge as well as another process added to your recording. You should let your producer know that you have it in your plans to make CD's and ask if you will be recording at the 44.1 kHz sampling rate or not.

LISTEN TO THE DAT MASTER A NUMBER OF TIMES BEFORE YOU SEND IT IN FOR REPRODUCTION.

Listen for any glitches, make sure the song order is how you want it, check for any unwanted sounds or noises and make sure you're happy with the mix.

ANALOG

This is a format where the tape runs along a magnetic surface (heads) like the reel to reel or the cassette. The following is the procedure for duplication.

YOU MUST LEAVE AT LEAST A FEW FEET OF BLANK TAPE AT THE BEGINNING AND AT THE END OF THE TAPE.

Reel to reels need to be threaded into the machine and require extra tape..

WHEREAS DAT MAY NOT REQUIRE A CALIBRATION TONE, ANALOG REQUIRES A SERIES OF ALIGNMENT TONES.

The standard minimum tones are as follows.

a) 1 kHz

b) 10 kHz

c) 100 Hz

all at 0 dB operating level.

As I mentioned earlier, these tones are the means in which the equipment can be measured for functionality and calibration. The tones should be placed on the tape by a machine that is up and running for at least 15 minutes - 1/2 hour, at the beginning of the session and on the same taping machine the recording will be made.

- **IF THE TAPE IS DOLBY ENCODED WITH EITHER DOLBY A OR DOLBY SR (NOISE REDUCTION), YOU MUST PUT IN THE APPROPRIATE DOLBY TONES, OTHERWISE THERE IS NO WAY TO DECODE IT.**

- **REEL TAPE WILL OCCASIONALLY REQUIRE SPLICING. MAKE SURE THE SPLICING IS DONE BY A PROFESSIONAL, OTHERWISE THE TAPE MAY GET CAUGHT IN CERTAIN MACHINES.**

- **LOG SHEET**

  Just like the example on the previous page for DAT but unlike DAT you must include the tones as well as unwanted noises or false starts. This is just to indicate to the pressing engineer what is to be recorded and what is to be eliminated.

In both situations above, I recommend that you consult with your prospective recording engineer that you plan on making CD's and cassettes. They might even be able to recommend a manufacturing plant for you and will know what their requirements are. If not, then at some point during this process you should know who is going to manufacture for you so that the producer can prepare the tapes to their specifications.

Now that your tape is finished the next step is to submit it for pressing.

CHOOSING A MANUFACTURING COMPANY

You have worked very hard recording your demo and have spent countless hours laboring over the mix. It's as good as money and time will allow. But you are only halfway home. You need to find a reputable manufacturing company that will handle your work and reproduce it with the same attention and care you put into its recording.

We all know that the reproduction of the music is just one aspect of putting out a product. There is artwork to consider as well. Whether it's a J-card for cassette or a booklet for the CD, these will have to be designed and printed as well. There are many companies across the country that do everything from tape duplication to art and graphic design and some companies that do both. There are companies that are large in size and do volumes of work and there are smaller companies that take on less clients but give the ones they have quality time and attention.

What you initially have to figure out is what your needs are (tape duplication, graphic design or both) and then shop around for quality and price. The problem that arises sometimes is due to a lack of information; you are stuck using the mastering plants that you find listed in your local phone book. I'm sure that some of them are great companies but some of them are not. What distinguishes a good company from a bad one is that a good one can offer you the following options:

PHONE SUPPORT

Having an educated and patient staff that will guide you through the entire duplicating process.

FORMAT SELECTION

Since there are different formats available to duplicate music onto (CD, Cassette, Vinyl) you should look for a company that can handle any of these processes for all your different needs.

PACKAGING SELECTION

We are all aware of how expensive tape duplication can be. We are also concerned with the problem of deciding whether to make CD's or cassettes or for that matter vinyl. You should look for a company that offers different package deals for one price offering you the best options for your needs and budget.

PRODUCT SAMPLES

You should be able to request and receive samples of their work whether it be music or graphic design they have produced in the past. This is a very good way for you to see and hear their capabilities.

TEST SAMPLES

The production plant should supply you with a test sample before they begin reproduction. This should be a direct copy of your master, from your master, recorded at the same speed on the same machine that your finished product will be manufactured on. If you have any concerns about how your process is going, these test samples should tell you either that everything is okay or that something is not right and needs to be corrected.

PRODUCTION TIME

This is a really important qualification since many of you might want to plan a release party to launch the new music or have made some valuable contacts that are expecting to receive the tape sometime this century. After you have approved the test samples, cassettes should take about 1-2 weeks for completion and 3-4 weeks for CD's. Most of the duplicating companies do not hold themselves accountable for a late delivery so for your own protection plan all release related events well in advance.

In-House Work

I think that it is a very important criterion that the company you choose, perform all the work under their own roof and not send any of it out. If you were to inquire about how your artwork is coming along, you don't want to hear "call back in a week because the printer we sent the work to is on vacation."

A company that offers all the services from art and graphic design to tape duplication, mastering, shrink wrapping and shipping will probably cut you a better deal on price. Look for a company that assigns a personal customer representative to help you coordinate all these options. It will make the whole process easy and painless.

Here are some manufacturing companies in N. America.

DISC MAKERS

(Offices in 5 locations call for free catalog)

(800) 468-9353   www.discmakers.com

THE RECORD FACTORY

Santa Anna Ca (Ask for Sherry)

(800) 3RECORD (714) 241-8801

DIGI ROM N.Y.C.

(800) 815-3444 (212) 730-2111

HEALY DISC/TAG DESIGN GROUP

(Ask for Steve) Ontario Canada (800) 835-1362

DIGITAL DOMAIN NYC NY

(Specialize in Mastering) (800) 344-4361

http://www.digido.com

MEDIA WORKS

Nashville TN (615) 327 - 9114

TRUTONE

Hackensack NJ (201) 489-9180

OMNI SOURCE

PT Claire Canada 800 668-0098

WAVE

Ottawa (800)928-3310

AM Tech Montreal Canada

(800) 777-1927 www.amtechdisc.com

PIERCE RECORDING & MUSIC

Fredricksburg VA (800) 200-2629

DIGITAL FORCE NYC NY

(212) 333- 5953

HERE ARE SOME WEB SITES YOU CAN VISIT

Dynamic Cassette Dup   >http://www.dynrec.com

Oasis Duplication   >http://www.oasiscd.com

Broken Heart Store   >http://www.bheartstore.com (Offices in Tn., Tx., & Wash)

Olde West Recording   >http://www.oldewest.com   1800 739-3000

Opsonic Optic Media   >http://bitstream.com   1800 476-8211   (Minn Mn)

Big Swifty   >http://www.moonsite.com (Rockville CT) 860-871-8719

Tom Parham Prod.   >http://www.tomparham.com 1800 bin loop (California)

Bluehouse Prod.   >http://www.smart.net   301-589 1001

Jackson Sound   >http://wwwjacksonsound.com (Denver Co)

SHIPPING, HANDLING & STORING

BEFORE YOU ATTEMPT TO PUT ANY MASTER TAPE IN THE MAIL, A COPY SHOULD BE MADE AND STORED IN A SAFE PLACE IN CASE IT GETS DESTROYED OR MISPLACED IN THE MAIL.

Do not send the copy however for duplication. You did not spend all that money and time in the studio just to have your merchandise made from a second generation tape.

WHEN SHIPPING YOUR TAPE, NEVER SEND IT REGULAR MAIL.

Use one of the next day shipping companies like Federal Express or UPS that issue you a shipping or tracking number. The tape is fragile and is affected by many things such as extreme weather conditions and magnetic fields. Using these services will reduce the time the tape spends outside its natural environment (the studio). Be sure mark the package, "**FRAGILE**" and "**MAGNETIC MEDIA PLEASE KEEP CONTENTS AWAY FROM ELECTROMAGNETIC FIELDS**" across the envelope.

One of the ways to ruin a tape is to have it scanned with x rays or a metal detector. To ensure it's safety when going on a plane make sure you carry it by hand and give it to the person in charge for a hand inspection.

ARTWORK

The other key finishing touch to the music is the visual presentation of it. Most humans have now evolved to the point where they cannot recognize quality unless it is in a shiny, bright, interesting package. But like everything else there is a price to pay for 4 color art separation and a 10 page insert booklet with full lyrics and pictures. Unless you're Bill Gates, you have to consider and create interesting packaging that will not break your bank account.

This is one area where I feel you can scrimp a bit on production to save yourself money. Considering that cassette duplication will cost you many hundreds of dollars and CD's running into the thousands, you want to make sure that most of that cost goes into the reproduction of the music.

Part of your inquiry into the production plants will cover artwork. Find out how much artwork is part of the package and where the artwork will be featured. All of the places you will want art is as follows:

 CD

The CD itself

The CD insert (front)

The CD insert (back)

CASSETTE

Cassette Label

J-card (cassette insert)

Some manufactures will offer you a package with all this art included in the cost. In some cases you will need to supply the artwork and for an extra fee their graphic designers will do artwork for you. First and foremost consider for what purpose you are using these tapes. If you are going for a big release of your own independent album to be sold to the public, you will have to invest in sharp artwork and insert material. However, if your sole purpose is to shop this as a demo for a deal you should be more concerned about having the vital information like band name, song names and band contact information such as address and phone number. While it's true that a flashy package might get seen before a dull one, record companies face the same expense problems as you do and will certainly appreciate a band that submits a demo of great songs in a package that is creative yet done with an obvious attention to saving money.

Hopefully you have developed a band logo by now and perhaps even have an artist who is helping define your music visually. When sending in artwork remember to have it made camera ready so that the plant's art department can bypass this step that will require it first being sent back to you for approval before production can take place.

Aside from your logo and any visual art you want presented, the following is a checklist of all the information you need printed as well as where they should appear.

 BAND NAME - and contact number directly on the format of your choice: tape, CD, DAT, Vinyl and the packaging they are contained in.

 TITLE OF WORK - On the packaging

TITLE OF THE SONGS - On the Jacket

 CONTACT INFORMATION - (name, address, phone number) on the format and the packaging they appear in.

 COPYRIGHT SYMBOL "©" FOLLOWED BY THE YEAR COPYRIGHT WAS GRANTED - on the format and the packaging

These are the five primary categories that need to be included in the package. Some groups have chosen to put a very simple photograph on the front cover and then put the song titles and contact information directly on the CD or cassette which is a good money saver. Regardless of whether you opt for this style or go on further to a more elaborate set up, you should *always print you name and phone number on the cassette and CD.* Tapes get separated from the box it comes in, and if a music industry executive is a recipient of the tape and there is no name and number on it, it will more than likely end up in the garbage before it ever gets heard.

If you are going forward with a larger insert include the following:

 BAND MEMBER'S NAMES AND CORRESPONDING INSTRUMENTS.

 THE NAME OF THE PERSON WHO PRODUCED THE TAPE FOLLOWED BY THE NAME OF THE ENGINEER, FOLLOWED BY WHERE THE TAPE WAS RECORDED.

 COMPOSITION INFORMATION SUCH AS ALL SONGS WRITTEN BY JAY (track 3) **EXCEPT** (track 4) **WRITTEN BY JAY AND SILENT BOB.**

 RECOGNITION OF THE ARTIST OF THE BAND LOGO OR ART WORK AS WELL AS THE PHOTOGRAPHER.

Thanks and acknowledgments to friends, family members, fans and industry people that have helped you along.

This secondary list can be included with the above list for no extra cost provided that you include it all on the J card for the cassette or split it up between the disc and the front and back insert cards for the CD.

Of course if you do this you will begin to crowd all the information together and should utilize the graphic design capabilities of the duplication plant if you cannot do it yourself.

Finally, there are the lyrics. If you print your lyrics, you will probably have to go to a two or four page insert. Once again, look at all the option plans available to you and their corresponding prices.

You do not have to use the manufacturing plant for artwork. The other option available to you is to completely do it yourself. Take a photograph of something that symbolizes your work. Draw a picture yourself. Or if you have computer skills or know a friend that has, pick up a good graphic design program and design your own booklet. Take the finished copy to a printer and have them run off enough copies for your cassettes or CD's. Ask your manufacturing plant if they will insert your booklets if you ship it to them. This way you can have the tapes shrink wrapped and ready for sale when you get it.

The more together you are and the more planning you do in advance, even before you enter the studio, the better it is. By knowing what your costs are before you spend dime one, you will be able to outline your goals against what is reasonable and see where you might fall short. This will enable you to create a new plan within your financial means and then systematically work to achieve it. The most successful people in the world operate in the same fashion. It is a rare moment in time when everything just seems to work out perfectly without any thought or work.

CHOOSING A FORMAT

There are three standard formats to choose:

CASSETTE ✪ CD ✪ VINYL

Why one or the other?

CD

Perhaps the most popular medium right now. This is the most expensive format to manufacture so you need to examine your needs. I boil it down to three.

IF YOU ARE PLANNING TO MERCHANDISE AT YOUR SHOWS OR ARE TRYING TO GET AN INDEPENDENT DISTRIBUTION DEAL THIS IS THE WAY TO GO.

This is the most popular form of recording technology today. Music sounds better on CD and most music listeners own a CD player.

PROMOTION

If you are trying to promote your group, having a finished CD in your pocket shows that your group has passed some of the essential hurdles many bands need to before they begin to be taken seriously. A CD is a perfect medium for someone to flip from song to song and sample the band.

RADIO AIR PLAY

This requires an entire chapter in itself but suffice it to say there are hardly any stations that will play cassettes. Cassettes need to be set up on a cart and most station programmers do not want to be bothered with the task. CD's can be tracked easily and they sound better.

CASSETTES

Cassettes are the most practical format to use when soliciting clubs for gigs. CD's are much too expensive to just give away which is essentially what you are doing when you send it out to clubs. Cassettes are cheaper to manufacture (approximately $2 per cassette with J-card insert), therefore they retail cheaper and can help your merchandising if you play places where a $10 CD might be too big an expense for some fans.

There will be times that you'll want to pass out your music for free to fans to publicize your band. Again cassettes are cheaper. They make more sense as a promotional item.

VINYL

Vinyl still has it's place in various differnet aplications. Record labels have been using vinyl as a promotional tool for newly released rock groups. Vinyl is still the format of choice for clud D.J. mixing rap, hip hop, latin and dance. You can utilize this same marketing device for yourself. Since college radio stations still track vinyl records, instead of printing 500 CD's because you were going to approach 200 radio stations, you can opt for a cheaper package of less CD's and a few 7 or 12" 45's for radio stations and club DJ's.

OTHER OPTIONS

You can choose to have all CD's made so you can reach the most important people with the best format. You can then order blank cassettes along with the boxes and if you own a good tape deck, make copies yourself as you need them for sending out to clubs for gigs. Depending on which reproduction plant you use, they might be able to supply you with the blank cassettes and everything else you need with it (like labels and cassette boxes). Again the advantage to using a company that does it all under one roof is that if they are printing up the insert booklet for the CD, they will be able to print the information on cassette J cards as well as the labels that go on the cassettes itself, which you will then insert by hand.

DISTRIBUTION

If you recall, we briefly touched upon the retail aspect of your music in chapter 11. We discussed setting up a merchandising booth and displaying your products as well as arriving at the proper retail price for sale. But this is only one of many retailing options available to you.

As you know, all signed bands never sell their records at their live performances. To purchase a group's album you have to go to a record store. The task of getting your record on to a shelf in a record store is one of the hardest to accomplish. You do not necessarily need a record deal or have your record distributed by a major record distribution company to achieve this great feat.

There are hundreds of smaller distribution companies and rack jobbers all across the country that can get your music on the racks in record stores. While it may be difficult or unrealistic to get shelf space at Tower Records, Sam Goody's or many of the other major chain stores, there are thousands of smaller privately owned mom & pop stores that deal with the smaller distribution companies.

To understand this clearly let's begin with the major labels and work downward. When you sign a record deal you are essentially agreeing to borrow money from the label to record your music. You pay the label back from the profits that come in from the record sales. Since most bands never sell enough copies of their first record to pay back the label, record companies stand to invest and lose a great deal of money. So in exchange for the opportunity they grant a young band to get their chance at the big time, labels will on the average take about 88% of the sale profits of the record. This pays them back for the costs they incur which include: video, tour support and advertising.

Though you might not think it's fair, you should consider the opportunities that can come to groups from their label's effort that the label does not share in, such as live performance income, publishing and merchandising to name a few, any one of which can make millionaires of the members.

After the record company manufactures your album, they need to make an arrangement with their distribution company. Their job is to sell the record to the big buyers for all the music stores in the country. Record stores do not buy directly from the labels. Take for instance the five major distribution companies that distribute for the major labels. It would be impossible for them to service every single, big to tiny record store in the country. Therefore they distribute product to regional distributors that buy for and sell directly to the local retail locations.

If you think it's an easy sell, think again. Records stores are in the business of making money. To do that they need to purchase products that will sell. The major recording acts that sell millions of records like Madonna, Pearl Jam, The Stones, Garth Brooks etc., are easy records to stock. But what about the dozens of brand new bands releasing records every month. Most of the new groups are unknown except to their home town fans, so what would motivate any record store especially a small one, to lay out money and clear off shelf space to stock them? Combine all the new releases with all the major releases and you create some fierce competition.

This is the difficult task for the sales force of the distribution companies assuring the One Stop distributors and Rack Jobbers that a particular new band is great. They will need to provide the marketing plans as well as press info and any other important fact about the band to help generate sales.

This diagram plots out the path the record takes upon release:

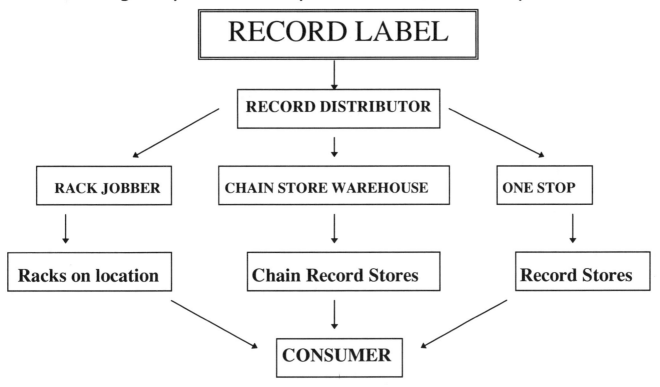

Major labels have little trouble getting their new artists onto the shelves at record stores. However, there is just not enough space in most record stores to carry every single title that is released, by every single record label. I'm sure that at one time or another you have gone into a record store to buy a new band's album only to find that the store does not have it. But if the album is requested or the band gains in notoriety, either through touring or radio play, so will the demand for their product create the supply from the retailer. This is commonly referred to as "supply and demand."

SELF DISTRIBUTION

With an understanding of how major distribution operates, an unsigned band can proceed to distribute their own record using similar means. Since most of the major chain stores are buying direct from their own warehouse, you should avoid the big stores and concentrate on the small, "mom and pop" shops. These intimate record stores, where the owners are behind the counter (unlike the big chain retailers), provide an opportunity for you to create a similar relationship that the major distribution salesmen do with their retailers. Through this relationship, you can create an opportunity to begin distributing your own record.

WHERE DO YOU START

If you remember back in chapter 6, I recommended that in between sound check and stage time you should be checking out record stores for future possibilities. Well the future is upon you now. Go over your list of all the places you've played especially where you are most popular. It is in these locations where you will start your sales campaign. After all, the small record stores are in business to do one thing and that is sell records. And if you are popular enough in the area, there is a good enough chance that you will sell records.

When approaching a store owner to make the sale, there are some basic techniques that you should obtain as well as a good sales kit to make your presentation.

 CALL IN ADVANCE AND MAKE AN APPOINTMENT TO MEET WITH THE BUYER

 HAVE A FORMULATED SALES PLAN. INCLUDE HOW MANY UNITS YOU WILL LEAVE IN THE STORE AND WHAT WHOLESALE PRICE YOU WILL SELL IT AT

 PRESENT A SIMPLE BAND HISTORY/ PRESS KIT WHICH YOU HAVE PREPARED SPECIFICALLY FOR THE RETAIL STORE

It should include press and touring information aimed at impressing the store manager. The hotter it looks, the more likely you will get your product in their store.

 PREPARE A MARKETING PLAN

This should be a simple outline of what your band's upcoming plans are. Included in this can be a condensed version of your bio, a description of the upcoming release with song titles, some press clipping quotes, and a projected view of your band's future touring plans for the next 3-6 months, highlighting the dates that take place in the areas the targeted record store is located in.

Remember you are facing some of the same problems that the big distributors face. Unless you know the store owner personally, you will need to back up your sales pitch with some strong evidence that you will sell records. (See sample on the next page.)

 ONCE YOU LAND AN ACCOUNT, LIST THEIR NAME AND ADDRESS IN YOUR MARKETING PLAN

This will keep it looking more and more impressive as you continue to build contacts.

"Substance & Soul"
Energy Records / Sel# NRG 81103-2/4

SONG TITLES:

1. Your Final Offering
2. Substance And Soul
3. It Will Find You
4. Temporary Mortuary
5. Sundays In The Womb
6. Let's Ride
7. Only I
8. Penance
9. Shoot For The Real Thing
10. Do You Really Know?
11. Intimate Loneliness
12. Whores
13. Wither In Fascination
14. 'Til The Break Of Day
15. Skin Deep

LAST TRIBE IS:

John Smith - vocals, guitar
Pete Jameson - bass
Rick Dobbelaer - guitar, vocals
Dave Ramie - drums

BIO/OVERVIEW

Capturing a band's focal point can be intricate and instinctive, like transforming a three-dimensional image into a flat photograph. So much of what one sees and hears depends on motion, perspective and the moment. The four young men in Last Tribe know that many elusive elements go into that image. For them, music is what defines their goals and their dreams. Having grown up together in the same suburban community, they found themselves bound by the same bonds and dilemmas. Ultimately, they were brought together by the music that had been brewing in their minds and souls--a tempestuous, vibrant mix of alternative, guitar-oriented rock. The closeness of the band's members was cemented by a steady, committed presence on the stage. To hone their skills as a band and sharpen their repertoire of about 60 songs, Last Tribe played over 300 shows in the last two years throughout the Northeast college circuit. Vocalist/guitarist John Smith gets into the spiritual essence of playing and he's not necessarily referring to a specific denomination: "It's a tool for communicating with people you will never know about feelings that they don't want to expose."

PRINT

Comprehensive campaign will include:
- Blanket advertising in key trade publications
- Follow-up strip ad campaign in key industry trade publications
- All major national consumer magazines
- Thorough regional co-op ad campaigns to follow release and tours

RADIO

Phase 1:
3/8 servicing of "Intimate Loneliness" 7" to college radio accounts
4/5 "It'll Find You"/Album add date
Phase 2:
- Includes servicing of commercial radio with potential AOR crossover

PRESS

- A strong presence at all college market publications as the band has a strong college following and plans to embark on a spring college tour.
- There will be a national press campaign to coincide with the albums release and subsequent growth.

VIDEO

The video for "It Will Find You" will be serviced to MTV and all other major video networks/mediums to coincide with the promotion blitz to commercial formats. There will be a servicing to clubs and retail accounts with a video set-up.

TOUR

After the band's East Coast college spring festival tour which will include Penn State and the WXRK Hoboken Classic, plans are underway for extensive national touring.

P.O.P / PROMOTIONAL TOOLS

- Limited Edition colored vinyl 7"
- 3-song "free cassette sampler" for key retail accounts
- Leather pouches serviced to key retail and radio accounts
- 40" X 60" oversize full-color poster
- 2' X 3' full-color poster
- 12" X 12" full-color album flats

CD $13.98	CASS $9.98
7 5235-81103-2 9	7 5235-81103-4 3

Energy Records

CONSIGNMENT

Once a record store owner agrees to carry your record, a deal will need to be made between the two of you. The most common arrangement is leaving your product there on consignment. This means that a space will be designated for your tape along with an arranged sale price. The owner will only pay you for the record after it has been sold. This way, they stand to lose nothing on merchandise that has not yet proven its market value.

Should you find some resistance from store owners about signing the contract, I would first suggest that you ask the retailer why. After all they are not signing their life away. They are just agreeing to carry your music and to sell it for the agreed price and at an agreed time they must return them to you in the same original condition along with your share of the profits. If they refuse to sign it don't leave any product.

A common financial arrangement on consigned merchandise is as follows. A full length CD should sell for **$12.00** retail. The store would generally keep on average **33%** of the retail price or approximately **$4.00**, leaving you with **$8.00**. Keep in mind that these figures are based upon full length CD's (10 songs or more) at the optimum situation. There are many other arrangements that can be agreed upon. (See rest of chapter for more details.)

In order to complete this arrangement, you should have the store owner sign a simple consignment document

Consignment Contract

THIS CONTRACT for the consignment of merchandise for sale is made on the _____ day of _____, 199___ between the undersigned,_____ herein called "Retailer" and the band _____, herein called distributor.

1. The distributor agrees to supply the retailer with _____ copies of his product _____ and the retailer agrees to display them in his store for sale.

2. The retail sale price of the product as set by the distributor will be $_____ for CD's, $_____ for cassettes and $_____ for vinyl.

3. The wholesale price as set by the distributor to be paid to the distributor by the retailer will be $_____ for CD's, $_____ for cassettes and $_____ for vinyl.

4. The retailer agrees to render payment to the distributor only for products sold in the form of a business check once a month on the first of the month.

5. The retailer may not alter the retail price of the product unless agreed upon by the distributor.

6. The products supplied to the retailer by the distributor are the sole property of the distributor. At any time said distributor may ask to have the product removed from the shelf and returned in the same condition it was received by retailer, with no penalty or cash payment.

7. The retailer is liable for all unpaid product supplied by distributor in his store in the event of a robbery, fire, earthquake, hurricane or any other act of God.

 8. THIS CONTRACT SHALL BE GOVERNED BY THE STATE OF

IN WITNESS WHEREOF, the parties hereto have set their names and seals on the and year first written above

_____

Retailers full name

_____

Signature of retailer

_____

Telephone

_____

Distributors full name

_____

Signature of distributor

_____

Telephone

The following is a consignment contract filled out:

CONSIGNMENT CONTRACT

THIS CONTRACT for the consignment of merchandise for sale is made on the **28th** day of **September,** 1995 between the undersigned: **Marcellus Wallace ,** herein called "Retailer" and the band **SUCTION,** herein called distributor.

1. The distributor agrees to supply the retailer with **5** copies of his product **PLUNGE OF ALLEGIANCE** and the retailer agrees to display them in his store for sale.

2. The retail sale price of the product as set by the distributor will be **$12.00** for CD's, **$8.00** for cassettes and **$6.99** for **12"** vinyl.

3. The wholesale price as set by the distributor to be paid to the distributor by the retailer will be **$8.00** for CD's, **$4.50** for cassettes and **$3.50** for vinyl.

4. The retailer agrees to render payment to the distributor only for products sold in the form of a business check once a month on the first of the month.

5. The retailer may not alter the retail price of the product unless agreed upon by the distributor.

6. The products supplied to the retailer by the distributor are the sole property of the distributor. At any time said distributor may ask to have the product removed from the shelf and returned in the same condition it was received by retailer, with no penalty or cash payment.

7. The retailer is liable for all unpaid product supplied by distributor in his store in the event of a robbery, fire, earthquake, hurricane or any other act of God.

8. THIS CONTRACT SHALL BE GOVERNED BY THE STATE OF NEW YORK

IN WITNESS WHEREOF, the parties hereto have set their names and seals on the and year first written above

MARCELLUS WALLACE

_____
Retailers full name

_____
Signature of retailer

_____
Telephone

MARC DAVISON MNGR.

_____
Distributors full name

_____
Signature of distributor

Telephone

RECORD STORE FILE

You should be creating a file directory of all the record stores you are supplying. This will help you keep track of the sales history. Why?

THE MORE ORGANIZED YOU ARE THE BETTER YOUR CHANCES ARE OF YOUR CAREER BECOMING PROFITABLE.

IF YOUR LONG TERM GOAL IS TO GET A RECORD DEAL, THIS IS IMPORTANT DATA TO SUPPLY TO THE LABELS.

Just because a band is a popular draw on the club circuit doesn't mean that they will sell a lot of records. A record company is in the business of selling records. While a young band might generate some interest from the labels based on their club track record, the interest goes no further if the group does not appear to have marketable songs. However, if you have tested the market yourself with your own independent release and have come up with some good sales numbers, you are going to find yourself being wooed by many labels.

To create a file:

Fiction Records

(RECORD STORE NAME)

Address: 1600 Utica Ave Brooklyn NY

Phone Number: (718) 623-5555   **Fax Number:** (718) 623 5550

Store Owner: Marcellus Wallace   **Store Buyer:** Jules Winnfield

Consignment yes

Date		Units	$ Amount	Total	Date	Total Sold	$ Collected	Units Returned
10/11	CD's	8	$6	$48	11/11	7	$42	0
10/11	Cass	5	$4	$20	11/11	2	$8	2
	Vinyl							

This chart should continue on as you re-supply the record store with product.

When you complete a page, on a separate sheet of paper create a summary totaling out all the columns. Staple both together and begin anew.

FIGURING OUT YOUR WHOLESALE AND RETAIL COSTS

To start, you must first figure out the true cost of your product. This cost must not only reflect the manufacturing costs, but must include the recording costs as well.

Let's start with a hypothetical scenario. You recorded 8 songs for a total recording cost of **$1,500.** This cost should include the cost of the tape as well as the incidentals like food, gas, equipment, etc.

Now let's look at manufacturing. You opted for a package that includes **500** CD's & **500** cassettes for a total cost of **$2,590.** Let's add **$200** for sales tax and shipping for a total cost of **$2,790. See figure 1 for total cost.**

figure 1

	$1500	RECORDING
+	**$2,790**	MANUFACTURING
=	**$4,290**	TOTAL COST OF TAPE.

To calculate the cost per unit see figure 2

figure 2

	$4,290	TOTAL COST OF TAPE
÷	**1000**	AMOUNT OF UNITS MANUFACTURED (500 CD'S + 500 CASSETTES)
=	**$4.29**	YOUR COST FOR EACH CASSETTE & CD

We have already determined, that the set market price for CD's is around **$10.** So if you sold **500** CD's at **$10,** you will gross **$5,000.** If you sold all **500** cassettes for **$8,** you will gross **$4,000. See figure 3.**

figure 3

500 (AMOUNT OF CD'S)	**500** (AMOUNT OF CASSETTES)
X **$10** RETAIL SALE PRICE	X **$8** RETAIL SALE PRICE
= **$5,000**	= **$4,000**

$5000 + $4000 = $9000 **TGP** (Total Gross Profit)

Figure 3 shows that if you sell each and every cassette and CD you have, you would earn a total gross profit of **$9000.** Gross profit though is not a true profit because you have not yet figured into the equation your cost of manufacturing. Once you subtract that figure from your gross profit you will arrive at your true profit or **net** profit. See figure 4

figure 4

	$9,000	GROSS PROFIT
-	**$4,290**	TOTAL COST OF TAPE (RECORDING & TAPE DUPLICATION)
=	**$4710**	TOTAL NET PROFIT

As figure 4 shows, once you pay back all the recording and duplication costs, the amount of money remaining, **$4,710**, is your net profit.

As we have discussed before, some of this product will be used for promotion and giveaway, which will cut into your net profit. **At the very least your financial concerns should be centered on recouping your costs** (or paying back the recording and duplication costs). This way if you borrowed money from anyone to make your tapes, you can pay it back. If you used your own money you can either pay yourself back or reinvest that amount back into a second pressing of tapes should you run out of the first **1000** tapes manufactured.

If you're really cost conscious and want to figure out exactly how many tapes you need to sell to recoup all your costs and how many tapes you can legitimately give away before you cut into your break even number, use these following formulas:

FOR CD'S

figure 5

How many you have to sell:

TOTAL COST OF TAPE ÷ RETAIL SALE AMOUNT = AMOUNT OF UNITS.

OR:

$4,290	TOTAL COSTS	
÷ **$10**	RETAIL SALE PRICE FOR CD'S	
429.	AMOUNT OF CD'S THAT NEED TO BE SOLD TO PAY FOR ALL YOUR COSTS.	

---

figure 6

What is left for giveaway:

TOTAL AMOUNT OF TAPE - AMOUNT NEEDS TO BE SOLD = GIVEAWAYS. **Or:**

500	TOTAL AMOUNT OF CD'S MADE
- 429	AMOUNT THAT NEEDS TO BE SOLD TO BREAK EVEN
= 71	AMOUNT LEFT FOR GIVEAWAYS

---

figure 7

TOTAL COST OF TAPE ÷ RETAIL SALE PRICE = AMOUNT OF UNITS. **OR:**

$4,290	TOTAL COSTS
÷ **$ 8**	RETAIL SALE PRICE FOR CASSETTES
= 536	AMOUNT OF CASSETTES YOU NEED TO SELL TO BREAK EVEN

****

Let's analyze all this information. If you sell **429** CD's (figure 5), you will pay back all your recording and manufacturing costs. You will have a balance of **71** CD's (figure 6) , which you can give away. Getting back to the original package you purchased, of **500** CD's and 500 cassettes (figure 7), you will have only used your CD's as sale product. After selling **429** CD's (figure 1), you paid back all your costs, (**$4,290**), leaving all the cassettes for giveaway or for sale at **$8** maximum price each, to increase profit.

Realizing that there is a need to use the CD as giveaway, especially for radio, record labels, managers, agents and press people, the **71** units you have left (figure 6) should be kept aside for just these situations, using the cassettes as freebies to fans etc. Of course, if you are shopping for a deal or for representation and plan on using more CD's than your free allotment, you should definitely sell some of the cassettes to offset the cost of the free CD's.

Keep in mind that although we talk about making profit, our main concern at the very least is to recoup the production costs, so that when the time comes to make a second pressing, the money is there.

If you analyze what happens when we figured out how many *cassettes* we need to sell to break even, we see that at **$8** per cassette (figure 7), we would need to sell more cassettes than we actually manufactured to recoup the recording costs (36 more cassettes to be exact). That is because the package we choose included the CD's which cost more to make. If we had chosen a package that gave us **1000** cassettes, the manufacturing cost would of course be much lower.

As a rule, if you are releasing CD's and cassettes, you must sell a bulk of the CD's to make back all your recording and manufacturing costs. If you want to make profit, give away less cassettes and sell them.

SELLING THROUGH RECORD STORES

Now CD's & cassettes typically command a set retail price at the store level as well. Most major releases sell between **$15.99 - $17.99,** depending on the group and the store. This price is determined by the cost incurred from all the different levels the product travels through to get to the consumer. An unsigned release such as yours, also commands an in store market price. That lies somewhere around **$10-$12** depending on the location, how many songs are on the tape and how much the group and store agree the tape can sell for.

If you sell the product through a store, you are going to cut into your profit margin because the store owner must make a profit as well. So we need to determine the best way to market through retail stores without cutting too much into your profit. If you are going to sell your product in the store at **$12** for the CD and **$8** for the cassette, to figure out what the wholesale price of the product should be, you must start at your cost of product and figure upwards.

We have already determined that each individual unit has cost you **$4.29.** When you sell your own product at shows for **$10**, you are making **$5.71** profit, at a markup of **133%** (a little more than doubling of your money). This amount of markup enables you to sell only **429** units out of the **1000** you made to recoup all your costs leaving the remaining amount for profit or giveaways.

When you wholesale to the store you are not going to be able to mark up your cost at **133%** because at a **$10** wholesale price to the store, the store will then only be able to make a **$2** profit on the sale if they sell it at **$12** which is only a **20%** markup. No store will want to sell your product and make such a little profit. Therefore you are going to have to adjust your costs as you are now acting as a wholesaler / supplier.

To help understand how you can lower your costs so that you can still recoup your expenses and possibly turn a profit you will need to adjust your initial cost of goods from the **$4.29** to a lower price.

Well how can you do that?

One way I know of is to devote some of the remaining giveaway to record store sales at a reduced price. Since these units were set aside for giveaway, you can conceivably offer them to a record store for a reduced rate so that they can sell at the store for the going rate. A good wholesale price to the store would be around **$4-$6** for the cassette and **$6-$8** for the CD. The only problem with this simple scenario is that for your first pressing you have paid the highest cost for your product. Therefore in my opinion it is best to try and sell as much as you can yourself at your shows so that you can generate the most amount of profit to pay off the recording cost.

This leads us to your second option. Wait until you have completely sold off the first pressing and then reinvest your money back into a second pressing. What will happen is that your second pressings costs are drastically reduced because your only cost here is the duplication fee. Remember that in your first pressing you had to figure in the recording cost of $**1,500** as well as duplication fee of **$2,790** (see figure 1). Well, once you pay back some, if not all of the **$1,500** recording costs, that cost of **$1,500** can be taken out of the equation giving you a reduced cost of goods. **See figure 8:**

figure 8

	$4290	ORIGINAL TOTAL COSTS OF GOODS
-	$1,500	RECORDING SESSION (INITIAL COST)
=	$2,790	NEW COST OF GOODS

Having sold out of your first pressing by selling them at shows and through your mailing list, you have paid yourself back all your initial cost. The **$1,500** is safely paid back and you have recouped your initial manufacturing cost of **$2,790**. Now you have no product left so you need to reorder. You send in the check for **$2,790** get your **500** CD's and **500** cassettes and the only amount you really need to recoup now to break even is the **$2,790**. This now sets you up for a number of great situations.

First, your new cost of goods is **2,790 ÷ 1000 = $2.79**. A big reduction from **$4.29** from the first pressing. With this savings you can drastically increase your potential for profit making from the sale of product at shows. Secondly at the new cost of goods price of **$2.79**, you can now begin to wholesale your product comfortably to retail stores, at a greater than **100%** profit and provide the retailer with a competitive cost of goods that they can mark up and make a profit themselves.

WHAT PRICE SHOULD YOU WHOLESALE AT?

For CD's a good starting price should be **$8.00** on a full length CD and **$6.00** on an EP which is a mark up of **115%-135%** from your **$2.79** cost (which by the way is slightly less than the **133%** markup you made initially selling the first pressing that cost you **$4.29** for **$10**).

The record store in turn can mark their cost up to **$12.00** which would profit them anywhere form **$4-$6.00** a unit. This is a fine deal for them especially since they are not responsible for any advertising or promotional costs.

By wholesaling the CD for **$6** for example, you need to sell **465** units to fully recoup your manufacturing costs leaving you with **35** CD's plus the **500** cassettes that you can either give away or continue to sell, generating you more profit. Obviously the more you can get for each unit the less product you need to sell in order to recoup your initial costs.

QUESTION -Why should you sell through record stores when you can make so much more money selling it at shows and through mail order?

   ANSWER - Because it's not always about making money. You are trying to set up a network that includes sales, promotion and recognition. The more you spread out and build your reputation, the more you will make of everything including money down the road. Think of all the things that having your product selling in stores provides you that selling on the road can't.

 LEGITIMACY

Listing the stores and compiling accounts gives you some very compelling statistics that can be directed towards record labels. After all they are in the business of selling records and if you are competing with them in some markets it may be your ace in the hole to landing a record deal.

★ IT IS A GOOD WAY TO PROMOTE YOUR BAND AND MAKE SOME SALES TO PEOPLE WHO MAY NEVER HAVE HEARD OF YOU BUT ARE THE TYPE OF CUSTOMERS THAT LIKE TO DISCOVER NEW MUSIC AT THE RECORD STORE.

★ IT IS A GREAT WAY TO KEEP YOUR RELATIONSHIP STRONG WITH RECORD STORES ESPECIALLY IF YOU END UP GETTING A RECORD DEAL.

Whatever you decide to do, remember one thing. Each time you give away a unit you are in a sense increasing the cost of each remaining unit. Many bands make the mistake of pressing CD's and giving so many away that by the time they are all out, they have recouped nothing and paid back no one for the loan they took out to make the tapes and the recording. The devastating thing about all this is that after a year or two, when you need to make a new tape, there will be no money to do so.

To succeed, you must act as your own manager, agent, lawyer, promoter and in this case your own record company. You have no choice. Who else can you rely on?

HOW TO PROMOTE YOUR RECORD

Earlier in the book (chapter 5) we spoke briefly about band promotion concerning the live show. I only touched upon a small part of promotion because I believe that there can exist an element of too much exposure. A young band just starting out, needs to understand that they are not all they are going be. A common mistake with young bands (I'm not necessarily referring to age only) is that they think they know everything and are ready to be signed even though they have only been together for six months and have five songs. That is like a ten year old wanting to enter college because he did well in 5th grade.

If you think you have written your best material in the first six months of being together, then how long of a career do you think you are going to have? Be realistic and patient. The longer you play together the better you will get. Therefore in the beginning of your band's career, you may want to regulate your promotions until you're good enough to impress the masses. But if you have gotten to this point and are releasing your first CD, you are going to need to sharpen your marketing techniques and expand your promotions.

PRINT

When you print up all your flyers, band newsletters and mailing list post cards, include the fact that you have a record out and where it can be purchased. When you print up flyers for gigs, make sure that at the bottom of the flyer you include something to the effect: "**Look for** BAND NAME **new release** Album Title **available at** Record Store Location etc.

Another idea is to print up mail order cards and leave them around at all the gigs you play. You can also begin a mail order section of your newsletter or gig announcement card. Below is a sample of a mail order card.

PLUNGE OF ALLEGIANCE

Mail Order: Suction, 630 E. 57th St Brooklyn NY, 11890

Item #	Description	Size	Qty	Color	Price	Total
CD 483	Plunge of Allegiance 10 Song CD				$10	
CS 484	Plunge of Allegiance 10 Song Cassette				$8	
T 100	Plunge (Red White & Brown) t-shirt, (L or XL)				$12	
T 101	Plunge It (L or XL) Red, Black or White				$10	
Order Total						
Sales Tax						
Shipping & Handling						$3.95
Total Enclosed						

Name_____

Address_____City_____State_____ Zip_____ Phone _____

Please include Check or Money order Made Payable to Suction.

As you may have noticed, I also listed some merchandise as well. As long as you are setting up a mail order business you might as well list all the merchandise you carry.

If you want to get really professional you can make arrangements with a credit card company to accept credit cards. If so add in a line for Account #, expiration date, name (that appears on credit card) and signature.

This order form should be printed on a standard 60lb post card stock. The other side of the card should have a larger graphic of your band's logo or cover art from the album cover.

If and when you print and mail your monthly gig calendar, be sure to list all the record stores or the mail order information somewhere on the postcard as well.

SAMPLERS

Perhaps the best form of advertising your music is the music itself. Record companies market what is called a sampler. A sampler contains a few selected tracks from the record usually recorded onto a cassette and distributed around as handouts at shows and other promotional outings. You can make the samplers yourself by recording off your CD onto blank cassettes. Affix a label on the cassette making sure you include your band name, address and phone number. Make a home grown J-card insert with your band logo on the front. Print in large letters both on the sampler label and the insert "from the CD (Name of CD) available at these record stores. *Make sure your name and phone number appear on the label that is on the cassette.*

Use every chance you get to hand these out at gigs, walking down the street or whatever your imagination comes up with. One year, I compiled a list of Frat houses for every college in New York. The guitarist in the band and I, stayed up for days and recorded over a hundred samplers, made J-cards and labels. I then enclosed each tape with a letter describing the popularity of the band, the scope of shows they had done and an 8x10 photocopied picture along with a price range for what the band would want to be paid to play. You cannot imagine how many calls I got back in response. Though it did not result in record sales since I had not placed product in any stores yet, we did receive a number of gigs that paid the band in some cases well over a thousand dollars a show.

COLLEGE RADIO

I can't even begin to tell you how important college radio is to your career. Suffice it to say that without college radio, mainstream radio might still be playing Tony Orlando & Dawn. I cover college radio in greater depth in chapter 15, so I just want to list it here as a focal point for your band's promotion. You will use college radio for band interviews, live performances and the rotation of your record. You will tie all these in with a strong attention to booking college gigs both on and off campus.

IN STORE PERFORMANCE

If you followed my advice and actively approached record store owners in the past during the free time at shows, as well as rehearsing the way I suggested for your recordings, you can now combine the two into one of the best ways to promote your band. The reference of "In Store" in the music business refers to bands making appearances at records stores to promote their record. This may include signing autographs or it may be more comprehensive and include a live performance of the group. I have orchestrated many of these events in the past and I can tell you that if you pull it off, it will make you look great.

You first start by contacting the store owner and letting them know that you have just released your debut and that the band will be coming through on such and such day for a show at the So and So club. You are interested in setting up an in-store performance at their store sometime in the early afternoon or early evening to help promote your show and record. Unless the store is really small or a franchise you will usually get a positive response. Especially after you assure them that you will send them a package in the mail which includes your CD and press kit along with a sample of promotional material. Once the owner gets wind of how focused you are they will see this as an opportunity to be in on the promotion because it just might get a bunch of people to come into their store to see you and hopefully buy some records even if it's yours, which of course you will supply and cut them in on the profits.

Once the owner accepts, you should create some flyers to send, and prepare a set that will feature some of the recorded songs. You will also need to decide whether or not you will perform the in-store acoustically or electrically. In this regard, you will be bound by the owner's needs and in most cases you will be asked to play acoustic. To pull this off, you will need to bring a small vocal PA which will amplify your vocals only. Guitarists need to bring acoustic guitars and small amps. Bass players can bring in their electric bass and amp rig unless they have an acoustic bass. Drummers can set up a simple kit and use brushes or other techniques for keeping the volume down. As an option you should consider bringing along chairs for the band members to sit on and a small portable riser to lift the drummer up.

Of course, you should schedule these in-stores with larger performances that you have scheduled for the same day. Did I just hear someone complain about performing twice in one day?.............. I didn't think so.

I can assure you that these are exciting to do and even if you do not think so, I ask that you try one before knocking it. Even if only ten people come to see you or just happen to be in the store when you play, if you are good, you have just made a fan from this. As a result of a successful in store, you will gain an important ally in the store owner, make a few new fans, which might translate into a more profitable gig later that night, as well as sell a few of your CD's.

INTERNET

click here

The INTERNET was a dedicated system designed years ago by the government to allow their computers to share information with each other. As time went by, the INTERNET became open to the corporate public. As we approach the twenty first century the Internet is open to anyone and everyone. There are millions of sites from government to corporate from private to personal. Anyone with access to a computer, modem and service provider can easily gain entrance and begin to scan everything in this electronic universe.

For our purposes here, the Internet can be a fantastic source for information. On one hand you can join any of the many services like AOL or Prodigy and get in on the conversation. On the other hand you can go straight into the World Wide Wed (www) and search out the endless sites available to the music business. See list below of recommended sites.

What may indeed be the most informative site for unsigned bands to visit is IUMA (www.iuma.com). IUMA is like a record store for unsigned bands where bands can post their music and merchandise for anyone clicking onto it to purchase. Due to IUMA's reputation, many major record labels frequent the site and demo the music. Their have been many bands that have signed major record deals, (Sublime as an example), just from being on this site.

Within IUMA there are other points of interest like industry publication listings and my personal favorite, **Sue Few's Sound Check.** This site (**http://www.iuma.com/IUMA-2.0/olas/extras/sue/**) is hosted by one of those rare music business people who understands your needs and is willing to share their expertise with you for free!!! Sound Check is like an industry newsletter geared right at unsigned bands containing among many things, a question and answer portion taken from your e-mails. Sue covers everything from booking your band to starting your own publishing company. The newsletters are short, informative and fun to read but most importantly they are written by someone who has done it all in at the record label level. Knowledge is the key to success and I guarantee that after reading her newsletters that date back to July of 1994, you will gain more knowledge and feel empowered to go out and make it. Now where else in this dog eat dog business can you go direct to the inside source and get help.

Well I'm glad you asked that question. As a client of mine you can go and visit my site at >**http://www.allareaaccess.com.** Here you can communicate directly with me as client and manager with your concerns, feedback, questions and dilemmas. This site will serve as your connection in the industry and further help guide you through your journey.

If you are unfamiliar with the Internet, become familiar. Just clicking on any site e-mail and requesting information can save you hundreds of dollars worth of magazine subscriptions, hours of directory research and instantly educate you on a topic you knew nothing about.

This is also a great way to build contacts. Many sites are sponsored by industry insiders and if you ask the right questions, you can build up enough of a rapport to send them your demo. Speaking of demo's, you know it's only a matter of time before you will be able to shop your demo to record labels directly through the computer.

To get you started, the following list contains some of the better and more important industry sites.

> http://www.allareaaccess.com (contains even more links to industry sites and other unsigned bands.

> http://www.iuma.com/

> http://www.iuma.com/IUMA-2.0/olas/extras/sue/

> http://www.sony.com/

> http://www.audionet.com/

> http://www.ssi.sony.com/SSI/

> http://www.halleonard.com/

> http://www.amrecords.com/

> http://technet.gtcc.cc.nc.us/pages/students/parkerj/index.htm

> http://pathfinder.com/@@BnX3iAQADijnTuyl/elektra/

> http://www.columbiahouse.com/

> http://www.bmgmusicservice.com/

> http://www.tvtrecords.com/toons/newtrax.htm

> http://www.emirec.com/

> http://pathfinder.com/@@5T1lOQUAITfjajHc/Discovery/

> http://www.warnerbros.com/

> http://atlantic-records.com/

> http://www.addict.com/

> http://www.RepriseRec.com/Default.html

> http://www.musicyellowpages.com/

> http://www.ubl.com/

> http://www.sony.com/Music/World.html

> http://www.rronline.com/

> http://www.geffen.com/

> http://www.hollywoodandvine.com/

> http://www.ticketmaster.com/talk/info/

> http://www.mammoth.com/

> http://www.liveconcerts.com/

> http://interjuke.com/jukebox

> http://www.rockthevote.org/

> http://www.live-online.com/

> http://www.infojapan.com/JWAVE/Welcome.html

> http://www.musicblvd.com/

> http://www.rockfetish.com/index.html

> http://pathfinder.com/@@5T1lOQUAITfjajHc/wmg-ca/

> http://www.manipulation.com/

> http://www.wwnet.net/~densmore/

> http://www.sonicnet.com/

> http://www.subpop.com/bands

"Hey Spike, I don't get it! I called Dave last month and told him we needed his van for the gig tonight."

13

ON THE ROAD

Son, it's a good idea," my father responded when I confronted him with my decision to leave home and travel across the country. Life had become mundane during the two years since my family moved from the city to a suburb thirty miles north of Manhattan. At age sixteen, it was a big culture shock leaving my friends and the neighborhood where I had grown up. Had it not been for the fact that David, one of my closest friends moved up the following year, I might have continued on with my plans to go off to college in September. But having virtually nothing else to do living here in the country, we would spend all of our time listening to and playing music.

During my junior year, I went to my first concert which was Hot Tuna and Kansas at Brooklyn College. By the end of my senior year, I had seen over thirty concerts including the Dead, the Allman Brothers and Emerson Lake and Palmer.

During the last year of high school, my studies took a complete back seat to music. I would sit in class and write lyrics into my notebook instead of taking notes. I would draw sketches of tour buses and stage designs. I was basically reverting back to the same antics of years ago in grade school. Music had once again resurfaced as the most driving force in my life. It was clear to me that I should begin to pursue down some avenue that would make it more than a diversion or hobby.

Dave and I had met some local musicians one day at the area's only music store and after a couple of jam sessions we began to seriously think about starting a band. So throughout the spring, we practiced playing cover tunes and some of my originals, in preparation for a big party planned in the summer.

After graduation I secured a summer job at my dad's travel company. I viewed the daily commute into New York City as an exhilarating experience, freeing me from the confines of country living. I remember also feeling overcome with anxiety every night sitting in rush hour traffic for two hours. My mind raced during that time, trying to weigh the effects of a decision I was about to make. I was clear on one thing: I did not want to spend the rest of my life stuck in a carpool commuting to a 9-5 day job. Though I had applied for and was accepted to college, I teetered on the brink of not going sometime in July, and on one muggy afternoon in August, sandwiched between my dad and Mr. Katzenstein, while stuck on the George Washington Bridge for what seemed like an eternity, I confirmed it. Approaching my father after dinner, he surprisingly agreed before I even finished telling him, which made me wonder if he was being supportive or anxious to finally get me and my "god damn noise" out of the house.

Next stop was to approach Dave with my grand plan. "California" I said, "that's were we should go." "San Francisco man, we'll move out there and start a band."

So we sold practically everything we owned to raise money, and on a cold November evening in 1974, three days before Thanksgiving, we said good-bye to our parents, and, with reckless abandon, headed west.

We drove through the night and into the next day. Time was at a standstill as we crossed off New Jersey, Pennsylvania and Ohio on the map. Throughout the day we drove through Indiana, where we witnessed a most spectacular sunset out past Indianapolis. Our quest to reach the Rockies in as quick a time as possible was our driving motivation, but sometime around 11:00pm, bug-eyed and spent, we pulled our chariot off the highway in search of a decent motel and a good night's sleep.

Having never been out of New York, we were somewhat naive to the cultural differences throughout the country. Not realizing the need to be discreet, we emerged from a cloud of sweet smoke from our car. With our long hair blowing in the wind, Dave and I entered into the small motel office asking in the thickest of NewYawk accents, if we could get a room.

The owners were a lovely couple and tried very hard to make us feel at home. As we filled out the register, the male counterpart took out his shotgun and began polishing it. It was downright nice of him to subtly share his concern for our safety and sure made us feel right at home. We bid them goodnight and bolted out the door. Room 14 was down at the end of a long one-story building. There were two blue lights hanging from the inside that lit the front part of the walkway, but our room was down at the other end encased in a blanket of darkness. As we preceeded down this concrete walk into nowhere, I was distracted by the neon sign by the roadside.

The words "No Vacancy," kept flashing on and off in a slow flicker. Each time it flashed on, a small bushy area to its immediate left would instantly illuminate and then disappear again when it flashed off. The shrubbery took on the likeness of a human being and I began having these horrible thoughts that the bush was really the owner's deranged half-brother, dressed in butcher's garb and eyeing us for the last and final ingredient needed for his home made sausage.

I slowly opened the door to the room and reached inside to feel along the wall for a light switch. I had no plan of employing any more of my body in until I turned the light on. As I searched the wall for the switch, Dave shoved me through the door. His sardonic laugh ceased immediately as he entered after me and switched on the light. We gazed in horror at this motel room from hell. The green and brown striped wallpaper fought hard to complement the blue shag carpeting. The light socket that hung loosely by white and red wires added a bizarre touch to the brown, stained ceiling. The 25 watt light bulb, dubiously screwed into the rusted socket, provided just enough light to see the huge concave dip that formed in the middle of the mattress, housing the room's only bed.

The bathroom was an archeologist's delight. Rings of sediment ran along the sides of the tub that led to a multitude of fragmented, fossil samples that lined the porcelain bottom. The bathroom gave off an odor that honored whatever died there millions of years ago. Man this was livin'. We got into bed, turned on Carson and tried to sleep. This was just the beginning of what turned into a strange but truly amazing trek around the country that I repeated later on, when I played in and managed bands.

******

Taking to the road is a turning point in a band's career. It is on the road, away from the comforts of home, that you will find out a lot about yourself and the group of people you are with. You will spend long hours driving and playing together. The road will be the true test of a group's endurance. As you get more popular you will find yourself traveling farther from home and staying out for longer periods of time. Your faith in the music needs to be at an all time high as well as the trust and commitment you share with the rest of the members of the band. The road is truly the place that can successfully lead you to fulfilling all your dreams or tear you apart and lead you back home to search for another way.

HOW TO BEGIN

Booking your band can very well be the most important function you can do aside from actually playing the gig. A lot more goes into booking than just picking up the phone and making a call. This is certainly true when booking outside your hometown.

Think for a moment about where you live. How many bars and clubs are within a thirty mile vicinity of your home? Now, how many of them would you want to play in? How many of them would you not want to play in? Now imagine you did not live in your town but wanted to play there. How would you know which ones to play in and which ones to steer away from? Another aspect to consider when booking is how far you intend on traveling. How much money will playing these gigs cost? How will you travel to the shows? What will the sleeping arrangements be? Can you afford to feed yourselves? If you have ever gone on vacation or traveled with your family you must be aware of all the planning that's required. Well, the same attention to detail will be needed to pull this off.

DEVELOPING A REGIONAL CIRCUIT

When you reach the point where you want to expand beyond your local environment, you must focus on why and how. The most common argument is, that there are just not enough clubs around to support all the dates you want to play. Well, that is certainly a good enough reason, although, it should not be the only reason.

If your ultimate goal is to get a record deal, you must try to make your group as signable as possible. Having good songs is a big part of it, as we have already established. But I know that many of you do not have faith in the music industry's capability of recognizing a good song or even worse, being able to get your music heard by the most important people. Therefore, you need to look at other ways to get their attention and at the same time increase your worth.

Developing a solid regional following is clearly the wave for bands right now. A regional following refers to a group's ability to tour a developed four to six state area. Regardless of where you live, you are surrounded by other states. Here on the east coast for example, it is not uncommon for unsigned bands to eventually develop a tour circuit that takes them from Maine down the eastern seaboard to the Carolinas, with many stops inland at colleges and smaller but vibrant cities like Burlington or Ithaca. Bands like PHISH or Blues Traveler did this extensively for years, which, even had they not been signed, would still have given them a career from all that touring.

By concentrating on expanding to at least four states and building up a following of at least 200-300 fans in each market, you are truly getting yourself on the musical map. This kind of exposure opens you up to countless press opportunities, college radio stations, club recognition and hopefully fan appreciation and merchandising sales.

These are all the potent ingredients in getting the attention of the music industry. In chapter 12 we spoke about record distribution and how difficult it is for a label to get a new band out to the public. Think how much easier you make their job if you are already popular in many major and minor sales and touring markets. Think how much more secure you will be in your record deal if you already have a tour circuit planned out that upon the release of your record, you can immediately go out on tour. You have no idea how difficult it is to land a major booking agent and how equally hard it is to get on a decent tour when you release your first record.

When a band first signs their deal, they are usually unknown to most markets in the country. When the album is released, the label begins working the single to radio but it can take six months or longer before it finds its way into steady rotation (that is if it gets any rotation at all). The band is expected to go out and make something happen, which translates into going out on tour so the label can sell records and start building a story.

This is the goal of every signed band: to get on a tour. To accomplish that, the band first looks for a booking agent. Labels do not assign booking agents to bands! Bands have to secure that for themselves. Yes, they may get recommended to one by their label or manager but in the end the agent has to believe in the band themselves if they are going to sign the band up.

Those beliefs are based on the following:

IS THE LABEL THE BAND IS SIGNED TO, CAPABLE OF MAKING THINGS HAPPEN?

We have agreed that without radio or MTV play you are not worth much on the tour circuit. To get on the air the label is going to have to do whatever it is they do. It may mean hiring independent promotion which is very expensive. It may mean having you perform at various seminars and conventions around the country that feature new artists to the radio programming industry. It may mean shooting a video which can cost the label $40,000 or more. It may mean putting up the necessary tour support dollars for you to travel around the country for years playing bars and small club dates that pay only $50-$200 a night.

The agent needs to know and feel that the label is committed to doing all these things and more to launch the band.

IS THE BAND GOOD ENOUGH TO RISE TO THE OCCASION?

Sometimes an agent will sign a group based on gut feeling. But that gut feeling still needs to be nourished by some sense of reality. Does the band have a prior tour history? Do they have a well developed circuit that the agent can take over and expand upon? If so what are they like live? Do they get the fans up and going showing some promise out there on the road in unfamiliar places?

Why would any busy agent sign up a band that is unknown with little or no tour history? Agents only make money from booking shows and nothing else. It's very hard to book an unknown band on a national club tour when the group cannot sell any tickets yet, as you may have already noticed if you have done it yourself. And why would a bigger national act want to drag a new group with them around the country as an opening act when the band has no fans outside their own home town so will probably not sell any tickets to the show?

The answer to these questions is they wouldn't and many times they do not. There are many bands that sign record deals and cannot get an agent to sign them. In these cases the band has got to get the job done themselves.

Think about it. If you had done the footwork prior to getting signed, if you had gone out on the road and developed a touring circuit you not only put yourself in a more powerful position to negotiate a deal but you greatly increase the amount of offers you get as well as accelerate the speed in which your career may take off.

Also, think about how this may increase your overall chances of being signed to a label. If you already have a large base of fans in many different markets that support your music you virtually take some of the guessing out of the game. If you have a mailing list of 3000 people, selling 50 CD's & 100 T-shirts a week, playing dates earning you over $500 steady, then my friend you have done a good job. Expect some kind of offer be it major or independent. Even if you don't get a deal, consider yourself an entrepreneur, working in your own business, calling your own shots, in an industry you love. The way I see it, you're miles ahead of the thousands of commuters you pass along the highway, going to work in a stuffy office, for a boss they hate and a job they hate even more.

WHEN DO YOU BEGIN

Though I champion the thought of playing everywhere and anywhere you can, I want you to take a more planned out approach at this stage of the game. When you play at home you have the support of family and friends as well as the comfort of friendly bars and clubs, but on the road things are not as cushioned. Therefore you should have a strong launching pad before you take off. In other words, before you head out of town you should first develop a good strong fan and press base at home. If you do not, on what basis then will you be booking yourself? You cannot really expect an out of town club to book you because you have a cool looking guitar.

What will get you booked is the fact that you are doing "business" in your own territory. Whether it's a healthy hometown following of 300 fans or more, or that you steadily play the top clubs as a headline act and have the press to prove it. If you do not have these stats behind you then you are either brand new, lazy or mediocre. If so then why would an out of town club hire you?

WHERE TO PLAY

(How to map out a circuit)

Sometimes the best place to begin your outreach may only be as close as 20 miles away and sometimes it could be as far as 500 miles away. Consider the possibility that you are a big hit in your home town. Friends of yours are away at college five hundred miles away. There are enough of them that if you were to play in a bar in town or on campus, a decent turnout would occur. If so, this is a great start. Ask your friends what the hot club in town is and have a bunch of them go there and tell the owner about your group. When you get the green light to call, reiterate to the club owner how popular you are at home, that many of your home fans are at the college nearby, and that a good turnout is inevitable. Even though it's five hundred miles away it's a great place for you to start because it's a place to start.

Outline a territory with your home town as starting point A, and the college town as finishing point B. Study a map to see what lies directly in between, give or take 75 miles off the highway. This will give you a visual indication of where to begin looking for places to play.

As I have mentioned, use POLLSTAR or other club directories such as newspapers or contacts, to locate the clubs in all these areas. It is important to note that these areas need not be big cities. Some of the best places to play are smaller towns that have at least one college nearby. Whether a big city or a college town, you will need to adopt some concept of what an important market is versus a non important market. In music business terms these important markets are places that matter in terms of record sales, concert ticket sales, popular radio stations and press contacts. New York, Boston, Chicago, Los Angeles, Austin, Nashville, Detroit, Seattle, San Francisco, Houston, Philadelphia, Miami and Atlanta are some important major markets for various different types of music. What makes them important is the population, the media exposure, the prestige club circuit and the presence of the "Industry." There are of course many smaller towns and cities throughout America that have happening musical scenes based mainly upon the presence of colleges and clubs. Towns like Boulder, Colorado or Lawrence, Kansas have tremendous student populations that support a healthy club scene. These places offer the chance for a band to find a niche with a crowd and possibly blossom.

Speaking of Boulder, Colorado, many bands from my area have gravitated there after building a strong following here. Many bands from the South have done the same thing, making this little city a major musical port for up and coming, unsigned acts.

So wherever you are from, you need to play your share of no name places just to build your buzz. Then you need to concentrate on working your way to the more important markets, so that you are taken more seriously.

Sometimes gigs and opportunities just pop up out of nowhere and when they do, consider all the ramifications then act upon them. You might be opening up for a band from out of town or they might be opening for you. Get to know all the acts you play with; you never know who they are and what they might bring to the table. They may be new in your town but they are from somewhere and can very well be popular there. If you hit it off you may ask to open for them in their hometown. Ask the booking agents of the clubs you presently play if they have contacts or if they can supply you with names and addresses of out of town clubs.

HOW TO PICK THE RIGHT CLUB

If I had a crystal ball, I would be at the track right now instead of at the computer typing away at three o'clock in the morning. There are many considerations you must go over to determine what the right club is. The truth is, unless you are in the club or know someone who has, when you are booking out of town it is sometimes a stab in the dark.

There are of course some criteria you can follow in the list below.

PICK A CLUB THAT FEATURES THE STYLE OF MUSIC YOU PLAY.

You can get an idea on what kind of music they feature by asking them directly or asking them to provide you with the name of the popular weekly or monthly newspapers in the area featuring the local music scene. Papers like BAM in LA or The AQUARIAN in New Jersey, Village Voice in NYC, Creative Loafing in Atlanta, all feature ads from many of the main clubs. You may even be able to tell by the names of the bands playing there what kind of place it is. When you contact these publications, ask them to send you a copy since you are considering placing an ad with them. You will learn a whole lot about a market by reading their papers.

PICK A CLUB THAT HAS AT LEAST A 75 PERSON CAPACITY.

Anything smaller and you will run the risk of being too loud or too cramped.

PICK A CLUB THAT HAS A REGULAR DRAW.

This means a club that on any given night has people there. It is virtually impossible for a band to develop a following out of town if they have to rely completely on drawing their own crowd. An alternative to a club that has a regular draw would be to make sure that the club has bands playing on a regular basis. Try to book yourself in a opening slot for one that has a good following, so that you can play to some sort of crowd.

PICK CLUBS THAT HAVE THEME NIGHTS LIKE "WED NIGHT ALL THE BEER YOU CAN DRINK FOR $10."

Since the beer is the main attraction, bands become the secondary act, but if you are good the club is doing you a favor by putting you in a room full of people. The pay might not be as good as a Friday night but the opportunity to build a following from this is what you are after.

PICK CLUBS THAT PUBLISH A MONTHLY CALENDAR.

Ask if they have a mailing list. If so, ask to be on it and ask if they can send you one. Once it arrives you can get a sample of what their monthly entertainment schedule looks like.

If you are really clueless about a town's music scene, call any club and ask them if they can supply you with a press sheet. Explain that you are interested in playing their venue and that you would like to explore all the press options in the area to make the show successful. The club can either fax you a press sheet or even read it to you over the phone. Once you obtain the list of editors, music critics and publications in the area, call them. Explain that you are from out of town and you are looking for a lead on the club scene. If they show any interest in helping you, explain what your band is like and ask which in their opinion would be the best club for you to play. Make sure that you take down their name and correspondence information because this is how you will expand your press contact list for each city. Call a few more names on the list provided to you to get a consensus of opinions. After you speak to a few people, you will get a much better idea as to where you would belong in that town. Make sure you thank them very much for their help and then send out a press kit and tape with a cover letter. When you finally book the gig, send a press release and invite them to the show by putting them + 1 on the guest list.

Another option is to ask the clubs if they advertise in the local music papers. Ask them which papers and if they can at least provide you with the phone number of that paper. Call the paper and inform them that you are an out of town band and are interested in playing in their area. Ask if they can send you a copy of the paper with some ad rates as you may be interested yourself in taking out an ad once a show is booked. They may indeed ask you what club you are playing at and you can respond by saying your not sure. That is one of the reasons why you want a copy of their paper so that you can see the ads all the clubs are taking out and what type of acts are playing .

If you cannot obtain a press sheet from any of the clubs, you may consider not bothering to perform there. After all, if clubs show no interest in helping you make it a good night, it can be an indication of other negative aspects of the clubs.

 **TRY CALLING LOCAL MUSIC INSTRUMENT STORES.**

You can obtain business phone numbers by calling the city's Chamber of Commerce. Call and explain that you are a traveling musical group and are trying to get some phone numbers of music instrument stores in their city. By calling these stores you can kill two birds with one stone. First, you really should have a list of stores like these in case you need to buy strings or get something repaired on the road. Secondly many times the employees of music stores are themselves musicians. Call and tell them you an out of town band on tour and you will soon be passing through. Perhaps he can suggest some clubs in the area that might be a good place for you to play. You might even be speaking with someone that is in a band and can offer you a gig opening up for them. You can in turn offer them a gig with your group in your home town. You might want to swap tapes via the mail just make sure you like their group. In any case be sure to take down their name as well as the address of the store.

 PICK CLUBS WITH A SOUND SYSTEM AND SOME KIND OF LIGHT BOARD WITH AT LEAST FOUR CANS.

If a club has neither it means that you will have to supply some of the production. This may not be such a bad thing especially if you own your own system and you think that you will draw a lot of people to the show. But if not, the production is expensive ($100 -$300 for a sound system and the same for lights) and that might make the night a big financial loss which you may not be able to afford.

ASK THE CLUB FOR SOME NAMES OF BANDS THAT HAVE PLAYED THERE RECENTLY.

You can tell a lot by the name of a band and you can get a feel for the clientele from the kinds of bands that play the clubs.

FIND CLUBS WITH STAGES AS OPPOSED TO PLACES WHERE YOU HAVE TO SET UP ON THE FLOOR WHERE THE POOL TABLE IS.

These are criteria that if all or some are included in the club, you are on the right track. However sometimes you may need to play a town that has only a bar and a college 15 miles away. This has happened to a client of mine once where I booked a town bar because it was on the way from point A to point B. The group was charting in the top five on the college station and it seemed a logical move even though the club met almost none of the requirements above. There was nowhere to play on campus, so I booked the one and only bar in town.

I cannot properly describe how bad this place looked when we entered. It was approximately 3 feet wide from the bar stools across to the wall which led into a main room that was about a total of 30 square feet. The bar had three old timers that were apparently permanently adhered to their bar stools since young adulthood. We arrived at three o'clock in the afternoon when we departed at four o'clock the next morning they were still there. The stage area which was not elevated, was distinguished by the mere fact that it housed the only electrical outlets in the place. Unfortunately the area was occupied by a small pool table with a biker playing on it.

I approached the area and presented myself to the gruff individual lost in a game of eight ball. In between shots, I asked that when the game was over to please alert us so that we can move the table over and set up the equipment. By the stare and body language that greeted my request, I wondered if perhaps I said something that was interpreted incorrectly. The entire room silenced as if I were E.F. Hutton. As this cretin turned to face me I recoiled in horror. *She* threw me a stare that made the hair on the back of my neck stand on end. I retreated backwards bumping into this corpulent mass of flesh that turned out to be her boyfriend. The band members were caught between their emotions. On one hand they felt "good, this is what he gets for booking us into this dice" but on the other hand they figured "it's four of us and only two of them, so we better move quick him out of here." Either way they didn't react fast enough. As I backed into Goliath, he let out this bellowing laugh that started way down in bottom of his gut and poured out like slow aged micro brew. I turned and looked straight up at this giant of a man and was humbled before him. The three remaining silver capped teeth that appeared to be only visiting his mouth rather than a permanent fixture, glistened from the beam of sunlight that lit the room and formed a halo around him. He reached down enveloping me with his arm in a brotherly shoulder wrap and turned to his tattooed, leather clad, goddess and proclaimed, "he's okay." I breathed a sigh of relief for had he not intervened on my behalf, I might have spent the rest of the night with a pool stick wedgie and an eight ball imbedded in my forehead.

The band was tentative all throughout sound check trying to alter their alternative musical compositions to sound like a Stevie Ray Vaughan meets the Black Crowes feel. This made it easier for my guardian angel to sing in key as he poised himself directly in front of the lead singer's microphone to assist in the vocal check. The band abruptly exited directly afterwards, not waiting for me or telling me where they were going. They must have figured I was now in good hands and gave me some time alone to bond with my new found friend.

As the hours passed, I wondered if perhaps they were 100 miles south on the Thruway, heading home. Around 9:00 I took my usual post near the door to begin collecting the three dollars admission for the show. My guardian angel parked himself right next to me making sure that I knew who his friends were as they entered so that I wouldn't make the grave mistake of charging them admission.

Around eleven o'clock, fifteen minutes prior to stage time the band pulled up, much to my relief. They were shocked to find that 200 plus people were already crammed in to see them. The group ended up playing until three in the morning and when all was told, four hundred people came in throughout the night paying $3 each.

The band learned a valuable lesson, in fact they made the most money out of any gig on that two week road trip. I of course received some heartfelt apologies but most importantly when we got back to the motel, I was given the honor of sleeping in my own bed.

HOW TO BOOK OUT OF TOWN CLUBS

Once you have established contact with the clubs you want to play, you now need to book the gig. Booking out of town clubs, is more difficult than booking local shows; after all, the local events have been booked off the familiarity of the group and a personal touch by you going down to see the booker. When approaching out of town clubs you are basically in the dark about them and they about you.

When you call you should have your facts ready and in front of you as reference. You do not have much time on the phone so know what you want to say and be prepared to write down any offer or instructions you receive. In front of you should be:

A NEW CLUB FILE FOLDER MADE UP FOR EACH NEW CLUB YOU CALL.

A DATA SHEET TO BE FILLED OUT LOGGING IN YOUR CONVERSATION.

A CALENDAR SO THAT YOU CAN SCAN THE DATES IN WHICH YOU ARE LOOKING TO BOOK AGAINST THE DATES YOU MAY BE OFFERED.

Make sure you are speaking with the correct individual that has the authority to book the bands. There usually is only one person that does the bookings and can make confirmations. The last thing you need is to get a casual okay from the bartender only to find out 2 days before the show when you call to advance it that the booking agent does not have you listed and has no idea who you are. If you have sent away for the club directories from POLLSTAR, you will notice that for each club listing they list the owner of the club as well as the booking agent for the club by name. Of course names do change as personnel changes, but for the most part if you have a current issue, you should ask for and only make deals with the names listed.

As experience has already shown you, booking a date takes time, patience and good phone rapport. If you have not displayed it up until now, this is the time to start. As I explained in chapter 5, personality goes a long way, and if you develop relationships easily, your job will be that much smoother. To obtain the booking, you will refer to all the techniques described in chapter 5 plus some.

Some of the differences in booking out of town gigs revolves around the need to work from an itinerary and the urgency to fill up loose dates. This will be compounded by the fact that you are probably an unknown entity.

If you have the 4th, 5th, 6th and 10th of a month booked, and these are gigs that are out of town, you obviously need to fill two of the three remaining dates (leaving one for a day off) during the 7th-9th. Since you will be away from home you cannot simply come back for an off day then return to the road (although if you are less than 75 miles from home and coming back is not in the opposite direction of the following show it is acceptable). Otherwise it will be just too costly in gas and van rental to spend a day or two without a gig. Furthermore you are going to want to make sure that the dates are booked in cities that are on the way to and from the dates they lie between. As the days go by and you still have no confirmations, you need to be more forceful in your approach and more creative finding places to play.

SEARCH FOR PERFORMANCE OPPORTUNITIES THAT YOU HAVE PREVIOUSLY EGLECTED

Take out a map of your touring region and search for off beat towns that may have a tourinst crowd or college. Where ever tourists and college are thie will be bars and clubs.

TRY CONTACTING SMALL COMMUNITY COLLEGES AND SEE IF YOU CAN BOOK AN AFTERNOON LUNCH TIME CONCERT LIKE THE "BENGAL PAUSE" AT BUFFALO STATE COLLEGE IN NEW YORK.

Perhaps you can perform at night in the student union. Even if they have never done anything like this before, convince them to make this the first time. All you need is enough money to cover transportation, production (sound and lights). Have them provide you with the dimensions of the performance room and some publicity. The idea here is to perform and make new fans

 TRY CONTACTING THE SCHOOL'S RADIO STATION AND SEE IF THEY WOULD BE INTERESTED IN PUTTING ON A BENEFIT CONCERT.

Offer a low admission and split the difference so that you can pay for your expenses.

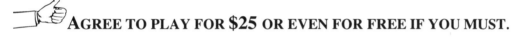

 IF THERE IS NOWHERE TO PLAY ON CAMPUS ASK ALL THESE PEOPLE YOU SPOKE WITH AT THE COLLEGE IF THEY CAN GIVE YOU THE NAME OF THE POPULAR BAR OR CLUB IN TOWN.

As you get closer to the dates in question you need to book them, otherwise there will be too much of a gap in your itinerary which will cost you a lot of money if you are not playing. Be creative in your ideas offering possibilities to clubs that might appear to be stubborn.

 AGREE TO BE THE THIRD BAND ON A BILL.

 AGREE TO PLAY FOR $25 OR EVEN FOR FREE IF YOU MUST.

Remember, this is not about money. It's about playing. That's why you are a band; bands play. Money must not be the most important driving force now or at any time in your career. It should place a strong second but only after opportunity and what is best for the band in their overall development. This holds true whether you are a club band or a stadium band. If you make decisions that are entirely financially based, I think you are being very short sighted. It's about getting out there and spreading your word even if three people see you and like you, that's okay.

It is going to take many return visits to a new club to really begin to build a new following. One of the ways to assure these return visit is to impress the club owner. And not just with the music! You need to impress him with your conscientious promotions whether it's working the mailing lists, or your spirited postering of the college nearby, as well as your business savvy. One way to guarantee never returning, is to ask for more money on your next booking, when you drew only eight people to the club. Do not make money an issue until you are making the club money.

Once you confirm the bookings try to get a confirmation from the owner. It should either be a signed contract or a confirmation by fax or mail from the club. This is important because you do not want to travel 300 miles, spend money on promotions and mailers to play a show only to find out that the person you booked it with was the bartender that got fired a month prior, and now you have no recourse from the club. A signed contract or confirmation at least gives you some legal leverage for the club to make some kind of reparation.

ONCE THE DATE IS BOOKED YOU NEED TO BEGIN YOUR FOLLOW UP. HERE IS A LIST OF ACTIONS YOU NEED TO TAKE:

 BEGIN IMMEDIATELY TO FOCUS IN ON PROMOTING THE SHOW.

Get the flyers printed and mailed out to the club. Get your mailing calendar going and set up for the printer.

 IF THERE IS A COLLEGE IN TOWN, CALL THE RADIO STATION AND TRY TO GET YOUR CD IN ROTATION AS WELL AS AN ON AIR INTERVIEW ON THE DAY OF THE SHOW.

Be relentless in your approach and excited about being in their city.

 CORRESPOND WITH THE CLUB OWNER OR BOOKER BY FAX, UPDATING THEM ON THE PROMOTIONAL PROGRESS YOU ARE MAKING.

Let the booker know you are doing a college radio spot or an in store.

 ASK THE BOOKER IF THEY CAN SUPPLY YOU WITH SOME FREE PASSES TO THE SHOW TO GIVE AWAY OVER THE RADIO OR AT THE RECORD STORE.

By coordinating all these events you are making noise and raising a lot of people's consciousness about your band. It is going to really impress people if you pull it all off, especially if you cap the night with a great live performance.

ROUTING

An important part of touring is the planning of the route you will travel. It would be a good idea for you to pick up one those large wall hanging maps and put it right over your desk. Pick up some colored thumb tacks. It was my practice to adhere white tacks to places I would call for bookings, replacing them with yellow as they became tentative and finally with a red one for confirmed. The tacks will serve as a quick reminder of where my acts were playing and what territories I was booking. It also helped to show a pattern for my routing.

As a rule I tried not to book the bands more than five hours' drive from their next gig. Where the very first show of a tour started didn't matter, as long as it was within a day's drive. The primary concerns are tying in personal appearances during the day, with sound check times, stage times and with driving times.

The one thing you want to avoid is backtracking. This occurs when you book one city on Monday, followed by Tuesday's gig in another city 200 miles away to the west and Wednesday's gig in a third city 300 miles back to the East. You basically want to push ahead rather than taking two steps forward one step back. On the other hand as you will come to find out, it is very difficult to book according to your map. Club bookers could care less that "You will be in Hartford on Thursday so you need a gig at their club in Boston on Friday." If they are booked up that's it. Now of course you can try and call other clubs in the area but you still may come up empty. This is why you need to take a peripheral view of the area and see what is 25 or 30 miles outside your target market. There may be a hip little town like Woodstock or Burlington, where you can do an acoustic set in a cafe and make a few bucks. Or there may be a community college that after some research you find that they have 6,000 students and an active student union.

When routing, try to use common sense and keep track of your traveling expenses. The cost of traveling backward to do a $50 gig may just be too high. You may be better off going straight on to the next destination to spend time there promoting the next show. On the other hand if you need to travel backward to play a big exposure show, of course do it. It once cost me $600 out of pocket to send my unsigned client to do three days opening up for the Darling Buds. They were a British band signed to Columbia records on a U.S. promotional tour. I received a call from their agent who asked if my act would want to open up the remaining three shows of the tour. The shows were taking place in New York City, Asbury Park, NJ and Washington, DC. I had two hours to make a decision and one day to coordinate the whole thing.

There were some heavy decisions to weigh. On the negative side, there would be no publicity, no road crew, I needed to rent transportation, arrange food and accommodations all on a $200 total compensation. On the positive side, Columbia Records reps were on the tour, the group would be playing in new clubs, to new fans. This seemed like an opportunity money usually can't buy. $600 seemed a small price to pay for this type of exposure.

Normally when I planned road trips, I usually have the groups perform a couple of big hometown shows to raise money to support the tour. In this case however being on such short notice that option was not available. But I felt very strongly about the circumstance, gave the band my credit card and called the agent back and agreed. Finally, I made sure to book a hometown show shortly after returning to recoup the expenses of this road trip.

PREPARING FOR THE ROAD

Once you have the majority of your dates booked, you should proceed to print up your gig calendar and mail it out to your mailing list. If time is getting short and a few dates are still tentative, list the date anyway and write tentative or TBA (To Be

Announced). Be sure to leave a hot line phone number so fans can call and find out where you are going to be.

TRANSPORTATION

Earlier when you were first starting out, you were probably renting vans or driving your cars. At this juncture, I want you to consider purchasing your own van. The money you will ultimately save on rental will allow you to take on lower paying gigs. You can probably find a decent van for under $1,000. It does not have to be beautiful in fact the more beat up the outside is, the less of a chance it has of becoming a target for thieves.

You need a van that runs well and is extended in size for all your equipment. Of course, you can look at other options like getting a ball hitch and renting a trailer for each show or even buying a trailer. You can then turn the back of the van into a comfortable place where you can all crash at night if you can not afford a motel room or on long day drives between shows.

The only other charge you need to worry about if you buy a van is the insurance. If you can, get someone over 25 years old to insure it. Insurance is rather high for a younger driver. If you must insure it yourself, take a driver's education course. That will reduce the monthly fee by 10%.

Make sure you secure the doors and locks on the van. If you are using the van for lugging equipment, make sure you put hard gauge metal screening over the back door windows. Do the same thing inside the van across the front dividing the seats and the back of the van. If you have the extra money, install a fuel line kill switch and buy "The Club" to further protect it from theft.

TOUR BUDGET

Before you get the motor running and head out on the highway, be sure you have analyzed the costs of your trip and are financially prepared to travel. This is a practice that will accompany you for all your touring days. To begin, I want you to make the following list of all the projected expense categories you are going to have. Once you design the list which will record each and every projected expense you expect to incur, you then should fill in the dollar amount that you expect to find on each item. You should do this for each day/show of the road trip. The totals of these approximate expenses will give you some indication of how much money you need to float the cost of the trip.

Here is a sample expense budget:

```
┌──────────────────────────────────────────────────────────────┐
│              EXPENSE BUDGET          DATE_____              │
│                                                                │
│  Motel                      _____                     │
│                                                                │
│  Transportation (Rental)    _____                     │
│                                                                │
│  Gas                        _____                     │
│                                                                │
│  Toll                       _____                     │
│                                                                │
│  Food                       _____                     │
│                                                                │
│  Transp. Expense (Repair)   _____                     │
│                                                                │
│  Entertainment              _____                     │
│                                                                │
│  Instrument Supplies        _____                     │
│                                                                │
│  Tips                       _____                     │
│                                                                │
│  Per Diem Payments          _____                     │
│                                                                │
│  Payroll                    _____                     │
│                                                                │
│  Postage                    _____                     │
│                                                                │
│  Laundry                    _____                     │
│                                         _____       │
│  TOTAL                                                          │
└──────────────────────────────────────────────────────────────┘
```

This list, gives you a visual presentation of what lies ahead expense-wise. Your goal now is to fill in the blanks next to each category by estimating as best as you can, how much you are going to spend for each show. Some of the expenses like transportation rental or motel rooms, are figures that you can arrive at with some precision. To calculate costs on food, entertainment and tips, you will need to determine exactly how much you want to allot for their expense. Will you expect to eat in fancy restaurants every night or will you agree to eat cheap at McDonald's? Will the band, fund your personal entertainment like video games, magazines or long distance phone calls or does this come out of your own money?

Gas is an expense that require an educated guess based on mileage. Check a map to determine what the mileage is from one city to another. Then based on what the gas mileage is of the vehicle you are driving, you can estimate how much it will cost you gas.

To figure out how many miles per gallon your vehicle gets consult this formula. See figure 1 ⟹

	FILL UP THE TANK TO THE TOP.
	SET YOUR ODOMETER TO 0
	DRIVE 50 MILES
	FILL IT BACK UP WITH GAS
	NOTE HOW MANY GALLONS IT TOOK TO FILL UP.
	DIVIDE THE AMOUNT OF MILES YOU DROVE BY THE AMOUNT OF GALLONS IT TOOK TO FILL THE TANK BACK UP.

figure 1

The amount you end up with is the amount of mpg your vehicle gets. See figure 2

figure 2

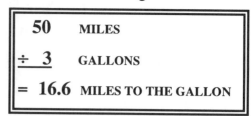

50	MILES
÷ 3	GALLONS
= 16.6	MILES TO THE GALLON

Now if there is a distance between two cities of 100 miles divide 100 by 16.6 (miles to the gallon). This will give you how many gallons of gas you will use on the trip. See figure 3.

figure 3

100	MILES FROM POINT A TO POINT B
÷ 16.6	MILES PER GALLON
= 6	GALLONS OF GAS USED ON THE TRIP

HOW MANY GALLONS OF GAS TO COMPLETE TRIP

If you take an estimate of what gas costs per gallon at gas stations in the area and multiply it by how gallons of gas you will use, you will arrive at a close approximation of what your gas costs will be. See figure 4:

figure 4

$1.39.9	PER GALLON
X 6	GALLONS OF GAS FOR THE TRIP
= $8.50	APPROXIMATE TOTAL GAS COST.

COST OF TRANSPORTATION FROM ONE GIG TO ANOTHER

Always cushion yourself with extra money, just in case something goes wrong like the van breaking down.

To figure out your bottom line, you should take the total estimated expense amount for the trip and minus it from the total dollar amount you are being paid from all the shows.

ROAD TRIP A

$650	**TOTAL GUARANTEE FROM CLUB**
- $890	**TOTAL ESTIMATED EXPENSES**
= **- $240**	**AMOUNT OF LOSS FROM TRIP**

or

ROAD TRIP B

$1,800	**TOTAL GUARANTEE FROM CLUBS**
- $ 865	**TOTAL ESTIMATED EXPENSES**
= **$ 935**	**PROFIT FROM SHOWS**

In example **A,** this road trip appears to be a financial loss. The balance (-$240) represents only an estimate of your expenses. To be safe you should add more money to this figure (about 50% more) or **$100** bringing the total up to **$340.**

In example **B,** you appear to be making a profit but again this is only based upon estimates. It might not seem necessary to bring money but you should anyway for a number of reasons **(a)** All your income amount is not in your hands until you play the shows and get paid. You will encounter certain expenses on your way to the first show like gas & tolls. **(b)** Your income amount is based upon the entire series of shows on the road trip. It does not take into account the fact that the first three shows might be the lowest paying of the bunch. Therefore you are going to need money to fund those three days.

This expense budget list should be created for each individual show but you must then add up the totals to get a complete view of the entire road trip.

Note: Shows that you have booked that do not have guarantee payments cannot be added to the budgets.

SLEEPING ARRANGEMENTS

Motels are expensive even the cheapest ones. Rooms around major cities are in the $50 & up range. In the outskirts and small rural towns you may still find places that are $15- $45 a night.

Below are some tips on how to save money on road accommodations.

 ASK THE CLUB BOOKER IF THEY HAVE ACCOMMODATIONS FOR THE BAND.

There are some clubs that have rooms above or connected to it where they do put touring bands up. It may not be offered so you should ask. On many occasions I asked if the band could crash at the booker's house since they were not paying us enough money to get a motel. Many times if the situation permitted the answer was yes.

 GET MOTEL RECOMMENDATIONS FROM THE BOOKER WHEN YOU ADVANCE THE SHOW.

Some clubs keep this information on file and will supply you the name and phone number. You should call these places and ask for room rates.

Try sticking with one room and two double beds. There is no reason to divulge how many there are in your party unless you are asked. If it is a reputable place there is not much cause for any concern but some of the smaller, off the main road establishments may either deny you a room or worse, up-charge you a radical amount per extra person. In order to protect yourself from getting ripped off, tell them only what they need to know.

You should sleep two people per bed and however many on the floor in sleeping bags. You can buy travel mattresses that are relatively inexpensive for those times when it's your turn to sleep on the floor.

If you have a credit card, book the room in advance. You always have the option to cancel should some other option arise. Fill this information out on your advance sheet along with directions to the motel from the club and from the highway. Find out how long in advance you have to cancel the room, without it getting charged to your credit card.

 FANS

Many times during or after the show, fans will come up to you and engage you in very friendly conversation. They may even invite you to stay over night at their place. If so, use your best judgment but don't turn it into a big party. It will certainly save you money and if you don't get the feeling that these people are deranged, go for it. It can solidify them as lifelong fans that will help promote you on your return visits. If this happens, do not get sloppy. Lock your van. Hide your money, and keep it in your pants. Paternity suits are a bitch, pregnancy will slow down your touring and I'm down on disease.

Word of caution. If you are staying in a hotel/motel don't tell anyone where you are. Don't invite fans back to your room. In a word..... theft. Money, clothes, equipment, whatever.

EQUIPMENT

Onthe road, bring extra equipment and supplies in case something goes wrong at the wrong time. Use the following as an addendum to your equipment checklist.

 BRING AT LEAST ONE BACK UP GUITAR AMP

 BRING AT LEAST ONE BACK UP GUITAR TO USE IF YOU BREAK STRINGS

 STOCK UP ON GUITAR STRINGS

Along with your supply of full string packs, you should purchase individual strings and store them in gauge order. Buy one of each guitar string for each gig you are going to play. Even though your habits might include changing your strings every night before a show, if you happen to break one during the show, why break up a fresh pack for one string that you will change anyway. Bass strings are rather expensive and do not break that often but you should stock at least one back up pair.

 STOCK UP ON DRUM HEADS

 BRING ALONG A SMALL VOCAL PA FOR IN-STORE PERFORMANCES OR FOR ROOMS THAT HAVE AN INFERIOR OR NO PA

 STOCK UP ON EXTRA CABLES

 BRING PLENTY OF DUCT TAPE

 CONSIDER RENTING A SMALL SMOKE MACHINE OR INVESTING IN SOME SPOT LIGHTS THAT YOU CAN USE IN THE EVENT THAT SOME OF THE CLUBS HAVE INFERIOR LIGHTING

For my last client I invested in 5 small spotlights which were set up on the stage floor. Three were placed directly under the microphones pointing straight up into the faces of the singers illuminating them with blue, green & purple beams of light. The other two were bright white, that sat at opposite sides of the stage crossing each other. We also had two large cones which sat behind the drummer pointing up with their beams crossing each other, illuminating his back with red and orange light for a dramatic fiery effect. The group rented and eventually bought a strobe light and smoke machine. This simple light show which we designed and ran, created wonderful effects especially in the small clubs that had very simplistic lighting. Unfortunately we never invested in a lighting board and all the effects were hooked up by many extension cords which led to 4 power surge protectors that I would click on and off during pre-designated portions of the music.

 BRING PLENTY OF EXTRA EXTENSION CORDS

 GUITAR PICKS

 DRUM STICKS

 CD'S OR CASSETTES OF YOUR FAVORITE MUSIC TO RUN THROUGH THE SOUND BOARD (IF YOU'RE ALLOWED) TO WARM UP THE CROWD

 BRING A GOOD VOCAL MIC, IN CASE THE CLUB'S ARE INFERIOR

 BRING A DECENT SIZED COOLER WHICH YOU KEEP IN THE VAN

In case there is extra food or drink from the club bring it in the van after the show with some ice from the bar to keep it fresh overnight.

HAVE ROAD CASES MADE UP FOR YOUR AMPS, EFFECTS, MERCHANDISE , ETC.

It will make your equipment a lot easier to move around especially if it's all on wheels, and will also keep everything protected.

If you think of anything else put it on the list and bring it.

FOOD FOR THOUGHT

If you never ate at McDonald's before, you will now. Unfortunately, traveling musicians cannot afford some of the luxuries the road has to offer. Let's face it, you are keeping long hours, sleeping on floors and not eating nutritious food. While this is in some narcissistic way, an exhilarating experience that you will never forget, it can also be hazardous to your health. Major acts that have all the comforts the business has to offer, have many times canceled shows due to exhaustion and sickness. While it is forgivable at that level, simply because you have enough resources to publicize a cancellation and refund tickets or reschedule, at your level of moving up the crowded ladder, you will most certainly drop down a rung by canceling a show.

Without food you cannot sustain your life. It contains vitamins, proteins and carbohydrates that are absorbed by your blood stream feeding your brain, heart, liver and lungs. If any of these vital organs should stop functioning, your life force disappears. The quality of the food you ingest will have some determination on the quality of your physical self. Let me ask you, would you pour chlorine into the gas tank of your car if you are low on fuel? Would you put olive oil into the crank case if you are low on oil? Of course not, it will destroy the engine! They why would you consider eating food that has no nutrition and may quite possibly shorten your life. I hate to think that you place more importance on your car than you do yourself. You are not indestructible. You may last longer eating crap than your car will with chlorine in the gas tank, but when you finally stop running, spare parts are harder to find.

Why am I so passionate about this? Well I myself got pretty damn sick on the road and it's no fun. Once I had food poisoning from bad food and the next night I was so sick that I could barely stand up. I needed to set up a garbage pail behind my amp and three times during the show I disappeared behind it and puked my brains out. For two days I could not eat anything and by the third I was so weak that we had to cancel shows so that I could go home and get admitted to the hospital.

The following suggestions will save money and be more nutritious.

 INVEST IN A LARGE COOLER. KEEP IT IN THE VAN AT ALL TIMES.

At the onset of your road trip, go to the supermarket and stock up on bread, cold cuts, fruit, salad items, dressing, peanut butter, purified water, juice and some home cooked meals.

Maintain the ice in the cooler so you can hang on to the contents for a number of days. Bring plastic utensils, napkins and a cutting board. For $40 you can feed five of you three times as opposed to once at McDonald's. When the food does run out, stop into another supermarket wherever you are and repeat the process.

MAKE SURE YOU EAT AT LEAST ONE SALAD PER DAY AND TWO PIECES OF FRUIT (APPLES, BANANAS, CANTALOUPE).

This will keep your plumbing in good working order.

TRY TO DRINK AT LEAST 7 GLASSES OF WATER A DAY. IT WILL HELP FLUSH OUT THE TOXINS ESPECIALLY THOSE INHALED IN SMOKY BAR ROOMS.

REDUCE YOUR INTAKE (SINGERS ESPECIALLY) OF DAIRY PRODUCTS

They produce mucous which can affect your voice and make colds worse.

INQUIRE AS TO WHETHER THE CLUB HAS A RESTAURANT.

Surely then you can expect some meal ticket. If they have a kitchen but it is only used at certain times ask if you can use it. If yes, have someone run to the market and buy some steaks, fish or pasta and cook it yourself.

Also inquire into having the booker arrange some form of catering. Arrange that they get some take out and have brought to the club for you. If they do not want to hassle with ordering, then ask for a food buyout which can be $5-$10 per band member so that you can buy your own food. It is common among touring national to have catering as part of their rider and club do provide this, however unless you ask you wont get..

BRING ALONG AN ELECTRIC FRYING PAN SO THAT IN THE MORNING YOU CAN COOK BREAKFAST IN THE MOTEL ROOM.

A dozen eggs costs $1.19. A loaf of bread is $1.69, butter 25 cents & half a gallon of OJ $1.99. If you went out to eat breakfast for five people it would cost you at least $15 plus a $3 tip. If you cook in your room it will cost you $5.12, a savings of at least $13. Multiply that by 14 days of a road trip and you saved yourself $182. Multiply that by 200 gigs a year and you get a savings of $2600. Now what can you do with $2600?

> *"When health is absent,*
>
> *Wisdom cannot reveal itself,*
>
> *Art cannot become manifest,*
>
> *Strength cannot be exerted.*
>
> *Wealth is useless,*
>
> *and Reason is powerless"*
>
> Ꮵerophilus, 300 BC

R_x

I know that the preceding section on food sounds good on paper and I know that many of you are going to try to do as much as you can. The truth is it's hard to eat right on the road and it takes a lot just to get by. Many of you may have never been away from home and it will take time before you master the regimen of taking care of yourself. Therefore I have compiled the following list on what to do to prevent illness and to restore nutrients to your body especially if you are not eating right.

This is a mixture of Homeopathy, Aromatherapy & Herbal Remedies which have absolutely no side effects and what is most important is that they support your immune system rather than dull it so that every time you get sick and treat yourself alternatively, your body ends up stronger and less susceptible to illness.

HERBAL MINT TEA OR GREEN TEA

Take with a Tbs. of honey when you feel low on energy or when you have an upset stomach. It is preferable to use fresh leaves rather than store bought dried tea.

Herbal Therapy is a very basic healing process though tea drinking is perhaps the weakest form. Herbal capsules are four times stronger than tea, but they are expensive. You still can get a lot out of tea if the leaves are fresh and you drink small amounts throughout the day rather than one big cup in the morning. Fresh leaves can be found at most health food stores.

CHAMOMILE TEA

To settle your nerves or treat stress at night after a long day of traveling and playing.

ROYAL JELLY

Comes in a jar packed in honey or in capsule form. Take at least 10,000 mg twice a day. Royal Jelly is the food that is fed to the queen bee from the head glands of the bee's nurse workers. It is a natural anti-biotic and a stimulant to the immune system.

NUX VOMICA

A Homeopathic remedy for upset stomach & headache. Available at most health food stores for about $4-$6 a bottle.

BELLADONNA

A Homeopathic remedy for any sudden outbreak of sickness that brings on a fever.

ACONITE

A Homeopathic remedy taken at the beginning stages of a cold. This remedy works miracles and if taken at the right time will reduce the cold by 80 -100%.

COLDS

You can also make a mix of 2 teaspoons apple cider and two teaspoons of honey in a glass of water in the morning, At night mix 2 Tbs. lemon and honey with one tsp. of grated ginger with a glass of water. If you are decongested try a Tbs. of grated horse radish with lemon juice and watch you sinuses clear right up. If you have a chest cold try taking grated ginger and pouring it in a bowl of very hot water. Dip a small towel in the water and let it soak up the mixture. Wring it out and apply it to your chest. No you won't end up smelling like a Chinese restaurant.

 ## KYOLIC GARLIC

You may have heard commercials about this product. You should take two a day as a steady diet but up it to six a day when you have a cold. This potent medicinal treatment will not leave the foul aftertaste that fresh garlic does, but will work wonders in the event that you are attacked by vampires.

 ## THE FLU

Unlike a cold the flu can be debilitating and cause the cancellation of shows. You will know you have the flu by its quick onset followed by aching bones and a high fever. Follow these simple remedies and please try not take any of the over the counter drug store medicines. They do not cure you! They only mask the condition. The following will help your body help itself by gaining strength and independence.

> DRINK PLENTY OF HOT DRINKS, SOUPS AND TEAS WITH HONEY.

> DRINK PLENTY OF JUICE MIXED WITH GREEN DRINK MIX. (SEE BELOW)

> AVOID EATING DAIRY AND SUGAR.

> TAKE BOIRON ASCILLOCOCCINUM. (This is impossible to pronounce but it works miracles). It is available at the health food stores that carry Homeopathic remedies. If they do not have, try BioForce.

> INFLUAFORCE (another miraculous remedy.)

> VITAMIN E 800IU DAILY

> DRINK GREEN TEA OR CALENDULA TEA 4 CUPS DAILY

> ECHINACEA - 10 DROP IN WATER. (SEE BELOW)

> GARGLE WITH A FEW DROPS OF TEA TREE OIL 4 TIMES DAILY.

Try to incorporate as many of these as you can. You will find that the flu will not be as severe and will dissipate quicker. The overall advantage is that you allowed your own immune system to fight off the flu making it stronger and more defensive against the next one.

 ## ARNICA

A Homeopathic remedy taken in the event that you should bruise or injure yourself. It will reduce shock to your system and also reduce swelling.

 ## GREEN DRINKS

You can not sustain life from eating death. I am not a pure vegetarian and I do not preach abstaining from meat. However, it is proven that while our bodies *crave* meat, they *need* green food, to enrich our blood. Green plants absorb the sun's light converting it into energy. Once digested by humans that energy is released into our blood stream returning back to us the essence of life.

On the road you are not getting nearly enough nutrients from the food you eat and wearing yourself down from the hours you're keeping. At least once a day you should consume some form of powdered green drink mixed in with juice or water. It's like adding STP to your gas tank. I recommend **Green Essence** which is powdered Barley, Alfalfa, Pepper, Broccoli, Shittake mushroom, Brown rice and more. Also try **Alfalfa • Barley • Chlorella** from Futurebiotics. These grains contain the highest concentration of proteins, amino acids, B vitamins and chlorophyll; more than any other food source. Alfalfa with its roots growing down to 130 feet deep, pulls up all of earth's resources from deep in the ground. Its chemical and mineral composition is almost identical to that of human blood.

Even if you eat well you still will benefit greatly from their consumption.

ECHINACEA - (Ika-nay-chia)

A natural antibiotic. This is a liquid extract from herbs and is a great immune system booster. It can be taken every day (a few drops in water with no bad taste) or when you are feeling physically run down but not yet sick. This will boost your immune system and probably keep you well or if you do get sick, it will be very mild. The brand I use is **Nature's Answer.**

MASSAGE

Have someone rub your back a few times a week to stimulate the nerve endings. It will ease tension and create better blood flow.

MISO SOUP

Purchased in powder form at most supermarkets and health food stores. This is a very basic medicinal food. It helps alkalize your system, lower cholesterol, help neutralize allergens and pollutants especially cigarette smoke.

This is just some of the many healthy alternatives to drug store, quick fix medicines that do not cure you at all. There are tons of good books that you can pick up at any health food book store that can further detail and educate you on natural healing.

The road will wear you down even after one week. I know some of you may probably smoke, drink and do whatever. If so, at least give yourself an edge to balance out your vices. Most of this stuff is priced from $4- $20, a small investment for big results.

ROAD CREW

There will come a time where you are going to need people to look after all the things that go into putting on a successful live performance so that you can concentrate on playing.

Some of things that will require looking after are:

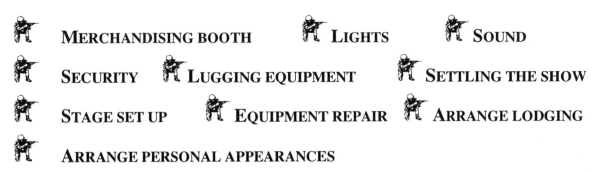

MERCHANDISING BOOTH   **LIGHTS**   **SOUND**

SECURITY   **LUGGING EQUIPMENT**   **SETTLING THE SHOW**

STAGE SET UP   **EQUIPMENT REPAIR**   **ARRANGE LODGING**

ARRANGE PERSONAL APPEARANCES

In the beginning you are probably going to split these jobs among the band members but let's face it, when you are on stage who will be minding the merchandise or changing a broken guitar string. Some of these things are just going to be avoided until you put together a small road crew.

This small crew may consist of only one person who is a good friend, fan or a sibling who just helps lug equipment and sit by the merchandising booth so nothing gets stolen. Or it is someone who may have started out this way but has graduated to a more responsible role of taking care of the equipment and settling the show for you while you mingle with the crowd.

The job descriptions of road personnel are:

ROAD MANAGER

RESPONSIBLE FOR THE ITINERARY OF THE ROAD TRIP ON A DAY TO DAY BASIS.

KEEP TRACK OF PERSONAL APPEARANCES AND TO MAKE SURE YOU GET THERE ON TIME.

KEEP TRACK OF THE NIGHT TIME ACTIVITIES FROM SOUND CHECK TIME TO STAGE TIME.

SETTLE THE SHOWS AND BE RESPONSIBLE FOR ALL THE MONEY.

TO LOOK AFTER THE MERCHANDISE.

MAKE SURE THAT ALL THE THINGS LISTED IN YOUR CONTRACT ARE HONORED.

ARRANGE YOUR SLEEPING ACCOMMODATIONS.

ADVANCE SHOWS FROM THE ROAD ESPECIALLY IF YOU ARE OUT FOR WEEKS AT A TIME.

 DO SOUND OR LIGHTS.

 POSITION THEMSELVES BY THE STAGE TO TAKE CARE OF ANY PROBLEMS THAT MAY OCCUR DURING THE SHOW.

 INSTRUCT YOU ON WHERE TO BE AND WHEN TO BE SO THAT YOU MEET ALL YOUR OBLIGATIONS.

SOUND MAN

The main function will be to man the sound board during the live performance. Clubs can at times be war zones of sorts. Sometimes when playing on another band's turf it might be a good idea to have someone on your side behind the board ensuring you a decent shot at a good sound mix.

Good sound men are hard to find. Try the following places for leads:

 INDEPENDENT SOUND COMPANIES LISTED IN THE PHONE BOOK.

 COLLEGES.

They are good places to look since they put on a lot of shows and usually have students that run the systems.

 CLUBS THAT OWN SOUND SYSTEMS HAVE ENGINEERS THAT RUN THEM.

Keep track of the club soundmen you meet along the way. Take down their name and phone numbers and store it in your gig file.

 LOCAL MUSIC STORES OR RECORD STORES THAT SEEM TO EMPLOY MUSICIANS MAY BE A GOOD PLACE TO LOOK.

Professional sound men generally command anywhere from $50 and up to mix a live show. If you bring someone on the road to mix your sound, you will need to work something out since you might not even get paid enough money to eat. You do not want to end off a road trip being in debt to a sound man.

Having gone out on road trips both with and with out soundmen, I can tell you that until the band is at a point where it is profiting money or headlining major venues, you do not really need one. As I mentioned in chapter 6, the club engineer should be able to give you decent mix since he knows the board and the acoustics of the room better than anyone. The more you travel and the more clubs you play, the more familiar you get with the many soundmen that are out there and the more comfortable you will be.

STAGE MANAGER

This persons office is the stage only. They are the caretakers for the band's equipment, duct taping all the cables, posting set lists, bringing you water or beer, fixing broken guitar strings and aiding any of the band members with whatever technical difficulty they have during the show. They will help assemble the stage prior to and disassemble it after the show is over. The mark of a good stage manager is one who keeps their eyes peeled on the stage throughout the set anticipating even the slightest problem like a guitar cable getting caught on a speaker monitor or a cymbal standing slightly out of place and then immediately mending the situation.

Unsigned bands that are earning average to minimum pay ($50 - $300) may need to do all these jobs themselves if they have no one to perform them for free. However, if you have some qualified friends that see this as a potential job opportunity and take it seriously, take out two people, one to stage manage and one to road manage. Both can help to watch the equipment while you go out to record stores or colleges or just a walk around town. It should be made known to the club owner that they are band personnel and are expected to receive whatever special treatment the band receives, including food, free admission to the club and back stage access.

COMFORTS OF HOME

Here is a small list of things you should bring with you in your luggage to make you more comfortable while you tour.

YOUR OWN PILLOW   SLEEPING BAG OR BLANKET   BOOK / MAGAZINES

WRITING PAD / JOURNAL   CAMERA   NINTENDO GAME BOY OR OTHER

PORTABLE TAPE PAYER / HEADPHONES   LONG DISTANCE PHONE CARD

TOOTH BRUSH / TOOTH PASTE   SHAVER/ RAZOR / SHAVING CREME   SOAP

MEDICINE, REMEDIES, TEAS ETC.   CARTON OF CIGARETTES.   MONEY

($10 PER DAY)   SUNGLASSES   EXTRA CLOTHES   YOUR OWN BATH

TOWEL   COOLER   FOOD   ELECTRIC FRYING PAN / SPONGE / SPATULA

DAILY ITINERARY

The member of the group that does all the bookings, should create some form of daily itinerary for the other band members. When you stop and think about all the conversations you may have had with the clubs and all the setting up of appearances, radio interviews etc., you must admit there's a lot of information. Perhaps more than you have been able to communicate with your group and certainly more than they will remember. Therefore you should type up a day to day itinerary so that they can read up on and familiarize themselves with what their day entails other than just eating, sleeping and playing.

This itinerary will borrow much of the information from your advance sheet.

FRIDAY MARCH 6

The Bayou Washington DC

11:30	Wake up
12:15	Breakfast
12:45	Depart Hotel (to destination 4 hour drive)
5:15	Load in
6:00	Sound Check
6:35	Interview with Music Scene Magazine
7:30	Dinner backstage at club
8:30	Personal appearance at WWDC radio for live interview. See advance sheet for directions
10:30	Meet backstage
11:00	Showtime 60 minute set
1:00	Load out
2:30	Check into Motel

Make an itinerary for each date of the road trip and have copies printed up and placed in a folder for each band member.

KEEPING TRACK OF ROAD EXPENSES

Throughout your days spent on the road, you will be holding, collecting and spending band money. This is a responsible job and requires careful documentation to ensure the safety of the money as well as its proper accounting so that all the expenses incurred both on the road as well as back home are taken care of. The proper way to account for all your expenses on the road is by collecting and saving all the receipts for everything you spend your money on. At the end of the day you should tally up all the totals of the receipts along with any income you produced that day and log them into a road report. These road reports will be your financial history of the road and allow you to analyze the flow of money over an extended period. This will be your best aid in designing budgets for future road trips as well as offering you ways to decrease some of those expenses that eat into your profit potential.

If you like you can flip over to chapter 16 where I discuss this subject in full detail as well as supply you with road reports (compliments of the Wlodinguer, Erk and Chanzis accounting firm in NYC) that you can use to fill in the proper numbers.

OTHER TIPS FOR THE ROAD

KEEP FILES OF ALL THE RECORD STORES, MUSIC STORES AND ALL THE OTHER TYPES OF PLACES YOU MAY WANT TO CALL UPON THE NEXT TIME YOU ARE IN TOWN.

Keep these files within the club file and update them as you continue to tour through these towns over and over again. The easiest way to do this is to get business cards from each place. Some of the listing you should save are:

- MUSIC STORES
- LAUNDROMATS
- HOTEL, MOTELS, INNS
- BANKS,
- WESTERN UNIONS
- RECORD STORES
- HARDWARE STORES
- RESTAURANTS
- ENTERTAINMENT PLACES
- SERVICE STATIONS
- SOUND EQUIPMENT COMPANIES
- IMPORTANT FANS
- SOUND MEN (You never know when you may need good soundman for an important showcase. You may resort to calling one from a club you have played in the past to come in for the day.

KEEP YOUR MONEY ON YOU AND SAFE AT ALL TIMES.

IF YOU NEED TO SEND MONEY HOME DO NOT SEND CASH.

Either have a bank, wire it into your account or get a bank check and mail it to yourself or financial representative at home to deposit it for you.

CHECK OUT YOU PREARRANGED LODGING.

If you pull into town earlier than expected and if you had previously reserved a motel, you should drive over to it and check it out.

You might find it to ritzy or too much of a dump. Use the time to scope out a more realistic place for you to sleep in that night.

IF YOU HAVE A FAR DISTANCE TO TRAVEL FROM ONE GIG TO ANOTHER, IT MIGHT BE WISE TO LEAVE AFTER THE SHOW AND DRIVE PART OF THE DISTANCE TO THE NEXT DESTINATION YOU ARE PLAYING.

You will always find a motel on the highway and this will allow you to sleep a little longer the next morning as well as cut down on your driving time. With the extra time you have the next day spend it by doing things to promote your group.

IF IT IS THE LAST NIGHT OF THE TRIP I WOULD LIKE TO SUGGEST THAT YOU TRY TO DRIVE STRAIGHT HOME WITHOUT GETTING A MOTEL ROOM, ESPECIALLY IF YOU ARE LOW ON CASH.

However, (and this goes for all after show drives) be aware of the time and your exhaustion level. I would prefer that you get a room and sleep off the gig arriving home with $80 less in cash, than arriving home in an ambulance.

 PLEASE DO NOT DRINK AND DRIVE.

 IF YOU ARE GOING TO BE OUT FOR WEEKS YOU SHOULD CALL THE CLUB YOU WILL BE PLAYING AT TWO DAYS BEFORE YOU GET THERE FROM THE ROAD.

This will be a quick call to check and see if any changes are made to your previously advanced information. Recheck load in time and sound check time.

 IF YOU NEED TO MAKE A PHONE CALL ALWAYS TRY TO ASK AT THE CLUB IF YOU CAN USE THEIR PHONE.

Keep it short but you can always sneak in a call to your significant other.

The last thing I want to say about being on the road is to realize and understand that you are a guest in someone else's town. Please try and bring with you the same respect and consideration you have for your own town and display it here as well.

Be mindful and courteous to others and stay out of trouble. The law enforcement people do not take kindly to strangers making trouble in their town. You are apt to face stiffer penalties for insignificant crimes that might otherwise go unnoticed or forgiven in your own home town. Even though America is one country, you will begin to realize just how diversified it is when you begin to travel. An out of state license plate can spell trouble if you are not careful.

14

COLLEGE TOUR CIRCUIT

With all the information you have received so far, you should now have been able to carve out a successful niche for yourself in the club circuit. If so, then first let me present you with this rock & roll high school diploma.

Go ahead, take a few days off, head to the shore and relax because when you return we will begin the second stage of your education, at the college of your choice. For some bands this is a breakthrough step that can launch them into a new dimension of touring and popularity.

The college tour circuit is not for every band. Though I have tried to be generic throughout the book, this chapter that may not pertain to certain acts whose music won't find a primary audience at the college level; where the relatively young crowds (18-23) are drawn toward the popular radio bands or the new up and coming college radio acts, whether rock, rap, metal or alternative.

Of the many college concerts that are booked throughout the year, a good portion feature national acts (bands with major label releases). The more popular nationals can earn upwards of $20,000 a show in the college circuit while the new up and coming acts can bank on a payment starting at around $500 to $2000. Since most college concert budgets can afford to hire the popular nationals for only a handful of shows a year, the rest of the events feature up & coming acts along with younger unsigned bands as openers. These are the events that you are going to focus on.

HOW TO BOOK A COLLEGE SHOW

There are thousands of colleges in America and many of them have college concert committees. These groups of students are given the prestigious task of spending a portion of the school tuition on hiring entertainment.

Some of the smaller community colleges have very small budgets and usually put on only one or two small events if any a year. But the bigger four year colleges and universities can add up to a gold mine of business if you play it right. There are a few ways to go about booking colleges so I will begin listing them below in no order of preference.

DIRECT CALLING

By obtaining the phone numbers of the college concert committees or student activities boards as they are sometimes referred to (use the Pollstar college directory), you can call and directly ask an activities board member for a gig. This is not the easiest of tasks since the students who sit on these boards keep slim office hours (like Tuesday from 2:15pm- 2:25pm). Their short period of office time is spent returning calls from agents and band managers, all of whom are requesting dates. The lesser known you are, the less of a chance you have getting your call returned. This is a fact of life but should not be a deterrent. Remember, patience and perseverance are key.

When you finally get through, you will encounter either a sweet, pleasant voice that is just as excited about booking you as you are about playing, or an obnoxious, arrogant, spoiled brat who gives you the run around. Keep in mind that these student bookers are just young people getting their feet wet in a very serious end of the music business. To most, this is not their eventual profession and they seem to fail to realize that for you, it very well may be. Therefore, counter their unprofessionalism with your professionalism, since chances are they are only one of many board members who will decide whether you will get the gig or not.

To land the gig, you will be required to send them your press kit and tape for final approval by the concert committee. So be nice and as soon as you hang up the phone go right to the post office and mail away your press kit and tape.

USING AN AGENT

Even though you might not be signed to a booking agency, you can submit your music to agencies for the college circuit only. There are many agents around the country that deal directly with colleges. These agents may represent some nationals, but they may also handle regional bands that are not signed but do well at colleges.

By using your directory, call around to the agencies. Do not expect the agents to jump out of their seats when you call, alerting them to your availability. You will have to endure the same lengthy ritual of sending in your press kits and tapes, calling back, calling back and calling back. In the end what will win you representation is if they have heard of your group's reputation either through the club circuit or through the press.

It would help to focus on booking and headlining venues that cater to college age crowds. For instance here in NYC there is a club called WETLANDS. It is a fairly popular club known around the country for booking alternative and counter culture bands as well as sponsoring and promoting social consciousness and environmental activism by hosting day time seminars from nationally renowned speakers.

The club attracts a strong college crowd and since it is located in NYC many of the participants in the audience are visiting from other places in the state and from other states. Many bands that have started out as very popular bands in Wetlands have gone on to become very popular college bands and some have gone even further to become very popular national acts like Blues Traveler.

If there are places similar to this in your town and if your music is conducive to the crowd that gathers there, it is imperative that you concentrate on becoming a fixture at the club. In time as your popularity grows you will be able to use that popularity to gain influence with the agents who book the college circuit as well as having your reputation spread far enough that those who sit on the booking committees at the colleges may eventually hear of you. This is why you need to always be thinking six months ahead. If you plan on booking the college circuit make it a point to book the type of clubs that will be a catalyst for the next stage rather than just randomly booking any old place.

USING THE CLUBS

Another angle in getting in on college events is to build up your reputation at the college by booking the clubs in the college town first. Here on the East Coast small towns like State College, PA or Burlington, have a large student body and plenty of town bars to choose from. This is what I call working your way from the inside. But it doesn't have to be a huge college town housing three universities. It can be a small town with one college and one bar. In 1992 I booked one of my clients into a tiny 75 capacity bar in Oswego. They played on a Friday night and the crowd was really receptive. I saw this place as a good once a month stop helping to fill up dates on their calendar as well as a way to position them for a possible spot for the Springfest concerts at the university in Oswego.

So I kept booking them throughout the year and sure enough by spring, they had become so popular that we were approached by members of the student committee who had become fans of the band after seeing many of the shows in that bar, to perform at the Springfest. They ended up opening up for the Smithereens, in front of 5000 people.

NACA

The **N**ational **A**ssociation of **C**ampus **A**ctivities comprises 1,200 colleges and universities all over the U.S. and Canada looking for the best entertainment and educational programs to present on campus. Affiliating with NACA opens you up to the many resources available to NACA members. NACA started about thirty five years ago when a few college entertainment buyers got together to purchase an act to perform at their respective schools. It seemed that if each school purchased the act separately, they would have had to pay a very high price for the one date. However by banding together and offering the artist a chance to perform multiple nights in different colleges they were able to procure the artist at a lower rate in exchange for consecutive work. The success of this venture gave birth to what is known as NACA today.

By joining NACA you will receive the names, addresses and telephone numbers of the talent buyers who program the events for their campuses. School members are also given your access information so that they can contact you directly.

Every year NACA has their national convention in Nashville. For four days you can mingle and meet with panels, school talent buyers committees and NACA affiliated agents (about 2000 representatives in all). There are live performance spots as well that enable your band to showcase themselves to all these various talent buyers.

NACA • 13 Harbison Way • Columbia, SC 29212-3401
1800 732-6222

The NACA office will be more than happy to supply you with all the registration and membership information you need. If you are interested in going to Nashville, NACA has a brochure prepared that lists all the registration information including fees, hotel reservations showcase and seminar categories. The brochure also comes complete with showcase applications and instructions.

Booking the college market is highly competitive given the nature of how many acts there are looking to this as a major source of work. You will be at a great advantage if you can hook up with a booking agent that has a NACA membership. Of course all the major booking agencies like CAA, ICM and William Morris, have memberships but there are many independent agencies that have membership and book only college concerts. They deal with the student buyers week in and week out and the student buyers prefer to deal with the members as a way of making sure that they get good, professional talent.

This does not mean that if you are not a member or do not have an agent that you will never get a gig. On the contrary you can but the problem is that many of the student buyers are not full time booking agents as we discussed at the opening of the chapter. They are full time students that may have office hours for 15 minutes on a particular day, one day, every two weeks. This means that you have about the same chance of getting them on the phone as OJ has of winning an Academy award. When the student buyer goes through their stack of messages they have enough time to just call back those they want to talk to, in this case the agents they deal with all year long. You would be very wise to investigate NACA further and when you can, make the investment to travel to Nashville for the convention.

WHEN IS THE BEST TIME TO BOOK COLLEGE

There are basically two booking periods throughout the college year. They are the fall season when many colleges host Fallfest (Late September-Early November) and Springfest (Late April-May) concerts. Though they might go by different titles depending on the school, they all occur during these times of the semester. Many of them are held outdoors and may feature a big name national act. But because they are all day events, there will be at least three if not more bands included on the bill. And one of them can be you.

FRATERNITIES / SORORITIES

Some of the very best shows (both emotionally and financially) that I attended and booked, were college frat parties. These are run by the students themselves and operate within the guidelines of their individual charters. In a way they seemed to mimic small countries run by Monarchies. They have certain codes of behavior that when looking in seem rather ludicrous but once you get to know these brothers and sisters, you will find them to be people who take friendship and honor very seriously.

At some colleges the frats have their own homes where as many as twenty to fifty people live. They will have kitchens, dining halls, bars and some of them have great rooms where bands can come and set up and play. Unlike a club situation where you are at the mercy of drawing a local crowd, when a fraternity throws a party everyone comes, including the keg delivery guy who will bring enough spirits to guarantee a wild night.

Frats have built an entertainment expense into their budget which is an accumulated amount of money from contributions of present and past frat brothers. These contributions keep the bills paid on the house they live in among other things. The best time to book a frat party is in the beginning of each semester when they start fresh with a new budget or at the very end of the semester when they have to spend the balance of what money's they have left.

HOW TO BOOK A FRAT PARTY

Unfortunately there is not a NACA organization for frat parties so booking one is going to take some connections and investigative know-how. First, you can call each college and ask for the phone number to the Greek Council. This will supply you with the names, phone numbers and address of the fraternities on campus and off campus. Some fraternities are more outgoing than others. There are fraternities that are made up mostly of athletes while there are some that are more academically oriented. Then there are some that are sort of a hodge podge and these are the ones you want to really zero in on.

To start with call the fraternity and ask to speak with the person in charge of fraternity events (also known as the "Social"). Inquire as to their policy regarding booking bands at the house and ask what a band needs to do to get to play one of their parties. If a frat house regularly has parties there is a good chance that they either hire DJ's or they already have a number of bands that they bring in whom they know and are assured of having a great time.

I can tell you that if no one at the frat house has heard of you, it is going to be a hard sell for you to get in. They want to make sure that for the money they pay which can amount to thousands of dollars, that they get a band that will keep them up and dancing all night.

You will need to have a good tape to present to them as well a good list of cover tunes. This is one time that I encourage original bands to resort to playing cover tunes (at least three per one hour set).

Aside from the usual politics of getting into a frat house you may indeed need to have an inside connection with the house. Like I mentioned earlier frats are a closed circle and sometimes it is very hard to even get the president to talk to you on the phone unless you have an in.

At many colleges, fraternities will hold "Greek Week." This usually occurs in the spring and can culminate with a big outdoor concert. At times the frats might combine all their resources together to put on a major event or they may each individually host their own block party or backyard concert. You should be aware of these events and pursue them with diligence because they pay well and are highly attended.

Due to the fact that the frats are not clubs and that they are not set up as performance halls, bands must be prepared to perform in a variety of uncharacteristically unusual situations. Whether it will be a performance held inside in a room with no lighting, stage or acoustically buffered walls or setting up outdoors on a slanted portion of their backyard, these must be considered only minor detractors from the overall benefit of playing the event. To minimize the inconvenience and be in more control of the environment use the following checklist:

 INQUIRE ABOUT THE SIZE OF THE ROOM YOU ARE PLAYING IN AND BRING ALONG AN APPROPRIATE SIZED PA SYSTEM.

If it is an outdoor show make sure that the frat has worked out the production (sound and staging).

BRING LIGHTING WITH YOU AT ALL COSTS.

The worst thing you can do is perform in a room under a fifty year old chandelier that emits a very bright light. Even worse is a room with a tall ceiling fitted with recessed lighting that only half the bulbs work. illuminating the room with a dull, yellow light. Use your imagination. I always carried a fresh supply of Christmas lights, both white and colored, large and small bulbs, that would replace the overhead lights creating a more intimate atmosphere.

BRING A LADDER

Or make sure that the frat house has one. You will use it to hang lights, banners, etc.

BRING RUGS

To set up on the stage area. It will help keep the drums from sliding around.

BRING PLENTY OF EXTENSION CHORDS

The older frat houses may not be able to handle all the amps going into the few outlets by where you are setting up. Therefore you will want to spread out the power around the house, especially if you are using a PA system.

MAKE SURE THAT YOU KNOW WHO IS PAYING YOU AND THAT IT IS AGREED THAT YOU WILL BE PAID PRIOR TO PERFORMANCE.

The very last thing you need, is to play for three hours and then spend the next three trying to find the guy who is supposed to pay you. When you finally do, he is running naked around the basement of the frat house, piss drunk, screaming out lyrics to your songs but has no recollection of who you are or where his urine soaked pants are with your check fermenting in it.

O MAKE SURE THAT IF PAYMENT IS GOING TO BE BY CHECK, THAT THE CHECK IS APPROVED AND CASHED PRIOR TO YOUR ARRIVAL.

This way you can receive the cash rather than having to cash the check at some other time. This is strictly for your convenience and insurance. A bounced check is worthless. Explain that you are on tour and you do not have the resources to cash checks out of town.

MAKE SURE THAT EITHER YOU OR THE FRAT PROVIDE A TAPE RECORDER OR STEREO THAT WILL PLAY MUSIC BEFORE AND AFTER EACH OF YOUR SETS.

MAKE SURE THEY PROVIDE FOOD, DRINK AND ROOMS FOR YOU TO CRASH IN BOTH DURING THE SHOW AND OVERNIGHT.

As they say, with a college education you can create bigger and better opportunities for yourself. Well that will be evident if you work at cultivating a good college following. From festivals and student union concerts to frat parties and college bars if you tie in T-shirts and tape sales, you can turn it all into a major financial resource that will help support your recording and touring endeavors. Parlay it all into one concise press kit with a strong 5 song CD and you may just get that recording contract, (diploma).

15

COLLEGE RADIO

Often throughout this book I have referred to college radio. I have done so because it is for an unsigned band, a pivotal medium to conquer. For starters, it may very well be the initial place for airplay that your record company will turn to when you release your first album. If you have developed college radio on your own with any kind of success, you will have paved the way for the label, which may indeed make your band more apt to get signed and, after releasing the record, advance to the next level at a more rapid pace.

To better understand the power and importance of college radio, let's first look at the overall importance of radio and its relationship with music.

In 1920, 55 years after James Clerk Maxwell discovered that electrical impulses travel through space at the speed of light, only 27 years after Edouard Branly invented a device that received a radio wave through a wire, only 25 years after Guglielmo Marconi sent radio signals through the air developing the first wireless telegraph, KDKA of Pittsburgh, and WWJ of Detroit, broadcasted the very first radio program. The few people that owned radios would don earphones and listen to broadcasts of phonograph records being played. By the late 1920's, stations were popping up everywhere, broadcasting everything from music and news to different forms of entertainment, like comedy, sports and advertisements.

In 1929, the first college radio station was founded. It functioned primarily as a regular station and was considered a college radio station simply because it was situated at a college.

For the next thirty years, radio rose in popularity to the point where in the late 1950's, an estimated 150,000,000 radios were fixtures in both homes and cars.

As television began to rise in popularity, radio's personality began to change. Different types of programming were needed to keep the interest of the commuter, housewife and vacationer. So as TV began to air the kind of programs that were first launched on radio, radio began to focus much more heavily on music, sports and news.

Though the first FM station began airing in 1933, most of the stations were broadcasting on the AM frequency and some broadcasted on both simultaneously. But, in 1966 the FCC declared that in the 65 major radio markets broadcasters could no longer send out their signal on both AM and FM frequencies.

By the end of 1967, FM radio began to rise in popularity due to a number of timely situations. The advent of stereo recording capability and stereo home receivers gave musicians a whole new palette of sound and possibilities on which to create, and FM was the logical place to broadcast their results. To cater to the ever expanding diversity of new music, radio stations began to spring up on the FM dial: these stations played the new releases that were recorded in stereo, offering the listener a new and heightened experience.

The face of rock and roll during this time had grown into two highly opposing images. The political and social climate that bathed the world during the 1960's had a profound effect on artists and musicians in both America and Europe, cultures which had influenced each other for years. What first began in the fifties with Elvis and then in the sixties with the Beatles and The Stones, these two cultures seemed to have spawned a musical offspring borne out of a marriage made in diode heaven. Music began to do more than just entertain, it began to enlighten and educate.

In 1967, FM radio had brought to the forefront a whole new genre of popular acts that were taking over the reins from the AM radio pop stars. Stations like WNEW FM in New York City came into being as their programming focused on this new rock and roll scene. Aside from the Beatles and Stones who transcended pop music and encouraged the experimental trends, acts like Bobby Sherman, B.J. Thomas, Three Dog Night etc., were losing credibility to artists like Bob Dylan, Richie Havens and Jimi Hendrix and bands like Creedence Clearwater Revival, Jefferson Airplane and others as more and more listeners were trading in their AM transistor radios for FM stereo receivers.

Although AM radio would after a time, play only a group's big hit single, FM was breaking new ground by playing other songs from the album thus the acronym: AOR (Album Oriented Rock).

The resulting popularity of this format launched into stardom certain bands that otherwise might never have found any success with AM. Thrust to the forefront by radio and then other forms of media, the public's social consciousness was drastically altered from the messages preached by these musical messiahs. Fashion, art, politics and alternative lifestyles of the musicians were welcomed with open arms by their loyal listeners. When Woodstock took place in 1969, millions of people converged in Bethel, New York to hear dozens of bands that were, for the most part, not even played on AM radio.

During this time the FCC released the lower areas of the FM frequency band for low wattage informational and educational programming. These were prime frequencies for college students to start their own radio stations, that would just broadcast on campus and not interfere with larger stations. The combination of musical renaissance, free form speech and lower band frequencies ignited an even more radical change in radio programming. Although college DJ's were playing much of the same music that was being heard on their big sister stations, college radio was very loosely programmed and became a free form voice for the burgeoning generation of the sixties. Whether DJ's were playing their own band's demo tapes, spinning some new Jazz or talking about the Vietnam War, college radio was off and running.

During its adolescence (1970's-early 1980), college radio formats were developing on every college campus. Somewhere during this time, the forerunners of the FM explosion seemed to have forgotten what their mission was and completely disregarded what was becoming the new wave evolution in music. What was once the underground, was now considered full-fledged mainstream and except for a few of the early "New Wave" bands like Devo, the early 1980's playlists still reflected what was on major FM. Artists such as Heart, The Who, Yes and Van Morrison, were the bulk of the stations music.

As "New Wave" started to gain its musical prowess in the mid eighties, college radio seemed to be going through its own metamorphosis. In rock and roll, there seemed to be two camps forming. On one hand, there were the mega rock bands like Boston, Fleetwood Mac and Foreigner, that seemed to be turning FM radio into purely hit-oriented broadcasting that AM once was, on the other hand, Punk and New Wave was taking a real stand in eventually changing the direction of rock music entirely. It was during this period of Black Flag and the Sex Pistols and, later on, REM, Gen. X, The Dickies and the Stranglers, that college radio began to shy away from big band rock and align itself with the new underground.

By the late 1980's commercial FM radio was going through a serious identity crisis. Programmers had no clue what to do to keep their listenership interested. Some chose to introduce comedy teams to goof around in between lame music and commercials while others resorted to going completely retro and broadcasting the hits of the sixties as if there were no new bands making good music anymore. I remember picking up a major national rock publication sometime in 1990 shocked to see on the cover Jim Morrison, who had died two decades earlier being touted along with "The Doors" as the poet of the new generation.

It was as if major radio had completely forgotten what its identity was and their aging, program directors were completely out of touch. This was not so at the bottom of the FM dial. The student population was discovering its own music despite what AOR radio was programming. Much of this music was being recorded on independent labels like IRS records who were signing up bands that the majors passed on due to the very same lack of vision that radio had.

Then, one day in 1991, when FM radio was broadcasting the best of Strawberry Alarm Clock and giving "Shadow Traffic" reports, and major labels were wondering why bands like Every Mother's Nightmare could not sell any records, Nirvana burst on the college radio scene with "Smells Like Teen Spirit." By late 1991 every rock formatted college radio station had Nirvana at number 1 on their playlist, and the flood gates had opened. They were like the musical roosters, cock a doodling right in the middle ears of A&R guys and major radio station program directors.

By the time of this writing, the music scene has seemingly benefited from what college radio spearheaded seven years ago or for that matter two decades ago. With the popularity of Hip Hop, Rap, Grunge and all the other labels you may want to stamp on music, the college philosophy of letting the DJ play what they like will always give the airwaves a true sample of what the people really want to hear.

With the popularity of college radio riding to the forefront, it seems as though major radio and record companies have spent more time looking in on their charts and even employing college-age staff members to scout out the new sound that is hip on the street level.

This has been a healthy injection of soul to the music business and has resulted in a variety of bands that have actually hit the big time, which may never have happened in previous environments. But the aftermath has yet to be written and I sometimes wonder if college radio will itself become complacent now that it has set the trend or will it continue to be a source of new music? Will the new found interest of record labels in the college radio format force the unsigned and indie bands off the air, making way for only the major label new releases? Will the major station programmers and A&R executives continue the search for new underground music or will they exploit and milk the crap out of whomever is popular at the moment and ruin every cool band that be happens to be popluar at any given moment. Bands need to take control of this exploitation, otherwise rock as we know it will get slick and complacent. If this happens one result is inevitable: Disco will return!!

CMJ

With all this action happening, CMJ (College Music Journal) was founded in 1978 to service, report and add credibility to college radio. In 1982, CMJ released its first publication, **THE NEW MUSIC REPORT,** which featured the top thirty playlists of all reporting college radio stations. As the publication grew, it began to compile sales figures along with these playlists and combined them to form the CMJ music charts. This, for the first time, gave programmers as well as their readership an insight into the popular and future trends of music; with great accuracy. As a subscriber, I have seen countless groups that were charting high on college radio, go on to become popular album sellers and major radio hitmakers.

Along with the charts from over 500 reporting college radio stations and about 100 major radio stations, the New Music Report also features music news and information, college radio station dialogue and several compilation CD's of new music, which are sent to the subscriber throughout the year. CMJ also publishes the

NEW MUSIC MONTHLY which is a consumer publication available at magazine outlets throughout the country. In every single issue, there is a CD with about 20 songs featuring the newest music of the month.

As you may now understand, this is valuable reading material for the industry (record companies, booking agencies and major radio), as well as managers and bands, especially unsigned bands. If you are listening primarily to what is programmed on the major radio stations, you are in effect two years behind musically. After all, that is about how long it takes for a young band to get signed, make a record, release it, tour it and finally get it to major radio. By then, the recording is several years old and the song itself may even be older than that. But at the college radio level, you're hearing the most recent recordings and may catch the newest trends in music.

For a subscription to CMJ NEW MUSIC REPORT send $295 to:

```
CMJ
11 MIDDLENECK RD
SUITE 400
GREAT NECK, NY  10021
OR CALL (516) 466-7471
```

CMJ also hosts a four day annual convention called Music Fest the week after Labor Day, at Lincoln Center in New York City. The convention is a way of crystallizing everything they do all year long in publication into a one on one social, media and music event.

What began in 1981 as a college radio gathering of 100 people with no live band showcases, had by 1997 evolved into a mega music event that included 6700 people hosting 55 panel discussions, as well as, 30,000 attending the 40 sponsoring clubs per night that showcased 487 bands which were covered by regional, national and international media, (Rolling Stone, CNN), retail buyers, record companies and radio stations.

The convention is made up primarily of daytime seminar activities, where members of the press, college radio programmers, commercial radio programmers, retail buyers and band members can partake in discussions and meet and greet situations. There is a registration fee so for more information call the phone number above.

At night, hordes of people converge on the numerous bars, clubs and theaters scattered throughout New York City to see various different unsigned and signed independent bands from all over the world. Great care is taken by the CMJ staff to choose bands from a vast array of different styles to perform. Along with the popular college radio bands that have been booked to perform (signed Indie bands and unknown major label bands), CMJ tries to give unsigned groups their chance to get heard. In the past years, bands like Silverchair, Hole, Jane's Addiction, Green Day and REM, unknown bands at the time, emerged from Music Fest as the hot bands of the year.

A minimum CMJ staff of three people (sometimes more) listen to and audition every single tape that is submitted. CMJ strives to find groups that have "attitude, forward thinking, edge and content to their music." They will on average discard about 30% of the applicants based upon the fact that they lack vision, walking already proven musical ground. By weeding out the wannabees, they can focus on the bands that are making some kind of artistic or political statement through their music and lyrics.

Submissions for performance spots are taken in January and all that is required is a tape (preferably cassette or CD), a contact name and number, bio, band instrumentation, press and history. While a full size press kit is helpful, the one thing that holds CMJ apart from many of its contemporaries is that it is not impressed by press kits that are loaded with hype. It truly is all about the music. I know many bands, together for a short time, that have landed a very good performance slot based entirely upon the quality of their music. No application fee is required and final selections are made by June 15 for international acts and July 15 for American acts.

There is no disputing the fact that Music Fest is one of the best opportunities for an unsigned band to come in completely unknown and leave having been seen by a label president, major press and countless radio people. You can truly manifest this opportunity into something spectacular if you concentrate on networking at the convention and succeed in getting people to come down and see your band perform.

All interested applicants can apply by sending their information to:

CMJ

MUSIC FEST

11 MIDDLENECK RD

SUITE 400

GREAT NECK, NY 10021

MAKING COLLEGE RADIO CONTACTS

The results of this performance can certainly lead you to picking up a few good contacts at college radio. If this is all you get out of the convention, it is certainly a windfall in itself. Remember that you are not only there to just play, but to network yourself and make contacts. This will save you from having to sell yourself over the phone to a complete stranger in months to come if you are trying to get played on college radio.

You will forward your CD over to these contacts in hopes of getting it added to the rotation. And, if you get enough airplay, you will get charted; and if they report to CMJ, it will be printed in The New Music Report. If this happens, you need to be aware of it. To do that, you should either have (a) formed a relationship with the station so that you can be forwarded a copy as it appears in the New Music Report, (b) have a subscription to New Music Report and watch the charts every week or (c) have access to a CMJ report through a friend who works in the business.

Knowing what we know about college radio, let's take that conversation one step further. Before Nirvana hit in 1991 and college radio was just a simple format run by college students it was relatively easy to get airplay. If you sent a decent recording to the station and a DJ or program director liked it, there was a good chance it would get played. If the audience responded favorably and requested it, the song would get more airplay. If other DJ's heard it and liked it, it would get even more airplay. When "Smells Like Teen Spirit" became a crossover hit, the industry, realizing that college radio was responsible, focused its attention in college radio's direction. Major record companies stepped up their calling of college DJ's and program directors, asking them what else was hot. College radio stations were soon deluged with material sent down from major labels to play on air. And along with the music came the kind of attention college DJ's had not seen before. National acts stopped in at college stations for interviews and even on air performances. Ticket giveaways and contests were offered. Cool merchandise was forwarded to radio programmers as incentives to play the newest releases. In many cases, these college students were getting a taste of the big time and a feeling of power.

By 1992, it became increasingly difficult to get a DJ or program director on the phone. By 1993, it became near impossible to get a college DJ to even listen to your single unless it was a major label or independently released recording with major label distribution. In a sense, the disease that flowed through the blood stream of the major music business, had now infected the once pure form that was college radio. Thankfully this disease is not terminal there are still many college stations that could offer your band air time if they like your music.

SO HOW DO YOU GO ABOUT GETTING AIRPLAY

STEP ONE

 YOU SHOULD NOT APPROACH COLLEGE RADIO UNTIL YOU HAVE A CD.

Once upon a time they played cassettes, but no longer. When you release your album, you should form your own small label to promote the record. Whether it's you, a manager or a friend on the other end of the phone, the DJ will be somewhat interested if the presentation has the look and feel of being professional.

 GET A DIRECTORY OF COLLEGE STATIONS

If you are using a good college directory like POLLSTAR, you will find listings of the college, the radio station phone number and the program or music director's name. When you call, you should have this information in front of you, but when the person picks up on the other end, instead of asking for the music director, you should first introduce yourself and ask the person on the other end of the phone what their name is.

This is because most program or music directors are in the studio only a short time each day. Since most college stations give the DJ's room to program their own music if one of the DJ's answer the phone, you might as well start a conversation with them and try to make a direct sell. If you were a legitimate and known record company you would definitely bypass the DJ and go straight to the music director. However you are not. Music directors are a bit jaded from dealing with bog labels and will probably not give you the time of day, but a DJ will. They will appreciate the attention and more importantly, if they spin the type of music you make, they would genuinely be interested in perhaps discovering someone new.

If you have ever tried working radio, you will have read this last paragraph and immediately think of all the snobby, arrogant, college DJ's that you have had the displeasure to meet. Well, I have known some myself and I always made it my job to work on those individuals the most, showering them with a great deal of attention, provided that they played my clients' type of music and had a decent listenership at a happening college.

On one such occasion, I worked this DJ on an Ithaca college radio station for an entire semester. Though he wouldn't spin my clients' record, we had developed a rapport and through repeated pestering on my part, combined with a support spot that I booked for my client opening up for Big Head Todd and the Monsters at The Haunt, Ithaca's most popular club, I got him to schedule a two hour broadcast of a live electric show done right from the studio. My clients arrived the day before the scheduled show and from 8-10:00 PM set up and performed live from the WICB radio station. Obviously I needed that kind of billing to get the broadcast but I also needed the broadcast to get the show.

It was a bit tricky coordinating these two events without promises from either party but that is what managing is all about. In the end, the broadcast went off in a big way and the club promoter, who had the radio tuned to the broadcast the night before, was very pleased with my clients, especially upon seeing a full house of new fans attracted by the broadcast.

WORK ON YOUR SALES PITCH

When you make your pitch to a college radio station, you should have your sales rap down. Consider not mentioning that you are in the band but rather assume the role of band representative. You can introduce yourself as the manager, or refer to yourself as someone calling on behalf of the band. This approach carries more weight and makes the band appear more professional. The following is a mock phone call similar to the way a record company radio person would do it.

"Hi, this is Troy calling about the group Suction from NY."   **"Yo what up"**

"Well I'm getting word out that they just released their debut album "Plunge of Allegiance" on Defense Records. I'd like to forward over the disc to your attention for airplay." **"Yawn"**

"The group is presently on tour and we are working on some bookings that will take them through your area (give a tentative date) and it would be great if we can get some airplay and build up some excitement about the upcoming show. If schedules can be worked out I would love to have them stop in to the studio for a brief on-air interview." **"What do they sound like?"**

" Hard edge sound, catchy melody lot's of samples" Kind of like Fun Loving Criminals,......Same Church, Different Pew" "The first single off the album is track 3, "Sway", but listen to the whole disc man and play what you like."

Amid all this rhetoric the DJ will hopefully be asking you questions about the group. Answer them honestly and try to refer to things that help get them on this radio station. For instance, if you have done your research and gotten a copy of CMJ, you would have looked up this station and checked their charts to see what kind of bands are in rotation. You may have noticed that the Fun Loving Criminals are in the top five and since you have heard that comparison before you might as well use it to your advantage. Secondly, the charts give you an indication as to whether this station would even be interested in your band.. Finally, by seeing their playlist of bands, you may notice that your band had played a show with one, which you should then mention in your conversation. This is called building the story. The more information you can supply to the programmer on behalf of the bands accomplishments the better chances you have of getting a shot at rotation.

There are other things you can mention to swing the DJ over to your side. Inquire as to where they are from or what their college major is. By personalizing the conversation, you may discover common interest between the two of you. After all, you are an unknown band on an unknown independent label and have very little to offer the station. By becoming more than just a voice on the phone, you increase your chances of getting on the radio.

The preceding approach is a direct one indeed, and you should not feel uncomfortable doing it. People tend to respond to an authoritative voice, especially if it is not overpowering and obnoxious. College radio music directors are used to this approach because this is how most label reps do it. If you feel uncomfortable with this type of rap, have someone do it for you or develop a rap that gets results. Again, I do not recommend that you call as a member of the band. It is a weak approach and you will be viewed by the station personnel as a band with no representation, i.e. unprofessional.

It's important to note that when you refer to "performing in town at some upcoming date," that you are indeed working on or have booked a show in the vicinity. Remember that at times you will need to have college radio play to get a booking in the town the college is in and sometimes you need to be booked in town to get college radio interested in putting your music into rotation.

This dilemma can be resolved by resorting to what I call "tentative truths," for the sake of getting what you want. Choose your words carefully like using the term "tentative". For instance, "We have some _**tentative**_ dates being discussed for a possible show in your area" or "we are looking over some available dates in our tour schedule to bring us through your area." These are common industry lines and are not lies provided that you *are presently* trying to book some dates.

I know first hand how difficult it is to get bookings in certain out of town locations unless the band has a huge reputation. But when I would tell the club booker that I had college radio play in their area and that I would have the band up at the station on the day of the show for an on air interview, I got the booking 100% of the time.

Of course it goes without saying that a show in the area will have some influence on getting some airplay on the radio station. Get those dates booked and let the radio station know about the dates so that you can get your band up to the station for an on air interview. Once they meet you in person and you impress them with your charm and presence, you will have a friend at that station for at least one full year. If you can knock out twenty or thirty of these stations and get your music played in enough rotations, and it is getting charted on CMJ on a regular basis, then you really are getting close to making it.

If you get the program director on the phone, you can follow the same format but you might not have as much time to schmooze. A program director has been through the mill already and has heard much of it before. You want to ask them to listen to the CD, especially the single and hopefully submit it for airplay. You will get the usual "I can't promise you anything."

Make sure that whomever you end up talking to, you get their office or on-air hours so that you have a better shot of reaching them when you call back. Take notes during the phone call and list some of the details that can be repeated back when you make your follow-up phone call. Put these notes in a radio file that corresponds to a club file so that you can have all this information at your disposal everytime you work this area.

After you hang up, get back on the phone and book a show in the town. Don't think "what if I don't get the radio play" or "what if no one shows up at the gig". That's negative thinking. Make sure you get on the air and work the show to get some people down to see you, even if it's only ten. If you are any good, that will turn into twenty then eighty and three hundred someday.

After you make all your contacts, file your information and get those tapes and press kits out in the mail. It wouldn't hurt to ask whomever you spoke with on the phone what clubs or bars they frequent or recommend that you perform in. You may find that they know someone at the club and can be instrumental in getting you a booking. In either case give it a week and call back to see if the CD got anywhere.

STEP TWO

AFTER THE INITIAL CONTACT WAIT A WEEK AND CALL BACK.

INQUIRE IF THEY RECEIVED YOUR PACKAGE.

Find out if they are going to put it into rotation.

GET THEM EXCITED TO MEET THE BAND.

Offer up some ways in which the music director or DJ can get involved with the upcoming event, be it an on-air interview, having the DJ announce the band at showtime, or turning the show into a station event by advertising it as "WKGB Presents," which some radio stations may appreciate since it can bring added awareness to the station. If you need a place to crash after the show, you can ask the DJ to help set you up with accommodations. This is another great way of bonding, which will result in added playlist rotation. If you have secured a show date somewhere nearby, let the DJ know about it and let your enthusiasm for coming to their town run rampant.

At this point, end the conversation expressing your gratitude and let them know that you will be in touch as the live date approaches. Depending on when the gig is, don't call again for about two weeks. When you do call back, make some small talk and then inquire about how well the single is doing. Find out what type of rotation it's in, light, medium or heavy. If it got into medium rotation, there is a good chance it may have gotten charted on CMJ and if so, inquire as to the status of that. If it did get charted, do whatever you can to get a copy of the charts as they appeared in CMJ.

For those of you who do not know, rotation refers to the amount of times your song is played in a day. Light rotation may mean 1-2 times a week, medium may mean 3-5 times a week and heavy means 6 and up. Songs get in rotation first because the DJ likes them and then by listener requests. So if you want to get good medium to heavy rotation, you should have a DJ that really likes the record and either some friends in the area to request the single or you can cheat and call the station yourself from time to time and request your own single. This may be okay initially, just to get enough airplay in order to get the record heard, but in the long run, it's bogus, especially if you hit heavy rotation because you called fifty times a week and nobody else did.

About a week or two before the scheduled gig, call the station and try to arrange an on-air interview for the day of the show. This should be pretty easy to accomplish, especially if you have been getting some airplay.

If you do get the interview, request that the DJ who has been charting you, conduct it. This should further improve their allegiance to your group. If they seem a bit shaky about it, ease them up by saying that you will supply them with a list of questions so things go smoothly. Once you get a conversation going, everything will be cool.

You can fax or mail the list of suggested questions you have compiled, along with a letter that encourages the DJ's own list of questions. This will give them time to study the questions so that at interview time, it won't sound like they are just reading questions off of a piece of paper. If you wish, ask if you can bring acoustic guitars so that you can do a song or two in the studio.

When it's all said and done, request the presence of the DJ or director to join the band for dinner after sound check as your guest. This is your way of showing thanks for their interest and help.

As any good employee of a record company would, you need to schmooze (a New York term meaning chill with) the DJ's to continue the charting of your record. You never know, that this geeky college DJ might graduate and become the next Howard Stern, so it pays to be friendly and appreciative to the person who is helping your band.

There is no question that this schmoozing is costly, especially if you are going after many radio stations. But, as I mentioned early on in the book, this is a business and it does require your continued investment. In the end it can pay off in a big way. Imagine a record company looking over your press kit, seeing dozens of college radio playlists cut out of CMJ along with a 175 per year tour date schedule, a self-released CD with sales reports and merchandising figures.

Imagine being visited after a show by a rep from Interscope, or SONY Records one day. They say that they have heard a lot about your band and after seeing you live would like to meet with you to discuss doing a record. Imagine all the hard work of the past few years, paying off in a very big way. Imagine this especially if you have made it all happen yourself. One thing is for sure, you will be in a much better position to direct your future and increase your worth, because you are on top of your game. Imagine that!

ACCOUNTING & MUSIC BUSINESS 101

As these past 15 chapters have stood as mile markers on your road to success, I'm sure that you have come across some serious financial road blocks along the way. From raising start up money to fund your very first gig, to plunking down the thousands of dollars for a recording session, the lack of available capital has, at times, rubbernecked your own musical career.

It has been a constant struggle to balance the weight of gigging, traveling and promoting, against the shortage of income the gigs produce and the high cost of advertising them. You may have even scratched your own head wondering: "How am I going to afford this?" or, even worse, been asked by your own band members in a rather confrontative matter: "Where does all the money we make go?"

As you will see, the money is spent in many different areas. Odds are that you will spend much more than you will make for much of your unsigned career. The costs of running the whole operation are very high when you figure in all the long distance calls for booking shows, postage, printing, gas and so much more. To fund your band business you will need to rely on investments from yourselves, parents, friends and possibly a manager.

The amount of debt that you can eventually go into can be quite high, not to mention what poor spending habits can result in. By creating some books detailing your cash flow, you will come face to face with the trail of money, which will heighten your financial awareness. But even more importantly, a business cannot properly function if its income and expenses are not documented and the money is not properly cared for.

A simple example is: you have a big show that you just booked. It's at a hot club and you are going to need to bring in a big crowd to really make an impression. So you make up some flyers and some postcards to mail out to your fans. You also call to reserve a van because the show is in the city thirty miles away. But wait, you check the band fund and find that there's no money in it. "How is that possible?" you ask yourself. "I thought we had one hundred dollars from the last gig we played two months ago." So now what do you do?

I have outlined an extreme case and I know that most of you know better than to be this careless. It certainly doesn't take a genius to figure out that you should have opened a bank account or at least kept the money separate from your own spending money. But just this alone is not enough.

What I want to do in this chapter is go a few steps further and show you how to keep books on your cash transactions as well as how to portion your money out so that you can take care of your present expenses and plan for future expenditures.

It is very important to keep records of your earnings and expenses day to day and month to month. By recording the information, you will be able to view it and find answers to your "where did all the money go" questions. By actually seeing the trail of cash flow you will come to understand the intrinsic relationship between earning and spending. The mastering of this relationship will result in improved spending habits and will force you to streamline them as well as to learn to shop around for better prices on many of the services and products you use. These records will also serve as income and expense documents for tax paying purposes.

DEVELOPING A CLEAR FINANCIAL PLAN

I want to emphasize the importance of building a strong financial base for the group and define some of what your long range plans may be. As band members, you are also, in a sense, businessmen. After all, your music is your product and the live performance of it is your service. When you provide the service (performance) of your product (music), you are going to get paid for it. This is no different than the business transactions of AT&T, Microsoft or McDonald's. These three businesses have created unique products and serviced the needs of masses of people, generating fantastic financial rewards, which is exactly what you are trying to do!

What do these three companies have in common? On a philosophical level, they all started out with a concept that they worked hard at for many years, focusing on little else. On a financial level they believed in their end result and put their money where there mouths were. They continually re-invested their capital back into their businesses, nurturing it until it grew up into the giant end result, rewarding them with a windfall of capital much greater than they ever dreamed possible.

I do not think that the men that started these companies saw money as their first priority. No, I think they were fueled by the realization of a dream and the desire to make a mark in the world. Their financial rewards came from their undying resolve to achieve their dreams, as well as a hard work ethic to create the best product they could. Somewhere in that spiritual mix there needed to be a deep understanding of finances and controlling the flow of money that ensured their growth. For you to succeed you need to become like them; to be consumed with the desire to make the best product you can, to work passionately at making it and to understand and control the flow of money. Without a handle on your finances you will not have the necessary funds to make a good recording or buy good equipment or afford a rehearsal space, all of which are things you need to make the best possible product you can.

By adapting some simple financial practices and philosophies, you will help yourself reach your goals and, if you do reach them, you may end up earning more money than you ever dreamed of. By then, you will have accumulated the knowledge to know what to do with the money so it won't get squandered.

KEEPING BOOKS AND RECORDS OF TRANSACTIONS

Throughout we have discussed what the many avenues of income are for the group. As you earn this income, you must also spend some of it in the form of expenses.

Let's take each income producing activity and break it down by its expense.

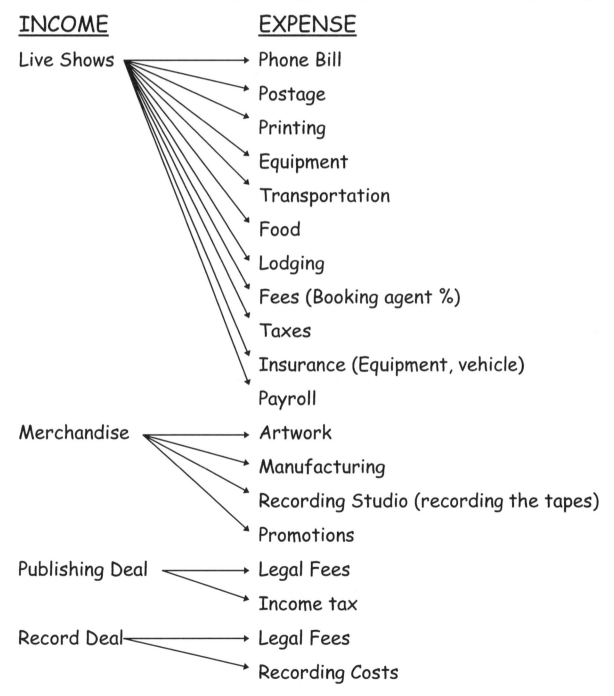

INCOME

Live Shows

Merchandise

Publishing Deal

Record Deal

EXPENSE

Phone Bill

Postage

Printing

Equipment

Transportation

Food

Lodging

Fees (Booking agent %)

Taxes

Insurance (Equipment, vehicle)

Payroll

Artwork

Manufacturing

Recording Studio (recording the tapes)

Promotions

Legal Fees

Income tax

Legal Fees

Recording Costs

By getting a clear picture of all the areas where you will have to spend money to make money, you will be in a position to budget out how much you want or can afford to spend on each category, thus increasing your chances of making money.

If you are unaware of what your expenses are going to be or for that matter what the items are that you have to spend money on, you will end up either spending money you don't have or losing money you have already spent. But if you focus on the costs you will be able to make sound financial decisions and minimize the losses.

Here's a very simple example. Suppose you go to the extent of booking an out of town show, which involved many long distance phone calls, mailing out your press kit and tape, finally getting the show and sending out your mailing list which has 500 names. All this work has cost you money. The cost may add up to the following:

$15 - Phone calls

$8 -   Press kit (includes printing cost for each page, photo, folder & tape)

$3 -   Postage

$40 - Postcards

$115 - Postage on 500 postcards

$85 - Van rental

$20 - Gas

$20 - Food

$306.00 Total

Now suppose the show is paying you **$200,** which leaves you with a **$106** cash debit. Question is, where are you going to come up with the **$106** balance to take care of expenses? Well you may have that money in your band fund left over from a previous show. Or you may need to take out a personal loan from the band members to fund the trip.

Now what if you have another out of town show in two days?

What if you receive a notice that your insurance payment is already a month late and if you don't make a payment in full tomorrow, they will cancel the insurance on your van?

What if you get the same notice from the phone company? The $15.00 dollar bill for the gig you just played was, in reality, 1/20th of the what the entire bill is.

What are you going to do now?

Has everyone in the band pooled together more of their own personal money to pay for everything?

How many times in the past have you done this already?

Is each member putting in their equal share or is there one member slacking off and not coming up with their share?

Has anyone been paid back any of the money they lent into the group?

Have you written and recorded each of the personal investments into your business?

The snowball effect that each one of these questions will create is enough to affect the future mobility of your band. No, there are no simple answers for how you can spend less than you earn because the simple fact is that booking, promoting and traveling to a show is an expensive ordeal and most shows do not pay enough to cover all the costs. The best insurance there is in preventing this avalanche is to have records of all your financial transactions. By becoming astute to all your expenses you will be in a better position to control the effects of cash flow and minimize the damage.

So when should you start doing all this? When should you be recording income and expenses? After all, you are not accountant. Well, you don't have to be an accountant and the time to start is right now!

I'm going to take you step by step from forming your band as a business entity to compiling spreadsheets and recording your transactions. So, in the immortal words of Ric Ocasek and The Cars, "Let's go!"

"Hey Rico, what do we do with all these receipts for beer and cigarettes"

FORMING THE BAND AS A BUSINESS ENTITY

When you form a band you are in a very real sense starting up a business. The rules and laws set up to govern your actions are the same for any group of people that form any type of business.

When you decide to conduct business and transact money, the first thing you need to do is register your business with the state and obtain a federal ID number. This is done mainly for tax purposes as well as obtaining a business checking account at the bank.

To form a business you first must decide what form of entity you will be. There are only three types of business entities, of which two are practical for a group. They are: (a) partnership or (b) corporation. (The third type is sole ownership which does not apply).

The basic difference between the two is that as a corporation you are not owners but employees of a larger business, whereas in a partnership you and your partners are the principal owners. This affects you in two major areas. (**a**) Tax liabilities (**b**) Insurance liabilities. Corporations pay a higher tax than partnerships, while partnerships are not protected in the event of a lawsuit. Should a suit be issued against a corporation, the individuals of that corp. are not personally liable as they would be if they were partners. There are many other differences and I will not venture to say which is better. That is for you to discuss with your lawyer and accountant, not a manager.

What is most important is that an open discussion take place between the band members and that certain agreements are made amongst you. These agreements should cover a wide range from what is expected from each band member, to the percentage ownership each member has in the group.

It is only logical that these agreements take place at the onset of the group rather than two years or ten years later. Each member should know, for instance, what their role is in this partnership and what their commitments are. If you decide to split everything equally, four ways for example, all for one and one for all, that means many things. Is the main songwriter therefore willing to share his publishing royalties with the rest of the band, or with one member who never had money to invest? Will you feel right about splitting your record contract advance equally with that person? Will they be asked to pay everyone back? How much money is that going to be? Or will they now be told that since they never put any money in, they have forfeited some of their equality and will now be offered a smaller percentage in band ownership?!

Imagine after your album has been at the top of the Billboard charts for 10 weeks, that the big publishing check that just arrived in time for the holidays, is being split by the two songwriters in the group and that you, the drummer, were never given any writer's credit and therefore are not entitled to any royalties. If this happens, you cannot blame anybody but yourself.

These and so many other questions need to be addressed and documented in some form of a partnership agreement. There are many matters that confront a band on a day to day basis and the band must make some friendly decisions regarding the entire scope of the band's operations. These agreements can be drawn up between the members and an attorney. In most cases it doesn't happen until the band is offered a record deal and in some unfortunate cases, even then it doesn't happen. And the effects can be truly formidable.

As a manager it would be my advice to you to create a simple agreement amongst yourselves by virtue of your own intelligence, as soon as you name your group and prepare to play out live. As you will see below, there are things that are intrinsic to a band that can be destructive should a band not have an agreement. After a while as things start to take shape, I would then recommend that the group see a lawyer and prepare a formal agreement listing do's and don'ts for the individual partners. Some of the categories that need immediate attention and discussion are:

 ## BAND NAME

This is a major asset of the band and its ownership must be known. What if you form a band and the bass player comes up with the name? What if you never discuss anything about name ownership and after three years the band is one of the hottest in the area? All you need to do is have the club put your group's name and logo in the paper and just by that alone hundreds of fans come to see you play. What happens if you have a major difference with the bass player and as a result they decide to leave the group and start another one? What if they want to take the band name to use for the new group? If you never discussed this, then I guess they might just be able to do that. And that would really suck for the rest of the band. Sure, replacing a bass player is difficult but what about a name that is so easily recognizable and in a sense has become a commodity for the user?

 ## PERFORMANCE PROFITS

These are the profits the band earns from live shows. Are they to be split up evenly among the members or are there two members that let's say are the creative force and do the majority of rehearsal and writing while the rest of the members are more in a part time situation? What is the split going to be? You certainly can't do things one way for five years and then one day say "Hey they are all my songs, I do all the work around here, so from now on, it's 50/50. I keep 50% and the rest of you split the other 50%." Or can you? If there's nothing in writing, then anyone can do or say whatever they want.

 ## INVESTMENT REQUIREMENTS

Are all the members of the band expected to invest equal amounts of personal money in exchange for an equal percentage split or not?

 PUBLISHING PROFITS

These are the profits earned from the sale and airplay of your written work. This is a major source of income for the writers of hit songs. Are you willing to share this money with your band mates? Do you ask that they contribute parts to your songs turning them into band songs or do you compose the entire song yourself and only require the players to play what parts you have written?

 MERCHANDISING

What is done with the earnings of T-shirt and tape sales? Are you the artist who designed the logo? Are you entitled to a larger share of the profits or will merchandise be part of the split that you have agreed on concerning publishing, touring etc.

 LEAVING BAND MEMBER

What happens if a member decides to leave the group three days before a tour? What are their liabilities? What are their responsibilities? Are they entitled to any money, profit sharing or credit?

As you can see things can get pretty hairy if you get into arguments and some members leave or decide to take control because their ego is inflated or because the rest of the band is slacking. It is best to tackle these things when you are in the best of times and all friends. The worst time to hash this out, is prior to signing a record deal and finding out for instance that the guitarist you have been playing with since grade school is not interested in splitting their song writing royalties with you.

Once you have some form of an agreement, you can now plow forward in harmony, each member knowing what their place is in the family.

BUSINESS REGISTRATION

To conduct business in America you must register with the town you live in as a business. This is done so that the town, city and state can collect taxes from the money you earn. Obviously if you do not register, then you are not a known entity and no one comes to collect taxes from you. But then you will not be able to open up a band bank account which will make depositing and cashing checks made out to the band impossible. Sure, you can open up a personal bank account, but then you would be liable to pay the taxes on the deposits of income into that account. These are just some of the things you need to think about before you go ahead and register or not register.

If you do register you will be asked to do a search of your company name to ensure that no one else is using that name. You will pay a fee of approximately $25.00 and receive a form. Once filled out you will get a business number and become a viable, tax paying, legitimate American business. For more information about starting and operating a business in America, send away to:

Basements to Backstage

22 Long Sands Road

Center Ossipee, NH 03814

603 539-6337

Ask for information concerning the series "**Starting & Operating a Business in...**" (Fill in your state). They have a different book available for each of the 50 states! The cost of the book is $24 plus shipping and handling.

Another book to inquire about is **"The Legal Guide for Starting and Running a Small Business."** This book helps answer many of the legal questions and problems that occur day to day. It's full of practical information to help you make sound business decisions. The book is $24 and they offer a software package for $39 for Windows or Mac.

INITIAL INVESTMENT

Going back to what we discussed in the beginning of the chapter, let's talk about the initial moneys brought into the group.

From the moment you start playing an instrument you are incurring expenses, whether it's buying equipment and sheet music or taking out an ad in the local paper looking for someone to jam with. The money you spend on these things is coming from your pocket and is yours to spend on your hobby as you like. It's not tax deductible and does not have to be paid back or matched by anyone else.

However, when you join a band and form a partnership, the money you spend on certain things will now be categorized as capital investment. I'm not referring to purchases that enhance your own personal equipment arsenal. Capital investment refers to money put into the band to be used to conduct the future business actions of that band, that benefit the entire band and not just one member. This money will be put into a fund commonly referred to as a *"BAND FUND."*

This money should be put into a bank account or given to a responsible person to hold onto and keep track of. The band may elect a treasurer if need be and that person will be in charge and responsible for the money and transactions. The band must also vote on what the money is to be used for. Is it available for the guitarist's string purchases or to be used for the printing of band flyers, vehicle rental and recordings? What is the maximum amount of money the treasurer is allowed to spend on band purchases before the rest of the members are asked to vote on that purchase?

Once the money is in the account, who is responsible for doing the daily and monthly recording of the expenditures and income? Have you registered yourself as a business with the town you live in? If you have, you will need to fill out quarterly tax returns. If so, you will need an accountant and they will need to see your books concerning your income and expenses.

SPREADSHEETS

So what are these alleged books I keep talking about? Simply, they are forms that document your daily cash flow. As you will see on the following pages, you will create a spreadsheet that records your income and categorizes the items of expenses broken down by each day of the month.

Everytime you purchase something be it a product or a service, you should get a receipt stating the amount you spent. The amount on the receipt should be entered into the spreadsheet under its correct category and then the receipt should be placed in a safe place until the end of the month. At that time, all the entries in the spreadsheet should be added up and totaled for the month. The totals should coincide with the receipts and the ending balance of cash on the spreadsheet should reflect the balance of cash your treasurer has on hand. If it all works out, then you have *"balanced"* out the month.

The expenses that are considered band responsibilities are as follows.

POSTAGE   For mailing lists, press kits or any other band correspondence.

PRINTER   For copies, flyers, press kits, logos etc.

PHONE   Monthly phone bill for the long distance calls related to the band

GAS   Band travel expense

TOLL Same as above

FOOD   Consumed on the road

SUPPLIES   Office supplies like press kit folders, staples, computer ribbon etc.

EQUIPMENT PA system or lighting etc.

RENT   Rent on the rehearsal hall

OTHER   Other expenses that may come up

SPREADSHEET

Day	Income	Postage	Printer	Phone	Gas	Toll	Food	Suppls	Equip	Rent	Other
1 Paradise	500.				$65		$25			$75/van	
2											
3 Press kits		$10									
4											
5 Rehearsal											$30
6 Put up flyers			$8.00		10.00	$2.10					
7											
8 930 Club	$50.				$35.00	$7.50				5/van	
9											
10 The Church	$25				$10	$2.10	$15			$55/van	
11 Press kits		$25									
12 Rehearsal											$30
13											
14 Phone bill				$250							
15 State College	$1,000				$25	$20	$25	$15.00	100/lights	85/van	
16											
17											
18											
19 Rehearsal											$30
20											
21 Press kits		$15.85									
22 Staples								$45.00			
23											
24 Mailing list		$100	$65								
25											
26 Rehearsal											$30
27											
28											
29 CBGB's	$85.00				$30	$10				$100/van	
30 Press Kits		$15.50									
31											
Total	$1885	$166.35	$73	$250	$165	41.70	$65	$60	$490		$120

TOTAL INCOME: $1885.00   **TOTAL EXPENSES: $1431.05**

This spreadsheet represents one month's worth of income and expenses.

What the spreadsheet above has portrayed for the month was that your income exceeded your expenses by $453.95 or in other words a positive cash flow. At the end of the month you should add up all you receipts again and count your remaining cash to make sure that these figures coincide.

BANK ACCOUNTS AND PETTY CASH

As you can see from the spreadsheet, there was quite a bit of cash activity. It would be rather tedious to be writing checks for each of these expenses, not to mention costly. Banks charge for checks and that will really start to add up if you are writing fifty checks a month.

The bank account should be used primarily for the saving of excess money.

A band bank account should require at least two signatures on a check for withdrawal of money. This is to protect the band from one member draining the account on their own.

Your bank activity should be held to a minimum for other reasons. There are monthly statements to fill out as well as the fact that most of your gigs will be paying you cash. And you should use this cash to pay for cash expenses.

Q. SO WHERE DOES THE CASH GO IF NOT INTO THE BANK?

A. For my last client, it went into a cigar box in a desk in the band's rehearsal room. The box was known as the petty cash box. Next to the box was another box that held all the receipts. The box rested on an accounting book that held the spreadsheet records for the month. In charge of the box was the guitarist, who acted as treasurer, and myself.

Since we were the two individuals that did most of the band's footwork, we were the only ones allowed to take money out. This made it very simple to track the movement of money. If there was a mistake or money missing it was either myself or the guitarist.

It was my elected job to do all the entries into the books. The system I had worked out to track the movement of money was very simple. The box that contained the money also had petty cash vouchers which looked like this:

PETTY CASH VOUCHER

DATE: _____

CREDIT AMOUNT : _____

FROM: _____

SIGNATURE: _____

- -

DATE: _____

DEBIT AMOUNT: _____

FOR: _____

SIGNATURE: _____

HERE'S ONE FILLED OUT

PETTY CASH VOUCHER

Money going in →

DATE: __DEC 10__

CREDIT AMOUNT : $300.00

FROM: __WETLANDS GIG__

SIGNATURE: _____

- -

DATE: Dec 14

DEBIT AMOUNT: $30.00

FOR: Postage

SIGNATURE: _____

Money going out
←

If money was to be taken out for an expense, the bottom half of the voucher would be filled out and signed and placed back into the cigar box. When the purchase was made the change would be put back in the box. If there was any deviation between the amount of money spent and the amount of money listed on the voucher, then it would be adjusted to reflect the true amount of what was used.

Then the receipt/s of the purchase/s would be placed in the other cigar box. Every few days I would go through the receipt box and enter the transactions into the spreadsheet. I would also keep a running tab of the vouchers to make sure that the money in the box was equal to amounts on the vouchers.

If money was to be added to the box (from a gig let's say) then the top half of the voucher would be filled in and placed back into the box along with the money.

The purpose here is to keep track of the in and out flow of money. If a voucher was not filled out or a receipt was not placed in the box it would cause a problem when I would go to balance the books. This is why I tried to enter the receipts in the spreadsheets every couple of days so that I could spot deviations and search our memories to find out where the money was spent and on what. After all, I had to make financial reports to the band once a month and I did not like being put into a spot of having to explain why money was missing.

For this exact reason, when the group was offered their record deal, the very first thing I did was send them into New York on six interviews with accounting firms. It's not a manager's place to keep a band's books since it can cause conflicts in an area where a manager is not an expert and does not belong. After all, it's the band's money, not the manager's.

By having records, receipts and vouchers you will have all the necessary documents to track your cash flow. At the end of the month if there is no money in the petty cash box, all the vouchers, if added up, would reflect the positive and negative cash flows that occurred.

When the month is complete, take the spreadsheet, the receipts and the filled out vouchers and put it all together in a file. This will be for your records so that if any band member should say "where did all the money go from last month", you can say "right here" and hand them the file.

If you have a computer with a spreadsheet program, that is excellent. If not, you should go to the stationery store and purchase an accounting book with the amount of columns you need for each category.

What do you do with the money that is not submitted to petty cash? Suppose you played a gig and got paid $1,000. You know that you do not need $1,000 lying around in a cigar box. By looking over your past spreadsheets, you can get a fair idea as to what your monthly expenses are. Take out what you need for the month, put it in the box along with a voucher and the balance should go into your bank account for safe keeping until such time that you need some cash, need to pay a big phone bill or make a big purchase like a PA system, recording a demo, manufacturing T-shirts or buying a van.

WHAT YOU DO WITH THE MONEY ONCE YOU MAKE IT

We are talking about the money you earn from your gigs and merchandise. If you recall in the beginning of the chapter, I spoke about reinvestment. Well, this is where we need to focus on what that was all about. From the start, you invested some money into the band. It could have been a small amount of **$50** each or it could have been a large amount of **$1,000** each. Did you invest your rent money or was it excess cash you put into a business to make it grow? Hopefully it was the latter. If it was rent money, then pay yourself back from the thousand dollar gig so that you can pay your rent; but don't do this again. A business should not drain you of every cent you have and, furthermore, if you are so under-funded that you need to use your rent money, then the writing is on the wall. It will be only a matter of time before something has to give. It will either be your apartment or the business.

I knew that somewhere in this book I was going to have to talk about working a day job. I had hoped to avoid it but I can't finish this section without stressing the importance of it. Listen, you have to have one, if for no other reason than to support your band. Money is going out on expenses faster than it is coming. I know, I've been in bands and managed them. So where is that extra float money going to come from? You can only borrow so much so it will have to come from *you,* the individual members of the band. And unless you are a whiz at the stock market or are independently wealthy, you will need that day job to keep you supplied with drum sticks, strings and clothes, as well as making investments into the band.

Q.   WHEN DO YOU PAY YOURSELF BACK ON THE INVESTMENT?

   A.   For the business to gain momentum, people must put some money into it that is not bled back out right away.

When you look at other businesses, whether restaurants or dry cleaning stores, when the owners open up for their first day of business, do you think that they take the money that came in that day and split it up to pay themselves back for all they spent to build the business? No freaking way! Do you think they split money the following week? No way again!! In fact, they might not even split, for months, any money for salary, let alone pay back any of the initial investment. The money that comes in is used to further build their business. Buy more stock or equipment, take out advertising and hire more help.

Over time, as the business grows and becomes established, the owners can begin to take salaries and, over more time, give themselves raises to eventually reach a point where the business is very successful and they are drawing a very nice salary. That initial **$25,000** they invested has now grown into a **$500,000** a year business and a **$75,000** a year salary.

A young band is just like a small business. The money that comes into the group must be invested back into the group without exception. The initial capital you invested in your band will be returned to you in ways other than fiscal. Consider it investment money for your life long dream.

You will be drawing income from a few different sources. Live shows and merchandising are two which we will concern ourselves with at the moment. Let's take a step back and go through the financial motions of these two endeavors.

GIG MONEY

In the beginning the money you will earn from the gigs will not equal what you are investing into the gig. A showcase that will net you **$0.00**, will cost you at least gas money if not van rental and food money and an assortment of other expenses. This is going to be funded by personal money from the band members or a loan from an outside source. If the next show you play nets you **$200**, do not pay yourselves or the loan back for the first show. If you do, where are you going to get funding for the third show that requires more flyers, another van rental, mailing list printing cost and postage? If you collected **$50.** from each band member as an initial investment, there is still no guarantee that this is the last time you will need to invest money. In the beginning, many of your shows will be for very little pay and you will have spent more on advertising them and getting there.

Keep these records on your spreadsheet. You title your personal investment by the category **CAPITAL INVESTMENT** and list it in the column along with the income. SEE BELOW:

SPREADSHEET

DATE	INCOME	POSTAGE	GAS	TOLL	RENTAL	FOOD	PRINTER	PHONE
1 Capital Inv.	$500							
2 Mail list		$100					$45	
10 AT&T								$245
14 Showcase	0		$10	$4.	$85			
19 Mail list		$50					$25	
25 Bob's Bar	$75		$5		$55	$15		

TOTALS   **$575**   **$150**   **$15**   **$4**   **$140**   **$15**   **$70**   **$245**

Total Cash   **$575**   -   Total Expense   **$639**   =   Balance deficit of **$64**

This is a fairly common example of a band's spreadsheet. From the looks of this month, the band will most likely have to invest further money into itself in order to cover the loss and fund operation for the next month.

Suppose the following month there is a positive cash amount of $200. Do you then begin to pay yourself back for the money you put in last month to cover the loss? My answer is no, not yet. You never know what the following month is going to look like. In fact, I would wait about 4-6 months before you pay yourself back. You want to see if this month's positive cash flow can be repeated again next month and the month after that. If your group is finding that after 4 consecutive months there is more money earned than spent, it may be a sign that you are over the loss period of your growing business. Consequently, you can begin to pay yourselves or your investors back. But do it slowly. Do not drain the pile all in one shot. Remember, you are saving up money for a recording session and T-shirts, a van and bigger promotion.

Another thing you can learn from the spreadsheet is how to sharpen your spending habits. Study the monthly spreadsheet. Do you see any area where you could have saved money?

If you noticed, on the 2nd and 19th of the month, two gig announcements were mailed out for a total of **$150** postage and **$70** printing fees. If you had known about both gigs at the beginning of the month, you could have put them both on one postcard and saved the **$25** printing charge as well as the **$50** postage charge. That **$75** could have been saved and the month would have then ended up with **$11** positive cash flow. If you can save even **$75** a month, that will be a total savings of **$900** for the year, which incidentally is the exact price the last group that I managed paid for a used van that lasted them three years on the road.

MERCHANDISE MONEY

This is the investment and income money earned in the making of your T-shirts and tapes. It is my belief that this money should be kept separate from the rest of your money, constantly recycling itself.

Once you make the investment into merchandise, you want to ensure that when you run out you will have the money to make more. Merchandise is extremely important in that it can be a good source of income down the road, it is a great way to promote your band and it signifies that a band has reached a certain level of maturity.

You should always have T-shirts and music for sale at your shows. Always!

Since you will be keeping this money separate from the rest, you should then have a separate spreadsheet to account for the money. Below is an example of what one should look like:

MERCHANDISING SPREADSHEET

October 95

Date	Location	T-SHIRTS Black $10.00	T-SHIRTS White $10.00	CD $10.00	CASSETTE $8.00	OTHER	TOTALS
5	CBGBS	3/ $30.00	7/ $70.00	1/$10.00	2/$16.00		$126.00
8	Mail Order	1/ $10.00					$10.00
12	The Church		3/$10.00		10/$80.00		$80.00
16	State College	5/45.00	1/$8.00	4/$10.00			$63.00
20	Mail Order	3/$10.00					$30.00
TOTAL		12	11	5	12		$309.00

This data gives you all the information of your merchandise sales for the month. The entries on this spreadsheet were taken from all the merchandise forms you filled out at the shows as well as an accounting of sales that take place outside the show, like mail order or if someone comes to your house to buy one.

Note the entry from State College where you sold some merchandise below sale price. You can, at any time, adjust the sale price of the merchandise, especially if a fan is a little short on cash or wants to buy more than one item. Just make sure that you record it so that your financial records match the cash amount at the end of the month.

Once again, put this money away in the bank or in safe keeping so that when you run out of merchandise, the funds are there to reorder.

EXPENSES

Expenses are a natural occurrence in the course of doing business. They are a terrible nuisance that you can learn to live with if you develop a respect for them and account for their existence.

The most important lesson is to never let yourself get a false impression of wealth. If you play a big college show and get paid $2,500, it does not mean that it is all yours to keep. To figure out how much of it is truly yours, you need to subtract the amount of money it cost you to make the $2,500. The balance is your net profit. By doing that in advance you will always have a fair idea as to what part of this amount is yours.

Previously, we learned how to create a tour budget. The budget outlines the expenses you will incur for a tour or for one show. When you go on the road, your road manager will be responsible for many financial transactions. For example:

 HOLDING THE FLOAT MONEY

 PAYING EACH AND EVERY EXPENSE

 RECEIVING PAY FROM THE CLUBS

 RECEIVING MONEY FROM MERCHANDISING

Hopefully, you have done a budget and are well-funded enough to complete the trip as well as arrive home with enough to pay off any outstanding bills incurred, like van or equipment rental.

Expenses can be handled two ways. They can be paid by credit cards and lumped all into one big payment that you make at the end of the trip. This is a smart and convenient way to run things, provided that you can pay off your card at the end of the month so that it does not build up into a big, interest-bearing debt. If you use a credit card, you will accumulate a lot of cash during a road trip and you must take precautions to protect it.

If you have a bank account, you can stop at any bank on the road and wire some of the money directly into your account. Just don't wire all of it, because you always need to have some cash just in case. If not, your road manager should have that money on their person at all times. If do not have a credit card then you will be paying cash out of expenses from all the cash you are taking in.

Remember what I said about a false sense of wealth. If you are doing four shows in a row and the first two will yield you $1000, do not get all pumped up and decide to stay in the Four Seasons Hotel on the third night. Most of that money is probably destined for some expense, and you should be doing your accounting every night, making sure that your receipts for the day are in order, that your road reports are completed and that you have put away money to pay off the bills when you get home. Remember, there's a big phone bill coming up, an insurance payment and perhaps another road trip that may not make you as much money as this one.

Having a handle on expenses is the smartest thing you can do because expenses are like termites to wood. They will eat away at your profits until there are none left with nowhere to go but bankruptcy.

PAYROLL

Payroll refers to the wages (salary) that you pay to anyone (soundman, lightman, roadie) you have hired to work for the band. Regardless of the amount of the payroll ($1.00 or $1,000), it should be reported to Uncle Sam and taxes paid on it. This is not a complicated process and it's in everyone's best interest to comply with the tax rules of the state.

As an employer, you are responsible for deducting certain taxes from an employee's wage. There is federal income tax, state income tax and social security tax. Depending on the amount of the wage (see below), an employer can pay the wage to the employee without deducting the taxes, leaving the responsibility of reporting the income to the employee.

Employees must file their tax returns (as should employers) to the IRS at the end of the year. Depending on how much they earned, they may need to pay further taxes or can quite possibly get some of it back.

In most cases, bands hardly make any money and neither do their employees. A common practice is for bands to pay their employees per diems, which becomes a band operating expense and not payroll. The recipient of the per diem ($5-$15 a day) does not have to declare the amount on their income tax.

If you are paying out a salary, whether it be to a soundman or road manager, you can give them a form 1099 (available from your accountant). This establishes them as separate independent contractors rather than employees of the band. They are in a sense in their own business contracting out their services of sound production or road managing to you. In this case you can pay them and not have to bother deducting any taxes because now it's a service charge not a wage. The responsibility to pay taxes is now on the individual whom you paid and they will do so by filling out the form 1099. If you earn under a certain amount per year ($600) you do not even need to file income tax. If you earn between $600 and $3,000 you must file but will not have to pay taxes. Amounts over $3000 will be subject to paying some income taxes.

ROAD REPORTS

We touched upon this briefly in chapter 13 and now I want to expand on it in detail. The road report is the documentation of your income and expense transactions that take place on the road. Throughout the day, you are spending money, whether on travel expenses like gas and tolls, or on per diems. At night you are collecting money in the form of payment from gigs and merchandising. You can't just take this money and shove it into your pocket. You need to keep track of it for all the reason we have so far discussed and for the following reasons:

KEEP TRACK OF YOUR AVAILABLE CASH BY MONITORING YOUR EXPENSES VS. WHAT YOU ARE EARNING.

KEEP AN ACCOUNTING RECORD FOR YOUR PARTNERS IN THE BAND SO THAT THEY KNOW HOW AND WHERE THE MONEY IS BEING SPENT.

IN THE EVENT THAT ONE BAND MEMBER OR MORE HAS LENT MONEY TO THE BAND TO COVER EXPENSES, A DETAILED LIST NEEDS TO BE RECORDED SO THAT THEY CAN GET BACK WHAT THEY ARE OWED.

KEEPING TRACK OF EARNINGS AND EXPENSES FOR THE GOVERNMENT.

I always found it easier to sleep if I took care of recording all this information at night, but I was the manager, not the performer, and I was able to find some quiet time after the show. You may choose to do this in the morning over breakfast but it must be done before you start the day. This will ensure that you do not mix up the receipts from different days or have lost a receipt. If too much time elapsed you might not remember where on what you spent the money. The road manager or assigned band member should follow these simple rules.

WEAR A FANNY PACK WITH TWO COMPARTMENTS IN IT.

Keep the cash in one compartment and the daily receipts in the other.

COLLECT RECEIPTS FOR EVERY THING THAT YOU SPEND MONEY ON.

IF YOU FORGET TO GET A RECEIPT RECORD THE AMOUNT ON A SHEET OF PAPER AND ADD IT TO THE OTHER RECEIPTS.

When you record the information, follow these steps:

TAKE OUT ALL THE RECEIPTS THAT YOU HAVE COLLECTED.

Things like gas, tolls, food, motel etc. They should be sorted into categories. Keep all the gas receipts together, toll receipts together, etc.

You should also have a receipt from the club stating the amount of money you were paid to perform that night and keep that in a separate file.

CREATE AND FILL OUT A ROAD REPORT SHEET.

Have these road report sheets typed out and run off so that you have a pile of them before you go out on the road. You can either use one sheet per show or you can format it in a way that there are more columns for accounting multiple days. I would not recommend however calculating more than three days worth of figures per report.

Print it up so that all three sections appear all on one page. Use both sides of the page so that you do not have to use two separate sheets of paper for one road report.

SECTION ONE

ROAD REPORT #_____   DATE PREPARED_____

1) LOANS TO THE BAND (ENCLOSE SCHEDULE) $_____

2) VAN EXPENSE (RENTAL, INSURANCE, REPAIRS) $_____

3) VAN EXPENSE (GAS, OIL, TOLLS $_____

4) HOTEL / MOTEL $_____

5) FOOD $_____

6 TAXIS & OTHER LOCAL TRANSPORTATION $_____

7) MUSIC INSTRUMENT SUPPLIES, RENTALS & REPAIRS $_____

8) TIPS $_____

9) SHIPPING & POSTAGE $_____

10)ENTERTAINMENT $_____

11)PAYROLL $_____

12) PER DIEM PAYMENTS $_____

13) TELEPHONE $_____

14) OTHER (EXPLAIN) $_____

   TOTAL CASH SPENT (DETAILED EXPLANATIONS

   AND ALL RECEIPTS MUST BE GROUPED TOGETHER) $_____

CHARGES: List all items that are charges on credit cards which will be paid back by check when you get home. Enclose the charge vouchers

1) _____ $_____   6)_____ $_____

2) _____ $_____   7)_____ $_____

3) _____ $_____   8) _____ $_____

4) _____ $_____   9) _____ $_____

5) _____ $_____   10)_____ $_____

****

SECTION TWO

PAY RECEIPTS

VENUE   _____

DATE   _____

INCOME:

A) PAYMENT   _____ $_____

B) OVERAGE   _____ $_____

C) MERCHANDISE   _____ $_____

D) TOTAL (A-C)   _____ $_____

DEDUCTIONS:

E) AGENCY DEPOSITS   _____ $_____

F) TAXES WITHHELD AT CLUB   _____ $_____

G) OTHER   _____ $_____

H) TOTAL (E-H)   _____ $_____

I) TOTAL CASH COLLECTED

   (H less D)   _____ $_____

SECTION THREE

BALANCE FROM LAST REPORT - NUMBER _____ ....$_____

CASH AMOUNT YOU BEGAN WITH .... FLOAT.............$_____

CASH COLLECTED FROM (I) ABOVE...$_____

LESS: TOTAL CASH SPENT (SEE EXPENSE TOTAL ABOVE)......................$_____

BALANCE...$_____

LESS AMOUNT SENT HOME...$_____

BALANCE CARRIED TO NEXT REPORT...$_____

When you fill this out be sure to detail on the dotted line the description of what the payment was for.

For any payment that you make that you do not have a receipt for, fill out a cash voucher in its place. You need to do this so that your records all reflect each and every cash payment you make. The voucher should look like this:

```
+-----------------------------------+
| VOUCHER                           |
| DATE:          _____ |
| AMOUNT:  $ _____ |
| PAID TO:       _____ |
| REASON:        _____ |
| SIGNATURE: _____ |
+-----------------------------------+
```

Here is a description of each category.

SECTION ONE

1) Since this is the first report of the trip you will be borrowing money to float you until the payment from the first show. This loan will either come from a band member or from the band's bank account.

2) If you are renting a van, the rental office should have given you a figure that will reflect each day's rental. This figure should also include the insurance as well. So in this space just fill in that amount and make a small receipt for it.

3) Save all the gas and toll receipts, add them up for the day and insert that amount.

4) If you are filling this out before you check out then ask the desk clerk for an exact room amount including tax.

5) Take all your food receipts from the day, add them up, and fill the amount in this space.

6) Unless you needed to use transportation other than your van, leave this blank.

7) Self explanatory.

8) This is for tips you may leave in the motel or if you slip the sound man ten bucks at a show. Don't forget to record the amount on a scrap of paper.

9) Any visit to the post office should be recorded.

10) Most of the time you will not use this line unless you are all going out on a day off and spending band money.

11) If you are employing anyone on the road, be it a sound man or roadie, their daily or weekly salary will be posted.

12) Per diem is an amount of money that each band member and crew gets per day to take care of personal expenses. A band taking to the road that is breaking even or losing money should not be taking per diems. This is really reserved for bands that are road dogs where the members do nothing else but tour. Therefore they are going to need some kind of small income to live. A band's salary will normally be paid to them by their accountant from money collected from prior tours and held in an account so that all their bills can be paid while they are on tour. The per diem is just a daily stipend so the individual can take care of day to day road expenses. A usual per diem is about $5 to $10 per person per day for an unsigned act. If you pay any per diems out you must fill out a voucher receipt acknowledging that you have paid out money.

13) For advancing shows or any band related phone expenses.

14) This is just an extra column for any miscellaneous expenses that may come up.

SECTION 2

Venue - Fill in name of club.

Road Report # - Start from #1 and proceed forward.

a) Fill in the contracted pay for the show.

b) Fill in any amount over the contracted pay; for instance, a bonus from the club.

c) Fill in merchandise sales.

d) Fill in the total of the last three figures.

e) If the club sent your booking agent a deposit on the show, that amount will be deducted from your total pay at the club. For instance, if the contracted price of the show was $1,000 ($250 of which was sent to you or your booking agent as a deposit), that amount would be written here.

f) If the club deducts state and local taxes from the pay, this amount will be written in here.

g) Any other money withheld by the club should be written here.

h) Add up the last three figures

I) Subtract (**h**) from (**d**) and you will get a total of how much you made on the night.

SECTION 3

- **BALANCE ON HAND.**
  (Fill this in starting from your second report.) This enables you to carry your financial figures from one show to another so that you can tie it all in together. (In this case since it is the first road report of the tour you would leave this section blank. However, the amount

that will appear at the very bottom, **BALANCE TO BE CARRIED TO NEXT REPORT**, would be filled in here on the following road report).

```
        Cash you started the trip out with
  +     Cash collected from ( I ) above.
  =     Total cash you have for the day
  -     Expenses
  =     Balance on the day
```

- **AMOUNT SENT TO HOME OFFICE.**

  If you have a big surplus of cash and want to send some home fill the amount here and deduct that from **BALANCE ON THE DAY.**

- **BALANCE TO BE CARRIED TO NEXT REPORT:**

  This is the amount you will fill in on your next report on the first line of Section Three.

When you are all done filling out the report, make sure that all your receipts are grouped and stapled together (all your gas receipts in one pile, food in another, etc.).

You should have with you a large envelope that you can fold the receipts and this tour report into, seal it and store it until you get home. Once you get home you will either transfer these records onto a spreadsheet for your accounting records or hand them over to an accountant for the same purpose.

Let's fill it out so that you can see how it's done:

ROAD REPORT   #1   **DATE PREPARED OCT 18, 1995**

1) LOANS TO THE BAND/STARTING AMOUNT.......*FROM BAND FUND*...........$400.00

2) VAN EXPENSE (RENTAL, INSURANCE, REPAIRS).......... *RENTAL*...................$65.00

3) VAN EXPENSE (GAS, OIL, TOLLS)....................................*GAS*..................$15.00

4) HOTEL / MOTEL..*MOTEL*................. $55.00

5) FOOD.. $20.00

6) TAXIS & OTHER LOCAL TRANSPORTATION............................ ....$0.00

7) MUSIC INSTRUMENT SUPPLIES, RENTALS & REPAIRS...................................$0.00

8) TIPS $0.00

9) SHIPPING & POSTAGE...$0.00

10)ENTERTAINMENT...$0.00

11) PAYROLL...$0.00

12) PER DIEM PAYMENTS...........................*2 CREW MEMBERS..$5.00 each*.......... <u>$10.00</u>

13) TELEPHONE..<u>$0.00</u>

14) OTHER(EXPLAIN)..<u>$0.00</u>

  TOTAL CASH SPENT (DETAILED EXPLANATIONS

  AND ALL RECEIPTS MUST BE GROUPED TOGETHER)......................<u>$565.00</u>

CHARGES: List all items that are charges on credit cards which will be paid back by check when you get home. Enclose the charge vouchers.

1) _____ $_____   4)_____ $_____

SECTION TWO

PAY RECEIPTS

VENUE   **THE BAYOU**   DATE   **OCT 18**

  INCOME:

A) PAYMENT (Contract)   _____   <u>$500.00</u>

B) OVERAGE   **Bonus for drawing over 400 people**   <u>$50.00</u>

C) MERCHANDISE   _____   <u>$100.00</u>

D) TOTAL (**A thru C**)   _____   <u>$650.00</u>

  DEDUCTIONS:

E) AGENCY DEPOSITS   _____   <u>$0.00</u>

F) TAXES WITHHELD AT CLUB   _____   <u>$0.00</u>

G) OTHER   _____   <u>$0.00</u>

H) TOTAL (**E thru G**)   _____   <u>$0.00</u>

I) TOTAL CASH COLLECTED (**H less D**) _____   <u>$650.00</u>

SECTION THREE

BALANCE FROM LAST REPORT - NUMBER _____...<u>$0.00</u>

CASH AMOUNT YOU BEGAN WITH ....FLOAT....................<u>$400.00</u>

CASH COLLECTED FROM (**I**) ABOVE ....<u>$650.00</u>

TOTAL CASH AVAILABLE..<u>$1050.00</u>

LESS: TOTAL CASH SPENT (SEE EXPENSE TOTAL ABOVE)............................<u>$565.00</u>

BALANCE...<u>$485.00</u>

LESS AMOUNT SENT HOME..<u>$0.00</u>

BALANCE CARRIED TO NEXT REPORT... <u>$485.00</u>

This balance of **$485** represents the **$650** you got paid less the **$165** in expenses you incurred that day. The **$400** that you started with should be used as the float for the next show and the next until such time as you have more than enough money from the shows to float the rest of the trip. If this is the case, you should consider stopping into a bank and wiring some of the money home into your bank account.

FEES

If you have hired a manager, agent or accountant, you must realize that they work for a percentage of your gross profits. That means that if you play a show that grosses you **$500** your agent will get **10%** or **$50**, your manager will get **15%** or **$75**, and your accountant will get **5%** or **$25**. This is a total of **$150** off the top which will yield you **$350** before other operating expenses.

This is by the book and in the real world a caring manager will probably not commission you (until you are earning more money) and your accountant will just bill you by their hourly wage. An agent on the other hand will definitely bill you and will expect their 10% fee within a short period of time after the show date is passed.

ASSIGNING YOUR MONEY TO SOMEONE ELSE

The band's money belongs to the band. Managers, accountants, lawyers and business managers are employees or consultants that you hire to work for you. These people may have some hand in the manipulation of your money or an opinion on its spending capacity, but they should not ever be in a position to spend a penny of it without your approval. Accountants are the only members of your team that should be physically handling your transactions concerning deposits, withdrawals, bill paying, payroll and taxes, and their financial advice should be considered heavily in any financial decision you make.

This includes any and all contracts, litigation's, major purchases, partnership agreements or corporation shareholders' agreements. Accountants are bright people who pay close attention to detail. Their job is to analyze figures and since you are in the *business* of music, you should use your accountant's advice as much as you can.

Managers have a vested interest in the band and at times may seem like a part of the band. But even in this highly influential position do not let the manager be the one or the only one to look after your money or make decisions concerning it. In fact, as I have stated earlier in the chapter, your manager should be as far away from your money as they can. It is in the band's best interest for the manager to work along side the accountant in many areas like budget planning, and contract negotiations as a good band representative should. Most mistakes that a manager will make can be overlooked or dismissed as human error. But a mishandling of the money is a sure fire means for losing trust from the band which may indeed lead to dismissal.

Perhaps, more than any other aspect of your career that is given over to someone else to handle, your financial records are the one area that should be monitored closely and receive as much scrutiny as possible by you.

Don't cop an attitude of "I can't get caught up in the business bullshit." You have worked so hard to finally be making money, be smart and look at your money as a necessary and vital part of your life. That's what all the other famous rock stars do, from Alice Cooper to U2, and from The Dead to Live.

Do not let the superfluous images that rock stars portray, fool you into thinking that they are only about sex, drugs and rock & roll. The ones that go by that credo alone, usually end up sick, strung out, broke and out of the business.

Many of the stars today are modem carrying, lap top using, super highway cruising businessmen, whose office is a tour bus and the mosh pit their executive conference table. When it comes right down to it, there is very little difference between the corporate heads of Fortune 500 companies and powerful entertainers like Madonna and Michael Jackson or bands like U2 and REM.

Whereas Bill Gates might thrive in an office high rise or in a power lunch sporting a $1,000 suit, rock stars conduct their business from their remote home offices or cell phones in dressing rooms, wearing cut off jeans, Doc Martens and T-shirts.

When you romanticize about what band members do backstage before or after a show, I can tell you that along with eating, mingling and interviewing, the successful ones are discussing, planning and designing their futures.

I know that I have made it a philosophical point to not always do things for money. I just want to make sure that you understand that there is a distinction between whoring yourself and taking care of your investments. At times you will have to put career moves ahead of financial gain and sometimes you will need to do the opposite. The most important point is that once you have earned money, take good care of it. It is the fuel you need to keep everything going. Do not put 100% trust in anyone but yourself. Learn about investments, mutual funds, real estate, the stock market, IRA's, etc.

Hire reputable accountants and business managers that serve you as consultants rather than parents or bosses. The final decisions on what to do with your finances should be based on your intelligent summations of the advice you are given.

> "*Live long and Prosper*"
> *Mr Spock - Starship Enterprise*

THE FOUR WISE MEN

Up until now, you have been doing all the work yourself. It has been a long road, but upon looking back you should feel a definite sense of pride for all your accomplishments, not to mention all the knowledge you have gained. It has been especially rough to not only play in the group, but to be responsible for moving the band's career forward. Many decisions were made off the cuff and along with the mistakes and bad calls there were plenty of good decisions as well.

But at some point you will realize that the burden of playing and managing your group is too heavy a load and that the group has grown to a level where the things you are making decisions about, are much more complicated and require a more professional hand. You will also find that there are some doors that are closed to you and with the proper representation, these doors can be opened and your path through them could be much smoother.

It is at this point in your band's career, that when you are either solicited by someone who wants to assume some executive role with the group or you begin to search for professional assistance to help further your career, you will need some reference to make the decision of whom to hire. These people you bring on board, are going to have a crucial influence in your musical career. Whether it is a lawyer, booking agent, manager or accountant, each person should be a specialist in their field and provide you with expertise in their specific area.

You will need to have a full understanding of what each one does so that you can decide where in your career you want to go next and which team member you would most benefit from.

Each of these members as they come on board will have a special relationship with the group. They will act as your consultant and confidant and be the instrument that guides and creates your future. The unique and beautiful thing about show business is that all members of the entertainment community whether they be actors, musicians, producers, directors, managers, agents or lawyers, all thrive on one thing: their desire to make it and be a part of a winning team. The sign of a winning team is when all the members of the team from artist to manager to record executive understands their role as well as respects the others and is locked into the same wavelength.

You will need to have trust in your team members and allow them certain freedoms in which to make decisions. But the bottom line is that they all work for you and have to answer to you and the more professional your team member is, the more they will adhere to this relationship.

The four team members we will cover in this chapter are:

 MANAGER

 **LAWYER**

 BOOKING AGENT

 **ACCOUNTANT**

While you are busy creating and performing music, you will not have the time even if you have the expertise, to handle all these areas of your career. But your knowledge of these positions by having worn many of these hats yourself will help you pick the best people to do these jobs for you and make sure that they are doing the best job they can.

It is hard to really say which of these you should look for first or in fact which might approach you first. It all really depends on the level your band is at and what your particular needs are.

Though each of the aforementioned professionals can individually help you with each of the different aspects of your career, they really should be limited to their own expertise and should never do the other team member's job. Throughout this chapter, I will define the roles of each of the team members and how to go about hiring one to work with your band.

MANAGER

I want to start here because the whole concept of this book is based on management and if there is one person that will spearhead the rest of your career for you it will be your personal manager.

The job of a manager is to create, maintain and secure a career for their client. The manager is the liaison between their client (the band) and booking agents, accountants, publicists, record companies and merchandisers, overseeing public appearances, contract negotiations, endorsements, video and recording budgets, touring as well as preserving a sound mental attitude in which the artist can create without worries. A band becomes very much dependent upon their manager to be their voice and the manger has a responsibility to use the power of their position for the advancement and betterment of their client and not use their client for their own personal advantage. For the manager to do a good job they must assimilate all your needs, talents and industry possibilities into a plan that will best suit your potential.

The relationship between a manager and a band is a very special one. Whereas a lawyer, booking agent or accountant may initially invest in or reject a client based purely upon financial qualifications, most managers manage their acts because they love the music and the band members. Their investment which is their time, will be a tremendous one and their return is usually put off until the band itself makes it.

Since there is no college degree offered in "Band Management," managers come from many different walks of life, some of them may not have even been related to music. A band and manager are many times thrown together by some weird twist of fate and only time and understanding can tell whether this will be a good or bad union.

The significant qualifications of a manager are that he/she be an astute businessman with the ability to nurture without butting in, exude confidence, resourcefulness, and have the ability to negotiate intelligently. There are three levels of managers available.

 ## TOP MANAGERS

These managers are very powerful players in the industry. They are powerful because they represent powerful clients. Some of them have been in the business for years and years working as attorneys, agents, promoters and so on. There are record company executives that have turned to managing, while others started out as unknowns and rose with a group all through the ranks to the top like Paul McGuiness U2's manager.

The top managers, considered to be the most powerful people in the music business, have a great deal of clout with record companies, radio, video, agents and press. If you are represented by one, there are many doors that can be opened to you. In many cases the benefits extended to you from these connections are based on the confidence in these managers to be able to pull all the strings. But the truth is that even with all the breaks and connections if the band isn't great they will never amount to anything.

Very few young groups ever get the chance to land such powerful representation from the get go. Young bands are somewhat volatile in that they are still unproven in many areas and it would not be worth the reputation of a top manager to get behind a young act until they are further along. Besides, a manager will put just as much time and energy into maintaining one of their superstars as they would to break a new act but for much larger financial return. So there is an obvious disadvantage to signing on a young act.

MIDDLE MANAGERS

These managers have one or more clients that are working, with a least one signed with national exposure. Though their acts might not be multi-platinum album sellers, they are working steady and earning income, which is a major feat in itself.

Middle managers are at times content with their present clientele especially if they have one that is out on tour promoting a very successful album. Some are constantly looking for new acts and if they get a spark from your band and the group has a big buzz going, you might have a chance getting picked up by one.

UNKNOWN MANAGER

This person may either be working in the industry in some capacity or can be your best friend from high school. In either case they will have little or no contacts in the business and may not even know very much about the business; kind of like you were when you started out.

The beauty of the music business is that even a person like this can possibly manage you successfully all the way to record deals and beyond. It can happen from the sheer effort of the individual overcoming their limitations and working hard to learn the business. Sometimes it occurs because the band is so great that their success just can't be denied. And sometimes it is the combination of the two.

The unknown manager is limited in most cases by their lack of clout. Not knowing anyone on the inside is a major drawback. This business is generated by contacts, favors and the good word of others. Contacts are the difference between calling a club and always getting an answering machine to having the call picked up immediately and getting action.

Having spent many years as an unknown manager, I recall one occasion when I tried for months to book a popular unsigned act from NY at a Washington D.C. club. No matter how many messages I left, the club owner would never return my call. Finally I turned to a friend of mine who is a powerful agent to make the call for me. Within ten minutes my act was booked for a Saturday night opening up for a touring British band.

I have a great deal of respect for the unknown manager because they have to work the hardest for their act with little or no return. Many times they get the act to a position where the act feels that a more powerful manager is needed to take them to the next level, so they leave their first manager behind. My advice to bands who have unknown managers is as follows: Before you devaluate the worth of your manager and before you start comparing yourselves to other groups that might be surpassing you, with thoughts like "if we only had a more powerful manager we would be further along," remember that if there's no line of powerful managers waiting to sign you up, consider yourself damn lucky to have your present manager.

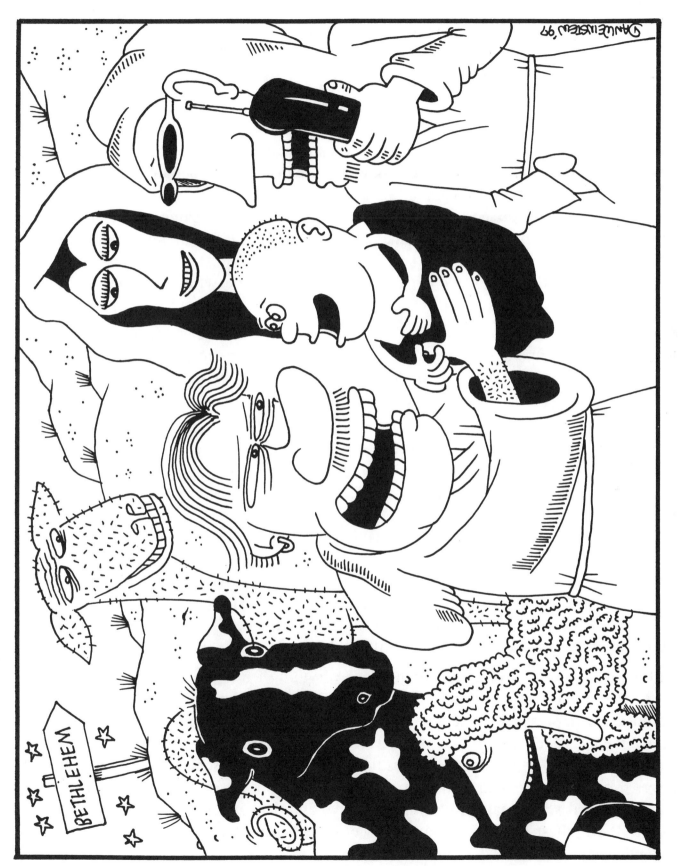

"Val, get Caesar on the phone. Find out the avails for June, I think I just discovered the next big thing!"

Do not judge your manager or your band by comparison to others, judge yourself by where you are now from where you were 6 months or a year ago. Every band grows at their own pace in their own time. Before you get all over your manager take a good look at yourselves and see if you are doing all *you* can to help *your* career.

A manager no matter what level they are at, must be someone that no matter how close they get with the band members, should always remain objective and give the band not always what they want, but what they need. A band must truly trust the manager's judgment and yet this relationship can only work if the manager trusts the band's judgment as well. In my opinion the reason why so many bands who perform great music do not make it is because they lack a certain fundamental understanding of the business and their manger is always perceived as someone who is making them do things they do not want to do. In this scenario, a struggle is constantly present and the group remains stagnant. On the other hand, many talented bands have a clear understanding perhaps even a vision of their direction and their manager is either not knowledgeable, not connected or just not in tune with the group and the same results occur.

This situation is compounded each time you take on a new team member and the existing balance of personalities and visions is at risk. It is therefore pretty clear why so few bands ever really make it to the very top and stay there long enough to spend a lifetime making a musical difference.

The manager's role will be to supervise and direct the activities of the rest of your team, and it is crucial that he hand pick some of the members and consult you on your choices. They will need to find people that share their same passion for your music. But unlike the rest of your team members, your personal manager must have direct insight into you as an artist and thoroughly understand your music. If your manager does not connect with the essence of what drives you or connect with your music, they will never be able to help you make good decisions on everything from which record company to sign with, what kind of tour to take, which songs to record, how to publicize yourself, etc. These are all such critical elements that are based upon each other to build a strong career. If a fault occurs in any one area, the foundation will crack and your career will tumble.

Without a comprehensive understanding of everything from international publishing deals and royalty rates to coordinating a 50 city stadium tour, tying in radio promotion with press advertisement, tour sponsorship and equipment and band travel arrangements, your manager can only service you to a certain extent. But since only a handful of the most powerful managers have this complete arsenal of knowledge and power, you probably will settle for someone who possesses less knowledge but makes up for it with tenacity, personality, drive and the capacity to learn. It's a long road to the highest level so it's a long way before you can feasibly attract the big time managers.

Remember, most big timers were once small timers and most bands are managed by small timers working their way up the ladder, learning as they go. As long as your manager uses smart business principles, listens to the advice of other qualified team members, keeps their ego in check and proceeds in a fashion that is calculated and accepted by the industry, if you are seeing weekly and monthly positive results then they are doing their job.

HOW TO FIND A MANAGER

Finding a manager is not an easy task. If it were, you would not need this book. Many bands start out either doing it themselves or if they show some promise might pick up a friend, family member or club owner to assist in some of the duties and whatever happens, happens. To get picked up by a real manager, some bands need to really reach a level of popularity where music industry professionals or full time managers are now responding to a buzz and are seeking out the band. Sometimes a band will first hire an attorney if they do not have a manager to help solicit for a record deal, which if one results, a manager will be introduced to them. When you reach a point where you feel it is time to get a full manager so that you can concentrate entirely on creating music, use the following list to guide your search:

 POLLSTAR

4333 NORTH WEST AVE

FRESNO CA 93705

1800-344-7383

CALIF (209) 224 2631

> Publishes a separate artist/manager guide that lists all the signed artists and their managers. The non subscription rate is $140 and $150 if you live in California.

RECORDING INDUSTRY SOURCEBOOK

6400 Hollis St

Emeryville Ca 94608

1800 233 9604

> Comprehensive listing (over 15,000 in fact) of industry contacts as well as descriptions of who and what they are. Published annually & mailed by written request for 74.95 which includes shipping.

YELLOW PAGES OF ROCK!

Album Network

120N. Victory Boulevard

Third Floor, Burbank, CA 91502

818 955-4000 or (818) 955-4000

> Somewhat like a telephone directory of the entire music business including, record distributors, radio stations, retail outlets, publicists as well as directories of labels and the names of the executives, managers, lawyers, agents and so on.

BILLBOARD MAGAZINE

The International Buyers Guide

$114

(212) 764-7300 or (1800) 344-7119

> Aside from their music business news publication which is available on news stands and stationery stores, they also publish a directory guide.

LOOK AT THE CD'S IN YOUR ALBUM COLLECTION AND CHECK THROUGH THE CREDITS.

In most cases the manager's name will be listed.

GO TO THE LIBRARY OR THE BOOK STORE AND READ BIOGRAPHIES ON BANDS.

Read interviews in Rock and Roll publications with bands you admire. Most if not all mention their managers.

ATTEND ALL THE MAJOR MUSIC INDUSTRY SEMINARS LISTED IN CHAPTER 2.

Arm yourself with copies of your latest recording and pass them out. Hopefully you will be performing sometime during the seminar so make sure that you pass out flyers promoting your show as well.

STAY ACTIVE ON THE CLUB SCENE.

Hang out at the more popular clubs in your area especially ones that feature touring national acts. Get friendly with all the club booking agents so that you can get guest listed for all these events. If your band has a good reputation, the club booker may introduce you to some of the managers they deal with.

All these suggestions will take some detective work and hustle on your part. I know it may be easier if you live in a big city, but for those of you that live out in the middle of nowhere, you're going to have to be more diligent because you aren't going to just bump into one of these guys at the local 7-11.

As I keep reinforcing, do not be so hung up on finding a manager. You need to do all this stuff yourself first and within time as you get good and start getting a lot of exposure, people are going to approach you. Your concern should not be: how are we ever going to find a manager, but how are we going to distinguish a good one from a bad one.

Lastly, the one thing that ultimately distinguishes a manager from the rest of your team members is that they be there for you day or night to help rejoice in your celebrations and console you in times of despair. This is your one team member that should take your calls and not leave you on hold for extended periods of time or return them three days later. Managers are your anchor of sanity in the crazy sea of the music business and if you reach for your anchor and it's not there, you will drift away.

MANAGER CONTRACTS

The common manner in which a band and a manager will consummate their relationship is via a signed management agreement. This is the manager's responsibility to provide to the band. It should contain a very detailed outline of their duties as well as the percentage cut they will take from the band for performing these duties. This is how managers get paid. They commission an agreed percentage from the many different areas of the artist's income. The standard percentage today is 20% of the gross. There are also deals where the manager gets a percentage of the net rather than the gross or is on a salary rather than percentage.

Managers should commission only that income which is earned and not from money that is borrowed or loaned which has to be paid back; like for instance recording costs, producer costs or tour support.

Managers can commission live performances, record sales, merchandising sales, publishing and endorsements. The reason being is that through the manager's efforts all these deals have come to pass and for that work they take their commission. The commission is usually taken off the top of the gross before expenses. There are some exceptions like live performances where some managers will take their percentage after the production expense. (Sound and lights).

Be aware that under a standard 20% gross commission, a manager may indeed earn more money from let's say a live show than each of the members of the band. For example if the show grosses $5,000 the manager will receive 20% or $1000. If there is an agent involved they will typically receive 10% off the $5000. There will be some expenses involved as well like payroll, traveling expenses, etc. The remainder which can end up being $1500 will then be split up between the band members. If there are 5 members in the band, each one gets $300.

Aside from the percentage, managers may bill certain expenses to their clients. Expenses such as certain phone calls, certain travel expenses etc. These are expenses that the manager incurs on behalf of the band and it's the band's responsibility to pay them.

Now all this is one variation of a manager/client agreement. Every band has a unique relationship with their manager thus one deal will differ greatly from another. There are some managers that are considered a member of the band and split everything equally with the band including sharing in all the expenses, while there are other managers that have a limited relationship with a very spelled out contract detailing criteria for the manager to meet for the band, otherwise the band can pull the contract and then there are some bands that have only a verbal agreement.

If you have been operating without a manager for a while and then enter into a relationship with someone who wants to manage you, you should not sign a contract for at least six months to see what this individual can do for you. If they are willing to extend you that time to prove their worth, you should ask for a copy of their standard contract and spend those 6 months studying it. This way when the trial time is over and you decide to keep this person you are not thrown off by the element of the contract.

Sometimes bands become a little put off by their manager that has been working for them for a period of time and then asks you for a signed contract. For this I say remember one thing. If you're a young band, chances are your manager is working full time trying to build you a career and getting nothing in return. Probably because there is nothing to commission or whatever money coming in is getting reinvested back into the band. While you are sleeping late after the gig, and hanging out doing whatever it is you're doing, the manager is on the phone slugging it out with some club owner for a gig or pleading with some press writer to come down to the show for a review, or endlessly writing letters and sending in press kits to record companies and booking agents. The least you can do if you like this person is to sign a piece of paper that in some way says, "Thanks I appreciate what you're doing, I'm in it with you."

TERMS (OF ENDEARMENT)

Contracts generally run somewhere around three years to five years. Managers would lean toward the longer end and bands prefer to keep it as short as possible. My contracts are three year contracts with a two year continuing option based on earning minimums built in for the band. This means that I need to create x amount of income for the band each of the three years I'm their manager. If the artist earns these amounts the contract continues, if not they can terminate the contract.

"Earn" is very ambiguous word that that needs further definition. Legitimate offers that are made to the group but are turned down by the band are considered earned income. I'm not talking about offers to perform at your manager's, daughter's nursery school once a month, but legitimate offers in the realm of what the band has been offered in the past. By receiving these offers the manager has done their job. If by the end of the year the band looks at their numbers and decides that they didn't make as much money and wants to terminate their manager, then the manager can calculate in the offers they refused and be allowed to continue. They may also choose not to, seeing how you first turned down work and then tried to retire their contract. There is recourse a manager can take so I advise you not to try and outsmart him.

Managers will build into the contract their deal if it is terminated. The terms generally revolve around receiving compensation for deals that were made while they managed you. Though technically sound, the bottom line is that you can conceivably be paying a manager for years after they are gone. Therefore, a good lawyer will work out some kind of escalating reduction of payment over a certain period of time to a point where it all ends. There are as many different ways to make deals as there are deals and since I don't want to dedicate this whole book to any one subject (and this can be the subject in itself) I advise you as an artist to have and hire your own attorney that negotiates with a potential manager and their attorney.

LAWYERS

While you may have relied on your manager to set up the showcase that ultimately got you signed, when you received the 150 page document outlining how you will live and breathe for the record company and receive nothing substantial in return, until you sell ten gazillion albums....... Uh, I mean your record contract, you will rely on none other than your attorney for protection against making a bad deal and negotiating a fair and decent one.

For anyone aspiring to be in show business, a lawyer is as necessary as an oxygen tank is when scuba diving. Promises are made frequently in this business that many times disappear in the wind the second they're spoken. For any promise to have real currency, it should be in written form, in a language that is clear and not assumed and signed by both parties. The only person qualified to create and distinguish this language (contract), is a lawyer.

In my experience I have found that none of the music attorneys I have met, got their start in the music business, but switched to it out of their genuine love for music. Music Business Law is not a primary subject in law school as is tax law or divorce. The music business is ever changing and new deals are negotiated every day creating new precedents all the time. A lawyer's expertise revolves around their ability to not only be up to date on what has transpired in past decades, but on what new angles they can create and protect against, tomorrow. While it is true that there is a lot of money to be made in music, the stark reality is that it is made by only a handful of artists represented by a smaller handful of lawyers and the rest out there are just getting by.

A lawyer's main function is to negotiate deals that require contractual obligations. A good lawyer is one that understands their client's needs and can advise the client on what direction to take that would be in their best interest. But there are other functions that lawyers need to bring to the table in today's music business. In the music business there are different levels of attorneys that all provide a different style of service for the client.

At the top level there are the big gun/personality lawyers. Their power is accumulated from years of hard work successfully representing successful clients. They are very much like performers in their own right, cultivating their reputation and making sure they know all the important people.

They not only negotiate deals, but they are expected to find deals for their clients as well. The combination of who they represent and who they know determines who is most powerful. And the attorney with the most power when they die.......wins.

Often a band will hire an attorney to shop them a record deal. These high profile attorneys do not take on every client that offers a retainer for a few phone calls to major label executives. They know that much of their reputation is synonymous with the reputation of their client and are therefore very picky with whom they represent. You may need to showcase yourself for this type of attorney before they will take you on as a client. But once they do, your tape will be heard by a number of top record company executives. Your association with this lawyer will lend credibility to your group though it still won't guarantee you a deal.

To hire such an attorney you are shopping in the hourly rate area of at least $175 an hour and up. To find out who they are you can check with same sources that are listed at the beginning of the chapter. At the other end of the spectrum there are the lawyers that may know as much about the inner workings of a contract as the "Big Guns." I call them "Contract Attorneys." The basic difference is that this individual tends to be more low key or more comfortable behind the scenes and behind their desk than at all the parties hob nobbing with the phony and powerful. The drawback is that these lawyers may not have as big a black book and may not be in a position to call the heads of every record company and "do lunch." But at a considerably cheaper fee, they would be able to negotiate and advise you on any deal that you or your manager procure. There are also many combinations of the two that can suit any of your needs. In choosing an attorney you should hold them in the same regard and with the same criteria as you would choosing a manager.

AS YOU INTERVIEW A POTENTIAL LAWYER LISTEN TO THEIR DIALOGUE AND SEE IF YOU CAN SENSE IF THEY ARE ETHICAL AND HAVE HONORABLE POLITICS.

Are they shrewd or plain dishonest.

ARE YOU INTIMIDATED OR DO THEY CONVEY A THERAPEUTIC LIKE QUALITY THAT ENABLES YOU TO TALK AND MAKE YOU FEEL COMFORTABLE.

A good attorney is one that does little talking and a lot of listening. After all, how can they advise you on what to do if they don't listen to find out what you are all about.

THEY SHOULD LIKE YOUR MUSIC AND UNDERSTAND YOU AS AN ARTIST.

Once when showcasing my client to a powerful attorney who was on retainer and shopping them a deal, he sat stone-faced throughout most of the set like he was judging a chess game. The band was smoking but he was in a trance, applying Scanner-like mind control, desperately trying to keep his feet from tapping out the beat. At times I thought the veins in his temples were going to explode all over his $800 Italian suit. I distanced myself a bit so that I could further enjoy the set when suddenly, while the band was in the middle of performing a cover of the song "He Said She Said" by the Beatles, he turned to me breaking his code of silence and said, "That's a catchy song, did the singer write it?" Though he did recognize it as a hit song, it was discouraging that he was so far removed that he didn't recognize that it was a Beatles song. As it turned out he was not moved by the group and although he was willing to represent them, they felt it would be in their best interest to part ways in search of a more inspired counselor.

FIND OUT WHO ELSE THEY REPRESENT.

This will be a good indication of what their career is like as well as his success rate.

PAYMENT

Lawyers bill by time. Since much of their work is consultation that might never result in a deal to be commissioned, time is the service for which they get paid. Whether they are on the phone with you or at important meetings disguised as lunches, lawyers will keep track of every minute of their time and bill you by the hour.

Lawyers are expensive and at $100-$300 an hour, you better have good reason to use them. For instance:

IF YOU ARE BEING SUED

IF SOMEONE IS INVESTING MONEY IN YOU AND REQUIRES A SIGNED CONTRACT SUCH AS:

Publishing deal, Record deal, Production deal, Endorsement deal.

TO NEGOTIATE OR DRAFT A BUSINESS AGREEMENT SUCH AS:

Partnership agreement, Manager contract, Agent contract.

HOW TO HIRE AN ATTORNEY

If there is a deal pending or an agreement to be drafted, all that is required in hiring an attorney is finding one that has the time and paying their fee. Make some calls and ask for a consultation appointment so that you can interview the attorney and explain what you have going down. When you find one you like, ask how much they charge per hour and to please estimate how many hours the job should take.

If you are looking for a lawyer to shop a record deal for you, your approach will be the same as with any other executive in the music business. After an initial contact you will be instructed to forward a press kit and tape to their office. After listening to the music, they will likely want to see the band live. If they feel you have something, they may indeed take you on as a client. Just remember that this is not a sure thing that you will get a deal. What is a sure thing is that you will be billed for each hour the attorney works for you whether you get signed or not. If you do not have a manager, your attorney may field some of the manager's responsibilities like setting up record company show cases or helping you make some crucial career decisions.

BOOKING AGENT

It is my own personal feeling that booking agents never get the respect so many them greatly deserve. I watch a lot of rock and roll award shows and among all the thank you's, I rarely hear the agent's name mentioned.

A booking agent's job is to procure live performance work for the band. Bands earn money from record sales (but only a small percentage), from their merchandising (again only a percentage), but their touring and live engagements are the bulk of their income. Like any other team member there are different levels of agent. The very powerful agents are those that represent very powerful clients. Clients that tour and sell out stadiums and arenas earning anywhere from $100,000 a night and up.

One of the ways these agents got to be so powerful is that they just don't book shows. They use their insight into the artist and their ability to manipulate all the possibilities of the industry and come up with the best possible live scenario that would make their clients happen. This would include decisions concerning:

WHAT BANDS TO INCLUDE ON A TOUR TO CREATE A COOL BILLING.

WHAT TYPE OF VENUES TO BOOK THE ACT IN.

Venues have personalities much in the same way bands do. A clever match of the two can sometimes result in magical moments.

CHOOSING THE RIGHT PROMOTERS TO BOOK THE BAND THROUGH.

Promoters usually buy the act from the agent and then take care of all the publicity, ticket sales, production hospitality and venue. Promoters are a lot like bacteria. There's some good ones and some that will make you ill. Good agents know who to do business with and who is poorly funded, crooked and short sighted, in the markets they books around the country.

 ## Choosing or even creating the promotional concepts to help sell the show.

Powerful agents have the ability to call other agents and get their acts on some sought after tours. This will help motivate your record company (who have many other acts they are working with) to step up on their publicity, tour support and radio campaigns.

These agents are impossible to get signed to unless you have a major recording deal and are currently touring earning at least $500 and up a night. There are exceptions of course. If you are signed to a powerful manager who has a relationship with a powerful agent who just that day had lunch with your powerful attorney, you might find yourself with powerful booking representation.

While landing a powerful agent is a major addition to a band's team, there are some disadvantages especially to a young band just starting out. Unless the agent really has developed their own love for you and your music, you will probably be booked by one of the assistants in the company until you begin to show some real income ....I mean promise. You will probably not get the choicest tours as they will be given to the more popular acts.

Agents are your best friends when you are making money and will become the hardest ones to reach when you are not. But this is okay because it's still up to you to make the best of every situation. So instead of complaining about your agent as so many groups tend to do when they are not selling tickets, work harder and show your agent you are worth it. Agents do not create crowds, and they do not create demand for bigger and better shows, bands do!

Good agents are the most tenacious of salesmen. They will tend to hype a band to the point where they totally believe the hype themselves to get the best possible positions for the group. If I had a dollar for every time an agent said, "You have to check out this band, they're going to be the next...." I could spend the rest of my life in a strip bar. Many times the bands do not pan out, but when they do, if you trace the band's road upward you will undoubtedly find the agent was the one in the passenger seat with the road map driving all night with the manager of course behind the wheel.

The middle agents and lower level agents are just as committed but through life's fate, have just not yet inherited the one great band that can raise them to the top.

These agents are like the young managers, in that they have to work even harder to get results. They rely on the bands to do the footwork, managers to coordinate with the record companies and promoters to give them good pay and decent nights. Young bands are a major expense especially to the smaller booking agencies because the pay for young acts is rather low leaving a sometimes minuscule percentage for the agent which can be translated into a loss when you factor in long distance calls and the mailing of press kits and tapes.

HOW DO YOU FIND ONE

Using the sources I have described previously, as well as using the same basic method of sending your tape and press kit and inviting them down to a show. The thing about agents is that they will be very interested in your press kit because press kits are generally performance oriented. And if you have a very strong tour history that encompasses a large region of the country working at least 15 dates a month, you will find many interested agents. Bands like Big Head Todd, The Mighty Mighty Bosstones and The Dave Matthew's Band had well developed sections of the country where they sold out big venues despite not having a record deal and were able to get signed to agents that very successfully booked them and increased their popularity. And due to this relationship and the fact that these are great bands, they ultimately got signed to major recording contracts.

As you begin showcasing for agents and as they begin to show interest perhaps even make you offers for representation, your ability to sort through these offers and see which one is designed to engage your career rather than exploit it, will give you an indication who your agent should be.

AGENT DEALS

 AGENTS COMMONLY RECEIVE 10% (SOMETIMES MORE) OFF THE VERY TOP FOR EVERY LIVE ENGAGEMENT THEY BOOK.

They are not entitled to commission any other part of your career income. To confirm a booking they will require 50% of the agreed pay from the promoter up front and then deduct their commission from that.

 THEY WILL WANT TO SIGN YOU FOR THREE YEARS BUT IN MANY CASES CAN BE NEGOTIATED DOWN TO ONE YEAR.

 THEY WILL ASK FOR THE EXCLUSIVE RIGHT TO PROCURE LIVE ENGAGEMENTS AND WILL BE ELIGIBLE TO RECEIVE COMMISSION ON PERFORMANCES BOOKED WITHOUT THEM.

They will also be very mad at you if you book a show without them and rightfully so.

Finally if you have a personal manager, it is likely that they will be the ones spending most of the time dealing with your agent. So even though in the end the final decision is yours, if your manager has inroads with a particular agent you should go with it.

ACCOUNTANT

Your accountant is the only member of your team whose job it is to handle your money. Not your manager, lawyer, agent, or fellow band members. An accountant's job is to analyze numbers, calculate income, figure expenses and pays taxes. They are schooled in these areas and have degrees which is their license to practice.

A rock and roll band, is a money machine much in the same way any other business is. You will have payroll to meet, business expenses, generate income and most definitely need to pay taxes.

Unsigned bands generally lose money and to stay afloat they rely on the big show every once in a while as well as personal investment. With all the transactions of money going on from gig to gig and from investments, who is keeping track of it, depositing it and paying taxes on it. **Do you know that you must be registered with your state as a business and if you are earning over a certain amount of money a year you must by law pay taxes? What do you do with the checks you get as pay from clubs? Did you give them your social security number? If you did, do you know that the amount of the check (which is the band's income) will now show up as your personal income for which you might have to pay the taxes?**

An accountant is in a sense your financial lawyer insofar that they can protect you from breaking state income tax laws as well as protect you financially from your record company, booking agent, personal manager and <u>yourself</u>. They must act as a sane voice in an insane business where way too much money is made in way too short of a time by inexperienced people who tend to throw way too much of it away.

WHO SHOULD YOU HIRE

As an unsigned band, whether you are either making moderate money to perhaps losing money, you should consider hiring a local accountant or bookkeeper that has experience doing the books for a retail service business. In sense this is what you are. Some of your deductions might be different than let's say a sporting goods store, but the general rules of accounting still apply.

If you're about to get signed to a record deal, I strongly recommend hiring an accountant that deals in the music industry. The particular nuances of record deal advances, recording budgets, producer budgets, interstate tax laws, tour budgets, income tax returns, royalty computations for mechanical royalties on record sales and publishing royalties, payroll and much, much more are way too specialized for the average accountant to do.

HOW TO FIND AN ACCOUNTANT

Many of the big accounting firms that handle music are located in NY, LA and Chicago. If you need to find one on your own, looking through the yellow pages of these cities will yield you phone numbers for accounting firms which when you get them on the phone you can inquire if they represent any entertainers and musicians.

Look through your CD collection and check the credits. They usually give thanks and mention the name of their financial representatives. To find out where they are located put on your Sherlock Holmes hat and do the following. If the bands list somewhere in the credits, a fan club hotline or the location of their management office, this can be an indication as to where the rest of their team is based. It is not uncommon that a band will choose their representatives that are all based in the same location. Once you have a destination, get that area's area code and call information.

Ask your attorney if they can recommend a good accountant. Most attorneys can and usually have very symbiotic relationships with accountants. It is not uncommon especially when going through a major contract such as a record deal, that you would want both your accountant and attorney scrutinizing it together.

HOW TO HIRE AN ACCOUNTANT

The accountant does not need to hear your tape and see a press kit to do your books. He needs to be paid. So therefore you must approach them in the same exact way you would if you were hiring an employee or a subcontractor that does a job for you. You will set up appointments with each prospective accountant and interview them to find out the following information.

HONESTY

You cannot tell always if a person is honest when you speak to them. Ask for a client list so that you can call and get some references.

EDUCATION

An accountant must be a college graduate with a degree in accounting. Inquire about their background to see if they are an accountant or have taken and passed a CPA exam making them a certified public accountant. At least you know to what degree their expertise lies.

FEES

The range is from 5% of your gross to hourly fees, flat fees or a combination of all three. Who in the firm does your work can determine the height of the fee. You need to be concerned about fees because in the beginning you might not be earning much money, yet if you are signed there are many financial details that should be handled by a professional. Accountants may defer payment until a later date which is a good short term remedy but unless you're making big bucks down the road the debt will come back to haunt you.

REPORTS

How often will you be receiving reports of your transactions, (deposits, expenses etc.).

WILL THEIR SERVICES INCLUDE TOUR BUDGET PREPARATION, PAYROLL, TOUR REPORTS, TAX RETURNS AS WELL AS ARRANGE PERFORMING AN AUDIT OF YOUR RECORD COMPANY ROYALTY STATEMENTS.

Speaking of audits will they object to you performing an audit on them? If they object, then just end the conversation right there and leave. A reputable accountant will have no problem with that question for two reasons. It is extremely expensive to audit ($5-10,000) so it is kind of a deterrent for you and secondly if they are reputable they have nothing to hide.

CONTRACT

Most accountants do not ask for a contract but some might. It's not a terrible thing since it spells out what they will do for you. The one thing I would not want to see in a contract is term limits. You should be free to leave that firm and use another accountant at any time.

JUST A WORD ON BUSINESS MANAGERS

The title "Business Manager" is very ambiguous and can either be synonymous with an accountant, a financial advisor/investor, or a sleaze bag that thinks they know a lot about investing money but in reality is just a swindler.

You will not need a business manager for a long time. You will be well protected by the four wise men in the previous pages. When the time comes for you to start investing your millions and diversifying your portfolio, you will by then have met many upstanding people as a result of introductions from your four wise men.

Just remember this: you have worked way to hard for your money. You want someone to invest it, but wisely and conservatively. It should all be there for you when you are too old to get up on stage and rock or if you have just run out of material and want to stay home and raise your children.

18

SHOPPING FOR A RECORD DEAL

Contrary to what the chapter title implies, landing a recording contract involves much more than just an afternoon of shopping. For most of us the process of shopping a record deal comes after years of hard work, living like a bum, eating pretzels and drinking cheap beer, playing your guts out in smoky bars, knocking on industry doors until your knuckles bleed and never letting up.

For the tens of thousands of bands around the world who are dreaming of a deal, relatively few ever get picked up by a record company. Not surprisingly, a relatively low percentage of these bands that get signed ever break out from anonymity to become nationally or internationally successful. Every year a select few new bands rise from anonymity and make it to the top of the charts, but in truth this represents only the tiniest percentages of all who try. Almost all these bands have been on the scene, struggling for years before it all comes together.

But one step at a time. The big question is: how do those few bands ever get to the stage of being offered a record deal?

WHAT IS A RECORD DEAL

Before we tackle the process of getting a deal I want to briefly explain what a deal is and isn't. I also want to tackle the very first psychological symptoms that occur from a signing and to do this you need to fully understand the basic premise of a contract.

A record deal is the arrangement made between a record company and a recording artist stating that the company will lend (advance) the band money to record an album. For the most part, that's it. Everything else in that 100 page document are treatments on this one basic premise. What you need to understand is that by signing a contract, you are in essence agreeing to borrow anywhere from $5,000 - $250,000 to make that record. The key word is borrow because you must pay this money back; and the way you do that is from your portion of royalties from the sale of the record.

For the top end advance of $250,000, you are going to have to sell quite a bit of records before you reach a break-even point to where you can start making money. If you are a part of a five man band this will mean that after all the debts are paid the money that comes in from the percentage of sales that represents the band's earnings, (usually around 8-12% before producer fees for new bands) you will only receive 1/5th of the royalties but only after your manager, accountant and others take their cut.

Now you can see why so few bands ever really make it even though they have signed a deal. They may have indeed been good bands but the serious financial problems that occur are enough to sour anyone's desire to continue. But that's the good news.

The bad news is that all this financial mess can be avoided if the label decides not to release your record. Oh yes, they can do that. You can sign a deal, get all this money and make a record, only to find out after your release date has been pushed back for months, that the label has decided not to release the damn thing and subsequently drops you from the contract.

The reason why I paint such a bleak picture is that I want you to understand that while signing a deal is cause for celebration, it is not an excuse to walk on air and forget all that has brought you to this point. The moment you sign a deal you have in essence leaped off a diving board taking you from the top of the unsigned band heap on a headfirst dive into the bottom of the signed band pool. All the hard work that has propelled you to the point of getting signed will be practice for what you will need to do now to get off the bottom and swim back to the top.

You will need to start over again building newer, more prestigious contacts, as well as creating a professional aura around yourself enabling you to compete against all the other signed bands in the national arena.

A record deal represents a chance. It is a moment of serenity in the window of opportunity. The wind that blows through is yours to capture. It is your decision whether you choose to ride on it toward success or to be blown away by it, and drown in the sea of failure.

WHEN ARE YOU READY TO LOOK FOR A DEAL

I know that in many young artists' minds they are ready for a deal the minute they finish writing their very first song. But as we all know it is a far-fetched dream to imagine that happening. It is the rarest of rare situations where an artist gets signed from a demo of material made in their bedroom without ever having done anything in the business. And if this has happened the chances are that they had a very strong connection in the industry. So how do you know when you are ready? The answer is you don't. But I do think you can use certain milestone markers as barometers of your ascension to readiness.

Getting signed means a number of things. It means you are about to enter into a negotiation. It means you have to hire professional representatives. It means you will determine the next five years of your life and put it in writing. You will be committing yourself to touring, recording, interviewing, performing and working twenty hours a day at times for no pay. You will be testing your constitution, flirting with all sorts of temptations. You will be homeless at times, living on a bus surrounded with the same people day in and day out. You will become business partners with other individuals

"Okay, we've got 2 1/2 songs not including the Stairway to Heaven
cover, 6 fans and we know someone who got a record deal with
Columbia House, it's time to get signed bro!"

and be asked to make decisions whose outcome will affect your life and the lives of those around you.

My belief is that a person cannot truly be ready for something that they have not had a chance to experience, let alone master. The same holds true for a band. If getting signed to a record deal means all I mentioned above, than disaster awaits any band that gets a deal before it has had a chance to experience doing these things I have just listed. How can you hire a group of professional attorneys, managers and agents when you never even hired a roadie? How can you be expected to successfully tour for sixteen straight months when you have never played outside your home town?

If you have negotiated club dates, bookings and compensations you are ready to handle the next stage of negotiations, like a record deal, manager or booking agent. If you have successfully prepared the books on the band's accounting for all the income and expenses, then you are ready to hire an accounting firm to work for you and quite possibly be ready to understand the financial ramifications of your record deal. If you have been touring for at least a year and have spent time with your band members and get along, then you may very well be ready to enter into the next phase of a touring band's life. Have you dealt with temptations and have you conquered your vices before they have conquered you?

Hopefully, you manifested a sense of yourself and an awareness of the realities of what the music business is, so that when the wind of opportunity comes and sweeps you off your feet, you have the knowledge and will land standing upright when it dies down.

How do you know when you are ready? The truth is you never really know so you must constantly be in the preparation mode. Record deals may come to you unexpectedly while you are just playing a gig and an A&R guy from some big label might be in the audience. Be prepared and try to learn everything about deals from the time you decide it is something to want to get. This way when you're approached backstage you will be prepared to engage in the conversation. This list below is a readiness gauge. It is divided into four categories, A-D. If you can check yes to 3 things out of each category, it may indicate that you are ready to shop for a deal.

- YOU SHOULD BE PLAYING AT LEAST **150** DATES A YEAR

- YOU SHOULD HAVE OPENED UP FOR SOME NATIONAL ACTS

- YOUR CAREER SHOULD BE AT LEAST TWO YEARS OLD

- YOU SHOULD HAVE AN ACTIVE, UP TO DATE MAILING LIST OF **1000+** FANS

- YOU SHOULD BE HEADLINING SOME OF THE PRESTIGIOUS CLUBS IN YOUR AREA

- YOU SHOULD BE TOURING AROUND IN AT LEAST **6** STATES

- YOU SHOULD HAVE FAVORABLE PRESS FROM ALL THE AREAS THAT YOU HAVE PLAYED

- YOU SHOULD HAVE BEEN IN THE RECORDING STUDIO AND HAVE MADE AT LEAST ONE DEMO TAPE

- YOU SHOULD HAVE RECEIVED FAVORABLE PRESS ON YOUR DEMO

- YOU SHOULD HAVE A PROFESSIONALLY WRITTEN PRESS KIT THAT INCLUDES A BIO PHOTOGRAPH AND TOUR HISTORY

- YOU SHOULD HAVE SHOPPED YOUR DEMO AROUND TO COLLEGE RADIO STATIONS AND RECEIVED AIRPLAY ON AT LEAST ONE OF THE SONGS

- YOU SHOULD HAVE A SMALL BUT LOYAL AND PROFESSIONAL ROAD CREW

- YOU SHOULD HAVE PREVIOUSLY RELEASED AT LEAST ONE CD OF YOUR ORIGINAL MATERIAL AND HAVE SOLD 3000 UNITS

- YOU SHOULD OWN YOUR OWN TOURING VEHICLE

- YOU SHOULD HAVE FILMED YOUR OWN INDEPENDENT PERFORMANCE VIDEO

D

- YOU SHOULD HAVE ENOUGH FINANCIAL BACKING TO PUT ON A SHOWCASE

- YOU SHOULD HAVE A MANAGER

- YOU SHOULD HAVE A PARTNERSHIP AGREEMENT

- YOU SHOULD HAVE A PUBLISHING DEAL

Though I personally know some bands that have been signed with no other credentials than a demo and a manager, I should point out that in all these cases they had a very powerful manager. In one recent example, a group was signed to a major label without having any of the things listed except for a demo and a manager. Their manager brought the demo to a renowned performer and producer, who shopped it to a major record label. The label signed the band and put them into the studio. When the recordings were done, the label decided not to release the album and passed on the band's contract. You have to wonder, if this band had developed a career from the list above with a strong fan base and tour circuit, would the label have been so quick to decide not to release the record? Since we will never know, it would safe to assume their chances would have been improved. If the label still chose to drop the act, the band would still have a career. In the example above what can this band now do other than sit around and wait for the phone to ring?

But what if you are not ready? What if your manager, lawyer or an eager band member is thinking with their heart and not their head and is pushing you into showcasing for the record companies? The consequences can be severe. All I can say is that the music community is small and word gets around fast. If you appear at a showcase and bomb on stage, you may eternally ruin your chances of getting signed. If you are rushing this process you have to ask yourself why. Do you have a deadline? If you don't make it by a certain date, then what will happen? Will you have to go back to school? Get married? Or worst of all, get a real job?

If this is the case get out of the business now! You will never make it. You can't rush a true lifelong dream and you will undoubtedly make irreversibly bad decisions if you rush forward trying to beat out a deadline.

ALL ABOUT RECORD COMPANIES

A record company is set up just like any other big corporation selling a product. There are different levels of executives all working together to make your music, which is their product, a success. For this entire process to become successful, two criteria must be met:

1 THE GROUP SHOULD FIT IN WITH THE LABEL'S EXISTING ROSTER

2 EVERYONE AT THE LABEL SHOULD BE EXCITED ABOUT THE PROJECT

This is a very important point to make and understand. Record labels have identities similar, if not analogous, to the groups that are signed to them. A band should be careful when approaching or being approached by labels that have something in common with each other. If not, it can lead to many disagreements that will end in no deal. For example, Tommy Boy Records which has signed mostly rap and hip-hop acts, would probably not be the right place for a country rock band to be on. If you are a country rock band, a label like MCA, which has an entire roster of country artists, would indeed be a more suitable move.

Defining yourself and associating with labels that may understand you more than with labels that won't, will also help get the whole company to rally around your group. This is important since labels are divided up by many different departments that handle different aspects of a band's career. When all these departments are in sync, the chances of success for the band are greatly improved. Speaking of label departments, let's look at some of the most important ones concerning you.

PRESIDENT

The person occupying this position oversees the entire operation of the company. Their main function is to oversee the financial end of the business, however many presidents will involve themselves in different departments based on their personal expertise. You may find that at one label, the president oversees all new acts signed to the label while at another, the A&R department has free rein while the president is more involved with promotion and marketing.

ARTIST & REPERTOIRE (A&R)

The A&R people, also known as the ears of the label, assume the role of liaison and coordinator of all label-band relations. While you may imagine that A&R people spend most of their time listening to tapes of unsigned bands, the truth is that they spend most of their time taking care of the careers of the acts they have signed to the label. With respect to unsigned acts, A&R are usually introduced to new acts via inside solicitation, by scouting acts at various national seminars or by responding to buzz on a hot act. Their job covers a wide range of duties which includes overseeing the recording, touring and video budgets as well as rallying the rest of the label departments around the group.

PROMOTIONS

This department will cater to your media exposure. From putting together press kits, arranging publicity shots, interviews and feature articles, the promotions department's job is to get the band exposure.

SALES

This department deals mostly with the record stores and the label's distribution arm. Their job is to coordinate the shipments of your records to the various different markets. As I explained in chapter 12, when a new band puts out their first record, not all the record stores are going to immediately order it. It is up to the sales department to work with promotions to get the retailers interested in the group. They will work with retailers providing them with P.O.P.'s (point of purchase displays; promotional band posters), trade advertisements and all other avenues that will raise customer awareness.

RADIO

There are essentially two ways to encourage record sales. One is through ardent touring by the band which is handled by the band and their agent. The other is through radio. In most cases radio is the true catalyst that will launch record sales and beef up touring potential, so the label needs to really put strong emphasis on this. The people in this department have telephone headsets strapped on their heads all day, calling station after station trying in amiable fashion to get airplay.

At times the radio department may need to employ professional independent radio promoters to help secure airplay. Let's face it, there are way too many albums being released each month and only a handful of openings in radio station playlists for new material. It's at this level that labels will have their new bands perform at national functions so that radio promoters and station directors get to see and meet and greet.

These five main departments and their respective department heads are the most influential people at the label.

Some of the Other Departments include:

PRODUCTION

This department coordinates the production of the album,   including manufacturing as well as shipment to the distributors.

PRODUCT MANAGEMENT

These individuals focus in on all the different divisions of the label coordinating all their efforts on keeping the collective ball rolling. Their main function is to make sure every department is pulling together on a group because each division's efforts are only as strong as their counterparts. After all, if the radio department is hyping all the stations on the band, and then turns to promotions to give them the okay to mail out the single, only to find out that production failed to tell them that the single's pressing is held up for two weeks, a major problem will arise.

LEGAL

The legal department is responsible for all company contracts dealing with artists, foreign licenses, publishing and record sales clubs.

*****

This is the basic breakdown by job description. It is very common in many labels that one executive might assume some of the other duties above. This is most common at the independent level where there may be one or two people running the entire operation.

The most significant difference between major labels, mini majors and independents is their distribution arm. The major labels all distribute their own records whereas the mini majors all use the distribution arm of their major label affiliates like Radioactive Records using the UNI distribution arm of MCA records or Epitaph using Sony's distribution.

The true independent labels have no affiliation with the majors so their operations are completely self-funded by the investment of the owners. Their records are distributed by independent distributors that cater to certain specialized markets like rap or death metal. In certain ways these types of distribution work much more effectively than the major labels would.

With all the label possibilities out there, there is a home for just about any style of music recorded. Research the labels and study their roster of bands. Focus only on labels that have bands signed to them that record similar music to yours. Do not limit yourself to major labels either. Sometimes they can be the worst place for a band. There are many good indie labels who just by the sheer fact that they are small and committed, will be able to help cultivate your group into one day becoming a major label act. Many young bands started on these labels with a five figure advance and have risen to platinum status (Smashing Pumpkins, Nirvana, Offspring) while many young band members signed to major labels are now working in the landscaping business.

RECORD LABEL INFORMATION

Aside from just looking at your CD collection to see what labels your favorite bands are on, and aside from the publications listed in chapter 17, below is a publication that I highly recommend for all band members to own and read.

MUSIC CONNECTION MAGAZINE:

4731 Laurel Canyon Blvd N. Hollywood Ca 91607

Phone: 818 755-0101

E-Mail: muscon@earthlink.NET

Web site is: http//www.musicconnection.com

This publication is available on newsstands but depending on where you live it may be hard to find so call and get a subscription. As of this writing the rates are: **13 issues for $22.00.... 25 issues (1 year)for $40.00...50 issues (2 years) for $65.00**

WHAT DO LABELS LOOK FOR IN A BAND?

Everyone has their own musical likes and dislikes, but from a business standpoint there are certain inherent qualities that all label reps judge new bands by. These are qualities that are possessed by every single successful band. Labels know that if they are going to risk big money on a young group, the group must possess all of these qualities. In today's music business, labels are there to distribute and market the record. They are not interested in developing young bands that may have some good songs but no clearly defined image or honed stage show.

Labels want developed acts with a proven sales, tour and radio history.

Their belief is: if the band has drummed up a modest career for themselves then imagine what can be accomplished with some backing. Yes there have been some exceptions but those exceptions never went further than one single. Very few acts can carve out a long successful career if they were signed based on just one good song and nothing else, so if you base you entire career on being the exception, then good luck!

The following are five of the most important qualities a label looks for:

DO THEY HAVE GREAT SONGS?

This is the single most important quality. Great songs lead to radio airplay which leads to sales which lead to happy label and artist. **What is a great song?** Though it is impossible to describe what makes a song great, when we hear one we know. I can tell you that the ingredients that make up a great song are: lyrics that are interesting, funny, clever, provoking; music that is familiar yet different; a presentation that is exciting and high quality.

Before you submit material to a label, you better be sure that the material is great. How do you do that? Look around. Are you getting any airplay? Are you packing every club you book? Do people you don't know come up to you after shows and offer their management, agent or legal services? Have you been approached by any label reps? Do you have an active merchandising mail-order business? Are the record stores that are carrying your demo tape re-ordering because they have sold out? If you can answer "yes" to these questions, then your songs may indeed be great. But what if you answer "no?" Then you better ask yourself why. Is it that you are not playing out or stocking record stores, submitting to radio and selling merchandise? If you are not then you need to start, after all how can you prove to the labels that your material is great when you have no proof? If you are playing out, submitting to radio stations, stocking record store shelves and nothing has been happening, perhaps there is something about the band that is not clicking. If this is the case it may not just be the songs. Read on and study the other qualifications and see if they apply to you.

MUSICAL FOCUS

Is the music cohesive and stylistic or is there a collage of songs acting as diplomatic representatives from every genre of the musical landscape? Labels need to classify music into categories so that they can target their promotions in a specific area. It is impossible to sell a band that writes and performs a heavy metal song, a rap song, country western and Latin. Bands that do this are better off becoming a cover band and playing various styles for bar crowds. If you are an original band hoping for a record deal, you must write music that has continuity and fits into one specific style.

UNIQUE SOUNDING VOCALIST

Think about this a minute. Think about every band you hear on the radio right now. Don't the most oft-played records have a unique sounding singer? Isn't it true that the bands with most unique sounding, most provocative and most personable singers, are in fact the most successful bands? Let's face it, how many Bono's do you know walking around the mall? He is a truly unique individual and always was. Even as a kid, people flocked around him and were compelled by him. To anyone that knows him, they know that it's no accident that he is as famous as he is.

Now I know that all you guitar or bass players, drummers and keyboard players are saying "hey what about us." After all, lead singers already have swelled heads and here I come inflating them even more. But the reality is, the singer is the one speaking directly to you, the listener. If they don't say anything interesting, will you really care what the rest of the band sounds like? Furthermore, if the lead singer's appearance is dull and their stage performance cheesy and lifeless, regardless of how good the rest of the band is, their chances of making it are slim.

If, on the other hand, the singer is charismatic, with compelling lyrics and a great entertainer, if the rest of the band is mediocre the chances of them making it are good as long as the songs are good. Now, if the musicians in the band behind the singer possess the same qualities as the singer, then your chances of ranking up there with the superstars are much better.

BAND IMAGE

If you look at your photo and notice that you all look like a bunch of geeks (Weezer), then that's an image. It may not be a great one or one that a label will believe in but at least the band looks unified. Just as a band's sound needs to form continuity, so should their appearance. This image is what will be used to attract like-minded fans who will relate to that image, and buy into what the group is selling.

Image is more than just a photograph. It is a vibe, an expression, an attitude that comes off the record and the live show as well. It is a statement about the group that can be summed up into one short phrase like The Black Crowes - "Seventies Southern Rock" or Coolio - "Thought-provoking Rap." If the band in question needs an entire bio to describe itself because the demo tape doesn't really do them justice, then no A&R executive will risk one penny of the label's money to help the band learn to define itself.

ORIGINALITY

If a band is sporting all the positives but they sound just like a rip-off of another major act, the only conclusion you can come up with is that they are really good at impersonating. I know that all of you can cite examples, like Silverchair's obvious resemblance to Pearl Jam. All I can say is that while it is true they sounded an awful lot like P.J. on their first big hit, the rest of the album did not. And besides, there is always an exception to the rule but I would not risk my career betting on long shots like Silverchair.

These are the qualities that every label looks for. No ifs, ands or buts. If you don't possess these qualifications, you are shooting at stars with wet linguini for arrows.

HOW TO PITCH YOUR BAND TO A LABEL

So now that you know what labels are looking for in a band, how do you begin to present these qualities to the label?

In reality, the entire focus of this book may indeed boil down to this next section. It could very well be that you have spent the last few years working your ass off, cultivating your band and now after spending a few thousand dollars to make a great demo the best you can come up with is to mail it off to some A&R guy whose name you got out of a directory. Well if you think that you are going to get a deal this way forget it. The heaps of unsolicited tapes are so high at record companies that Evel Knievel is thinking of jumping them for his next stunt.

The only way you are going to get signed is by reaching the heads of the five major departments that I mentioned earlier. These are the people that are the most influential at the label and truly have the power to get you signed. So, there you are, sitting in car, in some small town in the middle of nowhere, listing to your demo in the car stereo and thinking, **"How the hell am I ever going to get my tape into the hands of someone important?"** Well, I'm about to tell you how.

There are two ways to accomplish this:

1) BY THEM COMING TO YOU

2) BY BEING SOLICITED TO THEM BY RESPECTED INDUSTRY PROFESSIONALS

Let's begin by learning how to make them come to you, which in a sense will help pave the way for attracting other industry insiders who can represent you to the labels.

THE BUZZ

This is something that you can create right in own home town. To begin with, if you have read and followed everything in this book, then you have done everything possible to build a reputation in your home town. Now the question is, has it panned out? After all the gigging, press and marketing your group has done, are the songs good enough and the band interesting enough to have created an excitement everytime you play? Are you packing the clubs in your area at each and every booking? If you answer yes to these questions then you have created what is known as a buzz. The strength of the buzz and how far out it reaches will determine who picks up on it and responds.

You are certainly aware that fans are buying your tapes, reading the articles and lining up outside the club to see you play. But what you may be unaware of is that industry insiders may also be reading these articles or hearing about you from club owners or many of the other sources that make up the vast music business grapevine. The more they hear, the more they take notice After all, labels don't like taking any risks. If they see a young band proving themselves against all odds in the unsigned arena, they will be prone to taking that group and trying to duplicate their success on a large scale.

If your group has achieved headlining status at the various popular clubs in your big city by attracting a large following, has been charting on college radio stations, has been written up in some of the more popular music trade papers, and played in some of the popular conventions that take place around the country, you can safely say that you are creating that buzz. But can you be sure that the most important people on the inside know about you? Well not really. After all it is a big industry and if you are not located near the major musical Mecca's like New York, Nashville or Los Angeles, then you need to take some steps to ensure that they know about you.

HERE ARE SOME STEPS TO INSURE THAT YOUR BUZZ IS LOUD ENOUGH

GIGS,GIGS GIGS AND MORE GIGS

As I mentioned earlier in the book, repetition is recognition. Label reps read the local music sections of their city's rock and roll rag every week. If your name keeps coming up month after month, in the ads of the city's prestigious clubs, then at some point their curiosity may rise as to who this band is that is always playing. Constant gigging is good only if you are playing in many different places. You should try to limit your gigs in one market to two a month otherwise you may be thought of as a house band. Keep in mind that the major labels have satellite offices in some of the smaller markets as well. Targeting those markets as places to perform regularly is something you should look into. Many cities have summertime festivals, like The Fells Point Festival in Baltimore, or The Hoboken Festival in Hoboken, NJ, that are booked by the local club promoters. By playing their clubs during the year, you stand a better chance of getting on the bill which my indeed feature a big name headliner and can draw some of the local label reps to the show, not to mention the thousands of fans that attend.

As you begin spreading out your tour circuit, conquering city after city, work the press like discussed. When you get some favorable mention, send copies to any and all of the contacts within the industry that you have made. If you have selected a label or two that you feel would best serve your band, look up in any of the industry directories that I listed and select the A&R person of that label and begin a correspondence by mail.

Start off with some clippings along with a simple introductory letter. Make sure these clippings are really inspiring mentions, touting your band as the next big thing. Do not send mundane ads or one-liners. Keep your correspondence alive by occasionally sending out interesting matter to these label contacts. Never call though, it's way too early in the game. If you get a CMJ listing, mail it in. Finally when you book the very big show, headlining at one of your city's biggest venues, send in a postcard inviting that person to the show. Tag along a brief note that greets them and says they will be guest listed at the door should they decide to come down.

Do not call after the show to make contact. If they came and liked you they will contact you. After all this is the part of the book called "How to make them come to you." So all I want you doing right know is setting the bait.

USE YOUR MAILING LIST

Every name of every industry contact you ever made, should be listed in your mailing list. Now that you are performing in prestigious venues and receiving great press, you should be forwarding this information out to these contacts. Your correspondence should have a very professional appearance, remember, you are trying to impress the hell out of these people.

Impress is the key word here. Remember I told you about the charity events I booked my clients to play at their high school. The press I received from these events was very impressive because it showed that the band knew how to create media attention. I made copies of all the local press they got from these events and sent them to the attention of my contacts. I felt that this was a big enough move in the band's career, and that the label people should be aware of it. Keeping the band in their consciousness, with these kinds of articles is very important in starting that buzz.

Therefore, I want you to think up ways that you can do more with your bookings. Playing Friday night at the hot club is great but it's not newsworthy. If you can turn your shows into events by coming up with a creative angle, that's the stuff that gets label reps buzzing. How can you make these shows an event? Big question. For every band there is a different angle. One such angle I used one time was the following.

My client was playing a series of consecutive shows in New York State. In an unprecedented move, I conjured up a Be in an MTV video contest and added an extra show on the tour to sponsor it. I copied an MTV logo from the paper and created a flyer that read:

WANNA BE IN A

MTV

VIDEO

4 people will be chosen from the audience to appear

in an upcoming video by the group X#$@&%(*

Drawing will be held at

Kenny's

Thursday, March 18th

I targeted a small college town about one hour west of Albany where the band had played before to an average of about 30-50 people. I called some of the names off the group's mailing list and informed them that I was shopping the band to many labels and it was inevitable that the band would be getting a deal. It was our desire to hold a contest in their town and the winners would get cameo roles in the eventual video we would shoot for MTV. I asked them if they would like to volunteer to help put posters up around the college. After enlisting five gracious helpers I printed up 5000 flyers and mailed them each 1000. I booked the biggest room in that town and called up the biggest production company in Albany and arranged for a massive sound stage and lighting to be brought up for the show.

Within days after the poster placement began, a buzz was clearly generating all over town about the show. When the tour began a month and a half later, the band was tentative about the whole thing. They felt that I was committing a great deal of money to something never tried before and what if it doesn't work out. I assured them that if that happens, I will pay for everything out of my pocket and never do this again.

The first two nights of the tour were uneventful. They opened up for the Judybats (a band on Sire Records) to lukewarm audiences. The third night my clients were on their own, headlining the contest gig. As we pulled up to the venue, we saw a big production truck parked in front. The $500 stage sound and light package I ordered was already set up when the band prepared to load in. Though they did not admit it at the time, I could tell that there was an excitement in the air. After all they had opened up for so many national headliners in the past, but this was the first time that they would own the stage, production and the night. Even if there wasn't a big turnout, the chance to play through a great sound system would be worth it.

Sound check went well and afterwards the band went out for dinner. I stayed back at the club to watch the gear and prepare for what I expected to be a big night. Needless to say, by 9:00pm, there were hundreds of people lining up to get in. I had set up a big table in front of the door way behind the bouncers. I had stacks of color coded paper for the males and females to sign their names and addresses on. I explained as they would step up that each name was going to go into a barrel and two of each color would be picked at the end of the second and last set. This virtually guaranteed that all the people would stay and see the entire show, (which disappointed hundred of girls that dressed to kill, expecting us to hand pick from the audience.)

To make a long story short, three hours and 1200 paid people later, four fans were chosen. I gave them each a contract that promised them all spots in the first video the band shoots for their label. The band remained somewhat uncomfortable with the ambiguous nature of the contest but in my heart I knew that the band would someday get signed and make a video. In the end the band signed their deal and two months after the record came out I took out the contracts and called each of the winners and invited them down. The night was an amazing success. The bar broke every record in drinks served because no one left to bar hop as is customary at college towns. We brought in thousands of dollars at the door and 1200+ names to our mailing list.

OTHER IDEAS INCLUDE:

 PERFORMING AN UNPLUGGED, ACOUSTIC SET.

Invite members from the area's popular bands to sit in with you. Perform covers, and perhaps even collaborate with them on an original song. This would be a great way to meet the other bands, create a scene and bring in a new crowd.

PLAN AN OUTDOOR FESTIVAL OF YOUR OWN

Get the necessary permits from the town. Encourage some of the local merchants to set up concessions and include other popular local acts on the bill.

CREATE CONTESTS AT YOUR EVENTS

Like a Holloween costume contest.

BOOK A BIG OUT OF TOWN VENUE AND INVITE YOUR HOMETOWN FANS BY ARRANGING BUS SERVICE.

Call the local school bus company and see how much it costs to rent buses. Take the amount and divide it by the number of seats and that is what you charge the fans. Include the admission cost if there is one and send out the idea in your mailing list. Encourage people to respond by phone and collect reservations and money in advance.

Arrange a place like a big shopping center, where your fans will meet the bus. It's great when this works out. Imagine pulling up to a club 200 miles away from home with 95 paid fans in tow. The club booker will have an orgasm and if you work the press correctly you will have made a good story about an unknown out of town band that packed a local club.

There's many more good ideas out there. Use your imagination.

THE PRESS

The biggest ally you have in generating a buzz is the press. The press reaches thousands more people than you could ever hope to with you mailing list. If you use the press in the right way, you can make great strides in getting out the subtle message that you are a happening band.

We spoke about the two ways of using the press in chapter 7. One way is to advertise yourself. What I advise you to do is to take out small inexpensive ads that not just advertise the gig you're playing, but include two or three other dates near the one in that city. This is a good way of making the group seem happening especially if the other gigs are at well-known venues. If you are sharing the bill with an even bigger known act include that as well because that may very well bring in a new audience that was unaware that the bigger act was playing.

The second method is to utilize the editorial press. Contact writers and editors that have written about you in the past. I'm sure that you have compiled their names and addresses. But now I want you to also begin to look at the local and national music publications like CMJ New Music Report and look for a writer who pens articles on bands that are like yours. Put their names and addresses in your mailing list. Contact them by selectively mailing announcements of prestigious gigs in their area. There is no need to call them unless you want to confirm the correct spelling of their name or their address. Many of these writers are freelancers and have mailboxes at the paper so it would help to have that number.

Remember that when shopping for a deal, you need to be armed with as much inside weaponry as possible. What impresses label reps most are acknowledgments from other members of the musical community. By gaining mention in respected music publications, by respected writers and then faxing them over to label reps, you are once again casting that bait to bring them in to see you.

When you have the killer demo that you are preparing to send to the labels, begin first by sending it to everyone in the media list. At this juncture you can begin calling everyone from who you know to those you only corresponded with by mail. Break the ice by asking if they received your package and if there is a chance of a review.

Follow up with a second call in a few weeks again to make contact. You want to personally invite them to see a performance or to just ask about the review. Just don't demand anything from these people. I know you are anxious but you have come this far so be patient.

There may be some disappointing phone calls. You may encounter some arrogant writer that has no time to talk to you. Big deal, it's their loss. Remember them when you are a big star and refuse to give them the exclusive. You may encounter some negative comments. This may be the best thing because these people are just one stop away from the labels. If they don't like your tape ask them politely why. You may find some of their constructive criticism helpful in making your product better. Don't take everyone's advice but on the other hand allow for the possibility that you don't know everything yet. Mail in any positive press you receive on the demo to all the industry contacts you have. This will establish you in the eyes of the industry as a serious band.

RADIO AIRPLAY

As you can see, the pattern is forming. All the things we have done throughout the book are now coming to closure here. Labels need to sell records to be successful. To do that they need to get songs on the radio. So utilize everything you learned in chapter 15 to get your music played on the radio. But don't stop at college radio. Now is the time to send that CD in to a select number of the smaller, hip radio stations in your regional touring area that play unsigned bands. Don't go nuts mailing out tapes. It can get very expensive. Do ten at a time so that you can follow up with phone calls and keep track of things without getting overwhelmed.

Once you get a few stations playing and charting your music, use that to encourage ten more stations to do the same. Send them the playlists along with any press you received from that area and any upcoming gigs you have booked in that area.

Encourage your fans to call and request your songs in all your flyers and postcards. Print up separate postcards if you can, listing all the radio stations you are being played on along with their request line phone numbers. Make copies of those playlists. Getting on the radio is the hardest thing to do in the business as any label radio person knows. If you can do that on your own, you are not only buzzing, you're tripping!

MUSIC SALES

Compiling the outstanding figures of the sales of your musical products in your press kit tells a very compelling story to all those that review you. Once again record sales are the sole directive of any record company and if you are racking up impressive numbers on your own, that will perk up some interest. When you are really putting on the push to get signed, try and pump up your record sales. How do you do that? Do what record stores do to sell records. Advertise! Create incentives for people to buy your record. Sell two for one at your shows. Offer discounted rates to record stores so that you can print up 10% coupons and mail them out to new fans to promote the record. The more records you sell the closer you get to issuing a second, third and fourth pressing. The bills you get from the pressing plant is proof alone, but if you are moving product out of record stores you can be sure that the record store owners will probably tell some of the label reps that call them about this unsigned band they know that is selling good numbers in their store. If those same reps hear it from a few more store managers you can bet that news will start to travel up through the label. Hey, if a sales rep can find the next big thing, a job promotion can be theirs.

YOUR FOUR WISE MEN

In the last chapter we learned about the four wise men. You all know how valuable each one can be in helping attract a deal. But more importantly, record labels will never give a band the kind of money they do if the band does not have representation. Labels do not want to develop bands; that's what management teams do, and no matter how developed a band is at signing they are still going to need further development after the record comes out. A band that has a road crew, a manager, a lawyer and accountant is a band that is thinking wisely about their future and shows the necessary responsibility and maturity that warrants an advance of 1/4 of a million dollars.

Now that your band is touring, merchandising, getting press, being booked and managed, what the hell do you need a record company coming and taking 88% for? For one thing, 12% of millions will make you a lot more comfortable than 100% of thousands. Secondly, an unsigned band's shelf-life is only as long as they can keep up the touring. The mild success you generate as an unsigned act usually lasts only as

NEW YORK
BEVERLY HILLS
NASHVILLE
LONDON
ROME
SYDNEY
MUNICH

EST. 1898

XXXX

WILLIAM MORRIS AGENCY, INC.
1350 AVENUE OF THE AMERICAS · NEW YORK, N.Y. 10019 · (212) 586-5100

Cable Address:
"WILLMORRIS"
TELEX 620165
FAX:
(212) 246-3583

WRITER'S DIRECT DIAL NO.
(212) 903- 1360

October 29, 1990

Michael Caplan
VP of A&R
EPIC RECORDS
51 West 52nd St.,13th Floor
New York, NY 10019

Via NY Messenger

Dear Michael:

Please find enclosed a tape of two songs a friend of mine
submitted for consideration on TOWER OF POWER's forthcoming
record. Although the first cut's intro is a bit long, the
song itself is pretty good; the second cut however I really
like. Both were recorded on a simple four-track w/ a drum
machine. These guys have more quality material under their
belts than most writers come up with in a lifetime. There is
an additional song on here (the third cut) written about the
homeless. Although not really suited for TOWER, it is a
beautiful song nonetheless. Perhaps you could use it for
another act.

The person who submitted this to me is the guy you met in
the hotel room with Michelle Zarin and my family after our
softball game in August. His name is Marc Davison, and he
also manages a terrific young band called Last Tribe, which
I sent you a copy of their tape a while back. There is a
definite buzz starting on this act. Have you listened to it
yet? If so, I'm curious what you thought.

Please don't hesitate to give me a call if you need any
further information on the enclosed tape or on Last Tribe.
I'll speak to you soon.

Sincerely,

WILLIAM MORRIS AGENCY, INC

J   N

J :haz
enclosure

long as the shopping for a record deal process takes. Once an unsigned act has been passed over by the labels the chances of them ever getting signed are as thin as OJ's alibi, and the chances of them staying together much longer are even thinner. Unsigned bands will never get the kind of radio play majors can promise and the money signed acts earn from publishing can be enough, if properly invested, to last for generations.

So getting back to the buzz, if you are doing all these things, you can bet that you have gotten the attention of the record companies. Like I mentioned earlier you may not know it's happening but in the offices of those high rise city buildings, around the cushy lounges or on transatlantic phone calls, label people are asking and talking about your band. You may not know it's happening but you better be ready, for at any given time, a label may send some scouts out to see the band live. Whether or not the scouts make their presence known is entirely up to them. Typically if the band is really hot, the scouts might just approach and ask you when your next gig is without letting on to who they are. This way they can come back again and see if the first show was a fluke or if you can repeat the same level of quality. On this return visit they may bring their boss, who is A&R.

The scenario above is a nice one and has indeed happened, especially for bands located in the big cities where the industry has a musical presence. **It is in a way, much easier for bands in NY, LA or Nashville to flirt with the labels, but what about bands from small cities and towns far away from the beaten path.** Make sure that no matter where you are from, you book periodic gigs at these major music Mecca's and build on your contacts. This brings us to second method of getting a record deal.

HOW TO SOLICIT ON YOUR OWN

As you have read in the previous chapter, employing an attorney or manager to represent you in these matters, will make a big difference. It is not a common occurrence that a band member can get on the phone, dial up their favorite record company, get the head of A&R on the phone and make an appointment to come down and visit. In reality, unless they know you, your chances of getting A&R on the phone are about as slim as Kate Moss. But what if you don't have a manager or are a young, inexperienced manager trying to break a baby band?

The following list is a step by step plan on how to make the necessary contacts.

Before you begin, make sure you have the very best, most professional looking press kit and professional and produced sounding demo. There is no room at this point for mistakes or excuses. The songs should be your very best songs that have commercial appeal yet are fresh. Remember, the listener will only give the song fifteen seconds before they fast forward to the next so you better make sure that the first 15 seconds are interesting enough to keep the listener tuned in longer. With a great demo and press kit in hand, you now need to begin ascending the contact ladder to the top. Where do you start? At the bottom rung of course.

WORKING THE LOCAL SCENE

Wherever you live, there must be a club, music store, radio station, booking agent, newspaper columnist, studio engineer and other bands. If you live in or near a big city we will take it for granted that your choices are greater than for those that live in remote towns. Nonetheless the process is the same. Any or all of these establishments have people who will, if nothing else make themselves available to listen to and critique your music. This is a very crucial first step in (**a**) establishing whether your material is any good and (**b**) acquiring further assistance in the area of their expertise. Both of these are necessary since you really need to hear comments from complete strangers and you need to make contacts. With this action you will have made five new contacts that you didn't have before.

If your tape is really good, good enough that these five people are impressed to the point where they either do a story, or ask you to be their opening act, etc., you have just stepped onto the first rung of the ladder. If by chance they know someone in the business that they can pass your tape onto, the by George you are about to step onto the second rung. And this is what you had hoped to get out of this meeting.

If they were not impressed with your tape, they will let you know in a variety of cowardly ways. They may not receive or return any of your phone calls, or they may give you back the tape, say it's good and change the subject to sports. If this is the case, I want you to ask them what they did not like about the tape. I am not saying that you should take their comments seriously unless their comments are echoed by a few others that listened. Could it be that you need to go back and refine your sound? Well, perhaps it does. And there is nothing wrong with that. Even the big stars do that. That is why it takes sometimes years in-between albums

BEYOND THE LOCAL SCENE

If you live in or near NY, Nashville or LA, or some of the other big cities like Chicago or San Francisco where the music industry has a presence, your local music scene will supply you with all the contacts you need to work your way up the ladder. But what if you do not live near a big city? How can you make the next set of contacts that will take you into the belly of the business?

The answer is simple. Go to the city. Wherever you are in America, you are within a day or two of a major musical city. And that is where you will find the bigger club promoters, the music publishing house, managers, lawyer, accountants, press contacts and so on. Make a business trip once every two months to come to NY or LA and book some shows for your band. Bring lots of press kits and walk the streets with your club directory. It pays to call in advance to make sure what the club booker's office hours are. This way you're not just passing out bios to bar tenders.

Meeting people is the next step in networking yourself in the business. Though club bookers may be only the second rung on your way up, the clubs are the places where you will begin to play to urban crowds (a good test of a band's quality is their ability to turn on an urban crowd). You also need to secure some good club contacts in the event that they may need a good opening act for a young national act on tour and for further down the road when you want to showcase your group to record companies.

Aside from clubs there are the Music publishing organizations like BMI, ASCAP, SESAC. These profit free organizations function not only to collect royalties for their clients but to cultivate new talent as well. Their association with other songwriters, publishing companies and producers make them vital contacts for you. These organizations also partake at many of the seminars as wellas hosting their own seminars as well. Here they will feature some of their young talent showcasing them to the upper echelon of the industry. Make an appointment to meet a rep face to face and play them your tape.

REPRESENTATION

Record companies get hundreds of tape submissions a day, five days a week. It's too much to absorb. There are people at the labels who listen to these tapes but you can imagine how difficult it can be to pick a gem out of a huge heap of garbage. It can be done, but the tape better have a "My Sharona" on it. The way to get the A&R to notice you is by having your music solicited to them by someone they know, whose musical judgment they trust. At this juncture you may consider retaining a lawyer, signing to a manager or a publisher or being signed to a name producer. These four representatives have the necessary clout to reach the signing powers that be at the labels. If they take you on as a client your shopping duties are now over and you need to concentrate solely on performing. For a piece of the pie they will make all the calls and take care of all the arrangements. But if you decide to bypass this step and step right up to the label on your own you need to proceed with caution.

The big cities are where most of the industry's lawyers, managers and accountants are located. It may be more difficult to meet with managers, but you can set up appointments with attorneys and accountants for consultation. Explain that you are in a band and how long you've been together. You are looking for representation and would like to come and meet with the firm. You will be expected to drop off a tape since these professionals will like to hear the music and determine for themselves if they want to represent you or not. If they like your material and express interest in representing you, you can assume two things:

    ∇ **THAT YOUR INSTINCTS ARE GOOD AND YOU REALLY HAVE VIABLE MATERIAL.**

    ∇ **YOUR MUST MAKE A DECISION WHETHER YOU ARE READY TO HIRE AND PAY THESE REPRESENTATIVES TO SOLICIT YOUR MATERIAL.**

If you do not have any representation (no manager) hiring an attorney who is well known in the industry can do wonders for you. As we learned in chapter 17, these deal makers know all the important A&R people and the A&R people know them and trust their judgment. There is no guarantee that you will get a deal, but your chances of having your name and tape passed around the business are very good.

SEMINARS

Okay, so you booked some gigs, interviewed some attorneys and met some people at BMI. Great, but that is only the start. The key thing in this business is repetition and recognition. You need to keep meeting these people over and over again so that they begin to think that you are a part of the scene. The one place to meet these very same people and many more like them is at the seminars and conventions that I listed in chapter 2. Every facet of this business is represented at the seminars. Agents, publicists, A&R executives, lawyers, etc. Furthermore most of them are wearing badges with their name and position written on them.

Any smart band would pool their money and attend these conventions. Not just the ones that take place nearest you. Don't skip South By Southwest if you live in New York. And don't skip CMJ in New York if you live in Austin. The same people attend both events and others like it. Make yourself a fixture at all the events, local and national, that you can. Hopefully you will find some of the industry reps looking at you with recognition as you pass them in the hotel lobby.

Sit in on the seminars and workshops. The information is invaluable. Raise your hand and ask questions. The panels are usually occupied by important industry reps. Introduce yourself as so & so from the band whatever. Make an incisive comment or ask a question. Do what you can to make yourself stand out. After the workshop ends, approach one of the panelists with whom you've made eye contact and ask for their business card (which you will add to you mailing list as soon as you get home). You have just made an important industry contact. Give them your business card. And give them an invitation to see you at one of the performance spots that I taught you about in chapter 2. After all, at night is when all the A&R guys are buzzing around trying to find the next great group. Going to these seminars is great but you will really score some points if your band is performing.

If you are nervous about what to say when you meet these people here is one suggestion.

Collect and read as many industry publications as you can. R&R, CMJ, Billboard and Rolling Stone. By reading these papers you will become that much more educated about the business end of the music business. This will help you immensely when you come face to face with an industry bigwig. If all you can talk about is your band, you will become a bore. But if you can talk shop, perhaps discuss the latest label merger or the effects that the new copyright protection law has on the newly released recording technology, you may find that this individual will become more interested in you as a person, thus more interested in what you have to say musically. A lengthy conversation may ensue and now you have not only made a contact, you have perhaps made a friend and fan. This can only help get you that edge over the tens of thousand of bands trying to get noticed.

Okay, so in just a few short pages you have gone from knowing no one to meeting with and exchanging business cards with the vice president of A&R at Mercury Records. Rung three. What's next?

FINDING OUT IF THERE IS ANY LABEL INTEREST

So far so good, you are taking all the right steps to meeting people. The seminars are perhaps the best place of all to network and make contacts. If you are diligent, you should have passed out a few hundred tapes to all levels of industry insiders in a one-year period. What should happen next is that you should be getting all sorts of feedback from many of the people you have been meeting. Some of the feedback may come immediately at the seminar showcases by them approaching you after the show and handing you their cards. Some may come in letter form thanking you for your submission (SEE PAGE 356).

From all these responses you now need to weed out the negative ones from the positive ones. Unless you have already been approached by a label executive instructing you to have your attorney or manager contact the label for contract negotiations, you are going to have to flirt and dance with the positive responses a little while longer to take their interest to the next level.

Starting with the negative responses, and be prepared for some, I would like you to listen to everything they say with an open mind. You are smart enough to know when someone is trying to make you fit a mold without giving your project any credibility, and you are also smart enough to know when someone is really tuned in and is making legitimate criticisms. Either way, just take the advice and thank them very much. There is no need to argue or try to change their opinion. Give them respect and you will have secured them as a contact down the road.

The positive responses are the vibes we need to work off of. For the most part they will be in the form of "loved your tape, I would like to hear more," or "when are you playing again, I would like to bring some other people down to see you." Before you go rattling off a load of dates expecting them to remember, play it cool by taking their card, letting them know that you appreciate their interest and you will get back to them. I advise this because I want you to not act desperate and I also want you to be composed and submit the information they requested in a proper and professional way. The proper way is to regroup with your band at home and begin working on setting up a record company showcase.

USING INTEREST TO CREATE MORE INTEREST

Things are pretty good right about now. You have some interest and you are about to set up a showcase date. This is a great opportunity to try and use this momentum to generate more interest. Your first step is to gather together all those names of individuals who either rejected the band in the past or those who have criticized but not necessarily rejected you.

Secondly, I want you to scour through all those directories I asked you to get, (see chapter 17). Start digging through them and compile a list of every important label executive that works with bands that play a similar style of music that you do. Why use what little resources you have in inviting members of the musical community that have no influence in the genre you're looking to make it in? It is true that the directories only give you names and phone numbers and not the likes and dislikes of industry members. Therefore it would be wise to scour through all your favorite albums, reading the credits to find people that work with bands like yours. Once you locate their names then you can look up in the directory under the label that the band has recorded for to get their direct fax line and phone number.

What do you do with all these names?

Under no circumstances should you call them on the phone. If you call a label and the A&R person does not recognize your name, you will never be put through. Even if you were, what would you say: "Hi, you don't know me but I'm from the band Drool and I'd like to invite you out to see my band." You'll be hearing a dial tone faster than an agent can calculate percentage points. What you will do is forward over to them an invitation to the upcoming record company showcase. (**SEE INVITATION in next chapter.**) This process is like blowing hard on a small spark to turn it into a large fire.

Marc Davison
PO Box 127
Pearl River NY
18965

Dear Marc,

Thank you for submitting your material to
Atlantic Records.

We appreciate the time and effort involved in the
completion of your project. After careful
consideration by our A & R Department, we have
decided to pass on this project.

Good luck on your future endeavors and please
keep Atlantic Records in mind for any other
projects.

Regards,

Wendy Berry
A & R Representative

WB:js
Enclosure

Marc! Thanks so much for letting me finally
hear this band as there has been excitement about
them for quite some time - Unfortunately music.
like that at CB's But please keep me posted on
ongigs. The songs were not knocking me
out but I hear some super ideas
Best wishes with Everything!

After all, you have some label interest, let the other labels know that. Some will naturally become interested in you simply because others are. It's human nature.

REJECTION

You will encounter some rejection along the way. It is a fact of life. Art is subjective and not everybody will find favor in what you do. Every signed band has experienced rejection whether it was from fans, press people or labels. In many cases bands have signed on to the very last labels they have solicited to. So the moral of the story is, the more rejections you experience, the closer you get to getting signed.

Just keep plugging away and use the rejection to help you learn more about the business, more about what you need to do to improve yourself and further your contacts in the industry.

JAKE SLADE

PRESENTS A

recordcompany
SHOWCASE

FEATURING

THURSDAY, JULY 10 @ THE HORIZONTAL BOOGIE BAR 557 AVENUE A
COMPLIMENTARY AND IMMEDIATE ADMISSION FOR 2 WITH THIS INVITATION
OPEN BAR FROM 7:00 TO 8:00 PM
DOORS OPEN AT 7:00 PM (212)666-9856
SHOWTIME 8:15
FOR ADDITIONAL INVITES OR GUEST LIST INFO CONTACT US AT
http://www.suction.com

19

THE RECORD COMPANY SHOWCASE

After all the solicitations are made, all the contacts have been contacted, the day has arrived where you have to book this special show to host all the interested parties. This show of shows is called the "Record Company Showcase." Why is this night different than all other nights? For this show, everything from your set list to the invitations, to the type of venue you play in, must be planned as meticulously as possible. On this night your future may be determined as no other has in the past. This chapter will detail for you every step you need to take to plan the party.

PICKING THE RIGHT CLUB

Depending upon where you live and where you have decided to host your showcase, your first decision needs to be made on which club you will book at. As we have discussed many times already, the label's main offices are located in the three main music centers, New York, Los Angeles and Nashville. Unless you have express confirmation that certain executives with signing power are traveling first class to your home town, I strongly suggest that you book this event in one of these major cities, preferably the one in which you played in before. I might add here that when you are soliciting executives for interest, you do so from only one of these cites so that when you book your showcase and send out your invitations, their appearance won't depend on taking a limo out to the airport during rush hour to catch a flight into another city.

Having booked these major cities before, you know that there are dozens of clubs to choose from. Up until now your concern was to get a gig in these cities and try to get some attention. Now, you really need to examine the clubs and find the ones that cater to bands and their showcases as well as places where label executives like to hang out.

A club should meet the following criteria:

 ### REPUTATION

The club should have a good reputation of being kind to bands. All too many club owners still treat bands like they were 30 cent an hour sweat shop employees. When you are showcasing to the industry, you want to book a club that will give you an unlimited industry guest list, which for a showcases can be very extensive. You want the club to work with you giving you an early show time, making sound check available, dressing room privileges and everything else to make the night go well. If you have done your homework and booked yourselves in the clubs in the city, you stand a better chance of knowing who these clubs are and having them respect you by a past relationship.

A good way to spot a popular club, is by checking the papers to see where all the younger national acts are playing on tour. Tours are booked by major booking agents and they tend to know more about the club scene than anyone else. Don't concentrate so much on the big theaters or large 1000 capacity rooms. Even if you have played them before, the size alone makes them too impersonal for a showcase. Concentrate on the 150-500 capacity club.

 SOUND & LIGHTS

The room should be known for having decent sound and lighting. You do not want anything overpowering or it will take away from the show. But you do want to make sure that the room has an adequate sound and monitor system with enough lighting so that you do not take on the extra burden of bringing in your own production.

 THE STAGE

The room should have a stage if for no other reason than just to elevate you above the rest of the crowd, so that everyone in the audience can see your performance.

 FAMILIARITY

There's a lot to be said for a club where you have played several times already. You will feel more comfortable in a familiar surrounding without the worries of how to adjust your volume to compensate for the room's acoustics, where the dressing room is, where the good restaurants are, will your fans will know where the club is, your familiarity with the house sound man, lightman, manager and so on.

BOOKING THE SHOWCASE

Setting up a showcase is a giant undertaking. The following pages will attest to that. Your first step after getting some commitment from the labels is to arrange a date and venue. You should inform the club that this is a record company showcase and not a regular booking. The reason you need to mention that is (**a**) that they understand the importance of the event and (**b**) that they give you a date that has no chance of being canceled and at an earlier time away from the rest of the evening's events.

Record company showcases should take place somewhere between 8:00 and 10:00 at the very latest on either Tuesday or Wednesday with Monday and Thursday being secondary days.

Why? For starters, label executives do not want to hang around the city until midnight to see a band they have never seen before, especially when they have to be at work at 9:00 the next morning. (Although, if the group is hot and there truly is a lot of interest from many other labels, executives will stay out until 3:00 AM if they have to.) In addition, most who are employed in the executive branch of the business do not really get out of work until 7:00pm.

Also, these showcases are not really gigs, although you can and should invite your fans. It's just that for the price of admission that clubs may charge, your showcase, which will be a performance of no longer than 35 minutes, may not be worth the admission for anyone but your die hard fans. Lastly, as this is meant for record company viewing, having this take place at night when the room is filled with people might not give the invited guests the best advantage to see the group.

You should try and secure a date within three weeks from the time you find out about an interested party. You know the saying, "out of sight out of mind?" It can apply here. When a label shows interest, you need to respond and put something together soon so that you do not lose your window of time.

Once you have one interested party you should try and use that to influence the interest of others. When lawyers or managers are shopping a deal they will call everyone they know and start spreading the word by saying something like, "I've got a group showcasing on the 12th, they already have interest from Electric and Mustang Records. I'm sending out a tape by messenger so call me after you give it a listen." If you do not know anyone in the business on this personal level you will need to create a buzz on your own with your showcase invitations in order to get others to come down.

THE INVITATION

Once you have the date secured, it's time to send out the invitations. Yes, you can call on the phone. But phone calls become obscure messages written on "While you were out" pads. Your important call about a showcase date will spend its life recycling itself to the bottom of the pile of messages until it is routed on its final destination. I can picture it now, folded up like a mini-basketball, and flung with precision into the black cylindrical hoop like a set shot from the free throw line. You can mail it but you know how the mail is, especially in an office where nobody ever gets their mail.

So how do you do it?

This is the way that people in the business communicate with each other. Many executives have direct line fax machines and every time it goes off, their interests are peaked and they check it out.

SCRIBING THE INVITATION

The fax should be succinct and give definitive information.

 Management • PO Box 210 •NYC NY10010
(212) 555-1234

MARCH 25th, 1995

Bob Newfield

Director of A&R

Defense Records

1245 Ave of the Americas

34th Floor

NYC, NY 10010

RE: SUCTION/ INDUSTRY SHOWCASE WED APRIL 2, CBGB'S 8:30PM

Dear Bob:

Please be advised that "Suction" will performing an industry showcase this coming Wed, April 2nd at CBGB's 215 Bowery. Showtime for this showcase is 8:30 PM.

Suction's unique blend of music has been stirring quite a buzz here in the northeast. They have been doing great business everywhere they play and are ready to take the next step. I have forwarded a press kit and tape for your perusal.

If you are interested in seeing this amazing live band, please contact me at 914 555-1234 as I will be coordinating the guest list.

Sincerely,

SHAA Management

Marc Davison

MD:ld

The function of this fax is two-fold. It is to remind those people who have expressed interest in seeing the band as well as alert them to the date time and venue. It is also to create interest from others in the industry from whom you are trying to get interest. The fax should have a look of professionalism. Use band or management letterhead. Insert the date and follow it by listing the name, address and position of the person you are sending it to. Follow that by a bold heading stating the purpose of the fax.

Insert a brief press release/bio on the group. This is done so that person receiving the fax gets the impression that they are not the only ones getting the invitation.

Finish the fax with your name. The two initials followed by two lowercase initials after your name at the bottom, signifies the person who typed this letter; a secretary or assistant. It gives the letter the appearance that it came from an office which will give your band a more professional image. In many ways appearance is the first attraction in a courtship and if you haven't figured it out by now, that is exactly what this whole game is about. A courtship which will hopefully lead to dating, romance and marriage.

The letter should be faxed one week prior to the showcase date. All the faxes that are being to sent to new contacts should be followed up by a press kit and tape, sent by Fed Ex. Include in the fax that a press kit and tape are to follow.

CONFIRMING THE INVITATION

The faxes are out and press kits and tapes are out. Have a file prepared that contains all your faxes and all your invites. Your next step is to contact everyone you faxed, and find out if they will be coming to the showcase. The purpose of this is to (**a**) begin making out your guest list, (**b**) once again remind them of your showcase, (**c**) to just make contact. You should make your call 24-48 hours before the date of the showcase. Sooner than that would allow for too much time in between that call and the date. There are a lot of things in an A&R person's schedule that may sidetrack their thoughts on your show for something else. You want this date to be fresh in their mind and stay as a top priority. To confirm the invitation, take out your file and begin calling the direct number to your invited guest. When the assistant answers the phone begin by saying the following:

---**"Hi my name is _____ and I represent the band _____."**

                    Your Name   Band's name

"I faxed _____ an invitation concerning _____'s

             Name of person you sent kit to   Band's name

showcase next week. I am putting together the guest list for tomorrow night. Can you please tell me if they will be coming?"

---"Please Hold".."Yes it has; Mr. Newfield received it and he will be coming."

---**"Will he be bringing any guests?"**

---"Yes he will be bringing along two guests."

---**"If he has any questions he can reach me at (914) 555-1234. I look forward to seeing him at the show. Thank You, Good bye."**

Chances are, the call will seem a bit rushed, although there is a chance you may just hear "hold on one second" followed by "Hello this is Bob Newfield, can you tell me a little about the band." So be prepared when you call in case this happens and if it does, immediately after the call go to the nearest stationery store and play Lotto!

After you have made all your calls create a file that lists all the names of all the invited guests that agreed to come. This will represent your industry guest list. Take a good look at it. Pretty impressive. And just six months ago you didn't have one contact in the business. Great work!

All this faxing, mailing and phone calling is going to cost a good deal of money. Sending an overnight package that contains a press kit and tape will cost around $10-$13. Depending on whether you own a fax machine or not, the cost will range from the price of a long distance phone call to the going rate of a fax at the local Mail Boxes, Etc. that sells faxing services. In my hometown it's about $3 a page.

When your guest list is complete call the club and confirm with the manager your list and the amount of people you have on it. Never let a manager tell you that there are too many names on the list. That would be absurd if they should deny you an unlimited industry list, for no other reason than the obvious benefit to the club to have all these industry people in their club and at the bar drinking.

If for any reason at all they deny you your full guest list, you will have to offer to pay for the extra names, provided that they are all present the night of the show. I must say that this should only be your very last resort as well as the very last time you ever play at the club again.

SHOWCASE REHEARSAL

Please be very prepared for this performance. This is the scrimmage before the big game. Do not leave anything to chance.

REHEARSE A SET OF 7-8 SONGS (30 MINUTES TOPS) FOR TWO WEEKS.

IF YOU CAN, PERFORM IT AT YOUR REHEARSAL HALL FOR FRIENDS AND MAKE SURE THE SONGS ARE IN A GOOD ORDER.

USE SONGS OFF THE TAPE THAT GOT YOU INTEREST FOR THIS SHOWCASE.

DO NOT PLAY ANY NEW SONGS UNLESS TRIED AND TESTED LIVE ON A PREVIOUS AUDIENCE WITH A GREAT RESPONSE. THIS MEANS NO NEW SONGS THAT HAVE NOT BEEN PLAYED OUT LIVE.

THE SHOWCASE SHOULD CONTAIN SONGS THAT DEFINE THE PERSONALITY OF THE BAND BUT ALSO HAVE VERY MEMORABLE PARTS.

This is what the audience is there to find out. Do you have material that is fresh, interesting and catchy? They are in the record business. Not the touring business or the experimental music business. They are in the business of selling records. The way they do that is by getting the songs played on the radio. Bottom line, read chapter 3.

DO NOT EXPERIMENT AT THIS SHOW AND NO MATTER WHAT DO NOT DO ANYTHING THAT HAS NOT BEEN REHEARSED TO DEATH.

THE SHOWCASE

I know there is a lot going on right now and I wish I could be there to help you along. Please know that much of me is here with you on these pages and in these words you are reading right now. I have been right where you are now both as a performer and as a manager. I know that all you want to do is crawl right into your amp and forget about this industry bullshit. Trying to wear six different hats to impress a bunch of suits when all you want to do is make music is becoming a burden. What I want to tell you is that it's really not like what it appears to be. You are at this point for a reason and it is no different for you than it was for any big name band when they were showcasing for a deal.

In fact you have been at this point many, many times, everytime you played in front of a new audience in a new town. That was a showcase in a way. The only difference really between the two is that this time you can be offered a record deal when other times you weren't. But for both shows you had to do your share of work to get people to respond.

This is the moment you have lived your life for; to get the recognition and respect from the music business. Just getting interest from the labels and now coordinating the showcase is a magical time in your career. Don't freak out and don't blow it.

Everything rests right now on the performance. To make the best of it follow these simple do's don'ts and you will be okay:

Unless you incorporate audience interaction, minimize your conversation to brief introductions of songs and greetings to the crowd.

 Do not address each song with a long story behind it and do not sing happy birthday to your friend's dog.

 Be yourself.

Don't look for a new persona during the show and do not over-emphasize your performance. Your invited audience are showcase veterans and they will see through the contrived aura and the pretense. Allow the show to breathe and be what it always is: natural.

 Don't deviate from the set list. Play your set thirty minutes, thank the audience and leave the stage.

THE GAMES PEOPLE PLAY

Showcases are social events and they are great opportunities for colleagues from the different labels to see each other and schmooze. Sometimes they forget that they are there to see the band that put this whole party together, but that is just the way it is.

Do not be discouraged if you see two A&R guys over by the bar engrossed in friendly conversation during your solo. They may just be telling each other how great you sound. In fact, do not let anything you see in the audience from the stage adversely affect you in any way. You may see two reps walk out after the third song. It may mean they didn't like it or it may mean they have an AA meeting in half an hour and had to leave but plan on contacting you in the morning. Just don't offer them a drink.

BOTTOM LINE: don't pay any attention to the floor once you start playing. Just go into the set and get lost in the music. If you honestly feel that you are losing the audience then do what all the years on the road has taught you to do: get them back with your charisma, sense of humor and music.

One Sunday in 1994, I went with a friend of mine who was an agent at William Morris to see the band Quicksand play a showcase at Wetlands. They were already signed to Polygram Records and they were showcasing before a group of booking agents, hoping to get signed. When the band started playing most of the audience gathered by the stage except a small contingent who remained at the bar. I recognized all of them as agent reps from the various major booking agencies. In fact only a few months back I had many of them attend the record release party for one of my acts.

As the band started playing, the speaking volume at the bar rose to a holler so that we could hear each other speak about our most recent signings and good fortunes. But as each song ended and a new one started, our attention was drawn from our conversation to what was going on on-stage. The band was mesmerizing and all the schmoozing came to a halt by the third song. The end of their set met with everyone's approval and the whispered words that they would be the next big things were echoing throughout the club. To my surprise the band never really hit and unfortunately they broke up in 1995, but not before releasing two great albums on Polygram Records.

THE KISS GOODNIGHT

What do you do at that awkward moment after the set ends? Do you walk around the club searching for label people or do you hang back in the dressing room, chain smoking cigarette after cigarette nervously hoping that an A&R person comes in waving a record contract? Well either is good if it makes you comfortable. The reality is that even if you impressed people you may not know it by their behavior. If any of the invited guests feel the need to talk to you, they will know where to look. After all you are probably going to have to clear your equipment from the stage so within two minutes you will be back in the room anyway.

Besides, many reps do not always approach band members the night of the show. After seeing you they may want to listen to the tape again to formulate a better opinion. Or they may look for your manager or representative who invited them. In any case do not feel any resentment or anger. Keep in mind that all these people are in this business because they love music. They just show their appreciation a little differently than the average fan.

After the stage is cleared off, walk around the club. Grab a beer and just stay visible. Either way, make follow-up phone calls to get their responses; they know that, so they may feel more comfortable speaking with you during their work hours when they haven't spent two hours fixed to a bar stool.

Whatever you do, make sure that soon after your set is done, you proceed to the front door and get your guest list so that you can see what names were checked off. Make sure you bring this list home so that you can follow up with those that came to the show and find out why those that said they were coming didn't. And that's it. Go home and try to get some sleep.

THE DAY AFTER

If you have a manager they should have the guest list and begin calling the guests that were checked off to find out what they thought. If you do not have a manager then you must do this yourself. There is no need to delay the news. If it is negative, my best advice is not to explain yourself, not argue that they didn't understand what you were trying to do or whatever. Just thank them for their criticism, thank them for coming down and in the friendliest of voices let them know that after taking into account what they just said, you will consider making some improvements and hope to see them back at your next showcase.

That's it. Not everybody is going to like your band the very first time they see you play. But it's a funny thing about human psychology. Many times a band is liked because of the kind of people they are and once someone becomes more familiar with the individual members of a group, the more they may begin to appreciate the music. That's why I suggest you do not burn any bridges with label reps by arguing or disagreeing. Instead, win them over with your professionalism and know that you have at least made a potential friend or contact in the industry where the day before you had none.

What if they tell you they thought you were great and want to take it to the next step? Great, now find out what the next step is. It may mean another showcase, it may mean a desire for you to record another demo for them or it may mean they want to sign you. If for any reason these three scenarios present themselves, it's time to sit down with a good music attorney if you do not have a manager, and have them take over the correspondence.

THE PROPOSAL

If you get an offer it will usually come as a verbal commitment, first in the form of "How would like to make a record?" As your exuberance lifts your consciousness completely out your body, practice this following response so that it is spoken without any thought process needed: "Great, here's my attorney's address. Please forward the paper work over to their office."

It will be their job to receive the paper work and begin the tedious task of going through the offer and negotiating out the many points that can bind you for years. Your attorney may also want to make some more calls and let some of their colleagues at other labels know that you just received an offer and perhaps they may even want a crack at seeing you before you accept.

The plan here is to get more interested parties so that you have more leverage in your negotiation. With only one offer standing you are not in the strongest of positions to stack the contract in your favor as you would be if let's say you have four strong offers. With more offers on the table you stand a much better chance of making a deal that doesn't leave you at a complete disadvantage. During this time you may even be asked to play another showcase or two for other labels while the negotiation is taking place.

MEETING THE FAMILY

It is very important that when you consider an offer from a record company, you consider the company and how well you fit in as well as who the person is that is offering you the deal. I know we spoke about this before so I will briefly add on to it.

It is very important that the label have a track record as a record company as well as a track record with a band that makes music like yours. While all the major labels seem to have a variety of artists signed to them it is important for you to focus on who of all those artists are the ones that are successful and what format they fit into.

Take MCA Records for example; at the time of this writing, their strength as a label is not grounded in rock but rather in dance and country music. If you are an all-female band that writes feminist anthems you may find that MCA, although they are offering you a deal may not be a logical place for you to find a nurturing home. You may want to look for offers from Electra or Island Records, whose rosters are more eclectic and seem to have a more liberal policy with alternative bands.

So why would MCA be offering you a deal? Well it could be that the company has recently decided to change its direction and broaden the roster. It could be that your A&R person is a feminist (nothing wrong with that) and is trying to make a statement for the label. It could be that you're a great band and that there is a bidding war going on between many other labels and MCA is making the highest offer just to win out over the competition.

So how do you analyze this information? For starters, you must get a good read on the A&R executive who is making the offer and see how powerful they are in the company. The last thing you need is to get signed by a young A&R executive who has little clout or experience. (To find out their position at the company, just ask them who else on the roster they have signed and are responsible for.) The less powerful and responsible this person is, there more risky the signing is. This is only true for the major labels since the minors or independents usually have a small staff with only one or two A&R people.

A&R executives who are lower down on the corporate totem pole may not have the ability to rally the rest of the label behind your group. In the worst case scenario you may sign with this person only to find somewhere along the way they are dismissed from the company. This will leave you virtually isolated at the label where no one else understands your work and may unfortunately end in your eventually getting released from your contract.

Take a wide angle look at all the offers and all the labels. There are many possibilities and many offers. Some will be big financial offers from big labels and some will be smaller offers from smaller labels. The most important factors in deciding which label to sign with is how you feel about the people at the label and if these people truly convey sincerity about their focus and commitment to your band.

THE VOWS (MAJOR POINTS OF A RECORD DEAL)

I hesitate to offer this next section but I would be remiss if I neglected to point out some major points of a contract. Under no circumstances should you assume after reading this that you know anything about a record contract that you could negotiate one on your own.

A record contract binds you to the company for a set amount of recordings. A five record deal for instance actually may mean something quite different. It may mean a one-record deal with options on four more records, provided the first album sells a designated amount which would then automatically enact the funding of a second record.

On the other hand, if your record does not reach certain specified sales amounts, you can be dropped from the label. These are called options, referring to the record company reserving the option to fund your next record. The options are set up in the contract alongside specific sales amounts that you must reach. A schedule of sales figures may look something like this:

First Album	**50,000 units**
Second Album	**50,000 units**
Third Album	**125,000 units**
Fourth Album	**350,000 units**
Fifth Album	**500,000 units**

These units represent more than just whether the label will pick up your option or not. They are also tied into the amount of advance money you will receive for each new album you make. The advances are the loans you get to make the album which are paid from the sales. The bigger the advance the more you have to spend on the record's creation as well as the more bonus money band members may receive. The advances are determined by the performance of the preceding album as you will see further in this chapter in "Formula for Advances."

The unit amount figures indicate the amount of records you indeed need to sell to automatically have the option picked up. If you do not meet these sales numbers the label can choose to still pick up the option provided that there is still strong backing of your band from the company.

This is how first deals are designed and the only choices you have is either not accepting the deal or trying to reduce the amount of options to the lowest number possible. You see signing an eight album recording deal is much worse than a three album deal. The more options the label has the longer you are tied into the record company and bound by the initial financial schedules of the contract. If you sign a three record deal and by the third album you are a platinum selling band, you will be in a great position to re-negotiate a contract. If, however, you are selling a million records by your third album but you are under contract for eight albums, the royalty payments for this album as well as the next is still predetermined in the original contract and for the most part will be a low number.

Of course if you should sell a million albums at any point in your career, you will be able to re-negotiate any contract you're under. The point is that if you were to exceed the sales figures of your option by only a small percentage you may not be in a position to re-negotiate and you will be bound by the contract. This can really prove disastrous if your label does not let you out of your deal and there are still many options left to pick up. Another negative reason for long options is what if the label does not understand your music and has not shown a clear vision of how to market you. What if the label loves you but does not have competent personnel or clout in the industry to move you along. This will prove to be a tremendous hindrance especially if you are a really good act. An eight album deal may keep you in their embrace for eight to ten years before you are free to find another label. By then bands are usually broken up or their music has become stale.

FUNDS

If you recall, I explained that the label agrees to lend you money to pay for recording an album. This is commonly referred to as a recording fund. This amount is usually a set figure somewhere between **$5,000** and **$250,000** depending on the band and label. A small percentage of this money may be deducted as an advance for the band (an amount that is split up among the band members) but the bulk of this figure is to be used in making the album.

This fund is paid back to the label from the sales of the record should it get released. A standard deal will spell out for you the set amount of recording funds the label will provide for each consecutive record you release. Alongside this number is the royalty percentage you will be paid by the label for each unit that is sold.

A standard percentage is about **8-12%** of the suggested retail list price of your record. You will not see your percentage until enough albums have been sold to pay back the label for all the funds they advance you. That is how you pay the label back or in industry terms this is known as the label "recouping" their recording costs. Your record contract will define your royalty rate for the full extent of your contract. It will look something like this:

ALBUM NO.	PERCENTAGE
1	8%
2	8%
3	8.5%
4	8.5%

5	9%
6	9.5%
7	10%
8	11%

This schedule shows that as you record more albums your percentage will go from **8%** on the first album to **11%** by the time you record album #7. This may be okay if you never sell more than **50,000** albums and the truth is that from these percentages you will never make any money from record sales.

But what happens if you sell **750,000** albums on your second release? According to this schedule you will only receive a **0.5%** increase on your third record, a measly rise considering how much money you just made for the label. This is the basic problem with long option deals especially ones that do not have formulas built in. The contract will also contain the schedule of advances you will receive for each album. It may look something like this:

ALBUM NO	RECORDING FUND
1	$75,000
2	$75,000
3	$100,000
4	$100,000
5	$125,000
6	$150,000
7	$175,000
8	$200,000

Now the same question applies here as well. What happens if on the third album you sell **1,000,000** records? Are you still locked in to the small advances for the next record?

FORMULA FOR ADVANCES

Formulas are equations that adjust advances in the event that you sell well over certain predesignated amounts. Formulas are not necessarily a part of a contract as they work only in favor of the band and not the record company.

The formula states that based upon royalties earned from the last album a minimum of a set percentage (let's say **50%**) must be awarded to the band as an advance for recording the next album. So if the album earns **$1,000,000** in royalties on the third album and it has a **50%** formula, you will be entitled to a **$500,000** advance as opposed to the **$100,000** stated in the contract. There are as many variations on formulas as there are contracts and hopefully you will have a good attorney to make sure you get one that works in your favor.

There are many other sub-topics in the contract dealing with international royalties, publishing, ownership, mechanical royalties, tour support, video support, distribution agreements and much more. This all hinges on the basic premise that the label is going to pay you fairly for the albums you have sold and will reflect that in your royalty percentage and advances for the next album.

I do not want to spend too much more time on the contract itself simply because there is a different contract made for each signing and it could take an entire book to define a full record contract. It is imperative that when you are offered a deal, you read it through and redline everything in it you do not understand. There are some good books on record deals that you can take out of the library like:

 THIS BUSINESS OF MUSIC By Shemel and Krasilovsky

 ALL YOU NEED TO KNOW ABOUT THE MUSIC BUSINESS by Donald Passman

They explain in detail the inner workings of a record contract. My goal is to help you land one, not negotiate it.

I DO

If all is well and your lawyer, manager and the band have agreed on all the contract points, then sign on the dotted line and let me offer my sincerest congratulations!

20

A WORD TO THE WISE

Throughout this book is the culmination of answers and techniques that I have shared with many young up and coming artists that have called upon me for advice. Much of what I have written is just that, advice, I want to make it clear that it comes with no guarantees that if you follow this advice, you will make it big.

And so for the first commandment of this chapter, never believe anyone or sign anything with anyone that guarantees you that. Only *you* can make it for yourself. Believe these words and believe in yourself.

There are very few professions in the world that reward you with the likes of huge money, fame, adulation and power. Yes, it is very sweet at the top, but beware because on this road to riches there is going to be bumper to bumper traffic. The very thing missing from all those who got caught in the traffic, was the token of legal knowledge that would put them in that express lane to success.

Ignorance is not a defense nor is it an excuse and you cannot always rely on an attorney for two very simple reasons.

ALTHOUGH ATTORNEYS KNOW THE LAW, THEY CAN'T ALWAYS TELL WHICH VARIATION OF IT WOULD BEST SUIT YOUR NEEDS. BY UNDERSTANDING SOME SIMPLE LEGAL GUIDELINES YOU WILL BE IN A BETTER POSITION TO UTILIZE THE ADVICE YOU ARE GIVEN

LAWYERS CHARGE FOR THEIR ADVICE AND IF YOU NEED TO CALL ABOUT EVERY SINGLE ISSUE IT CAN GET VERY EXPENSIVE.

The following is a list of all the things I think you need to be aware of, so that you can think before you act and have a basis for finding out about what you should get advice for.

BUSINESS AND BAND AGREEMENTS

At the beginning then, if you are doing business as a solo artist or with a group then you first must become aware of the laws, statutes and regulations of your particular city and state regarding your business activities. This includes registering yourself as a business, receiving tax information, understanding performance liabilities (like what your problems might be if in a moment of performance ecstasy, you throw yourself into the audience and landing on a fan and break their arm), being aware of local ordinances regarding residential rehearsing or loud parties, etc.

Each state has statutes and laws on the books that regulate the way you do business, how you pay taxes and what your legal responsibilities are. If you are caught breaking them, the judgment against you could be damaging to your life and career. When you perform work and get paid you are in business and you must consult your local county clerk office to find out all you can about what your obligations are.

Learn about partnership agreements made between you and your band members. Know that there are verbal contracts that are binding, as there are written contracts that are binding. Most groups are not aware that even though there are no formal contracts signed among the members, you are bound together in some way as a working partnership. These obligations are once again defined by the law of the state in which they live. The workings of a partnership affect you most significantly when they are not spelled out in a contract, in such areas such as financial responsibility, music ownership and group commitment.

Choose your band members carefully because these people are your *business partners*. At the proper time (the very latest being prior to signing a record deal) get an attorney and create a proper partnership agreement between band members.

Each member of the band unless other wise determined, has equal say and is an equal percentage partner of the band, sharing in all band assets and debts. In English this means that if you write a song and it goes to number one and makes 1 million dollars, the band member that plays tambourine whom you've put up with but can't wait for a chance to replace when the time is right, is justified in sharing an equal amount of that one million along with the other members in your group unless otherwise spelled out. So, if there are seven members in your band your share of a $1,000,000 mechanical royalty check for the album featuring all your great songs, is worth only 1/7th or $143,000 instead of a potentially larger cut . And that's before Uncle Sam becomes your partner.

Bands incur many commitments as time goes on. If you were to disband or if a member should leave, think of the ramifications it would have on gig commitments, bills and debts and so on. Without a written agreement detailing the way in which a member can leave a group and what they are entitled to, you could be paying this tambourine player after you cut them from the group for years after the dismissal.

What about responsibility to band debt by leaving band members?

A band may indeed incur debt even if it's just from loans made to each other from the band fund. And debt certainly will take on a more imposing role once you are signed and owe money to the record company. What are some debts a band may incur?

Ψ **EQUIPMENT**

Has it been purchased by you or for you from a loan? This equipment can range from an amp to a PA system to transportation.

Ψ **RECORDINGS**

If you borrowed money for a recording session what is the liability of a leaving member? Is the loan to be paid back equally by all band members?

Ψ **MERCHANDISE**

Who paid for it? How do you split the profits? Was there an outside artist involved that did the artwork that hasn't been paid and is owed money?

Ψ **YOUR BAND NAME/LOGO.**

The name you choose for your group carries with it an intrinsic value. Who does the name belong to? Can a leaving band member use it? Can the remaining band members continue to use it? Have you protected it so that other bands can't use it?

Does it sound like or resemble another band's name or for that matter another trademarked name that you may be infringing on? Do you know about trademarks searches? Do you know that you should use an attorney who specializes in trademark searches? Do you know that it costs around $245 to do a trademark search? Do you know that this price does not include the attorney's hourly fee?

With regard to the band name, being a readily identifiable and tangible money-making commodity, its use is guarded with certain criteria. Record companies for one as well as the individual band members have a vested interest in the name. Certain obvious provisions should be addressed in your partnership agreement that cover this extensive topic.

Some other important points to a band partnership agreement are:

VOTE

As you progress and as you find that your career is moving ahead, more and more important decisions will need to be voted on. The result of the vote will determine the action you take. If your band is set up as an equal partnership, do each of the equal partners have an equal vote?

If you are all equal partners and there are an even number of members you may end up with a deadlock (where an even number of votes has decided yes and no). In this scenario is it wise to perhaps have one member that has power of an extra vote in a deadlock? Is there perhaps a team member like a lawyer, manager or accountant that is granted a vote in case of a tie?

You should also decide what type of vote it takes for a decision to be made. Does it take a majority vote or a unanimous vote. There may be some very serious situations that come up that may need a unanimous vote like, should we sign a contract with a particular record company, while certain decisions like should we play Joey's Pizzeria only require a majority vote.

HOW IS THE MONEY TO BE SPENT

This is something you are going to do just about every day if you are a busy band. The last thing you need is a manager or a band representative spending away on promotional activities or equipment without some band intervention.

HOW IS THE MONEY TO BE SPLIT

Remember there are many places you may earn money from. Splits may not necessarily be equal in all areas of your income. For example publishing vs. live performance income.

BOOKINGS

Who does the bookings for a band? Do you know that it is a conflict of interest for a manager to book their band and it can lead to a breach of contract?

If the band is without representation which member/s will do the bookings? How will they be compensated for the expense i.e. phone bills, travel, postage, etc.?

BAND SPOKESMAN

Should you have one member of the band who is the official schmoozer when it comes to the industry?

There are many ways to work these scenarios out. With all the ramifications of partnerships that there are, the two most important factors are:

WORK THEM OUT! AND PUT THEM IN WRITING.

DO IT EARLY ON IN YOUR BAND'S LIFE, WHEN THERE ARE NO PRIMADONNAS IN THE BAND, AND YOU ALL ARE FRIENDS.

Nothing can be properly discussed when you are at each other's throats. Some of the things discussed in partnership contracts might seem distasteful to discuss like when a married couple needs to draw up a will. But believe me as time goes on, things left unsaid cause more problems. Once you make your deal, members now have their roles defined and that will always make for a healthier relationship.

Aside from internal legal protection, the following are some categories on external protection.

FOR ALL AGREEMENTS YOU MAKE WITH PRODUCERS, PHOTOGRAPHERS, CLUB OWNERS, AGENTS, MANAGERS AND MERCHANDISERS, WHETHER FOR A TWO HOUR OR 20 YEAR COMMITMENT, GET A SIGNED CONTRACT.

DO NOT PLAY ANY LIVE EVENTS OUTSIDE YOUR OWN HOMETOWN WITHOUT SOME FORM OF SIGNED CONTRACT OR CONFIRMATION FROM THE CLUB BUYER, LISTING YOUR PAID COMPENSATION FOR THE SHOW.

You are legally protected as a hired employee of the club to be paid for your services. Without a contract, your document of employment may be a newspaper ad or flyers advertising the show. If you belong to the musicians' union and pay your yearly dues, they will act in your defense and be very successful in collecting what is owed you.

DON'T SIGN ANY CONTRACT OF AGREEMENT UNLESS YOUR ATTORNEY LOOKED AT IT FIRST.

YOU DON'T NEED TO HAVE A RECORD DEAL TO COLLECT ROYALTIES FROM RADIO AIR PLAY.

You can release you own independent CD, publish it yourself and register it with BMI or ASCAP. Air play on college radio can yield you some air play royalties.

PROTECT YOUR SONGS BY FILLING OUT COPYRIGHT FORMS AND MAIL THEM IN TO THE LIBRARY OF CONGRESS WITH THE $20 APPLICATION FEE.

I can't stress how important it is to know your rights as they apply to you in life and in business. There are many great books in the library or in the book store on music business law. It is your choice whether to search out the information or not, ultimately deciding on how smart and informed you want to be.

Nothing in here is new, obviously some bands have figured out how to make it long before this book was ever written. It just saddens me to know that there were so many groups who should have made it and could have given the world some great music if they were just, wiser.

Your mind is like a stereo. When it's turned on it stays on, until someone or something turns it off. My hope is that I have been able to turn your mind on. And as long as it never gets turned off, no matter what in life you set out to do, you will find success.

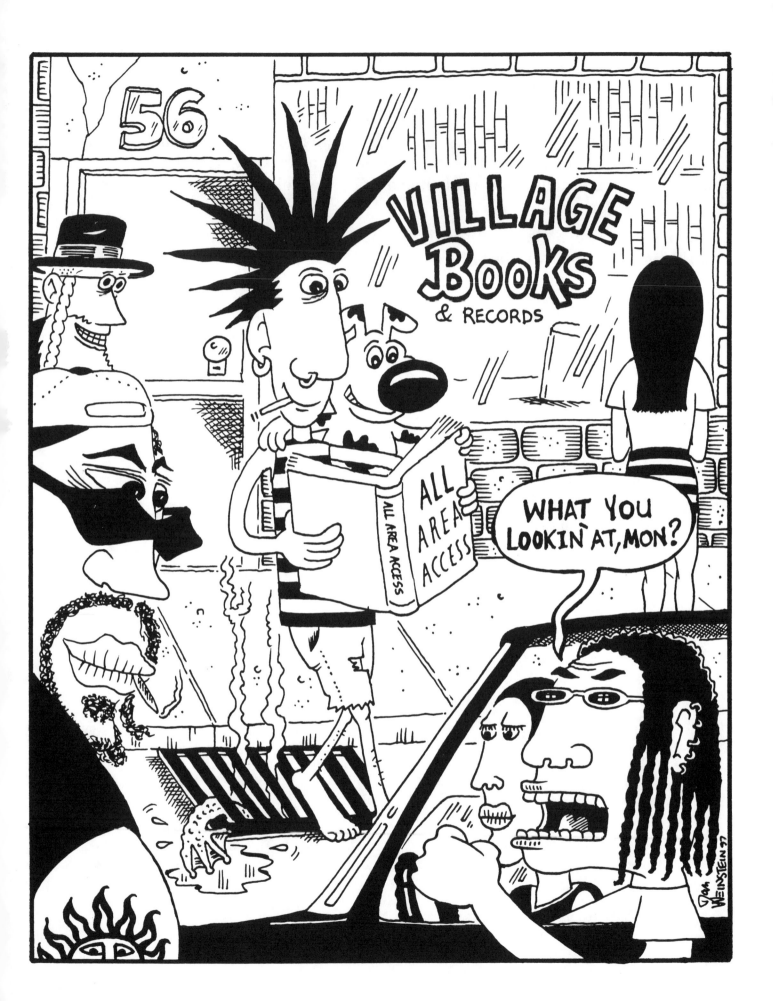

Books About the Music Business from Hal Leonard

GET IT IN WRITING
The Musician's Guide to the Music Business
by Brian McPherson

Confused by today's music business? Did you ever wish that that some super-knowledgeable music attorney would sit you down and explain the whole thing to you? Well, that's what this book is all about. *Get It in Writing* is actually three books in one: 1) An overview of the entire music business and the players involved; 2) Interviews with top industry professionals; and 3) A huge collection of sample agreements with extensive commentary from the author. This indispensible book covers: recording contracts, demo deals, copyrights and trademarks, music publishing, performance rights, motion pictures & TV, artist management, producers, band partnerships, and plenty more. All of this info coupled with expert insider advice makes this book every musician's best tool for success in the music business.
00330239   (352 pages, 8-1/2" x 11")................................$29.95

GOING PRO
Developing a Professional Career in the Music Industry
by Kenny Kerner

Everything musicians need to know to go pro, including information about personal managers, music attorneys, business managers and booking agents, record companies, A&R, publishing, songwriting, demo tapes and press kits, self-promotion, and much more.
00695322   (200+ pages, 6" x 9") $19.95

MAKING A LIVING IN YOUR LOCAL MUSIC MARKET - REVISED EDITION
Realizing Your Marketing Potential
by Dick Weissman

You can survive happily as a musician in your own local music market! The newly revised and expanded edition of this book will show you how. It includes detailed analysis of the latest regional music scenes that have developed; an extensive new section (written by Ron Sobel - vice president of ASCAP in Los Angeles) on opportunites for musicians and composers in developing and selling music in new mediums including the Internet, Greenhouse Channels, Theme Parks, and Desk Top Films; info on how music distribution and retailing is changing to meet the challenges of the 21st century; and many more essential tips. Also features a new appendix and a helpful Resources section after each chapter.
00330421   (304 pages, 6" x 9") $14.95

FILM AND TELEVISION COMPOSER'S RESOURCE GUIDE
by Mark Northam and Lisa Anne Miller

Many musicians are finding a new market for their music scoring for films and television. This comprehensive resource guide provides all the practical tools and information needed about how to organize and run a film and television music business. Section I contains helpful marketing materials, such as sample letters, brochures, postcards, resumes, and product packaging. Section II provides forms, documents and examples for the management, production, recording and delivery of music for projects. Section III features frequently used sample contracts and agreements, and Section IV lists other composer resources, such as a glossary of terms and abbreviations, info on performing rights organizations, attorneys and agents, listings of different markets to tap, internet resources, and much more. Essential for any musician interested in a career in film and television music.
00330420   (198 pages, 8-1/2" x 11")...............................$34.95

ALL AREA ACCESS
Personal Management for Unsigned Musicians
by Marc Davison

Success in the music business isn't the result of a whimsical journey fueled by a few good tunes; it's a destination reached after a long and well-planned trip over a road filled with potholes, detours, and speed bumps. This book is your road map. It tells you what you need to know and to do, step by step, to market your act and your music. Topics include starting a band, booking gigs, press and the media, recording, copyright laws, merchandising, touring, finances, managers and agents, and record deals. Author Marc Davison draws on his twenty-five years of experience - from playing and touring with bands to booking and managing them - to give you *All Area Access* to musical success.
00330295   (348 pages, 8-1/2" x 11") $24.95

YOU GOT THE

BOOK

ALLAREAACCESS

NOW GET THE

SHIRT.

Thanks for buying the book! Here's how you can stay in touch:

I'D LIKE TO KNOW WHO YOU ARE

Name:_____

Address:_____

_____

Are you a musician or artist rep? _____

What instrument do you play? _____

What style of music do you play? _____

Other industry related topics you'd like to learn more about: _____

_____

_____

Did you enjoy the book?_____   Do you own a computer? _____

Please fill out and send to:

Marc Davison c/o Shaa Management Group • 16 Dalewood Drive Suffern NY 10901